The King's English

—

H.W. & F.G. Fowler

Wordsworth Reference

This edition published 1993 by Wordsworth Editions Ltd,
8b East Street, Ware, Hertfordshire.

Reprinted 1994.

Copyright © Wordsworth Editions Ltd 1993.

ISBN 1-85326-304-4

Printed and bound in Finland

PREFACE

THE compilers of this book would be wanting in courtesy if they did not expressly say what might otherwise be safely left to the reader's discernment: the frequent appearance in it of any author's or newspaper's name does not mean that that author or newspaper offends more often than others against rules of grammar or style; it merely shows that they have been among the necessarily limited number chosen to collect instances from.

The plan of the book was dictated by the following considerations. It is notorious that English writers seldom look into a grammar or composition book; the reading of grammars is repellent because, being bound to be exhaustive on a greater or less scale, they must give much space to the obvious or the unnecessary; and composition books are often useless because they enforce their warnings only by fabricated blunders against which every tiro feels himself quite safe. The principle adopted here has therefore been (1) to pass by all rules, of whatever absolute importance, that are shown by observation to be seldom or never broken; and (2) to illustrate by living examples, with the name of a reputable authority attached to each, all blunders that observation shows to be common. The reader, however, who is led to suspect that the only method followed has been the rejection of method will find, it is hoped, a practical security against inconvenience in the very full Index.

Further, since the positive literary virtues are not to be taught by brief quotation, nor otherwise attained than by improving the gifts of nature with wide or careful reading, whereas something may really be done for the negative virtues by mere exhibition of what should be avoided, the examples collected have had to be examples of the bad and not of the good. To this it must be added that a considerable proportion of the newspaper extracts are, as is sometimes apparent, not from the editorial, but from the correspondence columns; the names attached are merely an assurance that the passages have actually appeared in print, and not been now invented to point a moral.

The especial thanks of the compilers are offered to Dr Bradley, joint editor of the *Oxford English Dictionary*, who has been good enough to inspect the proof-sheets, and whose many valuable suggestions have led to the removal of some too unqualified statements, some confused exposition, and some positive mistakes. It is due to him, however, to say that his warnings have now and then been disregarded, when it seemed that brevity or some other advantage could be secured without great risk of misunderstanding.

The *Oxford English Dictionary* itself has been óf much service. On all questions of vocabulary, even if so slightly handled as in the first chapter of this book, that great work is now indispensable.

H. W. F.   F. G. F.

PREFACE TO THE SECOND EDITION

IN this edition new examples have been added or substituted here and there.

PREFACE TO THE THIRD EDITION

AT the end of a quarter century, during which the sales of our book have maintained a yearly average of nearly two thousand copies, I am bound, in presenting a third edition, to thank the public for so unexpected a continuance of favour. To authors so didactic as ourselves, however, a greater joy than that of surviving a quarter century would· be any evidence of having proved persuasive. But such evidence is extremely difficult to find, or to rely upon when found. It has sometimes seemed to us, and to me since my brother's death, that some of the conspicuous solecisms once familiar no longer met our eyes daily in the newspapers. Could it be that we had contributed to their rarity? or was the rarity imaginary, and was the truth merely that we had ceased to be on the watch? I do not know; but a glimmer of hope has made the present revision, with occasional notes and changes, an agreeable task.

H. W. F.

September, 1930.

CONTENTS

PART I

CHAPTER I. VOCABULARY, pp. 11–63

PART II. pp. 300 to the end

EUPHONY, §§ 1–10

QUOTATION, ETC., §§ 11–19

GRAMMAR, §§ 20–37

CONTENTS

CHAPTER I
VOCABULARY
GENERAL

ANY one who wishes to become a good writer should endeavour, before he allows himself to be tempted by the more showy qualities, to be direct, simple, brief, vigorous, and lucid.

This general principle may be translated into practical rules in the domain of vocabulary as follows:—

Prefer the familiar word to the far-fetched.
Prefer the concrete word to the abstract.
Prefer the single word to the circumlocution.
Prefer the short word to the long.
Prefer the Saxon word to the Romance.[1]

These rules are given roughly in order of merit; the last is also the least. It is true that it is often given alone, as a sort of compendium of all the others. In some sense it is that: the writer whose percentage of Saxon words is high will generally be found to have fewer words that are out of the way, long, or abstract, and fewer periphrases, than another; and conversely. But if, instead of his Saxon percentage's being the natural and undesigned consequence of his brevity (and the rest), those other qualities have been attained by his consciously restricting himself to Saxon, his pains will have been worse than wasted; the taint of preciosity will be over all he has written. Observing that *translate* is derived from Latin, and learning that the Elizabethans had another word for it, he will pull us up by *englishing*

---

[1] The Romance languages are those whose grammatical structure, as well as part at least of their vocabulary, is directly descended from Latin—as Italian, French, Spanish. Under Romance words we include all that English has borrowed from Latin either directly or through the Romance languages. And words borrowed from Greek in general use, ranging from *alms* to *metempsychosis*, may for the purposes of this chapter be considered as Romance. The vast number of purely scientific Greek words, as *oxygen*, *meningitis*, are on a different footing, since they are usually the only words for what they denote.

his quotations; he will puzzle the general reader by introducing his book with a *foreword*. Such freaks should be left to the Germans, who have by this time succeeded in expelling as aliens a great many words that were good enough for Goethe. And they, indeed, are very likely right, because their language is a thorough-bred one; ours is not, and can now never be, anything but a hybrid; *foreword* is (or may be) Saxon; we can find out in the dictionary whether it is or not; but *preface* is English, dictionary or no dictionary; and we want to write English, not Saxon. Add to this that, even if the Saxon criterion were a safe one, more knowledge than most of us have is needed to apply it. Few who were not deep in philology would be prepared to state that no word in the following list (extracted from the preface to the *Oxford Dictionary*) is English:—*battle, beast, beauty, beef, bill, blue, bonnet, border, boss, bound, bowl, brace, brave, bribe, bruise, brush, butt, button.* Dr Murray observes that these 'are now no less "native", and no less important constituents of our vocabulary, than the Teutonic words'.

There are, moreover, innumerable pairs of synonyms about which the Saxon principle gives us no help. The first to hand are *ere* and *before* (both Saxon), *save* and *except* (both Romance), *anent* and *about* (both Saxon again). Here, if the 'Saxon' rule has nothing to say, the 'familiar' rule leaves no doubt. The intelligent reader whom our writer has to consider will possibly not know the linguistic facts; indeed he more likely than not takes *save* for a Saxon word. But he does know the reflections that the words, if he happens to be reading leisurely enough for reflection, excite in him. As he comes to *save*, he wonders, Why not *except*? At sight of *ere* he is irresistibly reminded of that sad spectacle, a mechanic wearing his Sunday clothes on a weekday. And *anent*, to continue the simile, is nothing less than a masquerade costume. The *Oxford Dictionary* says drily of the last word: 'Common in Scotch law phraseology, and affected by many English writers'; it might have gone further, and said ' "affected" in any English writer'; such things are antiquarian rubbish, Wardour-Street English. Why not (as our imagined intelligent reader asked)—why not *before, except,* and *about?* Bread is the staff of life, and words like these, which are common and are not vulgar, which are good enough for the highest and not too good for the lowest, are the staple of literature. The first thing a writer must learn is, that he is not to reject them unless he can show good cause. *Before* and *except,* it must be clearly understood, have such a prescriptive right that to use other words instead is not merely not to choose these, it is to reject them. It may be done in poetry, and in the sort of prose that is half poetry: to do it elsewhere is to insult *before,* to injure *ere* (which is a delicate flower that will lose its quality if much handled), and to make one's sentence both pretentious and frigid.

It is now perhaps clear that the Saxon oracle is not infallible; it will sometimes be dumb, and sometimes lie. Nevertheless, it is not without its uses as a test. The words to be chosen are those that the probable reader is sure to understand without waste of time and thought; a good proportion of them will in fact be Saxon, but mainly because it happens that most abstract words—which are by our second rule to be avoided—are Romance. The truth is that all five rules would be often found to give the same answer about the same word or set of words. Scores of illustrations might be produced; let one suffice: *In the contemplated eventuality* (a phrase no worse than what any one can pick for himself out of his paper's leading article for the day) is at once the far-fetched, the abstract, the periphrastic, the long, and the Romance, for *if so.* It does not very greatly matter by which of the five roads the natural is reached instead of the monstrosity, so long as it *is* reached. The five are indicated because (1) they differ in directness, and (2) in any given case only one of them may be possible.

We will now proceed to a few examples of how not to write, roughly classified under the five headings, though, after what has been said, it will cause no surprise that most of them might be placed differently. Some sort of correction is suggested for each, but the reader will indulgently remember that to correct a bad sentence satisfactorily is not always possible; it should never have existed, that is all that can be said. In particular, sentences overloaded with abstract words are, in the nature of things, not curable simply by substituting equivalent concrete words; there can be no such equivalents; the structure has to be more or less changed.

1. Prefer the familiar word to the far-fetched.

The old Imperial naval policy, which has failed conspicuously because it *antagonized the unalterable supremacy of Colonial nationalism.* —*Times.*
(stood in the way of that national ambition which must always be uppermost in the Colonial mind)

Buttercups made a sunlight of their own, and in the shelter of scattered coppices the pale *wind-flowers* still dreamed in whiteness.— E. F. BENSON.

We all know what an *anemone* is: whether we know what a *wind-flower* is, unless we happen to be Greek scholars, is quite doubtful.

The state of Poland, and the excesses committed by mobilized troops, have been of a far more serious nature than has been allowed to *transpire.* —*Times.* (come out)

Reform converses with possibilities, *perchance* with impossibilities; but here is sacred fact.—EMERSON. (perhaps)

Tanners and users are strongly of opinion that there is no room for further enhancement, but on that point there is always room for doubt, especially when the *export phase* is taken into consideration. —*Times.*
(state of the export trade)

Witchcraft has been put a stop to by Act of Parliament; but the mysterious relations which it *emblemed* still continue.—CARLYLE. (symbolized)

It will only have itself to thank if future disaster rewards its *nescience* of the conditions of successful warfare.—*Outlook.* (ignorance)

Continual vigilance is imperative on the public to ensure . . .—*Times.* (We must be ever on the watch)

These manœuvres are by no means new, and *their recrudescence is hardly calculated to influence the development of events.*—*Times.* (the present use of them is not likely to be effective)

'I have no particular business at L——', said he; 'I was merely going *thither* to pass a day or two.'—BORROW. (there)

2. **Prefer the concrete word** (or rather expression) to the abstract. It may be here remarked that abstract expression and the excessive use of nouns are almost the same thing. The cure consists very much, therefore, in the clearing away of noun rubbish.

The general poverty of explanation as to the diction of particular phrases seemed to point in the same direction.—Cambridge University Reporter.
(It was perhaps owing to this also that the diction of particular phrases was often so badly explained)
An elementary condition of a sound discussion is a frank recognition of the gulf severing two sets of facts.—Times.
(There can be no sound discussion where the gulf severing two sets of facts is not frankly recognized)
The signs of the times point to the necessity of the modification of the system of administration.—Times.
(It is becoming clear that the administrative system must be modified)
No year passes now without evidence of the truth of the statement that the work of government is becoming increasingly difficult.—*Spectator.*
(Every year shows again how true it is that . . .)
The first private conference *relating to the question of the convocation of representatives of the nation* took place yesterday.—*Times.*
(on national representation)
There seems to have been an absence of attempt at conciliation between rival sects.—Daily Telegraph.
(The sects seem never even to have tried mutual conciliation)

Zeal, however, must not outrun discretion in changing abstract to concrete. *Officer* is concrete, and *office* abstract; but we do not *promote to officers*, as in the following quotation, but to *offices*—or, with more exactness in this context, to *commissions.*

Over 1,150 cadets of the Military Colleges were *promoted to officers* at the Palace of Tsarskoe Selo yesterday.—*Times.*

3. **Prefer the single word** to the circumlocution. As the word *case* seems to lend itself particularly to abuse, we start with more than one specimen of it.

Inaccuracies were *in many cases* due to cramped methods of writing. —*Cambridge University Reporter.* (often)

The handwriting was on the whole good, with a few examples of remarkably fine penmanship *in the case both of* boys and girls.— *Cambridge University Reporter.* (by both boys . . .)

Few candidates showed a thorough knowledge of the text of 1 Kings, and *in many cases the answers* lacked care.—*Ibid.* (many answers)

The matter will remain in abeyance until the Bishop has had time to become more fully acquainted with the diocese, and to ascertain which part of the city will be most desirable for *residential purposes.*—*Times.* (his residence)

M. Witte is *taking active measures for the prompt preparation of material for the study of the question of the execution of the Imperial Ukase dealing with reforms.*—*Times.*
(actively collecting all information that may be needed before the Tsar's reform Ukase can be executed)

The Russian Government is at last face to face with the greatest crisis of the war, *in the shape of the fact that* the Siberian railway is no longer capable . . .—*Spectator.* (for) or (:)

Mr. J—— O—— has *been made the recipient of* a silver medal.— *Guernsey Advertiser.* (received)

4. Prefer the short word to the long.

One of the most important reforms mentioned in the rescript *is the unification of the organization of the judicial institutions and the guarantee for all the tribunals of the independence necessary for securing to all classes of the community equality before the law.*—*Times.*
(is that of the Courts, which need a uniform system, and the independence without which it is impossible for all men to be equal before the law)

I merely desired to point out *the principal reason which I believe exists for the great exaggeration which is occasionally to be observed in the estimate of the importance of the contradiction between current Religion and current Science put forward by thinkers of reputation.*—BALFOUR.
(why, in my opinion, some well-known thinkers make out the contradiction between current Religion and current Science to be so much more important than it is)

Sir,—Will you permit me to *homologate* all you say to-day regarding that selfish minority of motorists who . . .—*Times.* (agree with)

On the Berlin Bourse to-day the prospect of a general strike was cheerfully *envisaged.*—*Times.* (faced)

5. Prefer the Saxon word to the Romance.

Despite the unfavourable climatic conditions.—*Guernsey Advertiser.* (Bad as the weather has been)

By way of general rules for the choice of words, so much must suffice. And these must be qualified by the remark that what is suitable for one sort of composition may be unsuitable for another. The broadest line of this kind is that between poetry and prose; but with that we are not concerned, poetry being quite out of our subject. There are other lines, however, between the scientific and the literary styles, the dignified and the familiar. Our rendering of the passage quoted from Mr Balfour, for instance, may be considered to fall below the dignity required of a philosophic essay. The same might, with less reason, be said of our simplified newspaper extracts; a great journal has a tone that must be kept up; if it had not been for that, we should have dealt with them more drastically. But a more candid plea for the journalist, and one not without weight, would be that he has not time to reduce what he wishes to say into a simple and concrete form. It is in fact as much easier for him to produce, as it is harder for his reader to understand, the slipshod abstract stuff that he does rest content with. But it may be suspected that he often thinks the length of his words and his capacity for dealing in the abstract to be signs of a superior mind. As long as that opinion prevails, improvement is out of the question. But if it could once be established that simplicity was the true ideal, many more writers would be found capable of coming near it than ever make any effort that way now. The fact remains, at any rate, that different kinds of composition require different treatment; but any attempt to go into details on the question would be too ambitious; the reader can only be warned that in this fact may be found good reasons for sometimes disregarding any or all of the preceding rules. Moreover, they must not be applied either so unintelligently as to sacrifice any really important shade of meaning, or so invariably as to leave an impression of monotonous and unrelieved emphasis.

The rest of this chapter will be devoted to more special and definite points—malaprops, neologisms, Americanisms, foreign words, bad formations, slang, and some particular words.

MALAPROPS

Before classifying, we define a malaprop as a word used in the belief that it has the meaning really belonging to another word that resembles it in some particular.

1. **Words containing the same stem, but necessarily, or at least indisputably, distinguished by termination or prefix.**

'She writes *comprehensively* enough when she writes to M. de Bassompierre: he who runs may read.' In fact, Ginevra's epistles to her wealthy kinsman were commonly business documents, unequivocal applications for cash.—C. BRONTË.

The context proves that *comprehensibly* is meant.

The working of the staff at the agent's disposal was to a great extent voluntary, and, therefore, required all the influence of *judicial* management in order to avoid inevitable difficulties.—*Times.* (judicious)

A not uncommon blunder.

By all means let us have bright, hearty, and very *reverend* services.— *Daily Telegraph.* (reverent)

Not uncommon.

He chuckled at his own *perspicuity*.—CORELLI.

If the writer had a little more *perspicuity* he would have known that the Church Congress would do nothing of the kind.—*Daily Telegraph.*

Perspicuity is clearness or transparency: insight is *perspicacity.* *-uity* of style, *-acity* of mind. Very common.

Selected in the beginning, I know, for your great ability and *trustfulness*.—DICKENS. (trustworthiness)

Wise, firm, faithless; secret, crafty, passionless; watchful and inscrutable; acute and *insensate*—withal perfectly decorous—what more could be desired?—C. BRONTË.

Apparently for *insensible* in the meaning *hardhearted.* Though modern usage fluctuates, it seems to tend towards the meaning, *stupidly unmoved by prudence or by facts*; at any rate *acute* and *insensate* are incompatible.

In the meantime the colossal advertisement in the German Press of German aims, of German interests, and of German policy *incontinently* proceeds.—*Times.*

The idiomatic sense of *incontinently* is *immediately*; it seems here to be used for *continually*.

I was *awaiting* with real curiosity to hear the way in which M. Loubet would to-day acquit himself.—*Times*. (waiting)

Awaiting is always transitive.

But they too will feel the pain just where you feel it now, and they will *bethink* themselves the only unhappy on the earth.—CROCKETT.

There is no sort of authority for *bethink*—like *think*—with object and complement. *To bethink oneself* is to remember, or to hit upon an idea.

And Pizarro . . . established the city of Arequipa, since *arisen* to such commercial celebrity.—PRESCOTT.

Arethusa arose; a difficulty arises; but to greatness we can only rise—unless, indeed, we wake to find ourselves famous; then we do arise to greatness.

Of many other such pairs those chiefly needing attention are perhaps *alternate* and *alternative*, *definite* and *definitive*, *policy* and *polity*, and *practical and practicable*.

2. **Words like the previous set, except that the differentiation may possibly be disputed.**

The long drought left the torrent of which I am speaking, and such others, in a state peculiarly favourable to *observance* of their least action on the mountains from which they descend.—RUSKIN. (observation)

Observance is obedience, compliance, &c. The *Oxford Dictionary* recognizes *observance* in the sense of watching, but gives no authority for it later than 1732 except another passage from Ruskin; the natural conclusion is that he accidentally failed to recognize a valuable differentiation long arrived at.

It is physical science, and experience, that man ought to consult in religion, morals, *legislature*, as well as in knowledge and the arts.—MORLEY. (legislation)

Legislature is the legislative body—in England, King, Lords, and Commons. To call back the old confusion is an offence.

The apposite display of the diamonds usually stopped the tears that began to flow hereabouts; and she would remain in a *complaisant* state until . . .—DICKENS. (complacent)

Our Correspondent adds that he is fully persuaded that Rozhdestvensky has nothing more to expect from the *complacency* of the French authorities.—*Times.* (complaisance)

Complaisant is over polite, flattering, subservient, &c. *Complacent* means contented, satisfied.

In the spring of that year the privilege was withdrawn from the four associated booksellers, and the *continuance* of the work strictly prohibited.—MORLEY.

Continuation is the noun of continue, go on with: *continuance* of continue, remain. With *continuance* the meaning would be that the already published volumes (of Diderot's *Encyclopaedia*) were to be destroyed; but the meaning intended is that the promised volumes were not to be gone on with—which requires *continuation.* Again the next two extracts, from one page, show Mr Morley wrongly substituting *continuity*, which only means continuousness, for *continuance.*

Having arrived at a certain conclusion with regard to the *continuance* . . . of Mr. Parnell's leadership . . .—GLADSTONE.

The most cynical . . . could not fall a prey to such a hallucination as to suppose . . . that either of these communities could tolerate . . . so impenitent an affront as the unruffled *continuity* of the stained leadership.—MORLEY.

The Rev. Dr. Usher said he believed the writer of the first letter to be earnest in his inquiry, and agreed with him that the topic of it was *transcendentally* important.—*Daily Telegraph.*

Transcendently means in a superlative degree: *transcendentally* is a philosophic term for independently of experience, &c.

Until at last, gathered *altogether* again, they find their way down to the turf.—RUSKIN. (all together)

At such times . . . Jimmie's better angel was always in the ascendency. —*Windsor Magazine.*

Was in the *ascendant*: had an *ascendancy* over.

The inconsistency and *evasion* of the attitude of the Government.— *Spectator.*

Evasiveness the quality: *evasion* a particular act.

The *requisition* for a life of Christianity is 'walk in love'.—*Daily Telegraph.*

Requisite or *requirement*, the thing required: *requisition*, the act of requiring it.

We will here merely chronicle the *procession* of events.—*Spectator*. (progress or succession)

I was able to watch the Emperor during all these interviews, and noticed the forcible manner in which he spoke, especially to the Sultan's uncle, who came from Fez *especially*.—*Times*. (specially)

As it stands, it implies that he came chiefly from Fez, but from other places in a minor degree; it is meant to imply that he came for this particular interview, and had no other motive. The differentiation of *spec-* and *espec-* is by no means complete yet, but some uses of each are already ludicrous. Roughly, *spec-* means particular as opposed to general, *espec-* particular as opposed to ordinary; but usage must be closely watched..

That it occurs in *violence to* police regulations is daily apparent.— *Guernsey Advertiser*. (violation of)

In the field it aims at efforts of unexpected and extreme violence; the *research* of hostile masses, their defeat by overwhelming and relentless assault, and their wholesale destruction by rigorous pursuit.—*Times*. (discovery)

The object of research is laws, principles, facts, &c., not concrete things or persons. Entomological research, for instance, does not look for insects, but for facts about insects.

3. **Give-and-take forms,** in which there are two words, with different constructions, that might properly be used, and one is given the construction of the other.

A few companies, *comprised* mainly *of* militiamen.—*Times*. (composed of? comprising?)

The *Novoe Vremya* thinks the Tsar's words will undoubtedly *instil* the Christians of Macedonia *with* hope.—*Times*. (inspire them with hope? instil hope into them?)

He appreciated the leisurely solidity, the leisurely beauty of the place, so *innate with* the genius of the Anglo-Saxon.—E. F. BENSON. (genius innate in the place? the place instinct with genius?)

The speeches in the present volume are *prefixed* by a clear and connected account of . . . Lord Curzon's government.—*Westminster Gazette*. (are prefaced by? have prefixed to them?)

The perfect safety and freedom enjoyed by the Congregation . . . and

by its single members is a demonstration of the respect in which they are now *entertained.—Speaker*.
(in which they are held? which is entertained for them?)

4. Words having properly no connexion with each other at all, but confused owing to superficial resemblance.

Mr. Barton walked forth in cape and boa, to read prayers at the workhouse, *euphuistically* called the 'College'.—ELIOT.
(euphemistically)

Euphemism is slurring over badness by giving it a good name: *euphuism* is a literary style full of antithesis and simile. A pair of extracts (*Friedrich*, vol. iv, pp. 5 and 36) will convince readers that these words are dangerous:

Hence Bielfeld goes to Hanover, to grin-out *euphuisms*, and make graceful court-bows to our sublime little Uncle there.—CARLYLE.

Readers may remember, George II has been at Hanover for some weeks past; Bielfeld diligently grinning *euphemisms* and courtly graciosities to him.—CARLYLE.

Troops capable of *contesting* successfully against the forces of other nations.—*Times*.

Though there is authority, chiefly old, for it, good general usage is against *contest* without an object—contest the victory, &c. And as there is no possible advantage in writing it, with *contend* ready to hand, it is better avoided in the intransitive sense.

In the present *self-deprecatory* mood in which the English people find themselves.—*Spectator*. (self-depreciatory)

Depreciate, undervalue: *deprecate*, pray against. A bad but very common blunder.

'An irreparable colleague,' Mr. Gladstone notes in his diary.—MORLEY. (irreplaceable)

No dead colleague is reparable—though his loss may or may not be so—this side the Day of Judgement.

Surely he was better employed in plying the trades of tinker and smith than in having *resource* to vice, in running after milkmaids, for example.—BORROW. (recourse)

You may indeed have recourse to a resource, but not vice

versa. You may also resort to, which makes the confusion easier.

What she would say to him, how he would take it, even the vaguest *predication* of their discourse, was beyond him to guess.—E. F. BENSON. (prediction)

Predication has nothing to do with the future; it is a synonym, used especially in logic, for *statement*. The mistake is generally whipped out of schoolboys in connexion with *praedĭcere* and *praedĭcare*

5. **Words whose meaning is misapprehended without apparent cause.** The hankering of ignorant writers after the unfamiliar or imposing leads to much of this. We start with two uses of which correct and incorrect examples are desirable: *provided*, where *if* is required; and *to eke out* in wrong senses. *Provided* adorns every other page of George Borrow; we should have left it alone as an eccentricity of his, if we had not lately found the wrong use more than once in *The Times*.

Provided is a small district in the kingdom of *if*; it can never be wrong to write *if* instead of *provided*: to write *provided* instead of *if* will generally be wrong, but now and then an improvement in precision. So much is clear; to define the boundaries of the district is another matter; we might be wiser merely to appeal to our readers whether all the examples to be quoted, except one, are not wrong. But that would be cowardly; we lay down, then, that (*a*) the clause must be a stipulation, i.e., a demand yet to be fulfilled, (*b*) there must be a stipulator, who (*c*) must desire, or at least insist upon, the fulfilment of it.

Ganganelli would never have been poisoned *provided* he had had nephews about to take care of his life.—BORROW.

There is no stipulator or stipulation. Grammar would have allowed Providence to say to him 'You shall not be poisoned, provided you surround yourself with nephews'.

The kicks and blows which my husband Launcelot was in the habit of giving me every night, *provided* I came home with less than five shillings.—BORROW.

Launcelot, the stipulator, does not desire the fulfilment. If *kisses* are substituted for *kicks and blows*, and *more* for *less*, the sentence will stand.

She and I agreed to stand by each other, and be true to old Church of England, and to give our governors warning, *provided* they tried to make us renegades.—BORROW.

The stipulators, she and I, do not desire the fulfilment. *Not* to give warning, provided they did *not* try, would be English. There is similar confusion between the requirements of negative and positive in the next:

A society has just been founded at Saratoff, the object being, as the members declare in a manifesto to the Liberals, to use violent methods and even bombs *provided* the latter do so themselves.—*Times*.

In these circumstances the chances are that the direction to proceed to Vladivostok at all costs, *provided* such instruction *were* ever given, may have been reconsidered.—*Times*. (if indeed . . . was)

There is no stipulation; it is only a question of past fact.

What will the War Council at the capital decide *provided* the war is to continue? . . . The longer Linevitch can hold his position the better, provided he does not risk a serious action.—*Times*.
(if, or assuming that)

There is no stipulation, stipulator, or desire—only a question of future fact. The second *provided* in this passage is quite correct. The *Times* writer—or the Russian War Council, his momentary client—insists that Linevitch shall not run risks, and encourages him, if that stipulation is fulfilled, to hold on.

To *eke out* means to increase, supplement, or add to. It may be called a synonym for any of these verbs; but it must be remembered that no synonyms are ever precise equivalents. The peculiarity of *eke out* is that it implies difficulty; in technical language, agreeing with *supplement* in its denotation, it has the extra connotation of difficulty. But it does not mean to make, nor to endure. From its nature, it will very seldom be used (correctly), though it conceivably might, without the source of the addition's being specified. In the first of the quotations, it is rightly used; in the second it is given the wrong meaning of *make*, and in the last the equally wrong one of *endure*.

A writer with a story to tell that is not very fresh usually *ekes* it *out* by referring as much as possible to surrounding objects.—H. JAMES.

She had contrived, taking one year with another, to *eke out* a tolerably sufficient living since her husband's demise.—DICKENS.

Yes, we do believe, or would the clergy *eke out* an existence which is not far removed from poverty?—*Daily Telegraph*.

Next, some isolated illustrations of our present heading:

'There are many things in the commonwealth of Nowhere, which I rather wish than hope to see adopted in our own.' It was with these words of characteristic *irony* that More closed the great work.—J. R. GREEN.

The word *irony* is one of the worst abused in the language; but it was surely never more gratuitously imported than in this passage. There could be no more simple, direct, and literal expression of More's actual feeling than his words. Now any definition of irony—though hundreds might be given, and very few of them would be accepted—must include this, that the surface meaning and the underlying meaning of what is said are not the same. The only way to make out that we have irony here is to suppose that More assumed that the vulgar would think that he was speaking ironically, whereas he was really serious—a very topsy-turvy explanation. *Satire*, however, with which *irony* is often confused, would have passed.

A literary tour de force, a *recrudescence*, two or three generations later, of the very respectable William Lamb (afterwards Lord Melbourne), his unhappy wife, Lady Caroline Lamb, and Lord Byron.—*Times*. (reincarnation, avatar, resurrection?)

Recrudescence is becoming a fashionable journalistic word. It properly means the renewed inflammation of a wound, and so the breaking out again of an epidemic, &c. It may reasonably be used of revolutionary or silly opinions: to use it of persons or their histories is absurd.

A colonel on the General Staff, while arguing for a continuation of the struggle on *metaphysical* grounds, admitted to me that even if the Russians regained Manchuria they would never succeed in colonizing it. . . . The *Bourse Gazette* goes still further. It says that war for any definite purpose ceased with the fall of Mukden, and that its *continuation is apparent* not from any military or naval actions, but from the feeling of depression which is weighing upon all Russians and the reports of the peace overtures.—*Times*.

We can suggest no substitute for *metaphysical*. Though we have long known *metaphysics* for a blessed and mysterious word, this is our first meeting with it in war or politics. The 'apparent continuation', however, seems darkly to hint at the old question between phenomena and real existence, so that perhaps we actually are in metaphysics all the time.

> In a word, M. Witte was always against all our aggressive measures in the Far East. . . . M. Witte, who was always supported by Count Lamsdorff, has no share in the responsibility of all that has *transpired*. —*Times*. (happened)

As a synonym for *become known*,[1] *transpire* is journalistic and ugly, but may pass: as a synonym for *happen*, it is a bad blunder, but not uncommon.

> It was, of course, Mrs. Sedley's opinion that her son would *demean* himself by a marriage with an artist's daughter.—THACKERAY.

> The actors who raddle their faces and *demean* themselves on the stage.—STEVENSON. (lower, degrade)

To *demean* oneself, with adverb of manner attached, is to behave in that manner. The other use has probably arisen by a natural confusion with the adjective *mean*; one suspects that it has crept into literature by being used in intentional parody of vulgar speech, till it was forgotten that it was parody. But perhaps when a word has been given full citizen rights by Thackeray and Stevenson, it is too late to expel it.

> 'Oxoniensis' approaches them with courage, his thoughts are expressed in plain, unmistakable language, *howbeit* with the touch of a master hand.—*Daily Telegraph*.

Albeit means *though*: *howbeit* always *nevertheless*, beginning not a subordinate clause, but a principal sentence. A good example of the danger attending ignorant archaism.

> In a word, Count von Bülow, who took a very rosy view of the agreement last year, now suddenly discovers that he was slighted, and is indignant *in the paulo-post future tense*.—*Times*.

This jest would be pedantic in any case, since no one but schoolmasters and schoolboys knows what the paulo-post-

---

[1] As in the second quotation from *The Times* on p. 14.

future tense is. Being the one represented in English by *I shall have been killed*, it has, further, no application here; *paulo-ante-past tense*, if there were such a thing, might have meant something. As it is, pedantry is combined with inaccuracy.

6. **Words used in unaccustomed, though not impossible, senses or applications.** This is due sometimes to that avoidance of the obvious which spoils much modern writing, and sometimes to an ignorance of English idiom excusable in a foreigner, but not in a native.

No one can imagine non-intervention carried through so desperate and so *consequential* a war as this.—GREENWOOD.

If *important* or *fateful* will not do, it is better to write *a war so desperate and so pregnant with consequences* than to abuse a word whose idiomatic uses are particularly well marked. A consequential person is one who likes to exhibit his consequence; a consequential amendment is one that is a natural consequence or corollary of another.

Half of Mr. Roosevelt's speech deals with this double need of justice and strength, the other half being a *skilled* application of Washington's maxims to present circumstances.—*Times*. (skilful)

Idiom confines *skilled*, except in poetry, almost entirely to the word *labour*, and to craftsmen—a skilled mason, for instance.

It is to the Convention, therefore, that reference must be made for an *intelligence* of the principles on which the Egyptian Government has acted during the present war.—*Times*. (understanding)

No one can say why *intelligence* should never be followed by an objective genitive, as grammarians call this; but nearly every one knows, apart from the technical term, that it never[1] is. Idiom is an autocrat, with whom it is always well to keep on good terms.

Easier to reproduce, in its *concision*, is the description of the day.—H. JAMES. (conciseness)

Concision is a term in theology, to which it may well be left. In criticism, though its use is increasing, it has still an exotic air.

[1] What, never? Well, hardly ever. *O.E.D.* calls it 'Now *rare* or *Obs.*', but finds specimens. H. W. F. 1930.

7. Simple love of the long word.

The wide public importance of these proposals (customs regulations) has now been conceived in no *desultory* manner.—*Guernsey Advertiser*.

We have touched shortly upon four dozen of what we call malaprops. Now possible malaprops, in our extended sense, are to be reckoned not by the dozen, but by the million. Moreover, out of our four dozen, not more than some half a dozen are uses that it is worth any one's while to register individually in his mind for avoidance. The conclusion of which is this: we have made no attempt at cataloguing the mistakes of this sort that must not be committed; every one must construct his own catalogue by care, observation, and the resolve to use no word whose meaning he is not sure of—even though that resolve bring on him the extreme humiliation of now and then opening the dictionary. Our aim has been, not to make a list, but to inculcate a frame of mind.

NEOLOGISMS

Most people of literary taste will say on this point 'It must needs be that offences come; but woe to that man by whom the offence cometh'. They are Liberal-Conservatives, their liberalism being general and theoretic, their conservatism particular and practical. And indeed, if no new words were to appear, it would be a sign that the language was moribund; but it is well that each new word that does appear should be severely scrutinized.

The progress of arts and sciences gives occasion for the large majority of new words; for a new thing we must have a new name; hence, for instance, *motor, argon, appendicitis*. It is interesting to see that the last word did not exist, or was at least too obscure to be recorded, when the *Oxford Dictionary* began to come out in 1884; we cannot do without it now. Nor is there in the same volume any sign of argon, which now has three pages of the *Encyclopaedia Britannica* to itself. The discoverers of it are to be thanked for having also invented for it a name that is short, intelligible to those at least who know Greek, free of barbarism, and above all pronounceable. As to barbarism, it might indeed be desired that the man of science should always call in the man of Greek composition as godfather to his gas or his process; but it is a point of less importance. Every one has been told at school how *telegram* ought to be *telegrapheme*; but by this time we have long ceased to mourn for the extra syllable, and begun seriously to consider whether the further shortening into *wire* has not been resisted as long as honour demands.

Among other arts and sciences, that of lexicography happens to have found convenient a neologism that may here be used to help in the very slight classification required for the new words we are more concerned with—that is, those whose object is literary or general, and not scientific. A 'nonce-word' (and the use might be extended to 'nonce-phrase' and 'nonce-sense'— the latter not necessarily, though it may be sometimes, equivalent to nonsense) is one that is constructed to serve a need of the moment. The writer is not seriously putting forward his word as one that is for the future to have an independent existence; he merely has a fancy to it for this once. The motive may be laziness, avoidance of the obvious, love of precision, or desire for a brevity or pregnancy that the language as at present constituted does not seem to him to admit of. The first two are bad motives, the third a good, and the last a mixed one. But in all cases it may be said that a writer should not indulge in nonce-words unless he is quite sure he is a good writer.

The couch-bunk under the window to conceal the *summerly recliner*. —MEREDITH.

The adjective is a nonce-sense, *summerly* elsewhere meaning 'such as one expects in summer'; the noun is a nonce-word.

In Christian art we may clearly trace a parallel *regenesis*.—SPENCER.
Opposition on the part of the *loquently* weaker of the pair.—MEREDITH.
Picturesquities.—SLADEN.
The *verberant* twang of a musical instrument.—MEREDITH.
A Russian army is a solid machine, as many *war-famous* generals have found to their cost.—*Times*.

Such compounds are of course much used; but they are ugly when they are otiose; it might be worth while to talk of a war-famous brewer, or of a peace-famous general, just as we often have occasion to speak of a carpet-knight, but of a carpet-broom only if it is necessary to guard against mistake.

Russia's disposition is aggressive . . . Japan may conquer, but she will not *aggress*.—*Times*.

Though *aggress* is in the dictionary, every one will feel that it is rare enough to be practically a neologism, and here a nonce-word. The mere fact that it has never been brought into common use, though so obvious a form, is sufficient condemnation.

She did not answer at once, for, in her rather *super-sensitized* mood, it seemed to her . . .—E. F. BENSON.

The word is, we imagine, a loan from photography. Expressions so redolent of the laboratory are as well left alone unless the metaphor they suggest is really valuable. Perhaps, if *rather* and *super-* were cancelled against each other, *sensitive* might suffice.

Notoriously and unctuously *rectitudinous*.—*Westminster Gazette*.

Some readers will remember the origin of this in Cecil Rhodes's famous remark about the unctuous rectitude of British states-men, and the curious epidemic of words in *-ude* that prevailed for some months in the newspapers, especially the *Westminster Gazette*. *Correctitude*, a needless variant for *correctness*, has not perished like the rest.

We only refer to it again because Mr. Balfour clearly thinks it necessary to vindicate his claims to correctitude. This desire for correctitude is amusingly illustrated in the *Outlook* this week, which . . . —*Westminster Gazette*.

All these formations, whether happy or the reverse, may be assumed to be conscious ones: the few that now follow—we shall call them new even if they have a place in dictionaries, since they are certainly not current—are possibly unconscious:

The minutes to dinner-time were numbered, and they *briskened* their steps back to the house.—E. F. BENSON. (quickened)

He was in some amazement at himself . . . *remindful* of the different nature . . .—MEREDITH. (mindful)

Remindful should surely mean 'which reminds', not 'who remembers'.

Persistent *insuccess*, however, did not prevent a repetition of the same question.—*Times*. (failure)

The best safeguard against any *deplacement* of the centre of gravity in the Dual Monarchy.—*Times*. (displacement)

Which would condemn the East to a long period of *unquiet*.—*Times*. (unrest)

Mere slips, very likely. If it is supposed that therefore they are not worth notice, the answer is that they are indeed quite unimportant in a writer who allows himself only one such slip in fifty or a hundred pages; but one who is unfortunate enough to make a second before the first has faded from the memory becomes at once a suspect. We are uneasily on the watch for his next lapse, wonder whether he is a foreigner or an Englishman not at home in the literary language, and fall into that critical temper which is the last he would choose to be read in.

The next two examples are quite distinct from these—words clearly created, or exhumed, because the writer feels that his style requires galvanizing into energy:

A man of a cold, *perseverant* character.—CARLYLE.

Robbed of the just fruits of her victory by the arbitrary and *forceful* interference of outside Powers.—*Times*.

All the specimens yet mentioned have been productions of individual caprice: the writer for some reason or other took a liberty, or made a mistake, with one expression; he might as well, or as ill, have done it with another, enjoying his little effect, or taking his little nap, at this moment or at that. But there are other neologisms of a very different kind, which come into existence as the crystallization of a political tendency or a movement in ideas. *Prime Minister, Cabinet, His Majesty's Opposition*, have been neologisms of this kind in their day, all standing for particular developments of the party system, and all of them, probably, in more or less general use before they made their way into books. Such words in our day are *racial*, and *intellectuals*. The former is an ugly word, the strangeness of which is due to our instinctive feeling that the termination -*al* has no business at the end of a word that is not obviously Latin. Nevertheless the new importance that has been attached for the last half century to the idea of common descent as opposed to that of mere artificial nationality has made *a* word necessary. Racial is not *the* word that might have been ornamental as well as useful; but it is too well established to be now uprooted. *Intellectuals* is still apologized for in 1905 by *The Spectator* as 'a convenient neologism'. It is already familiar to all who give any time to observing continental politics, though the Index to the *Encyclopaedia* (1903) knows it not. A use has not yet been found for the word in home politics, as far as we have observed; but the fact that intellect in any country is recognized as a definite political factor is noteworthy; and we should hail *intellectuals* as a good omen for the progress of the world.

These, and the scientific, are the sort of neologism that may fairly be welcomed. But there is this distinction. With the strictly scientific words, writers have not the power to decide whether they shall accept them or not; they must be content to take submissively what the men of science choose to give them, they being as much within their rights in naming what they have discovered or invented as an explorer in naming a new mountain, or an American founder a new city. *Minneapolis*, *Pikeville*, and *Pennsylvania*, may have a barbaric sound, but there they are; so *telegram*, or *aesthophysiology*. The proud father of the latter (Herbert Spencer) confesses to having docked it of a syllable; and similarly Mr Lecky writes of 'a eudaemometer measuring with accuracy the degrees of happiness realized by men in different ages'; consequently there will be some who will wish these long words longer, though more who will wish them shorter; but grumble as we may, the *patria potestas* is indefeasible. On the other hand, with such words as *racial*, *intellectuals*, it is open to any writer, if he does not like the word that threatens to occupy an obviously vacant place, to offer a substitute, or at least to avoid giving currency to what he disapproves. It will be remembered that when it was proposed to borrow from France what we now know as the closure, it seemed certain for some time that with the thing we should borrow the name, *clôture*; a press campaign resulted in *closure*, for which we may be thankful. The same might have been done for, or rather against, racial, if only some one had thought of it in time.

AMERICANISMS

Though we take these separately from foreign words, which will follow next, the distinction is purely *pro forma*; Americanisms are foreign words, and should be so treated. To say this is not to insult the American language. If any one were asked to give an Americanism without a moment's delay, he would be more likely than not to mention *I guess*. Inquiry into it would at once bear out the American contention that what we are often rude enough to call their vulgarisms are in fact good old English. *I gesse* is a favourite expression of Chaucer's, and the sense he sometimes gives it is very finely distinguished from the regular Yankee use. But though it is good old English, it is not good new English. If we use the phrase—parenthetically, that is, like Chaucer and the Yankees—, we have it not from Chaucer, but from the Yankees, and with their, not his, exact shade of meaning. It must be recognized that they and we, in parting some hundreds of years ago, started on slightly divergent roads in language long before we did so in politics. In the details of divergence, they have sometimes had the better of us. *Fall* is better on the merits than *autumn*, in every way: it is short, Saxon (like the other three season names), picturesque; it reveals its derivation to every one who uses it, not to the scholar only, like *autumn*; and we once had as good a right to it as the Americans; but we have chosen to let the right lapse, and to use the word now is no better than larceny.

The other side of this is that we are entitled to protest when any one assumes that because a word of less desirable character is current American, it is therefore to be current English.

There are certain American verbs that remind Englishmen of the
barbaric taste illustrated by such town names as Memphis and
those mentioned in the last section. A very firm stand ought
to be made against *placate*, *transpire*[1], and *antagonize*, all of
which have English patrons.

There is a real danger of our literature's being americanized,
and that not merely in details of vocabulary—which are all
that we are here directly concerned with—but in its general
tone. Mr. Rudyard Kipling is a very great writer, and a
patriotic; his influence is probably the strongest that there is at
present in the land; but he and his school are americanizing us.
His style exhibits a sort of remorseless and scientific efficiency
in the choice of epithets and other words that suggests the
application of coloured photography to description; the camera
is superseding the human hand. We quote two sentences from
the first page of a story, and remark that in pre-Kipling days
none of the words we italicize would have been likely; now,
they may be matched on nearly every page of an 'up-to-date'
novelist:

Between the snow-white cutter and the flat-topped, *honey-coloured*[2]
rocks on the beach the green water was troubled with *shrimp-pink*
prisoners-of-war bathing.—KIPLING.
Far out, a three-funnelled Atlantic transport with turtle bow and
stern *waddled* in from the deep sea.—KIPLING.

The words are, as we said, extremely efficient; but the impulse
that selects them is in harmony with American, not with
English, methods, and we hope it may be developed in America
rather than here. We cannot go more fully into the point in a
digression like this. But though we have digressed, it has not
been quite without purpose: any one who agrees with us in
this will see in it an additional reason for jealously excluding

[1] Even in the legitimate sense (see p. 26), originally a happy metaphor for
mysterious leaking out, but now vulgarized and 'dead'.
[2] Not that this word calls for censure in itself; but when packed into a
sentence with *snow-white*, *green*, and *shrimp-pink*, it contributes noticeably
to that effect of brief and startling exhaustiveness which is one variety of
what we have stigmatized as efficiency.

American words and phrases. The English and the American language and literature are both good things; but they are better apart than mixed.

Fix up (organize), back of (behind), anyway (at any rate), standpoint (point of view), back-number (antiquated), right along (continuously), some (to some extent), just (quite, or very —'just lovely'), may be added as typical Americanisms of a different kind from either *fall* or *antagonize*; but it is not worth while to make a large collection; every one knows an Americanism, at present, when he sees it; how long that will be true is a more anxious question.

And, *back of* all that, a circumstance which gave great force to all that either has ever said, the rank and file, the great mass of the people on either side, were determined . . .—CHOATE.

Hand-power, *back-number*, flint-and-steel reaping machines.—KIPLING.

Some of them have in secret approximated their *standpoint* to that laid down by Count Tisza in his programme speech.—*Times*.

We close the section by putting *placate* and *antagonize* in the pillory. It may be remarked that the latter fits in well enough with Emerson's curious bizarre style. Another use of *just* is pilloried also, because it is now in full possession of our advertisement columns, and may be expected to insinuate itself into the inside sheets before long[1].

When once *placated* the Senators will be reluctant to deprive honest creditors of their rights.—*Spectator*.

It is true the subject is American politics; but even so, we should have liked to see this stranger received ceremoniously as well as politely, that is, with quotation marks; the italics are ours only.

The old Imperial naval policy, which has failed conspicuously because it *antagonized* the unalterable supremacy of Colonial nationalism.—*Times*.

If Fate follows and limits power, power attends and *antagonizes* Fate.—EMERSON.

[1] It has done so. 'It would be difficult to say just how many weddings of famous people have been celebrated at St. George's Church, Hanover Square.'—*Westminster Gazette*.

Have you ever thought *just how much* it would mean to the home if . . .—*Advertisements passim.*

· FOREIGN WORDS

The usual protest must be made, to be treated no doubt with the usual disregard. The difficulty is that some French, Latin, and other words are now also English, though the fiction that they are not is still kept up by italics and (with French words) conscientious efforts at pronunciation. Such are *tête-à-tête*, *ennui, status quo, raison d'être, eirenicon, négligé*, and perhaps hundreds more. The novice who is told to avoid foreign words, and then observes that these English words are used freely, takes the rule for a counsel of perfection—not accepted by good writers, and certainly not to be accepted by him, who is some-times hard put to it for the ornament that he feels his matter deserves. Even with the best will in the world, he finds that there are many words of which he cannot say whether they are yet English or not, as *gaucherie, bêtise, camaraderie, soupçon*, so that there is no drawing the line. He can only be told that all words not English in appearance are in English writing ugly and not pretty, and that they are justified only (1) if they afford much the shortest or clearest, if not the only way to the meaning (this is usually true of the words we have called really English), or (2) if they have some special appropriateness of association or allusion in the sentence they stand in. This will be illustrated by some of the diplomatic words given below, and by the quotation containing the word *chasseur*.

Some little assistance may, however, be given on details.

1. To say *distrait* instead of *absent* or *absent-minded*, *bien entendu* for *of course, sans* for *without* (it is, like *I guess*, good old English but not good English), *quand même* for *anyhow, penchant* for *liking* or *fancy, rédaction* for *editing* or *edition, coûte que coûte* for *at all costs, Schadenfreude* for *malicious pleasure, œuvre* for *work, alma mater* (except with strong extenuating circum-stances) for *University*—is pretension and nothing else. The substitutes we have offered are not insisted upon; they may

be wrong, or not the best; but English can be found for all these. Moreover, what was said of special association or allusion may apply; to call a luncheon *déjeuner*, however, as in the appended extract, because it is to be eaten by Frenchmen, is hardly covered by this, though it is a praiseworthy attempt at what the critics call giving an atmosphere.

It was resolved that on the occasion of the visit of the French Fleet in August the Corporation should offer the officers an appropriate reception and invite them to a *déjeuner* at the Guildhall.—*Times*.

But speaking broadly, what a writer effects by using these ornaments is to make us imagine him telling us he is a wise fellow and one that hath everything handsome about him, including a gentlemanly acquaintance with the French language. Some illustrations follow:

Motorists lose more than they know by *bêtises* of this kind.—*Times*.

His determination to conduct them to a successful issue *coûte que coûte* might result in complications.—*Times*.

The gloom which the Russian troubles have caused at Belgrade has to some extent been lightened by a certain *Schadenfreude* over the difficulties with which the Hungarian crisis threatens the neighbouring Monarchy.—*Times*.

A recent reperusal . . . left the impression which is so often produced by the exhibition in bulk of the *œuvre* of a deceased Royal Academician —it has emphasized Schiller's deficiencies without laying equal emphasis on his merits.—*Times*.

'Spying strangers' is apparently to become a daily *divertissement* in the House.—*Westminster Gazette*.

The *va et vient* behind the scenes is the most interesting feature in the House of Commons.—*Westminster Gazette*.

The following are instances of less familiar French or Latin words used wantonly:

Sa'di himself visited Somnath, and has described his somewhat *saugrenu* experiences with a Hindu priest there.—*Spectator*.

So, one would have thought, the fever of New York was abated here, even as the smoke of the city was but a gray *tache* on the horizon.— E. F. BENSON.

Either we know that *tache* means stain, or we do not. If we do, we cannot admire our novelist's superior learning: if we do not, we must be doubtful whether we grasp the whole of his possibly valuable meaning. His calculation is perhaps that we shall know it, and shall feel complimented by his just confidence in us.

When the normal convention governing the relations between victors and vanquished is duly re-established, it will be time to chronicle the conjectures relating to peace in some other part of a journal than that devoted to *faits divers.—Times.*

It is true *The Times* does not condescend to an Odds-and-Ends, or a Miscellaneous column; but many other English newspapers do, under various titles; and the *Times* writer might have thrown the handkerchief to one of them.

But times have changed, and this procedure enters into the category of *vieille escrime* when not employed by a master hand and made to correspond superficially with facts.—*Times.*

In relation to military organization we are still in the flourishing region of the *vieilles perruques.—Times.*

The users of these two varieties, who, to judge from the title at the head of their articles, are one and the same person, must have something newer than *vieux jeu.* Just as that has begun to be intelligible to the rest of us, it becomes itself *vieux jeu* to them. It is like the man of highest fashion changing his hat-brim because the man of middling fashion has found the pattern of it.

The familiar gentleman burglar, who, having played wolf to his fellows *qua* financier, journalist, and barrister, undertakes to raise burglary from being a trade at least to the lupine level of those professions.—*Times.*

It is quite needless, and hardly correct, to use *qua* instead of *as* except where a sharp distinction is being made between two coexistent functions or points of view, as in the next quotation. Uganda needs quite different treatment if it is regarded as a country from what it needs as a campaigning ground:

For this point must be borne constantly in mind—the money spent to date was spent with a view only to strategy. The real development of the country *qua* country must begin to-day.—*Times.*

The reader would not care to have my impressions thereanent; and, indeed, it would not be worth while to record them, as they were the impressions of an *ignorance crasse.*—C. BRONTË.

The writer who allows Charlotte Brontë's extraordinarily convincing power of presentment to tempt him into imitating her many literary peccadilloes will reap disaster. *Thereanent* is as annoying as *ignorance crasse*.

It was he who by doctoring the Ems dispatch in 1870 converted a *chamade* into a *fanfaronnade* and thus rendered the Franco-German war inevitable.—*Times*.

We can all make a shrewd guess at the meaning of *fanfaronnade*: how many average readers have the remotest idea of what a *chamade*[1] is? and is the function of newspapers to force upon us against our will the buying of French dictionaries?

2. Among the diplomatic words, *entente* may pass as suggesting something a little more definite and official than *good understanding*; *démenti* because, though it denotes the same as *denial* or *contradiction*, it connotes that no more credence need be given to it than is usually given to the 'honest men sent to lie abroad for the good of their country'; as for *ballon d'essai*, we see no advantage in it over *kite*, and *flying a kite*, which are good English; it is, however, owing to foreign correspondents' perverted tastes, already more familiar. The words italicized in the following quotations are still more questionable:

The two Special Correspondents in Berlin of the leading morning newspapers, the *Matin* and the *Écho de Paris*, report a marked *détente* in the situation.—*Times*.

Entente is comprehensible to every one; but with *détente* many of us are in the humiliating position of not knowing whether to be glad or sorry.

All the great newspapers have insisted upon the inopportuneness of the *démarche* of William II.—*Times*. (proceeding)

The *entourage* and counsellors of the Sultan continue to remain sceptical.—*Times*.

[1] Readers of history are of course likely to be familiar with it; it occurs, for instance, scores of times in Carlyle's *Friedrich*. In such work it is legitimate, being sure, between context and repetition, to be comprehensible; but this does not apply to newspaper writing.

Mere laziness, even if the word means anything different from *counsellors*; but the writer has at least given us an indication that it is only verbiage, by revealing his style in *continue to remain*.

In diplomatic circles the whole affair is looked upon as an *acte de malveillance* towards the Anglo-French *entente*.—*Times*.

You have been immensely amused, cyrenaically enjoying the moment for the moment's sake, but looking before and after (as you cannot help looking in the theatre) you have been disconcerted and *dérouté*.—*Times*.

In spite, however, of this denial and of other official *démentis*, the Italian Press still seems dissatisfied.—*Times*.

In this there is clearly not the distinction that we suggested between *denial* and *démenti*—the only thing that could excuse the latter. We have here merely one of those elegant variations treated of in the chapter 'Airs and Graces'.

3. It sometimes occurs to a writer that he would like to avail himself of a foreign word or phrase, whether to make a genuine point or to show that he has the gift of tongues, and yet not keep his less favoured readers in the dark; he accordingly uses a literal translation instead of the actual words. It may fairly be doubted whether this is ever worth while; but there is all the difference in the world, as we shall presently exemplify in a pair of contrasted quotations, between the genuine and the ostentatious use. The most familiar phrase thus treated is *cela va sans dire*; we have of our own *I need hardly say, needless to remark*, and many other varieties; and the French phrase has no wit or point in it to make it worth aping; we might just as well say, in similar German or French English (whichever of the two languages we had it from), *that understands itself*; each of them has to us the quaintness of being non-idiomatic, and no other merit whatever. A single word that we have taken in the same way is more defensible, because it did, when first introduced here, possess a definite meaning that no existing English word had: *epochmaking* is a literal translation, or transliteration almost, from German. We may regret that we

took it, now; for it will always have an alien look about it; and, recent in English as it is, it has already lost its meaning; it belongs, in fact, to one of those word-series of which each member gets successively worn out. *Epochmaking* is now no more than *remarkable*, as witness this extract from a speech by a Lord Chancellor:

The banquet to M. Berryer and the banquet to Mr. Benjamin, both of them very important, and to my mind *epochmaking* occasions.— LORD HALSBURY.

The verb *to orient* is a Gallicism of much the same sort, and *the half-world* is perhaps worse:

In his quality of eligible bachelor he had no objections at any time to conversing with a goodlooking girl. Only he wished very much that he could *orient* this particular one.—CROCKETT.

High society is represented by . . . Lady Beauminster, *the half-world* by Mrs. Montrose, loveliness and luckless innocence by her daughter Helen.—*Times.*

The next extract is perhaps from the pen of a French-speaker trying to write English: but it is not worse than what the English writer who comes below him does deliberately:

Our enveloping movement, which has been proceeding *since several days.*—*Times.*

Making every allowance for special circumstances, the manner in which these amateur soldiers of seven weeks' service acquitted themselves compels one 'furiously to think'.—*Westminster Gazette.*

A warning may be given that it is dangerous to translate if you do not know for certain what the original means. To ask what the devil some one was doing in that *gallery* is tempting, and fatal.

Appended are the passages illustrating the two different motives for translation:

If we could take this assurance at its face value and *to the foot of the letter*, we should have to conclude. . . .—*Times.*

It will be observed (*a*) that *literally* gives the meaning perfectly; (*b*) that *to the foot of the letter* is absolutely unintelligible to any one not previously acquainted with *au pied de la lettre*; (*c*) that there is no wit or other admirable quality in the French itself. The writer is meanly admiring mean things; nothing could possibly be more fatuous than such half-hearted gallicizing.

I thought afterwards, but it was *the spirit of the staircase*, what a pity it was that I did not stand at the door with a hat, saying, 'Give an obol to Belisarius'.—MORLEY.

The French have had the wit to pack into the words *esprit d'escalier* the common experience that one's happiest retorts occur to one only when the chance of uttering them is gone, the door is closed, and one's feet are on the staircase. That is well worth introducing to an English audience; the only question is whether it is of any use to translate it without explanation. No one will know what *spirit of the staircase* is who is not already familiar with *esprit d'escalier*; and even he who is may not recognize it in disguise, seeing that *esprit* does not mean spirit (which suggests a goblin lurking in the hall clock), but wit. The American name for the thing is 'latter-wit'.

We cannot refrain from adding a variation that deprives *au pied de la lettre* even of its quaintness:

The tone of Russian official statements on the subject is not encouraging, but then, perhaps, they ought not to be taken at the letter.—*Times*.

4. Closely connected with this mistake of translating is the other of taking liberties with foreign phrases in their original form, dovetailing them into the construction of an English sentence when they do not lend themselves to it. In Latin words and phrases, other cases should always be changed to the nominative, whatever the government in the English sentence, unless the Latin word that accounted for the case is included in the quotation.

There is no legacy of the last Socialist Government which is more *damnosa.*—*Sunday Times*.

The whole party were engaged *ohne Rast* with a prodigious quantity of *Hast* in a continuous social effort.—E. F. BENSON.

German, in which so few Englishmen are at their ease, is the last among the half-dozen best-known languages to play these tricks with. The facetiousness here is indescribably heavy.

The clergy in rochet, alb, and other best *pontificalibus*.—CARLYLE.

The intention is again facetious; but the incongruity between a Latin inflected ablative and English uninflected objectives is a kind of piping to which no man can dance; that the English *in* and the Latin *in* happen to be spelt alike is no defence; it is clear that *in* is here English, not Latin; either *in pontificalibus*, or *in other pontificalia*.

The feeling that one is an *antecedentem scelestum* after whom a sure, though lame, Nemesis is hobbling. . . .—TROLLOPE.

Antecedens scelestus is necessary.

. . ., which were so evident in the days of the early Church, are now *non est.—Daily Telegraph*.

All things considered, I wonder they were not *non est* long ago.—*Times*.

Such maltreatment of *non est inventus*, which seems to have amused some past generations, is surely now as stale and unprofitable as *individual* itself.

5. A special caution may be given about some words and phrases that either are shams, or are used in wrong senses. Of the first kind are *nom de plume*, *morale*. The French for the name that an author chooses to write under is *nom de guerre*. We, in the pride of our knowledge that *guerre* means war, have forgotten that there is such a thing as metaphor, assumed that another phrase is required for literary campaigning, thereupon ascertained the French for pen, and so evolved *nom de plume*. It is unfortunate; for we now have to choose between a blunder and a pedantry; but writers who know the facts are beginning to reconcile themselves to seeming pedantic for a time, and reviving *nom de guerre*.

The French for what we call *morale*, writing it in italics under the impression that it is French, is actually *moral*. The other is so familiar, however, that it is doubtful whether it would not be better to drop the italics, keep the -*e*, and tell the French that they can spell their word as they please, and we shall do the like with ours. So Mr. Kipling:

The Gaul, ever an artist, breaks enclosure to study the morale [*sic*], at the present day, of the British sailorman.—KIPLING.

In the second class, of phrases whose meaning is mistaken, we choose *scandalum magnatum*, *arrière-pensée*, *phantasmagoria*, and *cui bono?*.

Scandalum magnatum is a favourite with the lower-class novelist who takes *magnatum* for a participle meaning *magnified*, and finds the combination less homely than *a shocking affair*. It is a genitive plural noun, and the amplified translation of the two words, which we borrow from the *Encyclopaedia*, runs: 'Slander of great men, such as peers, judges, or great officers of state, whereby discord may arise within the realm'.

Arrière-pensée we have seen used, with comic intent but sad effect, for a bustle or dress-improver; and, with sad intent but comic effect, for an afterthought; it is better confined to its real meaning of an ulterior object, if indeed we cannot be content with our own language and use those words instead.

Phantasmagoria is a singular noun; at least the corresponding French monstrosity, *fantasmagorie*, is unmistakably singular; and, if used at all in English, it should be so with us too. But the final -*a* irresistibly suggests a plural to the valorous writers who are impressed without being terrified by the unknown; so:

Not that such *phantasmagoria are* to be compared for a moment with such desirable things as fashion, fine clothes . . .—BORROW.

Cui bono? is a notorious trap for journalists. It is naturally surprising to any one who has not pushed his classics far to be told that the literal translation of it is not 'To what good (end)?' that is 'What is the good of it?' but 'Who benefited?'. The former rendering is not an absolutely impossible one on the principles of Latin grammar, which adds to the confusion. But if that were its real meaning it would be indeed astonishing that it should have become a famous phrase; the use of it instead of 'What is the good?' would be as silly and gratuitous as our above-mentioned *to the foot of the letter*. Every scholar knows, however, that *cui bono?* does deserve to be used, in its true sense. It is a shrewd and pregnant phrase like *cherchez la femme* or *esprit d'escalier*. *Cherchez la femme* wraps up in itself a perhaps incorrect but still interesting theory of life—that whenever anything goes wrong there is a woman at the bottom of it; find her, and all will be explained. *Cui bono?* means, as we said, 'Who benefited?'. It is a Roman lawyer's maxim, who held that when you were at a loss to tell where the responsibility for a crime lay, your best chance was to inquire who had reaped the benefit of it. It has been worth while to devote a few lines to this phrase, because nothing could better show at once what is worth transplanting into English, and what dangers await any one who uses Latin or French merely because he has a taste for ornament. In the following quotation the meaning, though most obscurely expressed, is probably correct; and *cui bono?* stands for: 'Where can the story have come from? why, who will profit by a misunderstanding between Italy and France? Germany, of course; so doubtless Germany invented the story'. *Cui bono?* is quite capable of implying all that; but a merciful writer will give his readers a little more help:

(Berlin) The news which awakens the most hopeful interest is the story of a concession to a Franco-Belgian syndicate in the harbour of Tripoli. There is a manifest desire that the statement should be confirmed and that it should have the effect of exciting the Italian people and alienating them from France. *Cui bono?—Times.*

6. It now only remains to add that there are French words good in some contexts, and not in others. *Régime* is good in the combination *ancien régime*, because that is the briefest way of alluding to the state of things in France before the Revolution. Further, its use in the first of the appended passages is appropriate enough, because there is an undoubted parallel between Russia now and France then. But in the second, *administration* ought to be the word:

Throwing a flood of light upon the proceedings of the existing *régime* in Russia.—*Times.*

He said that the goodwill and friendship of the Milner *régime* had resulted in the effective co-operation of the two countries.—*Times.*

The word *employé* is often a long, ugly, and unnatural substitute for *men*, *workmen*, or *hands*, one of which should have been used in the first two of the passages below. But it has a value where clerks or higher degrees are to be included, as in the third passage. It should be used as seldom as possible, that is all:

The warehouses of the Russian Steamship Company here have been set on fire by some dismissed *employés*.—*Times*.

The *employés* of the Trans-Caucasian line to-day struck work.—*Times*.

The new project, Article 17, ordains that all *employés* of the railways, whatever their rank or the nature of their employment, are to be considered as public officials.—*Times*.

Finally, even words that have not begun to be naturalized may be used exceptionally when a real point can be gained by it. To say *chasseur* instead of *sportsman, gun*, or other English word, is generally ridiculous. But our English notion of the French sportsman (right or wrong) is that he sports not because he likes sport, but because he likes the picturesque costumes it gives an excuse for. Consequently the word is quite appropriate in the following:

But the costume of the *chasseurs*—green velvet, very Robin-Hoody—had been most tasteful.—E. F. BENSON.

FALSE, UGLY, OR NEEDLESS FORMATIONS

1. As a natural link between this section and the last, the practice of taking French words and spelling them as English may stand first. With French words that fill a definite blank in English, the time comes when that should be done if it can. With some words it cannot; no one has yet seen his way to giving *ennui* an English look. With *dishabille*, on the other hand, which appears in the dictionary with spellings to suit all tastes[1], many attempts have been made. This word, however, well illustrates the importance of one principle that should be observed in borrowing from French. Unless the need is a very crying one, no word should be taken that offers serious difficulties of pronunciation. In *déshabillé* are at least two problems (*h*, and *ll*) of which an Englishman fights shy. The consequence is that, though its English history dates back some centuries, it

[1] The *Oxford Dictionary* has fourteen varieties.

is very seldom heard in conversation; no word not used in conversation becomes a true native; and *dishabille* is therefore being gradually ousted by *négligé*, which can be pronounced without fear. As *dishabille* is really quite cut off from *déshabillé*, it is a pity it was not further deprived of its final -*e*; that would have encouraged us to call it *dish-abil*, and it might have made good its footing.

Naïveté is another word for which there is a clear use; and though the Englishman can pronounce it without difficulty if he chooses, he generally does prefer doing without it altogether to attempting a precision that strikes him as either undignified or pretentious. It is therefore to be wished that it might be disencumbered of its diaeresis, its accent, and its italics. It is true that the first sight of naivety is an unpleasant shock; but we ought to be glad that the thing has begun to be done, and in speaking sacrifice our pride of knowledge and call it *navity*.

The case of *banality* is very different. In one sense it has a stronger claim than *naivety*, its adjective *banal* being much older in English than *naïve*; but the old use of *banal* is as a legal term connected with feudalism. That use is dead, and its second life is an independent one; it is now a mere borrowing from French. Whether we are to accept it or not should be decided by whether we want it; and with *common, commonplace, trite, trivial, mean, vulgar*, all provided with nouns, which again can be eked out with *truism* and *platitude*, a shift can surely be made without it. It is one of those foreign feathers, like *intimism, intimity, femininity, distinction* and *distinguished* (the last pair now banalities if anything was ever banal; so do extremes meet), in which writers of literary criticism love to parade, and which ordinary persons should do their best to pluck from them, protesting when there is a chance, and at all times refusing the compliment of imitation. But perhaps the word that the critics would most of all delight their readers by forgetting is *meticulous*.

Before adding an example or two, we draw attention to the danger of accidentally assimilating a good English word to a

French one. *Amende* is good French; *amends* is good English; but *amend* (noun) is neither:

Triviality and over-childishness and naivety.—H. SWEET.

Agrippa himself was primarily a paradox-monger. Many of his successors were in dead earnest, and their repetition of his ingenuities becomes *banal* in the extreme. Bercher himself can by no means be acquitted of this charge of *banality.*—*Times.*

It is significant that the only authorities for *banality* in the *Oxford Dictionary* are Sala, Saintsbury, Dowden, and Browning; but the volume is dated 1888; and though the word is still used in the same overpowering proportion by literary critics as opposed to other writers, its total use has multiplied a hundredfold since then. Our hope is that the critics may before long feel that it is as banal to talk about banality as it is now felt by most wellbred people to be vulgar to talk about vulgarity.

His style, which is pleasant and diffuse without being *distinguished,* is more suited to the farm and the simple country life than to the complexities of the human character.—*Times.*

His character and that of his wife are sketched with a certain *distinction.*—*Times.*

And yet to look back over the whole is to feel that in one case only has she really achieved that perfection of *intimism* which is her proper goal.—*Times.*

The reference to the English nonconformists was a graceful *amend* to them for being so passionate an Oxonian and churchman.—MORLEY.

And in her presentation of the mode of life of the respectable middle classes, the most *meticulous* critic will not easily catch her tripping.—*Times.*

2. **Formations involving grammatical blunders.** Of these the possibilities are of course infinite; we must assume that our readers know the ordinary rules of grammar, and merely, not to pass over the point altogether, give one or two typical and not too trite instances:

My landlady entered bearing what she called 'her best lamp' *alit.*—CORELLI.

This seems to be formed as a past participle from *to alight,* in the sense of to kindle. It will surprise most people to learn that there is, or was, such a verb; not only was there, but the form

that should have been used in our sentence, *alight*, is probably
by origin the participle of it. The *Oxford Dictionary*, however,
after saying this, observes that it has now been assimilated to
words like *afire*, formed from the preposition *a-* and a noun.
Whether those two facts are true or not, it is quite certain that
there is no such word as *alit* in the sense of lighted or lit, and
that the use of it in our days is a grammatical blunder.[1]

But every year pleaded *stronger* and *stronger* for the Earl's conception.
—J. R. GREEN.

Comparative adverbs of this type must be formed only from
those positive adverbs which do not use *-ly*, as *hard*, *fast*. We
talk of *going strong*, and we may therefore talk of *going stronger*;
but outside slang we have to choose between *stronglier*—poetical,
exalted, or affected—and *more strongly*.

The silence that *underlaid* the even voice of the breakers along the
sea front.—KIPLING.

Lie and *lay* have cost us all some perplexity in childhood. The
distinction is more difficult in the compounds with *over* and
under, because in them *-lie* is transitive as well as *-lay*, but in a
different sense. Any one who is not sure that he is sound on the
point by instinct must take the trouble to resolve them into *lie
over* or *lay over*, &c., which at once clears up the doubt. A
mistake with the simple verb is surprising when made, as in the
following, by a writer on grammar:

I met a lad who took a paper from a package that he carried and
thrust it into my unwilling hand. I suspected him of having *laid* in
wait for the purpose.—R. G. WHITE.

A confusion, perhaps, between *lay wait* and *lie in wait*.

I am not sure that *yours* and my efforts would suffice separately; but
yours and mine together cannot possibly fail.

The first *yours* is quite wrong; it should be *your*. This mistake
is common. The absolute possessives, *ours* and *yours*, *hers*,
mine and *thine*,(with which the poetic or euphonic use of the last

[1] *Alit* is due, no doubt, to mere inadvertence or ignorance: the form *litten*
('red-litten windows', &c.), for which the *Oxford Dictionary* quotes Poe,
Lytton, W. Morris, and Crockett, but no old writer, is sham archaism.

two before vowels has nothing to do) are to be used only as pronouns or as predicative adjectives, not as attributes to an expressed and following noun. That they were used by old writers as in our example is irrelevant. The correct modern usage has now established itself. We add three sentences from Burke. The relation between *no* and *none* is the same as that between *your* and *yours*. In the first sentence, modern usage would write (as the correct *no or but a few* is uncomfortable) either *few or no*, or *few if any*, or *no rays or but a few*. For the second we might possibly tolerate *to their as well as to your own*; or we might write *to their crown as well as to your own*. The third is quite tolerable as it is; but any one who does not like the sound can write *and their ancestors and ours*. It must always be remembered in this as in other constructions, that the choice is not between a well-sounding blunder and an ill-sounding correctness, but between an ill and a well sounding correctness. The blunder should be ruled out, and if the first form of the correct construction that presents itself does not sound well, another way of putting it must be looked for; patience will always find it. The flexibility gained by habitual selection of this kind, which a little cultivation will make easy and instinctive, is one of the most essential elements in a good style. For a more important illustration of the same principle, the remarks on the gerund in the Syntax chapter (p. 120) may be referred to.

Black bodies, reflecting *none* or but a few rays.—BURKE.

You altered the succession to *theirs*, as well as to your own crown.—BURKE.

They and we, and *their* and our ancestors, have been happy under that system.—BURKE.

3. Formations violating analogy.

And then it is its panache, its careless *a-moral* Renaissance romance.—*Times*.

But she is perfectly natural, and while perfectly *amoral*, no more immoral than a bird or a kitten.—*Times*.

A- (not) is Greek; *moral* is Latin. It is at least desirable that in making new words the two languages should not be mixed.

The intricate needs of science may perhaps be allowed to override a literary principle of this sort; and accordingly the *Oxford Dictionary* recognizes that *a-* is compounded with Latin words in scientific and technical terms, as *a-sexual*; but purely literary workers may be expected to abstain. The obvious excuse for this formation is that the Latin negative prefix is already taken up in *immoral*, which means contrary to morality, while a word is wanted to mean unconcerned with morality. But with *non* freely prefixed to adjectives in English (though not in Latin), there can be no objection to *non-moral*. The second of our instances is a few weeks later than the first, and the hyphen has disappeared; so quickly has *The Times* convinced itself that *amoral* is a regular English word.

There was no social or economic jealousy between them, no *racial* aversion.—*Times*.

Concessions which, besides damaging Hungary by raising *racial* and *language* questions of all kinds, would . . .—*Times*.

The action of foreign countries as to their *coastal* trade.—*Times*.

Her *riverine* trade.—*Westminster Gazette*.

It has been already stated that *-al* is mainly confined to unmistakable Latin stems. There is *whimsical*; and there may be others that break the rule, though the *Oxford Dictionary* (*-al suffix*, *-ical suffix*, *-ial suffix*) gives no exceptions. The ugly words *racial* and *coastal* themselves might well be avoided except in the rare cases where *race* and *coast* used adjectivally will not do the work (they would in the present instances); and they should not be made precedents for new formations. If *language* is better than *linguistic*, much more *race* than *racial*; similarly, *river* than *riverine*.

Bull baiting, bear baiting . . . were put down with the same *indiscriminating* severity.—J. R. GREEN.

We can only regret that his ideas are *indigested*.—*Times*.

It may safely be laid down that when adjectives ending in the obviously English *-ed* or *-ing* are to be negatived, the English *un-* is better than the Latin *in-*; *indigestible*, but *undigested*; *indiscriminate*, but *undiscriminating*.

What she was pleased to term their superior intelligence, and more real and *reliable* probity.—C. BRONTË (*Villette*, 1853).

It is absurd at this time of day to make a fuss about the word. It is with us and will remain with us, whatever pedants and purists may say. In such cases *obsta principiis* is the only hope; *reliable* might once have been suppressed, perhaps; it cannot now. But it is so fought over, even today, that a short discussion of it may be looked for. The objection to it is obvious: you do not rely a thing; therefore the thing cannot be reliable; it should be rely-on-able (like *come-at-able*). Some of the analogies pleaded for it are perhaps irrelevant—as *laughable*, *available*. For these *may* be formed from the nouns *laugh*, *avail*, since *-able* is not only gerundival (capable of being laughed at), but also adjectival (connected with a laugh); this has certainly happened with *seasonable*; but that will not help *reliable*, which by analogy should be *relianceable*. It is more to the point to remark that with *reliable* must go *dispensable* (with *indispensable*) and *dependable*, both quite old words, and *disposable* (in its commoner sense); no one, as far as we know, objects to these and others like them; *reliable* is made into a scapegoat. The word itself, moreover, besides its wide popularity, is now of respectable antiquity, dating at least from Coleridge.[1] It may be added that it is probably to the campaign against it that we owe such passive monstrosities as 'ready to be availed of' for *available*, which is, as we said, possibly not open to the same objection as *reliable*.

I have heretofore designated the misuse of certain words as *Briticisms*. —R. G. WHITE.

Britannic, Britannicism; British, Britishism. Britic?

4. Needless, though correct formations.

The *sordor* and filths of nature, the sun shall dry up.—EMERSON.

As *candeo candor*, *ardeo ardor*, so—we are to understand—

---

[1] The *O.E.D.*, which had not reached R when this book was published (1906), now shows that *reliable* (or *raliabill*) goes back to the 16th century. H. W. F. 1930.

sordeo sordor. The Romans, however, never felt that they needed the word; and it is a roundabout method first to present them with a new word and then to borrow it from them; for it will be observed that we have no living suffix -*or* in English, nor, if we had, anything nearer than *sordid* to attach it to. Perhaps Emerson thought *sordor* was a Latin word.

Merely nodding his head as an *enjoinder* to be careful.—DICKENS.

As *rejoin rejoinder*, so *enjoin enjoinder*. The word is not given in the *Oxford Dictionary*, from which it seems likely that Dickens invented it, consciously or unconsciously. The only objection to such a word is that its having had to wait so long, in spite of its obviousness, before being made is a strong argument against the necessity of it. We may regret that *injunction* holds the field, having a much less English appearance; but it does; and in language the old-established that can still do the work is not to be turned out for the new-fangled that might do it a shade better, but must first get itself known and accepted.

Oppositely, the badness of a walk that is shuffling, and an utterance that is indistinct is alleged.—SPENCER.

This, on the other hand, is an archaism, now obsolete. Why it should not have lived is a mystery; but it has not; and to write it is to give one's sentence the air of an old curiosity shop.

Again, as if to *intensate* the influences that are not of race, what we think of when we talk of English traits really narrows itself to a small district.—EMERSON.

A favourite with those allied experimenters in words, Emerson and Carlyle. A word meaning *to make intense* is necessary; and there are plenty of parallels for this particular form. But Coleridge had already made *intensify*, introducing it with an elaborate apology in which he confessed that it sounded uncouth. It is uncouth no longer; if it had never existed, perhaps *intensate* would now have been so no longer, uncouthness being, both etymologically and otherwise, a matter of strangeness as against familiarity. It is better to form words only where there is a clear demand for them.

5. **Long and short rivals.** The following examples illustrate a foolish tendency. From the adjective *perfect* we form the verb *to perfect*, and from that again the noun *perfection*; to take a further step forward to a verb *to perfection* instead of returning to the verb *to perfect* is a superfluity of naughtiness. From the noun *sense* we make the adjective *sensible*; it is generally quite needless to go forward to *sensibleness* instead of back to our original noun *sense*. To *quieten* is often used by hasty writers who have not time to remember that *quiet* is a verb. With *ex tempore* ready to serve either as adverb or as adjective, why make *extemporaneous* or *extemporaneously*? As to *contumacity*, the writer was probably unaware that *contumacy* existed. *Contumacity* might be formed from *contumax*, like *audacity* from *audax*. The Romans had only the short forms *audacia*, *contumacia*, which should have given us *audacy* as well as *contumacy*; but because our ancestors burdened themselves with an extra syllable in one we need not therefore do so in the other.

> The inner, religiously moral *perfectioning* of individuals.—*Times*.
> She liked the quality of mind which may be broadly called *sensibleness*.—*Times*.

Broadly, or lengthily?

> M. Delcassé, speaking *extemporaneously* but with notes, said . . .—*Times*.
> And now, Mdlle St. Pierre's affected interference provoked *contumacity*.—C. BRONTË.
> It is often a very easy thing to act *prudentially*, but alas! too often only after we have toiled to our prudence through a forest of delusions.—DE QUINCEY.

Prudent gives *prudence*, and *prudence prudential*; the latter has its use: prudential considerations are those in which prudence is allowed to outweigh other motives; they may be prudent without being prudential, and vice versa. But before using *prudentially* we should be quite sure that we mean something different from *prudently*. So again *partially*, which should be reserved as far as possible for the meaning *with partiality*, is now commonly used for *partly*:[1]

The series of administrative reforms planned by the Convention had been *partially* carried into effect before the meeting of Parliament in 1654; but the work was pushed on.—J. R. GREEN.

That the gravity of the situation is *partially* appreciated by the bureaucracy may be inferred from . . .—*Times*.

Excepting, instead of *except*, is to be condemned when there is no need for it. We say *not excepting*, or *not even excepting*, or *without excepting*; but where the exception is allowed, not rejected, the short form is the right one, as a comparison of the following examples will show:

Of all societies . . . *not even excepting* the Roman Republic, England has been the most emphatically . . . political.—MORLEY.

The Minister was obliged to present the Budget before May each year, *excepting* in the event of the Cortes having been dissolved.—*Times*.

The sojourn of belligerent ships in French waters has never been limited *excepting* by certain clearly defined rules.—*Times*.

Excepting the English, French, and Austrian journalists present, no one had been admitted.—*Times*

Innumerable other needless lengthenings might be produced, from which we choose only *preventative* for *preventive*, and *to experimentalize* for *to experiment*.

On the other hand, when usage has differentiated a long and a short form either of which might originally have served, the distinction must be kept. *Immovable* and *irremovable* judges are different things; the shorter word has been wrongly chosen in:

By suspending conscription and restoring the *immovability* of the Judges.—*Times*.

---

[1] The use deprecated has perhaps crept in from such phrases as *the sun was partially eclipsed*, an adaptation of *a partial eclipse*; and to such phrases it should be restricted. 'The case was partially heard on Oct. 17' is ambiguous; and the second example in the text is almost so, nearly enough to show that the limitation is desirable. The rule should be never to write *partially* without first considering the claims of *partly*.

6. Merely ugly formations.

Bureaucracy.

The termination -*cracy* is now so freely applied that it is too late to complain of this except on the ground of ugliness. It may be pointed out, however, that the very special ugliness of *bureaucracy* is due to the way its mongrel origin is flaunted in our faces by the telltale syllable -*eau*-; it is to be hoped that formations similar in this respect may be avoided.

An ordinary reader, if asked what was the main impression given by the *Short History of the English People*, would answer that it was the impression of picturesqueness and *vividity*.—BRYCE.

In sound, there can be no question between *vividity* with its fourfold repetition of the same vowel sound, its two dentals to add to the ugliness of its two *v*'s, and the comparatively inoffensive *vividness*.

We conclude with deprecating the addition of -*ly* to participles in -*ed*. Some people are so alive to the evil sound of it that they write *determinately* for *determinedly* (Thurlow . . . applied himself determinately to the business of life.—*Southey*); that will not do either, because *determinate* does not mean *determined* in the required sense. A periphrasis, or an adjective or Latin participle with -*ly*, as *resolutely*, should be used. *Implied* is as good a word as *implicit*, but *impliedly* is by no means so good as *implicitly*. Several instances are given, for cumulative effect. Miss Corelli makes a mannerism of this.

Dr. John and his mother were in their finest mood, contending *animatedly* with each other the whole way.—C. BRONTË.

Where the gate opens, or the gateless path turns aside *trustedly*.—RUSKIN.

'That's not a very kind speech,' I said somewhat *vexedly*.—CORELLI.

However, I *determinedly* smothered all premonitions.—CORELLI.

I saw one or two passers-by looking at me so *surprisedly* that I came to the conclusion . . .—CORELLI.

I stared *bewilderedly* up at the stars.—CORELLI.

It should be added that to really established adverbs of this form, as *advisedly*, *assuredly*, *hurriedly*, there is no objection whatever; but new ones are ugly.

SLANG

The place of slang is in real life. There, an occasional indulgence in it is an almost necessary concession to our gregarious humanity; he who declines altogether to let his speech be influenced by his neighbours' tricks, and takes counsel only of pure reason, is setting up for more than man. *Awfully nice* is an expression than which few could be sillier; but to have succeeded in going through life without saying it a certain number of times is as bad as to have no redeeming vice. Further, the writer who deals in conversation may sometimes find it necessary, by way of characterizing his speakers, to put slang into their mouths; if he is wise he will make the least possible use of this resource; and to interlard the non-conversational parts of a book or article with slang, quotation-marks or no quotation-marks, is as bad as interlarding with French. Foreign words and slang are, as spurious ornaments, on the same level. The italics, but not the quotation-marks, in these examples are ours:

When the madness motif was being treated on the stage, Shakespeare (as was the custom of his theatre) treated it '*for all it was worth*', careless of the boundaries between feigning and reality.—*Times*.

But even this situation '*peters out*', the wife being sent away with her fate undecided, and the husband, represented as a 'forcible-feeble' person by the dramatist and as a feeble person, tout court, by the actor. . . .—*Times*.

M. Baron the younger is amusing as the '*bounder*' Olivier.—*Times*.

Asking ourselves this question about Mr. Thurston's play, we find that it has given us a ha'porth of pleasure to an intolerable deal of boredom. With its primary postulate, '*steep*' as it is, we will not quarrel.—*Times*.

They will find no subtlety in it, no literary art, no profundity of feeling; but they will assuredly find breadth, colour, and strength. It is a play that hits you, as the children say, '*bang in the eye*'.—*Times*.

They derive no advantage from schemes of land settlement from which the man who has broken the land in gets '*the boot*', the voter gets the land, the Government gets the vote, and the London labour market gets the risk.—*Times*.

The effect of using quotation marks with slang is merely to

convert a mental into a moral weakness. When they are not used, we may mercifully assume that the writer does not know the difference between slang and good English, and sins in ignorance: when they are, he is telling us, I know it is naughty, but then it is nice. Most of us would rather be taken for knaves than for fools; and so the quotation marks are usually there.

With this advice—never to use slang except in dialogue, and there as little as may be—we might leave the subject, except that the suggestion we have made about the unconscious use of slang seems to require justifying. To justify it, we must attempt some analysis, however slight, of different sorts of slang.

To the ordinary man, of average intelligence and middle-class position, slang comes from every direction, from above, from below, and from all sides, as well as from the centre. What comes from some directions he will know for slang, what comes from others he may not. He may be expected to recognize words from below. Some of these are shortenings, by the lower classes, of words whose full form conveys no clear meaning, and is therefore useless, to them. An antiquated example is *mob*, for *mobile vulgus*. That was once slang, and is now good English. A modern one is *bike*, which will very likely be good English also in time. But though its brevity is a strong recommendation, and its uncouthness probably no more than subjective and transitory, it is as yet slang. Such words should not be used in print till they have become so familiar that there is not the slightest temptation to dress them up in quotation marks. Though they are the most easily detected, they are also the best slang; when the time comes, they take their place in the language as words that will last, and not, like many of the more highly descended words, die away uselessly after a brief popularity.

Another set of words that may be said to come from below, since it owes its existence to the vast number of people who are incapable of appreciating fine shades of meaning, is exemplified by *nice, awful, blooming*. Words of this class fortunately never make their way, in their slang senses, into literature (except, of course, dialogue). The abuse of *nice* has gone on at any rate for over a century; the curious reader may find an interesting page upon it in the fourteenth chapter of *Northanger Abbey* (1803). But even now we do not talk in books of *a nice day*, only of *a nice distinction*. On the other hand, the slang use makes us shy in different degrees of writing the words in their legitimate sense: *a nice distinction* we write almost without qualms; *an awful storm* we think twice about; and as to *a blooming girl*, we hardly venture it nowadays. The most recent sufferer of this sort is perhaps *chronic*. It has been adopted by the massses, as far apart at least as in Yorkshire and in London, for a mere intensive, in the sense of *remarkable*. The next step is for it to be taken up in parody by people who know better; after which it may be expected to succeed *awful*.

So much for the slang from below; the ordinary man can detect it. He is not so infallible about what comes to him from above. We are by no means sure that we shall be correct in our particular attribution of the half-dozen words now to be mentioned; but it is safe to say that they are all at present enjoying some vogue as slang, and that they all come from regions that to most of us are overhead. *Phenomenal*, soon, we hope, to perish unregretted, is (at least indirectly, through the abuse of *phenomenon*) from Metaphysics; *immanence*, a word often met in singular company, from Comparative Theology; *epochmaking* perhaps from the Philosophic Historian; *true inwardness* from Literary Criticism; *cad* (which is, it appears, Etonian for *cadet*) from the Upper Classes; *psychological moment* from Science; *thrasonical* and *cryptic* from Academic circles; *philistine* from the region of culture. Among these the one that will be most generally allowed to be slang—*cad*—is in fact the least so; it has by this time, like *mob*, passed its probation and taken its place as an orthodox word, so that all who do not find adequate expression for their feelings in the orthodox have turned away to *bounder* and other forms that still admit the emphasis of quotation marks. As for the rest of them, they are being subjected to that use, at once over-frequent and inaccurate, which produces one kind of slang. But the average man, seeing from what exalted quarters they come, is dazzled into admiration and hardly knows them for what they are.

By the slang that comes from different sides or from the centre we mean especially the many words taken originally from particular professions, pursuits, or games, but extended beyond them. Among these a man is naturally less critical of what comes from his own daily concerns, that is, in his view, from the centre. *Frontispiece*, for face, perhaps originated in the desire of prize-ring reporters to vary the words in their descriptive flights. *Negotiate* (a difficulty, &c.) possibly comes from the hunting-field; people whose conversation runs much upon a limited subject feel the need of new phrases for the too familiar things. And both these words, as well as *individual*, which must be treated more at length in the next section, are illustrations of a tendency that we have called polysyllabic humour and discussed in the Chapter *Airs and Graces*. We now add a short list of slang phrases or words that can most of them be referred with more or less of certainty to particular occupations. Whether they are recognized as slang will certainly depend in part on whether the occupation is familiar, though sometimes the familiarity will disguise, and sometimes it will bring out, the slanginess.

To hedge, the double event (turf); *frontal attack* (war); *play the game, stumped* (cricket); *to run*—the show, &c.—(engine-driving); *knock out, take it lying down* (prize-ring); *log-rolling, slating, birrelling* (literature); *to tackle*—a problem, &c.—(football); *to take a back seat* (coaching?); *bedrock, to exploit, how it pans out* (mining); *whole-hogging, world policy* (politics); *floored* (1. prize ring; 2. school); *the under dog* (dog-fighting); *up to date* (advertising); *record*—time, &c.—(athletics); *euchred, going one better, going Nap.* (cards); *to corner*—a thing—(commerce)—a person—(ratting); *chic* (society journalism); *on your own, of sorts, climb down, globetrotter, to laze* (perhaps not assignable).

Good and sufficient occasions will arise—rarely—for using most of these phrases and the rest of the slang vocabulary. To those, however, who desire that what they write may endure it is suggested that, as style is the great antiseptic, so slang is the great corrupting matter; it is perishable itself, and infects what is round it—the catchwords that delight one generation stink in the nostrils of the next; *individual*, which almost made the fortune of many a Victorian humorist, is one of the modern editor's shibboleths for detecting the unfit. And even those who regard only the present will do well to remember that in literature as elsewhere there are as many conservatives as progressives, as many who expect their writers to say things a little better than they could do themselves as who are flattered by the proof that one man is no better than another.

'Skepsey did come back to London with rather a damaged *frontispiece*', Victor said.—MEREDITH.

Henson, however, once *negotiated* a sprint down his wing, and put in a fine dropping shot to Aubert, who saved.—*Guernsey Evening Press.*

Passengers, the guild add, usually arrive at the last moment before sailing, when the master must concentrate his mind upon *negotiating* a safe passage.—*Times.*

To deal with these extensive and purely local breeding grounds in the manner suggested by Major Ross would be a very *tall order.*—*Times.*

In about twenty minutes he returned, accompanied by a highly intelligent-looking *individual*, dressed in blue and black, with a particularly white cravat, and without a hat on his head; this *individual*, whom I should have mistaken for a gentleman but for the intelligence depicted in his face, he introduced to me as the master of the inn.—BORROW.

A Sèvres vase sold yesterday at Christie's *realized* what is believed to be the *record* price of 4,000 guineas.—*Times.*

You could not, if you had tried, have made so perfect a place for two girls to lounge in, to *laze* in, to read silly novels in, or to go to sleep in on drowsy afternoons.—CROCKETT.

Mr. Balfour's somewhat *thrasonical* eulogies.—*Spectator.*

A quarrelsome, somewhat *thrasonical* fighting man.—*Spectator*.

The *true inwardness* of this statement is . . .—*Times*.

We do not know what *inwardness* there may be in the order of his discourses, though each of them has some articulate link with that which precedes.—*Times*.

Such a departure from etiquette at the *psychological moment* shows tact and discretion.—*Times*.

He asserts that about four years ago there was quite an Argentine *boom* in New Zealand.—*Times*.

No . treatment of slang, however short, should omit the reminder that slang and idiom are hard to distinguish, and yet, in literature, slang is bad, and idiom good. We said that slang was perishable; the fact is that most of it perishes; but some survives and is given the idiomatic franchise; 'when it doth prosper, none dare call it' slang. The idiomatic writer differs chiefly from the slangy in using what was slang and is now idiom; of what is still slang he chooses only that part which his insight assures him has the sort of merit that will preserve it. In a small part of their vocabulary the idiomatic and the slangy will coincide, and be therefore confused by the undiscerning. The only advice that can be given to novices uncertain of their own discrimination is to keep carefully off the debatable ground. Full idiom and full slang are as far apart as virtue and vice; and yet

> They oft so mix, the difference is too nice
> Where ends the virtue, or begins the vice.

Any one who can confidently assign each of the following phrases to its own territory may feel that he is not in much danger:

Outrun the constable, the man in the street, kicking your heels, between two stools, cutting a loss, riding for a fall, not seeing the wood for the trees, minding your Ps and Qs, crossing the *t*s, begging the question, special pleading, a bone to pick, half seas over, tooth and nail, bluff, maffick, a tall order, it has come to stay.

PARTICULAR WORDS

Individual, mutual, unique, aggravating.

To use *individual* wrongly in the twentieth century stamps a writer, more definitely than almost any other single solecism, not as being generally ignorant or foolish, but as being without the literary sense. For the word has been pilloried time after time; every one who is interested in style at all—which includes every one who aspires to be readable—must at least be aware that there is some mystery about the word, even if he has not penetrated it. He has, therefore, two courses open to him: he may leave the word alone; or he may find out what it means; if he insists on using it without finding out, he will commit himself. The adjectival use of it presents no difficulty; the adjective, as well as the adverb *individually*, is always used rightly if at all; it is the noun that goes wrong. An *individual* is not simply a person; it is a single, separate, or private person, a person as opposed to a combination of persons; this qualification, this opposition, must be effectively present to the mind, or the word is not in place. In the nineteenth, especially the early nineteenth century, this distinction was neglected; mainly under the impulse of 'polysyllabic humour', the word, which does mean *person* in some sort of way, was seized upon as a facetious substitute for it; not only that; it spread even to good writers who had no facetious intention; it became the kind of slang described in the last section, which is highly popular until it suddenly turns disgusting. In reading many of these writers we feel that we must make allowances for them on this point; they only failed to be right when every one else was wrong. But we, if we do it, sin against the light.

To leave no possible doubt about the distinction, we shall give many examples, divided into (1) right uses, (2) wrong uses, (3) sentences in which, though the author has used the word rightly, a perverse reader might take it wrongly. It will be observed that in (1) to substitute *man* or *person* would distinctly weaken the sense; in the sentence from Macaulay it would be practically impossible. The words italicized are those that prove the contrast with bodies, or organizations, to have been present in the author's mind, though it may often happen that he does not actually show it by specific mention of them. On the other hand, in (2) *person* or *man* or *he* might always be substituted without harm to the sense, though sometimes a more exact word (not *individual*) might be preferable. In (3) little difference would be made by the substitution.

(1) Many of the *constituent bodies* were under the absolute control of individuals.—MACAULAY.

Regarding the general effect of Lord Kitchener's proclamation, everything so far as is known here points to the conclusion that the document has failed to secure the surrender of any *body of men*. Merely a few individuals have yielded.—*Times*.

The wise Commons, considering that they are, if not a French *Third Estate*, at least an aggregate of individuals pretending to some title of that kind, determine . . .—CARLYLE.

(2) That greenish-coloured individual is an advocate of Arras; his name is Maximilien Robespierre.—CARLYLE. (person)

Surely my fate is somehow strangely interwoven with that of this mysterious individual.—SCOTT. (person)

And, as its weight is 15 lb., nobody save an individual in no condition to distinguish a hawk from a handsaw could possibly mistake it for a saluting charge.—*Times*. (person)

The Secretary of State for War was sending the same man down to see what he could do in the Isle of Wight. The individual duly arrived. —*Times*. (he)

My own shabby clothes and deplorable aspect, as compared with this regal-looking individual.—CORELLI. (person)

In the present case, however, the individual who had secured the cab had a companion.—BEACONSFIELD. (man)

I give my idea of the method in which Mr. Spencer and a Metaphysician would discuss the necessity and validity of the Universal Postulate. We must suppose this imaginary individual to have so far forgotten himself as to make some positive statement.—A. J. BALFOUR. (person)

But what made her marry that individual, who was at least as much like an oil-barrel as a man?—C. BRONTË. (monstrosity)

He was a genteelly dressed individual; rather corpulent, with dark features.—BORROW. (man)

During his absence two calls were made at the parsonage—one by a very rough-looking individual who left a suspicious document in the hands of the servant.—TROLLOPE. (man)

(3) Almost all the recent Anarchist crimes were perpetrated by *isolated* halfwitted individuals who aimed at universal notoriety.— *Times*.

Which of these two individuals, in plain white cravat, that have come up to regenerate France, might one guess would become their king? For a king or leader they, as all *bodies of men*, must have.—CARLYLE.

Some apology is due for so heaping up instances of the same thing; but here, as with other common blunders to be treated of later, it has seemed that an effect might be produced by mere iteration.

The word *mutual* requires caution. As with *individual*, any one who is not prepared to clear his ideas upon its meaning will do well to avoid it; it is a very telltale word, readily convicting the unwary, and on the other hand it may quite easily be done without. Every one knows by now that *our mutual friend* is a solecism. *Mutual* implies an action or relation between two or more persons or things, A doing or standing to B as B does or stands to A. Let A and B be the persons indicated by *our*, C the *friend*. No such reciprocal relation is here implied between A and B (who for all we know may be enemies), but only a separate, though similar relation between each of them and C. There is no such thing as a mutual friend in the singular; but the phrase *mutual friends* may without nonsense be used to describe either A and C, B and C, or, if A and B happen to be also friends, A and B and C. *Our mutual friend* is nonsense; *mutual friends*, though not nonsense, is bad English, because it is tautological. It takes two to make a friendship, as to make a quarrel; and therefore all friends are mutual friends, and *friends* alone means as much as *mutual friends*. *Mutual well-wishers* on the other hand is good English as well as good sense, because it is possible for me to be a man's well-wisher though he hates me. Mutual love, understanding, insurance, benefits, dislike, mutual benefactors, backbiters, abettors, may all be correct, though they are also sometimes used incorrectly, like *our mutual friend*, where the right word would be *common*.

Further, it is to be carefully observed that the word *mutual* is an equivalent in meaning, and sometimes a convenient one for grammatical reasons, of the pronoun *each other* with various prepositions. To use it as well as *each other* is even more clearly tautological than the already mentioned *mutual friendship*.

If this be the case, much of the lost mutual understanding and unity of feeling may be restored.—*Times*.

Correct, if *mutual* is confined to *understanding*: they no longer understand *each other*.

Once their differences removed, both felt that in presence of certain incalculable factors in Europe it would be of mutual advantage to draw closer together.—*Times*.

Slightly clumsy; but it means that they would get advantage *from each other* by drawing together, and may stand.

. . . conversing with his Andalusian lady-love in rosy whispers about their mutual passion for Spanish chocolate all the while.—MEREDITH.

Surely you have heard Mrs. Toddles talking to Mrs. Doddles about their mutual maids.—THACKERAY.

Indefensible.

There may be, moreover, while each has the key of the fellow breast, a mutually sensitive nerve.—MEREDITH.

A nerve cannot respond to each other; nerves can; *a common nerve* would have done; or *mutually sensitive nerves*.

It is now definitely announced that King Edward will meet President Loubet this afternoon near Paris. Our Paris Correspondent says the meeting will take place by mutual desire.—*Times*.

Right or wrong according to what is meant by *desire*. (1) If it means that King Edward and M. Loubet desired, that is, had a yearning for, each other, it is correct; but the writer probably did not intend so poetic a flight. (2) If it means that they merely desired a meeting, it is wrong, exactly as *our mutual friend* is wrong. The relation is not one between A and B; it is only that A and B hold separately the same relation to C, the meeting. It should be *common desire*. (3) If *desire* is here equivalent to *request*, and each is represented as having requested the other to meet him, it is again correct; but only politeness to the writer would induce any one to take this alternative.

The carpenter holds the hammer in one hand, the nail in the other, and they do their work equally well. So it is with every craftsman; the hands are mutually busy.—*Times*.

Wrong. The hands are not busy *with* or *upon each other*, but with or upon the work. As *commonly* would be ambiguous here, *equally* or *alike* should be used, or simply *both*. *Mutually serviceable*, again, would have been right.

There were other means of communication between Claribel and her new prophet. Books were mutually lent to each other.—BEACONSFIELD.

This surprising sentence means that Vanity Fair was lent to Paradise Lost, and Paradise Lost to Vanity Fair. If we further assume for politeness' sake that *mutually* is not mere tautology with *to each other*, the only thing left for it to mean is *by each other*. The doubt then remains whether (1) Paradise Lost was lent to Vanity Fair by Paradise Lost, and Vanity Fair to Paradise Lost by Vanity Fair, or (2) Paradise Lost was lent to Vanity Fair by Vanity Fair, and Vanity Fair to Paradise Lost by Paradise Lost. This may be considered captious; but we still wish the author had said either, They lent each other books, or, Books were lent by them to each other.

A thing is *unique*, or not unique; there are no degrees of uniqueness; nothing is ever somewhat or rather unique, though many things are almost or in some respects unique. The word is a member of a depreciating series. *Singular* had once the strong meaning that *unique* has still in accurate but not in other writers. In consequence of slovenly use, *singular* no longer means singular, but merely remarkable; it is worn out; before long *rather unique* will be familiar; *unique*, that is, will be worn out in turn, and we shall have to resort to *unexampled* and keep that clear of qualifications as long as we can. Happily it is still admitted that sentences like the three given below are solecisms; they contain a self-contradiction. For the other regrettable use of *unique*, as when the advertisement columns offer us what they call *unique opportunities*, it may generally be assumed with safety that they are lying; but lying is not in itself a literary offence, so that with these we have nothing to do.

Thrills which gave him *rather* a *unique* pleasure.—HUTTON.
A *very unique* child, thought I.—C. BRONTË.
. . . is to be translated into Russian by M. Robert Böker, of St. Peters-

burg. This is a *somewhat unique* thing to happen to an English text-book.—*Westminster Gazette.*

To *aggravate* is not to annoy or enrage (a person), but to make worse (a condition or trouble). The active participle should very rarely, and the rest of the active practically never, be used without an expressed object, and that of the right kind. In the sentence, *An aggravating circumstance was that the snow was dirty*, the meaning is not that the dirt was annoying, but that it added to some other misery previously expressed or implied. But, as the dirt happens to be annoying also, this use is easily misunderstood, and is probably the origin of the notorious vulgarism; since it almost inevitably lays a writer open to suspicion, it is best avoided. Of the following quotations, the first is quite correct, the other five as clearly wrong; in the fifth, *aggrieved* would be the right word.

A premature initiative would be useless and even dangerous, being calculated rather to aggravate than to simplify the situation.—*Times.*

Perhaps the most trying and aggravating period of the whole six months during which the siege has lasted was this period of enforced idleness waiting for the day of entry.—*Times.*

There is a cold formality about the average Englishman; a lack of effusive disposition to ingratiate himself, and an almost aggravating indifference to alien customs or conventions.—*Times.*

Mrs. Craigie may possibly be regarding him with an irony too fine for us to detect; but to the ordinary mind he appears to be conceived in the spirit of romance, and a very stupid, tiresome, aggravating man he is.—*Times.*

'Well, I'm sure I'm very much obliged to you, Misses Brown,' said the unfortunate youth, greatly aggravated.—DICKENS.

Nevertheless, it is an aggravating book, though we are bound to admit that we have been greatly interested.—*Westminster Gazette.*

CHAPTER II

SYNTAX

CASE

THERE is not much opportunity in English for going wrong here, because we have shed most of our cases. The personal pronouns, and *who* and its compounds, are the only words that visibly retain three—called subjective, objective, possessive. In nouns the first two are indistinguishable, and are called the common case. One result of this simplicity is that, the sense of case being almost lost, the few mistakes that can be made are made often—some of them so often that they are now almost right by prescription.

1. In apposition.

A pronoun appended to a noun, and in the same relation to the rest of the sentence, should be in the same case. Disregard of this is a bad blunder.

But to behold her mother—*she* to whom she owed her being!—S. FERRIER.

2. The complement with *am, are, is*, &c., should be subjective.

I am she, she *me*, till death and beyond it.—MEREDITH.
Whom would you rather be?
To how many maimed and mourning millions is the first and sole angel visitant, *him* Easterns call Azrael.—C. BRONTË.
That 's *him*.

In the last but one, *him* would no doubt have been defended by the writer, since the full form would be *he whom*, as an attraction to the vanished *whom*. But such attraction is not right; if *he* alone is felt to be uncomfortable, *whom* should not be omitted; or, in this exalted context, it might be *he that*.

On *that 's him*, see 4, below.

3. When a verb or preposition governs two pronouns united by *and*, &c., the second is apt to go wrong—a bad blunder. *Between you and I* is often heard in talk; and, in literature:

And now, my dear, let you and *I* say a few words about this unfortunate affair.—TROLLOPE.

It is kept locked up in a marble casket, quite out of reach of you or *I*.—S. FERRIER.

She found everyone's attention directed to Mary, and *she* herself entirely overlooked.—S. FERRIER.

4. The interrogative *who* is often used for *whom*, as, *Who* did you see? A distinction should here be made between conversation, written or spoken, and formal writing. Many educated people feel that in saying *It is I, Whom do you mean?* instead of *It 's me, Who do you mean?* they will be talking like a book, and they justifiably prefer geniality to grammar. But in print, unless it is dialogue, the correct forms are advisable.   ·

5. Even with words that have no visible distinction between subjective and objective case, it is possible to go wrong; for the case can always be inferred, though not seen. Consequently a word should never be so placed that it must be taken twice, once as subject and once as object. This is so common a blunder that it will be well to give a good number of examples. It occurs especially with the relative, from its early position in the sentence; but, as the first two examples show, it may result from the exceptional placing of other words also. The mere repetition of the relative, or insertion of *it* or other pronoun, generally mends the sentence; in the first example, change *should only be* to *only to be*.

The occupation of the mouths of the Yalu, however, his Majesty considered undesirable, and should only be carried out in the last resort.—*Times*.

This the strong sense of Lady Maclaughlan had long perceived, and was the principal reason of her selecting so weak a woman as her companion.—S. FERRIER.

Qualities *which* it would cost me a great deal to acquire, and would lead to nothing.—MORLEY.

A recorded saying of our Lord *which* some higher critics of the New Testament regard as of doubtful authenticity, and is certainly of doubtful interpretation.

A weakness *which* some would miscall gratitude, and is oftentimes the corrupter of a heart not ignoble.—RICHARDSON.

Analogous to these are the next three examples, which will require separate comment:

Knowledge *to* the certainty of which no authority could add, or take away, one jot or title.—HUXLEY.

To is applicable to *add*, not to *take away*. The full form is given by substituting for *or* 'and from the certainty of which no authority could'. This is clearly too cumbrous. Inserting *or from* after *to* is the simplest correction; but the result is rather formal. Better, perhaps, 'the certainty of which could not be increased or diminished one jot by any authority'.

From his conversation I should have pronounced him to be fitted to excel *in* whatever walk of ambition he had chosen to exert his abilities.

A second *in* is required. This common slovenliness results from the modern[1] superstition against putting a preposition at the end. The particular sentence may, however, be mended otherwise than by inserting *in*, if *excel* is made absolute by a comma placed after it. Even then, the *in* would perhaps be better at the end of the clause than at the beginning.

Lastly may be mentioned a principle *upon which* Clausewitz insisted with all his strength, and could never sufficiently impress upon his Royal scholar.—*Times*.

The italicized *upon* (we have nothing to do with the other *upon*) is right with *insist*, but wrong, though it must necessarily be supplied again, with *impress*. It is the result of the same superstition. Mend either by writing *upon* after *insisted* instead of before *which*, or by inserting *which he* after *and*.

6. After *as* and *than*.

These are properly conjunctions, and 'take the same case after them as before'. But those words must be rightly understood. (a), *I love you more than him*, means something different from (b), *I love you more than he*. It must be borne in mind that the 'case before' is that of the word that is compared with the 'case after', and not necessarily that of the word actually

[1] I will not leave thee, until I have done that which I have spoken to thee of.—*Gen.* xxviii. 15.

next before in position. In (a) *you* is compared with *him*: in (b) *I* (not *you*) is compared with *he*. The correct usage is therefore important, and the tendency illustrated in the following examples to make *than* and *as* prepositions should be resisted— though no ambiguity can actually result here.

> When such as *her* die.—SWIFT.
> But there, I think, Lindore would be more eloquent than *me*.— S. FERRIER.

It must further be noticed that both *as* and *than* are conjunctions of the sort that can either, like *and*, &c., merely join coordinates, or, like *when*, &c., attach a subordinate clause to what it depends on. This double power sometimes affects case.

> It is to him and such men as *he* that we owe the change.—HUXLEY.

This example is defensible, *as* being here a subordinating conjunction, and *as he* being equivalent to *as he is*. But it is distinctly felt to need defence, which *as him* would not; *as* would be a coordinating conjunction, and simply join the pronoun *him* to the noun men. So, with *than*:

> Such as have bound me, as well as others much better than *me*, by an inviolable attachment to him from that time forward.—BURKE.

On the other hand, we could not say indifferently, *I am as good as he*, and *I am as good as him*; the latter would imply that *as* was a preposition, which it is not. And it is not always possible to choose between the coordinating and the subordinating use. In the next example only the coordinating will do, no verb being capable of standing after *he*; but the author has not observed this.

> I beheld a man in the dress of a postillion, whom I instantly recognized as *he* to whom I had rendered assistance.—BORROW.

A difficult question, however, arises with relatives after *than*. In the next two examples *whom* is as manifestly wrong as *who* is manifestly intolerable:

> Dr. Dillon, than *whom* no Englishman has a profounder acquaintance with . . .—*Times*.
> It was a pleasure to hear Canon Liddon, than *whom*, in his day, there was no finer preacher.

The only correct solution is to recast the sentences. For instance, . . . *whose acquaintance with . . . is unrivalled among Englishmen*; and . . . *unsurpassed in his day as a preacher*. But perhaps the convenience of *than whom* is so great that to rule it out amounts to saying that man is made for grammar and not grammar for man.

7. Compound possessives.

This is strictly the proper place for drawing attention to a question that has some importance because it bears on the very common construction discussed at some length in the gerund section. This is the question whether, and to what extent, compound possessives may be recognized. Some people say *some one else's*, others say *some one's else*. Our own opinion is that the latter is uncalled for and pedantic. Of the three alternatives, *Smith the baker's wife*, *Smith's wife the baker*, *the wife of Smith the baker*, the last is unmitigated Ollendorff, the second thrusts its ambiguity upon us and provokes an involuntary smile, and the first alone is felt to be natural. It must be confessed, however, that it is generally avoided in print, while the form that we have ventured to call pedantic is not uncommon. In the first of the examples that follow, we should be inclined to change to *Nanny the maid-of-all-work's*, and in the second to *the day of Frea, goddess of*, &c.

Another mind that was being wrought up to a climax was Nanny's, the maid-of-all-work, who had a warm heart.—ELIOT.

Friday is Frea's-day, the goddess of peace and joy and fruitfulness.—J. R. GREEN.

NUMBER

Very little comment will be needed; we have only to convince readers that mistakes are common, and caution therefore necessary.

1. The copula should always agree with the subject, not with the complement. These are wrong:

The *pages* which describe how the 34th Osaka Regiment wiped out the tradition that had survived since the Saigo rebellion *is* a typical *piece* of description.—*Times*.

A *boy* dressed up as a girl *and a girl* dressed up as a girl *is*, to the eye at least, the same *thing.—Times.*

People do not believe now as they did, but the moral *inconsistencies* of our contemporaries *is* no *proof* thereof.—*Daily Telegraph.*

It must be remembered that in questions the subject often comes after the verb and the complement before it; but the same rule must be kept. E. g., if the last example were put as a question instead of as a negative statement, 'What proof *is* the inconsistencies?' would be wrong, and 'What proof *are* &c.?' right.

Some sentences in which the subject contains *only*, a superlative, &c., have the peculiarity that subject and complement may almost be considered to have changed places; and this defence would probably be put in for the next three examples; but, whether actually wrong or not, they are unpleasant. The noun that stands before the verb should be regarded as the subject, and the verb be adapted to it.

The only *thing* Siamese about the Consul, except the hatchment and the flag, *were* his *servants.*—SLADEN.

The only *difficulty* in Finnish *are* the *changes* undergone by the stem.—SWEET.

The most pompous *monument* of Egyptian greatness, and *one* of the most bulky works of manual industry, *are* the pyramids.—JOHNSON.

The next example is a curious problem; the subject to *were* is in sense plural, but in grammar singular (*finding*, verbal noun):

Finding Miss Vernon in a place so solitary, engaged in a journey so dangerous, and under the protection of one gentleman only, *were circumstances* to excite every feeling of jealousy.—SCOTT.

2. Mistakes in the number of verbs are extremely common when a singular noun intervenes between a plural subject (or a plural noun between a singular subject) and its verb. It is worth while to illustrate the point abundantly; for it appears that real doubt can exist on the subject:—' "No one but schoolmasters and schoolboys knows" is exceedingly poor English, *if it is not absolutely bad grammar*' (from a review of this book, 1st ed.).

And do we wonder, when the *foundation* of *politics are* in the letter only, that many evils should arise?—JOWETT.

There is *much* in these ceremonial *accretions and teachings* of the Church which *tend* to confuse and distract, and which hinder us . . .—*Daily Telegraph*.

This sentence, strictly taken as it stands, would mean something that the writer by no means intends it to, viz, 'Though the ceremonies are confusing, there is a great deal in them'.

An immense *amount* of *confusion and indifference prevail* in these days. —*Daily Telegraph*.

They produced various *medicaments*, the lethal *power* of *which were* extolled at large.—*Times*.

The *partition* which the two ministers made of the *powers* of government *were* singularly happy.—MACAULAY.

One at least of the *qualities* which fit it for training ordinary men *unfit* it for training an extraordinary man.—BAGEHOT.

I failed to pass in the small *amount* of *classics* which *are* still held to be necessary.—*Times*.

The Tibetans have engaged to exclude from their country those dangerous *influences whose appearance were* the chief cause of our action.—*Times*.

Sundry other reputable *persons*, I know not whom, *whose* joint *virtue* still *keep* the law in good odour.—EMERSON.

The practical *results* of the recognition of this *truth is* as follows.— W. H. MALLOCK.

The Ordination *services* of the English *Church states* this to be a truth.—*Daily Telegraph*.

All special *rights* of *voting* in the election of members *was* abolished. —J. R. GREEN.

The separate *powers* of this great *officer* of State, who had originally acted only as President of the Council when discharging its judicial functions, *seems* to have been thoroughly established under Edward I. —J. R. GREEN.

3. *They, them, their, theirs*, are often used in referring back to singular pronominals (as *each, one, anybody, everybody*), or to singular nouns or phrases (as *a parent, neither Jack nor Jill*), of which the doubtful or double gender causes awkwardness. It is a real deficiency in English that we have no pronoun, like the French *soi, son*, to stand for *him-or-her, his-or-her* (for *he-or-she* French is no better off than English). Our view,

though we admit it to be disputable, is clear—that *they*, *their*, &c., should never be resorted to, as in the examples presently to be given they are. With a view to avoiding them, it should be observed that (*a*) the possessive of *one* (indefinite pronoun) is *one's*, and that of *one* (numeral pronoun) is either *his*, or *her*, or *its* (One does not forget *one's* own name: I saw one of them drop *his* cigar, *her* muff, or *its* leaves); (*b*) *he*, *his*, *him*, may generally be allowed to stand for the common gender; the particular aversion shown to them by Miss Ferrier in the examples may be referred to her sex; and, ungallant as it may seem, we shall probably persist in refusing women their due here as stubbornly as Englishmen continue to offend the Scots by saying *England* instead of *Britain*. (*c*) Sentences may however easily be constructed (Neither John nor Mary knew *his* own mind) in which *his* is undeniably awkward. The solution is then what we so often recommend, to do a little exercise in paraphrase (*John and Mary were alike irresolute*, for instance). (*d*) Where legal precision is really necessary, *he or she* may be written in full. Corrections according to these rules will be appended in brackets to the examples.

Anybody else who *have* only *themselves* in view.—RICHARDSON. (has . . . himself)

Ce n'est que le premier pas qui coûte, in novel-writing as in carrying *one's* head in *their* hand.—S. FERRIER. (one's . . . one's)

The feelings of the *parent* upon committing the cherished object of *their* cares and affections to the stormy sea of life.—S. FERRIER. (his)

But he never allowed *one* to feel *their* own deficiencies, for he never appeared to be aware of them himself.—S. FERRIER. (one's)

A difference of opinion which leaves *each* free to act according to *their* own feelings.—S. FERRIER. (his)

Suppose *each* of us *try our hands* at it.—S. FERRIER. (tries his hand; or, *if all of us are women*, tries her hand)

Everybody is discontented with *their* lot in life.—BEACONSFIELD. (his)

4. Other mistakes involving number made with such pronominals, or with nouns collective, personified, or abstract.

Inconsistencies, which effectually deprive the story of *all shred* of literary illusion.—*Outlook*.

No man can read Scott without being more of a public man, whereas the ordinary novel tends to make its *readers* rather less of *one* than before.—HUTTON.

And so *each* of his portraits *are* not only a 'piece of history', but ...—STEVENSON.

Le Roman d'un Spahi, Azidaye and Rarahu *each* contains the history of a love affair.—H. JAMES.

He manages to interest us in the men, who *each* in turn wishes to engineer Richard Baldock's future.—*Westminster Gazette*.

When *each* is appended in apposition to a plural subject, it should stand after the verb, or auxiliary, which should be plural; read here, *contain each*, *wish each in turn* (or, *each of whom wishes in turn*).

As the leading maritime *nation* in the world and dependent wholly on the supremacy of our fleet to maintain this position, *everyone* is virtually bound to accord some measure of aid to an association whose time and talents are devoted to ensuring this important object.—*Times*.

Every one is indeed a host in himself, if he is the leading maritime nation.

It is not in *Japan's* interests to allow negotiations to drag on once *their* armies are ready to deliver the final blow.—*Times*.

The personification of Japan must be kept up by *her*.

Many of my notes, I am greatly afraid, will be thought *a superfluity*. —E. V. LUCAS (quoted in *Times* review).

My notes may be a superfluity; many of my notes may be superfluous, or superfluities; or many a note of mine may be a superfluity; but it will hardly pass as it is.

5. Though nouns of multitude may be freely used with either a singular or a plural verb, or be referred to by pronouns of singular or plural meaning, they should not have both (except for special reasons and upon deliberation) in the same sentence; and words that will rank in one context as nouns of multitude may be very awkward if so used in another.

The public is naturally much impressed by this evidence, and in considering it *do* not make the necessary allowances.—*Times*.

The *Times* Brussels correspondent ... tells us that the *committee adds* these words to *their* report.—*Westminster Gazette*.

The Grand Opera Syndicate *has* also made an important addition to *their* German tenors.—*Westminster Gazette*.

The only political *party who* could take office was *that* which . . . had consistently opposed the American war.—BAGEHOT.

As *the race* of man, after centuries of civilization, still *keeps* some traits of *their* barbarian fathers.—STEVENSON.

The battleship Kniaz Potemkin, of which the *crew is* said to have mutinied and murdered *their* officers.—*Times*.

6. *Neither, either*, as pronouns, should always take a singular verb—a much neglected rule. So also *every*.

The conception is faulty for two reasons, neither of which *are* noticed by Plato.—JOWETT.

. . . neither of which *are* very amiable motives for religious gratitude. —THACKERAY.

He asked the gardener whether either of the ladies *were* at home.— TROLLOPE.

Were, however, may be meant for the subjunctive, when it would be a fault of style, not of grammar.

I think almost *every one* of the Judges of the High Court *are* represented here.—LORD HALSBURY.

Every Warwick institution, from the corporation to the schools and the almshouses, *have* joined hands in patriotic fellow-working.— *Speaker*.

7. For rhetorical reasons, a verb often precedes its subject; but enthusiasm, even if appropriate, should not be allowed to override the concords.

And of this emotion *was* born all the *gods* of antiquity.—*Daily Telegraph*.

But unfortunately there *seems* to be spread abroad certain *misconceptions*.—*Times*.

But with these suggestions *are* joined some very good *exposition* of principles which should underlie education generally.—*Spectator*.

Sir Henry Campbell-Bannerman has received a resolution, to which *is* appended the *names* of eight Liberal members and candidates for East London . . .—*Times*.

COMPARATIVES AND SUPERLATIVES

The chief point that requires mention is ill treatment of *the more*. In this phrase *the* is not the article, but an adverb, either relative or demonstrative. In *the more the merrier* it is first relative and then demonstrative: by-how-much we are more, by-so-much we shall be merrier. When the relative *the* is used, it should always be answered regularly by, or itself answer, the demonstrative *the*. Attempts to vary the formula are generally unhappy; for instance,

He was leaving his English business in the hands of Bilton, who seemed to him, the more he knew him, extraordinarily efficient.— E. F. BENSON.

This should run, perhaps: *whose efficiency impressed him the more, the more he knew him*—though it must be confessed that the double form is nearly always uncomfortable if it has not the elbow-room of a whole sentence to itself. That, however, is rather a question of style than of syntax; and other examples will accordingly be found in the section of the Chapter *Airs and Graces* concerned with originality.

The farther we advance into it, we see confusion more and more unfold itself into order.—CARLYLE.

Most readers will feel that this is an uncomfortable compromise between *The farther we advance the more do we see* and *As we advance we see confusion more and more unfold itself*. Similarly

She had reflection enough to foresee, that the longer she countenanced his passion, her own heart would be more and more irretrievably engaged.—SMOLLETT.

But it is when the demonstrative is used alone with no corresponding relative clause—a use in itself quite legitimate— that real blunders occur. It seems sometimes to be thought that *the more* is merely a more imposing form of *more*, and is therefore better suited for a dignified or ambitious style; but it has in fact a perfectly definite meaning, or rather two; and there need never be any doubt whether *more* or *the more* is right. One of the meanings is a slight extension of the other. (1) The correlative meaning *by so much* may be kept, though the relative clause, instead of formally corresponding and containing *the* (meaning *by how much*) and a comparative, takes some possibly quite different shape. But it must still be clear from the context what the relative clause might be. Thus, 'We shall be a huge crowd'.—'Well, we shall be the merrier'. Or, 'If he raises his demands, I grant them more willingly', i.e., The more he asks, the more willingly I give. This instance leads to the other possible meaning, which is wider. (2) The original meaning of the demonstrative *the* is simply *by that*; this in the complete double form, and often elsewhere, has the interpretation, limited to quantity, of *by so much*, or *in that proportion*; but it may also mean *on that account*, when the relative clause is not present. Again, however, the context must answer plainly in some form the question *On what account?*. Thus, He has done me many good turns; but I do not like him any the better; i.e., any better on that account; i.e., on account of the good turns.

The function of *the*, then, is to tell us that there is, just before or after, an answer to one of the questions, *More by what amount?*, *More on what account?*. If there is no such answer, we may be sure that the comparative has no right to its *the*. We start with a sentence that is entitled to its *the*, but otherwise unidiomatic.

We are not a whit *the less* depressed in spirits at the sight of all this unrelieved misery on the stage *by the reminder* that Euripides was moved to depict it by certain occurrences in his own contemporary Athens. *Times*.

The less is *less on that account*, viz., that we are reminded. But the preposition required when the cause is given in this construction by a noun is *for*, not *by*. Read *for the reminder*. The type is shown in *None the better for seeing you*. Our sentence is in fact a mixture between *Our depression is not lessened* by *the reminder*, and *We are not the less depressed* for *the reminder*; and the confusion is worse that *depressed by* happens to be a common phrase.

The suggestion, as regarded Mr. Sowerby, was certainly true, and was not the less so as regarded some of Mr. Sowerby's friends.— TROLLOPE.

The tells us that we can by looking about us find an answer either to *Not less true by what amount?* or to *Not less true on what account?*. There is no answer to the first except *Not less true about the friends in proportion as it was truer about Mr Sowerby*; and none to the second except *Not less true about the friends because it was true about Mr Sowerby*. Both are meaningless, and the *the* is superfluous and wrong.

> Yet as his criticism is more valuable than that of other men, so it is the more rarely met with.—*Spectator.*

This is such an odd tangle of the two formulae *as . . . so, the more . . . the more*, that the reader is tempted to cut the knot and imagine what is hardly possible, that *the* is meant for the ordinary article, agreeing with *kind of criticism* understood between *the* and *more*. Otherwise it must be cured either by omitting *the*, or by writing *The more valuable his criticism, the more rarely is it met with*. If the latter is done, *than that of other men* will have to go. Which suggests the further observation that *the* with a comparative is almost always wrong when a *than*-clause is appended. This is because in the full double clause there is necessarily not a fixed standard of comparison, but a sliding scale. The following example, not complicated by any *the*, will make the point clear:

> My eyes are more and more averse to light than ever.—s. FERRIER.

You can be more averse than ever, or more and more averse, but not more and more averse than ever. *Ever* can only mean the single point of time in the past, whichever it was, at which you were most averse. But to be more and more averse is to be more averse at each stage than at each previous stage. Just such a sliding scale is essential with *the more . . . the more*. And perhaps it becomes so closely associated with the phrase that the expression of a fixed standard of comparison, such as is inevitably set up by a *than*-clause, is felt to be impossible even when the demonstrative *the* stands alone. In the next two examples, answers to the question *More on what account?* can be found, though they are so far disguised that the sentences would be uncomfortable, even if what makes them impossible were absent. That is the addition of the *than*-clause in each.

But neither is that way open; nor is it any the more open in the case of Canada than Australia.—F. GREENWOOD.

The *the* might pass if *than Australia* were omitted, and there would be no objection to it if we read further (for *in the case*) *if we take the case*, and, better still, placed that clause first in the sentence: Nor, if we take the case of Canada, is the way any the more open. *The* then means *on that account*, viz, because we have substituted Canada.

I would humbly protest against setting up any standard of Christianity by the regularity of people's attendance at church or chapel. I am certain personally that I have a far greater realization of the goodness of God to all creation; I am certain that I can *the more* acknowledge His unbounded love for all He has made, and our entire dependence on Him, *than I could* twenty years ago, when I attended church ten times where I now go once.—*Daily Telegraph*.

In this, the answer to *More on what account?* is possibly implied in the last clause; it would perhaps be, if clearly put, Because I go to church seldomer. The right form would be, *I can the more acknowledge . . . for going* (or *that I go*) *to church only once where twenty years ago I went ten times*. Unless the *than*-clause is got rid of, we ought to have *more* without *the*.

This question of *the* is important for lucidity, is rather difficult, and has therefore had to be treated at length. The other points that call for mention are quite simple; they are illogicalities licensed by custom, but perhaps better avoided. Avoidance, however, that proclaims itself is not desirable; to set readers asking 'Who are you, pray, that the things everybody says are not good enough for you?' is bad policy; 'in vitium ducit culpae fuga si caret arte'. But if a way round presents itself that does not at once suggest an assumption of superiority, so much the better.

1. *More than I can help*.

Without thinking of the corresponding phrase in his native language more than he can help.—H. SWEET.

We don't haul guns through traffic more than we can help.— KIPLING.

These really mean, of course, more than he (we) can*not* help.

To say that, however, is by this time impossible. More than he need, if (when) he can help it, too much, unnecessarily, and other substitutes, will sometimes do.

2. *Most of any* (singular).

A political despotism, the most unbounded, both in power and principle, of any tyranny that ever existed so long.—GALT.

She has the most comfortable repository of stupid friends to have recourse to of anybody I ever knew.—S. FERRIER.

And they had the readiest ear for a bold, honourable sentiment, of any class of men the world ever produced.—STEVENSON.

Latin at any rate should be an essential ingredient in culture as the best instrument of any language for clear and accurate expression of thought.—*Times*.

The first chapter, which from the lessons it enforces is perhaps the most valuable of any in the present volume . . .—SIR G. T. GOLDIE.

Disraeli said that he had 'the largest parliamentary knowledge of any man he had met'.—BRYCE.

Though this is extremely common, as the examples are enough to show, there is seldom any objection to saying either *most of all* or *more than any*.

3. *Most* with words that do not admit of degrees.

Unique has been separately dealt with in the chapter on *Vocabulary*. *Ideal* is another word of the same sort; *an ideal solution* is one that could not possibly be improved upon, and *most* is nonsense with it; *an ideal and most obvious* should be read in the example:

That the transformation of the Regular Army into the general service Army and of the Militia into the home service Army is a most ideal and obvious solution admits, I think, of no contradiction.—*Times*.

RELATIVES

a. Defining and non-defining relative clauses.

For the purposes of b. and c. below, all relative clauses are divided into defining and non-defining. The exact sense in which we use these terms is illustrated by the following groups, of which (i) contains defining clauses, (ii) non-defining.

(i) The man who called yesterday left no address.

Mr. Lovelace has seen divers apartments at Windsor: but not one, he says, that he thought fit for me.—RICHARDSON.

He secured . . . her sincere regard, by the feelings which he manifested.—THACKERAY.

The Jones who dines with us to-night is not the Jones who was at school with you.

The best novel that Trollope ever wrote was . . .

Any man that knows three words of Greek could settle that point.

(ii) At the first meeting, which was held yesterday, the chair . . .

Deputies must be elected by the Zemstvos, which must be extended and popularized, but not on the basis of . . .—*Times*

The Emperor William, who was present . . ., listened to a loyal address.—*Times*.

The statue of the Emperor Frederick, which is the work of the sculptor Professor Uphnes, represents the Monarch on horseback.—*Times*.

Jones, who should know something of the matter, thinks differently.

The function of a defining relative clause is to limit the application of the antecedent; where that is already precise, a defining clause is not wanted. The limitation can be effected in more than one way, according to the nature of the antecedent. As a rule, the antecedent gives us a class to select from, the defining clause enables us to make the selection. Thus in our first example the antecedent leaves us to select from the general class of 'men', the defining clause fixes the particular man (presumably the only man, or the only man that would occur in the connexion) 'who called yesterday'. Sometimes, however, the functions of the two are reversed. When we have an antecedent with a superlative, or other word of exclusive or comprehensive meaning, such as 'all', 'only', 'any', we know already how to make our selection, and only wait for the relative clause to tell us from what class to make it. We know that we are to choose 'the best novel': the relative clause limits us to the works of Trollope. We are to choose 'any man' we like, provided (says our relative clause) that he 'knows three words of Greek'. In either case, the work of definition is done by the exclusion (implied in the relative clause) of persons or things that the antecedent by itself might be taken to include.

The point to notice is that, whichever way the defining clause does its work, it is essential to and inseparable from its antecedent. If for any reason we wish to get rid of it, we can only do so by embodying its contents in the antecedent: 'The man in Paris with whom I correspond' must become 'My Paris correspondent'. To remove the clause altogether is to leave the antecedent with either no meaning or a wrong one. Even in such extreme cases as 'the wisest man that ever lived', 'the meanest flower that blows', where the defining clause may seem otiose and therefore detachable, we might claim that future wise men, and past and future flowers, are excluded; but we shall better realize the writer's intention if we admit that these clauses are only a pretence of limitation designed to exclude the reality; it is as if the writers, invited to set limits to their statements, had referred us respectively to Time and Space.

This fact, that the removal of a defining clause destroys the meaning of the antecedent, supplies an infallible test for distinguishing between the defining and the non-defining clause: the latter can always, the former never, be detached without disturbing the truth of the main predication. A non-defining clause gives independent comment, description, explanation, anything but limitation of the antecedent; it can always be rewritten either as a parenthesis or as a separate sentence, and this is true, however essential the clause may be to the point of the main statement. 'Jones', in our last example above, is quoted chiefly as one 'who should know something of the matter'; but this need not prevent us from writing: 'Jones thinks differently; and he should know something of the matter'.

To find, then, whether a clause defines or does not define, remove it, and see whether the statement of which it formed a part is unaltered: if not, the clause defines. The test can be applied without difficulty to all the examples given above. It is true that we sometimes get ambiguous cases: after removing the relative clause, we cannot always say whether the sense has been altered or not. That means, however, not that our test has failed, but that the clause is actually capable of performing either function, and that the main sentence can bear two distinct meanings, between which even context may not enable us to decide. The point is illustrated, in different degrees, by the following examples:

> Mr. H. Lewis then brought forward an amendment, which had been put down by Mr. Trevelyan and which provided for an extension of the process of income-tax graduation.—*Times*.
>
> This was held to portend developments that somehow or other have not followed.—*Times*.

The former of these is quite ambiguous. The bringing forward of an amendment (no matter what or whose) may be all that the writer meant to tell us of in the first instance; the relative clauses are then non-defining clauses of description. On the other hand, both clauses may quite well be meant to define; and it is even possible that the second is meant to define, and the first not, though the coordination is then of a kind that we shall show under c. to be improper. Similarly, in the second sentence, 'to portend developments' may possibly be complete in itself; the whole might then be paraphrased thus: 'It was thought that the matter would not stop there: but it has'. More probably the clause is meant to define: 'It was held to portend what have since proved to be unrealized developments'. This view is confirmed, as we shall see, both by the use of 'that' (not 'which') and by the absence of a comma before it.

Punctuation is a test that would not always be applicable even if all writers could be assumed to punctuate correctly; but it is often a guide to the writer's intention. For (1) a non-defining clause should always be separated from the antecedent by a stop; (2) a defining clause should never be so separated unless it is either preceded by a parenthesis indicated by stops, or coordinated with a former defining clause or with adjectives belonging to the antecedent; as in the following examples:

> The only circumstance, in fact, that could justify such a course , . .
>
> It is he only who does this, who follows them into all their force and matchless grace, that does or can feel their full value.—HAZLITT.

Perfect types, that satisfy all these requirements, are not to be looked for.

It will occur to the reader that our last two examples are strictly speaking exceptions to the rule of defining clauses, since they tell us only what is already implied, and could therefore be removed without impairing the sense. That is true to some extent of many parallel defining clauses: they are admissible, however, if, without actually giving any limitation themselves, they make more clear a limitation already given or implied; if, in fact, they are offered as alternative versions or as reminders. Our next example is of a defining clause of the same kind:

This estimate which he gives, is the great groundwork of his plan for the national redemption.—BURKE.

The limitation given by 'this' is repeated in another form by the relative clause. 'This estimate, the one he gives, is . . .'

The reader should bear in mind that the distinction between the two kinds of relative is based entirely on the closeness of their relation to the antecedent. The information given by a defining clause must be taken at once, with the antecedent, or both are useless: that given by a non-defining clause will keep indefinitely, the clause being complete in sense without the antecedent, and the antecedent without the clause. This is the only safe test. To ask, for instance, whether the clause conveys comment, explanation, or the like, is not a sufficient test unless the question is rightly understood; for, although we have said that a non-defining clause conveys comment and the like, as opposed to definition of the antecedent, it does not follow that a defining clause may not (while defining its own antecedent) *contribute* towards comment; on the contrary, it is often open to a writer to throw his comment into such a form as will include a defining clause. It may even appear from a comparison of the two sentences below that this is the origin of the non-defining clause, (2) being an abbreviation of (1):

1. Lewis, a man to whom hard work never came amiss, sifted the question thoroughly.

2. Lewis, to whom hard work never came amiss, sifted the question . . .

In (1), a comment is introduced by 'a man' in apposition with Lewis; 'a man' is antecedent to a defining relative clause; separate them, and the antecedent is meaningless. But next remove the connecting words 'a man', and the relative changes at once its antecedent and its nature: the antecedent is 'Lewis'; the relative is non-defining; and the clause *is* a comment, and does not merely contribute to one.

b. 'That' and 'who' or 'which'.

'That' is evidently regarded by many writers as nothing more than an ornamental variation for 'who' and 'which', to be used, not indeed immoderately, but quite without discrimination. The opinion is excusable; it is not easy to draw any distinction that is at all consistently supported by usage. There was formerly a tendency to use 'that' for everything: the tendency now is to use 'who' and 'which' for everything. 'That', from disuse, has begun to acquire an archaic flavour, which with some authors is a recommendation. De Quincey, for one, must certainly have held that in exalted prose 'that', in all connexions, was the more dignified relative; his higher flights abound in curious uses of the word, some instances of which are quoted below.

This confusion is to be regretted; for although no distinction can be authoritatively drawn between the two relatives, an obvious one presents itself. The few limitations on 'that' and 'who' about which every one is agreed all point to 'that' as the defining relative, 'who' or 'which' as the non-defining. We cannot say 'My father, that left Berlin last night, will shortly arrive', and an examination of instances would show that we can never use 'that' where the clause is unmistakably non-defining. On the other hand, we cannot say 'All which I can do is useless'; this time, it is true, the generalization will not hold; 'which' can, and sometimes must, be used, and 'who' commonly is used, in defining clauses. But that is explained partly by the obvious inconvenience sometimes attending the use of 'that', and partly by the general tendency to exclude it from regular use, which has already resulted in making it seem archaic when used of persons, except in certain formulae.

The rules given below are a modification of this principle, that 'that' is the defining, 'who' or which' the non-defining relative; the reason for each modification is given in its place. We must here remind the reader of the distinction drawn in a. between defining and non-defining clauses: a defining clause limits the application of the antecedent, enabling us to select from the whole class to which the antecedent is applicable the particular individual or individuals meant.

1. 'That' should never be used to introduce a non-defining clause; it is therefore improperly used in all the following examples:

But by her side was kneeling her better angel, that hid his face with wings: that wept and pleaded for her: that prayed when she could not: that fought with Heaven by tears for her deliverance.—DE QUINCEY.

Rendering thanks to God in the highest—that, having hid his face through one generation behind thick clouds of war, once again was ascending.—DE QUINCEY.

And with my own little stock of money besides, that Mrs. Hoggarty's card-parties had lessened by a good five-and-twenty-shillings, I calculated . . .—THACKERAY.

How to keep the proper balance between these two testy old wranglers, that rarely pull the right way together, is as much . . .—MEREDITH.

Nataly promised amendment, with a steely smile, that his lips mimicked fondly.—MEREDITH.

It is opposed to our Constitution, that only allows the Crown to remove a Norwegian Civil servant.—NANSEN.

I cannot but feel that in my person and over my head you desire to pay an unexampled honour to the great country that I represent, to its Bench and Bar, that daily share your labours and keep step with your progress.—CHOATE.

'That I represent' is right: 'that daily share' is wrong.

As to dictionaries of the present day, that swell every few years by the thousand items, the presence of a word in one of them shows merely . . .—R. G. WHITE.

The sandy strip along the coast is fed only by a few scanty streams, that furnish a remarkable contrast to the vast volumes of water which roll down the Eastern sides.—PRESCOTT.

'That' and 'which' should change places.

The social and economic sciences, that now specially interest me, have no considerable place in such a reform.—*Times*.

If this is a defining clause, excluding 'the social and economic sciences that' do *not* interest the writer, the commas should be removed.

2. 'Who' or 'which' should not be used in defining clauses except when custom, euphony, or convenience is decidedly against the use of 'that'. The principal exceptions will be noted below; but we shall first give instances in which 'that' is rightly used, and others in which it might have been used with advantage.

In those highly impressionable years that lie between six and ten . . . —*Spectator*.
The obstacles that hedge in children from Nature . . .—*Spectator*.
The whole producing an effect that is not without a certain poetry.— *Times*.
He will do anything that he deems convenient.—BORROW.
The well-staffed and well-equipped 'High Schools' that are now at work . . . had not yet sprung into being.—*Times*.
Then, Sir, you keep up revenue laws which are mischievous, in order to preserve trade laws that are useless.—BURKE.

'That' should have been used in both clauses.

The struggle that lay before him.—J. R. GREEN.
There goes another sort of animal that is differentiating from my species . . .—H. G. WELLS.
There are other powers, too, that could perform this grateful but onerous duty.—*Times*.

In the following examples, 'that' is to be preferred to 'which'; especially with antecedent 'it', and after a superlative or other word of exclusive or comprehensive meaning, such as 'all', 'only', 'any'.

The opportunities which London has given them.—*Times*.
The principles which underlay the agreement.—*Times*.

One cause which surely contributes to this effect has its root in early childhood.—*Spectator*.

A meeting which was held yesterday, which consisted in the main of a bitter personal attack.—ROSEBERY.

'Which consisted' is right: but we should have 'that was held'; the clause defines.

The first thing which the person who desires to be amiable must determine to do is . . .—*Spectator*.

The most abominable din and confusion which it is possible for a reasonable person to conceive.—POE.

Reverential objections, composed of all which his unstained family could protest.—MEREDITH.

He required all the solace which he could derive from literary success.—MACAULAY.

All the evidence which we have ever seen tends to prove . . .—MACAULAY.

A battle more bloody than any which Europe saw in the long interval between Malplaquet and Eylau.—MACAULAY.

The only other biography which counts for much is . . .—*Times*.

The French Government are anxious to avoid anything which might be regarded as a breach of neutrality.—*Times*.

It was the ecclesiastical synods which by their example led the way to our national parliaments.—J. R. GREEN.

It is the little threads of which the inner substance of the nerves is composed which subserve sensation.—HUXLEY.

'Of which' in a defining clause is one of the recognized exceptions; but we ought to have 'that subserve'.

It is not wages and costs of handling which fall, but profits and rents.—*Times*.

It has been French ports which have been chosen for the beginning and for the end of his cruise.—*Times*.

Who is it who talks about moral geography?—E. F. BENSON.

3. We come now to the exceptions. The reader will have noticed that of all the instances given in (2) there is only one —the last—in which we recommend the substitution of 'that' for 'who'; in all the others, it is a question between 'that' and 'which'. 'That', used of persons, has in fact come to look archaic: the only cases in which it is now to be preferred to 'who' are those mentioned above as particularly requiring 'that'

instead of 'which'; those, namely, in which the antecedent is 'it', or has attached to it a superlative or other word of exclusive meaning. We should not, therefore, in the *Spectator* instance above, substitute 'the person that desires' for 'who desires'; but we should say

> The most impartial critic that could be found.
> The only man that I know of.
> Any one that knows anything knows this.
> It was you that said so.
> Who is it that talks about moral geography?

Outside these special types, 'that' used of persons is apt to sound archaic.

4. It will also have been noticed that all the relatives in (2) were either in the subjective case, or in the objective without a preposition. 'That' has no possessive case, and cannot take a preposition before it. Accordingly, 'the man that I found the hat of' will of course give place to 'the man whose hat I found'; and 'the house in which this happened' will generally be preferred to 'the house that this happened in'. The latter tendency is modified in the spoken language by the convenient omission of 'that'; for always in a defining clause, though never in a non-defining, a relative in the objective case, with or without a preposition, can be dropped. But few writers like, as a general rule, either to drop their relatives or to put prepositions at the end. 'The friends I was travelling with', the book I got it from', 'the place I found it in', will therefore usually appear as

> The friends with whom I was travelling.
> The book from which I got it.
> The place in which I found it.

5. Euphony demands that 'that that' should become 'that which', even when the words are separated; and many writers, from a feeling that 'which' is the natural correlative of the demonstrative 'that', prefer the plural 'those which'; but the first example quoted in (2) seems to show that 'those . . . that' can be quite unobjectionable.

6. A certain awkwardness seems to attend the use of 'that' when the relative is widely separated from its antecedent. When, for instance, two relative clauses are coordinate, some writers use 'that' in the first, 'which' in the second clause, though both define. This point will be illustrated in c., where we shall notice that inconsistency in this respect sometimes obscures the sense.

It may seem to the reader that a rule with so many exceptions to it is not worth observing. We would remind him (i) that it is based upon those palpable misuses of the relatives about which every one is agreed; (ii) that of the exceptions the first (numbered 3) and the last (numbered 6) result from, and might disappear with, the encroachment of 'who' and the general vagueness about the relatives; while the other two (numbered 4, 5), being obvious and clearly defined, do not interfere with the remaining uses of 'that'; (iii) that if we are to be at the expense of maintaining two different relatives, we may as well give each of them definite work to do.

In the following subsections we shall not often allude to the distinction here laid down. The reader will find that our rules are quite as often violated as observed; and may perhaps conclude that if the vital difference between a defining and a non-defining clause were consistently marked, wherever it is possible, by a discriminating use of 'that 'and 'which', false coordination and other mishandlings of the relatives would be less common than they are.

c. 'And who'; 'and which'.

[This discussion being complicated, the usual rule of thumb, insufficient as it is, may be stated for those who prefer risks to complications. It is: *And which* (or *who*), *but which* (or *who*), should be used only if another *which* (or *who*) has preceded.]

The various possibilities of relative coordination, right and wrong, may be thus stated: (i) a relative clause may be rightly or wrongly coordinated with another relative clause; this we shall call 'open' coordination; (ii) it may be rightly or wrongly coordinated with words that are equivalent to a relative clause, and for which a relative clause can be substituted; 'latent' coordination; (iii) a clause that has obviously no coordinate, open or latent, may yet be introduced by 'and' or other word implying coordination; for such offenders, which cannot be coordinate and will not be subordinate, 'insubordination' is not too harsh a term.

The following are ordinary types of the three classes:

(i) Men who are ambitious, and whose ambition has never been thwarted, . . .

Pitt, who was ambitious, but whose ambition was qualified by . . .

(ii) Ambitious men, and whose ambition has never been thwarted, . . .

An evil now, alas! beyond our power to remedy, and for which we have to thank the folly of our predecessors.

(iii) Being thus pressed, he grudgingly consented at last to a redistribution, and which, I need not say, it was his duty to have offered in the first instance.

A coordination in which 'and' is the natural conjunction may also be indicated simply by a comma; there is safety in this course, since the clause following the comma may be either coordinate or subordinate. But we have to deal only with clauses that are committed to coordination.

'Insubordination' will not detain us long; it is always due either to negligence or to gross ignorance; we shall illustrate it in its place with a few examples, but shall not discuss it. With regard, however, to open and latent coordination opinions differ; there is an optimist view of open coordination, and a pessimist view of latent, both of which seem to us incorrect. It is held by some that open coordination (provided that the relatives have the same antecedent) is never wrong, and by some—not necessarily others—that latent coordination is never right: we shall endeavour to show that the former is often wrong, and the latter, however ungainly, often right.

The essential to coordination is that the coordinates should be performing the same function in the sentence. It is not necessary, nor is it enough, that they should be in the same grammatical form: things of the same form may have different functions, and things of different forms may have the same function. If we say 'Unambitious men, and who have no experience', 'unambitious' and 'who have no experience' are not in the same form, but they have the same function—that of specifying the class of men referred to. Their grammatical forms (vocabulary permitting) are interchangeable: a defining adjective can always take the form of a relative clause, and a defining relative clause can often take the form of an adjective: 'inexperienced men, and who have no ambition'. 'Unambitious' is therefore the true grammatical equivalent of 'who have no ambition', and latent coordination between it and a relative clause is admissible.

On the other hand, among things that have the same grammatical form, but different functions, are the defining and the non-defining relative clause. A non-defining clause, we know, can be removed without disturbing the truth of the predication; it has therefore no essential function; it cannot therefore have the same function as a defining clause, whose function we know to be essential. It follows that open coordination is not admissible between a defining and a non-defining clause; and, generally, coordination, whether open or latent, is admissible between two defining or two non-defining coordinates, but not between a defining and a non-defining.

Our object, however, in pointing out what seems to be the true principle of relative coordination is not by any means to encourage the latent variety. It has seldom any advantage over full coordination; it is perhaps more apt to lead to actual blunders; it is usually awkward; and it does violence—needless violence, as often as not—to a very widespread and not unreasonable prejudice. Many writers may be suspected of using it, against their better judgement, merely for the purpose of asserting a right; it is their natural protest against the wholesale condemnation of ignorant critics, who do not see that latent coordination may be nothing worse than clumsy, and that open coordination may be a gross blunder. For the benefit of such critics it seems worth while to examine the correctness of various examples, both open and latent; on the other merits and demerits of the latent variety the reader will form his own judgement.

(i) Open coordination.

A few minutes brought us to a large and busy bazaar, with the localities of which the stranger appeared well acquainted, and where his original demeanour again became apparent.—POE.

Mr. Lovelace has seen divers apartments at Windsor; but not one, he says, that he thought fit for me, and which, at the same time, answered my description.—RICHARDSON.

All the toys that infatuate men, and which they play for, are the self-same thing.—EMERSON.

All these are correct: in the first both clauses are non-defining, in the others both define.

The hills were so broken and precipitous as to afford no passage except just upon the narrow line of the track which we occupied, and which was overhung with rocks, from which we might have been destroyed merely by rolling down stones.—SCOTT.

Wrong: the first clause defines, the second not.

From doing this they were prevented by the disgraceful scene which took place, and which the leader of the Opposition took no steps to avert.—*Times*.

Wrong. The first clause defines, the second is obviously one of comment: the 'scene' is not distinguished from those that the leader *did* take steps to avert.

They propose that the buildings shall belong . . . to the communes in which they stand, and which, it is hoped, will not permit their desecration.—*Spectator*.

Wrong. The communes that 'will not permit' are not meant to be distinguished from those that will. The second clause is comment, the first defines.

The way in which she jockeyed Jos, and which she described with infinite fun, carried up his delight to a pitch . . .—THACKERAY.

In the best French which he could muster, and which in sooth was of a very ungrammatical sort . . .—THACKERAY.

Peggy . . . would have liked to have shown her turban and bird of paradise at the ball, but for the information which her husband had given her, and which made her very grave.—THACKERAY.

All these are wrong. Thackeray would probably have been saved from these false coordinations if he had observed the distinction between 'that' and 'which': 'In the best French (that) he could muster, which in sooth was . . .'.

There goes another sort of animal that is differentiating from my species, and which I would gladly see exterminated.—H. G. WELLS.

Probably the second clause, like the first, is meant to define: if so, the coordination is right; if not, it is wrong. We have alluded to the tendency to avoid 'that' when the relative is widely separated from its antecedent; here, the result is ambiguity.

And here he said in German what he wished to say, and which was of no great importance, and which I translated into English.—BORROW.

Wrong: 'what (that which)' defines, the 'and which' clauses do not.

(ii) **Latent coordination,** between relative clause and equivalent, is seldom correct when the relative clause is non-defining; for the equivalent, with few and undesirable exceptions, is always a defining adjective or phrase, and can be coordinate only with a defining clause. The equivalent must of course be a true one; capable, that is, of being converted into a relative clause without altering the effect of the sentence. Neglect of this restriction often results in false coordination, especially in one particular type of sentence. Suppose that a historian, after describing some national calamity, proceeds: 'In these distressing circumstances . . .' Here we might seem to have two possible equivalents, 'these' and 'distressing'. First let us expand 'these' into a relative clause: 'In the distressing circumstances that I have described'. This, in the context, is a fair equivalent, and as often as not would actually appear instead of 'these'. But next expand 'distressing': 'In these circumstances, which were distressing', a non-defining clause. To this expansion no writer would consent; it defeats the object for which 'distressing' was placed before the antecedent. That object was to record his own sensibility without disparaging the reader's by telling him in so many words (as our relative clause does) that the circumstances were distressing; and it is secured by treating 'distressing' not as a separate predication but as an inseparable part of the antecedent. 'Distressing', it will be observed, cannot give us a defining clause; it is obviously meant to be co-extensive with 'these'; we are not to select from 'these' circumstances those only that are 'distressing'. Moreover, as 'these', although capable of appearing as a relative clause, can scarcely require another relative clause to complete the limitation of the antecedent, it follows that in sentences of this form coordination will generally be wrong. We have examples in the Cowper quotation below, and in the anonymous one that precedes it.

Juices ready prepared, and which can be absorbed immediately.— HUXLEY.

A deliberate attempt to frame and to verify general rules as to phenomena of all kinds, and which can, therefore, be propagated by argument or persuasion . . .—L. STEPHEN.

'Rules that shall be general, and that can . . .'

A painful, comprehensive survey of a very complicated matter, and which requires a great variety of considerations, is to be made.—BURKE.

The goldsmith to the royal household, and who, if fame spoke true, oftentimes acted as their banker, . . . was a person of too much importance to . . .—SCOTT.

'The man who was goldsmith to . . . and who'.

It is a compliment due, and which I willingly pay, to those who administer our affairs.—BURKE.

All these are correct, with defining coordinates throughout.

'A junior subaltern, with pronounced military and political views, with no false modesty in expressing them, and who (sic) possesses the ear of the public, . . .'—(Quoted by *The Times*.)

'Who has . . . views, and who . . .' 'Sic' is the comment of the *Times* writer. The coordination is correct.

While there, she had ample opportunity afforded her of studying fashionable life in all its varied and capricious moods, and which have been preserved to posterity in her admirable delineations of character.

I am sensible that you cannot in my uncle's present infirm state, and of which it is not possible to expect any considerable amendment, indulge us with a visit.—COWPER.

These are instances of false expansion alluded to above. The former is based on the non-defining expansion 'in all its moods, which are varied and capricious'; the true expansion being 'in all the varied and capricious moods in which it reveals itself', a defining clause, which will not do with the 'and which'. Similarly, the second is based on the non-defining expansion 'in my uncle's present state, which is an infirm one'; the true expansion is 'in the infirm state in which my uncle now is'. In both, a non-defining clause is coordinated with words that can only yield a defining clause.

Previous to the innovations introduced by the Tudors, and which had been taken away by the bill against pressing soldiers, the King in himself had no power of calling on his subjects generally to bear arms.—J.R. GREEN.

If the writer wishes us to distinguish, among the innovations introduced by the Tudors, those that had also been taken away, the 'and which' clause defines, and the coordination is right. But more probably the clause conveys independent information; the coordination is then wrong.

[The various arrangements of *pueri puellam amabant*] all have the same meaning—the boys loved the girl. For *puellam* shows by its form that it must be the object of the action; *amabant* must have for its subject a plural substantive, and which must therefore be, not *puellam*, but *pueri*.—R. G. WHITE.

Wrong. 'A plural substantive' can yield only the defining clause 'a substantive that is plural'. Now these words contain an inference from a general grammatical principle (that a plural verb must have a plural subject); and any supplementary defining clause must also be general, not (like the 'and which' clause) particular. We might have, for instance, 'Amabant, being plural, and finite, must have for its subject a plural substantive, and which is in the nominative case'. But the 'and which' clause is evidently non-defining; the inference ends at 'substantive'; then comes the application of it to the particular case.

He refused to adopt the Restrictive Theory, and impose a numerical limit on the Bank's issues, and which he again protested against in 1833.—H. D. MACLEOD.

Wrong. The 'and which' clause is non-defining; none of the three possible antecedents ('Theory', 'limit', 'imposition') will give a non-defining clause.

The great obstacle . . . is the religion of Europe, and which has unhappily been colonially introduced into America.—BEACONSFIELD.

This illustrates an important point. 'Of Europe' gives the defining clause 'that prevails in Europe'; the coordination therefore requires that the 'and which' clause should define. Now a defining clause must contain no word that is not meant to contribute to definition; if, then, the 'and which' clause defines, the writer wishes to distinguish the religion in question, not only from those European religions that have not been colonially introduced into America, but also from those European religions that have been introduced, but whose introduction is not a matter for regret; that is the only defining meaning that 'unhappily' can bear, and unless we accept this interpretation the clause is non-defining.—We shall allude to this sentence again in d., where the possibilities of parenthesis in a defining clause are discussed.

It may seem strange that this important place should not have been conferred on Vaca de Castro, already on the spot, and who had shown himself so well qualified to fill it.—PRESCOTT.

One of our 'few and undesirable exceptions', in which the clause-equivalent is non-defining ('who was already on the spot'); for a person's name can only require a defining clause to distinguish him from others of the same name. The sentence is an ugly one, even if we remove the 'and who' clause; but the coordination is right.

(iii) Insubordination.

The struggler, the poor clerk, mechanic, poorer musician, artist, or actor, feels no right to intrude, and who quickly falls from a first transient resentment . . .—*Daily Telegraph.*

Such a person may reside there with absolute safety, unless it becomes the object of the government to secure his person; and which purpose, even then, might be disappointed by early intelligence.— SCOTT.

All this when Madame saw, and of which when she took note, her sole observation was:— . . .—C. BRONTË.

To these we may add examples in which the coordinated relatives have different antecedents. In practice, nothing can justify such coordination: in theory, it is admissible when the antecedents are coordinate, as in the following sentence:

We therefore delivered the supplies to those individuals, and at those places, to whom the special grants had been made, and for which they were originally designed.

But in the following instances, one antecedent is subordinate to another in the same clause, or is in a clause subordinate to that of the other.

They marched into the apartment where the banquet was served; and which, as I have promised the reader he shall enjoy it, he shall have the liberty of ordering himself.—THACKERAY.

A large mineral-water firm in London, whose ordinary shares are a million in value, and which shares always paid a dividend before the imposition of the sugar-tax, have not paid any dividend since.— *Times*.

He very much doubted whether I could find it on his mine, which was located some five miles from St. Austell, Cornwall, and upon whose property I had never been.—*Times*.

But I have besought my mother, who is apprehensive of Mr. Love-lace's visits, and for fear of whom my uncles never stir out without arms, . . .—RICHARDSON.

It was of Mr. Lovelace that the uncles were afraid.

d. Case of the relative.

Special attention was not drawn, in the section on Case, to the gross error committed in the following examples:

Instinctively apprehensive of her father, whom she supposed it was, she stopped in the dark.—DICKENS.

That peculiar air of contempt commonly displayed by insolent menials to those whom they imagine are poor.—CORELLI.

It is only those converted by the Gospel whom we pretend are influenced by it.—*Daily Telegraph*.

We found those whom we feared might be interested to withhold the settlement alert and prompt to assist us.—GALT.

Mr. Dombey, whom he now began to perceive was as far beyond human recall.—DICKENS.

Those whom it was originally pronounced would be allowed to go. —*Spectator*.

But this looks as if he has included the original 30,000 men whom he desires 'should be in the country now'.—*Times*.

We feed children whom we think are hungry.—*Times*.

The only gentlemen holding this office in the island, whom, he felt sure, would work for the spiritual good of the parish.—*Guernsey Advertiser*.

These writers evidently think that in 'whom we think are hungry' 'whom' is the object of 'we think'. The relative is in fact the subject of 'are'; and the object of 'we think' is the clause 'who are hungry'; the order of the words is a necessary result of the fact that a relative subject must stand at the beginning of its clause.

It is interesting to notice that in *Matt*. xvi. 13 and 15, the revisers have corrected the A.V. grammar, writing 'But who say ye that I am' instead of 'But whom . . .'

(The same awkward necessity confronts us in clauses with 'when', 'though', &c., in which the subject is a relative. Such clauses are practically recognized as impossible, though Otway, in a courageous moment, wrote:

> Unblemished honour, and a spotless love;
> *Which tho'* perhaps now *know* another flame,
> Yet I have love and passion for their name.)

Some writers, with a consistency worthy of a better cause, carry the blunder into the passive, renouncing the advantages of an ambiguous 'which' in the active; for in the active 'which' of course tells no tales.

As to all this, the trend of events has been the reverse of that which was anticipated would be the result of democratic institutions.—*Times*.

'Which *it* was anticipated would be'. Similarly, the passive of 'men whom we-know-are-honest' is the impossible 'men who are-known-are-honest': 'men who we know are honest' gives the correct passive 'men who it is known are honest'.

Nor must it be supposed that 'we know' is parenthetic. In non-defining clauses (Jones, who we know is honest), we can regard the words as parenthetic if we choose, except when the phrase is negative (Jones, who I cannot think is honest); but in a defining clause they are anything but parenthetic. When we say 'Choose men who you know are honest', the words 'you know' add a new circumstance of limitation: it is not enough that the men should in fact be honest; you must know them to be honest; honest men of whose honesty you are not certain are excluded by the words 'you know'. Similarly, in the *Guernsey Advertiser* quotation above, the writer does not go the length of saying that these are the only gentlemen who would work: he says that they are the only ones of whom he feels sure. The commas of parenthesis ought therefore to go, as well as the comma at 'island', which is improper before a defining clause.

The circumstances under which a parenthesis is admissible in a defining clause may here be noticed.

(i) When the clause is too strict in its limitation, it may be modified by a parenthesis:

Choose men who, during their time of office, have never been suspected.

A whole class, excluded by the defining clause, is made eligible by the parenthesis.

(ii) Similarly, a parenthesis may be added to tell us that within the limits of the defining clause we have perfect freedom of choice:

Choose men who, at one time or another, have held office.

They must have held office, that is all; it does not matter when.

(iii) Words of comment, indicating the writer's authority for his limitation, his recognition of the sentiments that it may arouse, and the like, properly stand outside the defining clause: when they are placed within it, they ought to be marked as parenthetic.

There are men who, I am told, prefer a lie to truth on its own merits.

The religion that obtains in Europe, and that, unhappily, has been introduced into America.

The latter sentence is an adaptation of one considered above on p. 100. 'Unhappily' there appeared not as a parenthesis but as an inseparable part of the relative clause, which was therefore defining or non-defining, according as 'unhappily' could or could not be considered as adding to the limitation. But with the altered punctuation 'unhappily' is separable from the relative clause, which may now define: 'that obtains in Europe and (I am sorry to have to add) in America'.

In sentences of this last type, the parenthesis is inserted in the defining clause only for convenience: in the others, it is an essential, though a negative, part of the definition. But all three types of parenthesis agree in this, that they do not limit the antecedent; they differ completely from the phrases considered above, which do limit the antecedent, and are not parenthetic.

e. Miscellaneous uses and abuses of the relative.

(i) A relative clause is sometimes coordinated with an independent sentence; such coordination is perhaps always awkward, but is not always incorrect. The question arises chiefly when the two have a common subject expressed only in the relative clause; for when the subject is expressed in both, the independent sentence may be taken to be coordinate, not with the relative clause, but with the main sentence to which the relative clause is attached, as in the following instance:

To begin with, he had left no message, which in itself I felt to be a suspicious circumstance, and (I) was at my wit's end how to account plausibly for his departure.

Retain 'I', and 'I was' may be coordinate with 'he had left': remove it, and the coordination is necessarily between 'I was' and 'I felt'. In our next examples the writers are committed:

These beatitudes are just laws which we have been neglecting, and have been receiving in ourselves the consequences that were meet.—
Daily Telegraph.

The idea which mankind most commonly conceive of proportion, is the suitableness of means to certain ends, and, where this is not the question, very seldom trouble themselves about the effect of different measures of things.—BURKE.

Fictitious capital, a name of extreme inaccuracy, which too many persons are in the habit of using, from the hasty assumption that what is not real must necessarily be fictitious, and are more led away by a jingling antithesis of words than an accurate perception of ideas.—H. D. MACLEOD.

The first two of these are wrongly coordinated: the third, a curiosity in other respects, is in this respect right. The reason is that in the first two we have a defining, in the third a non-defining relative clause. A defining clause is grammatically equivalent to an adjective ('violated laws', 'the popular idea'), and can be coordinated only with another word or phrase performing the same function; now the phrase 'we have been receiving', not being attached to the antecedent by means of a relative, expressed or understood, is not equivalent to an adjective. We could have had 'and (which we) have been properly punished *for neglecting*', or we could have had the 'and' sentence in an adverbial form, 'with the fitting result'; but coordination between the two as they stand is impossible.

The Burke sentence is a worse offender. Coordination of this kind is not often attempted when the antecedent of the relative is *subject* of the main sentence; and when it is attempted, the two coordinates must of course not be separated by the predicate. If we had had 'the idea which mankind most commonly conceive of proportion, and very seldom trouble themselves about anything further', the coordination would have been similar to the other, and could have been rectified in the same way ('and beyond which they very seldom . . .', or 'to the exclusion of any other considerations'). But this alteration we cannot make; for there is a further and an essential difference. The *Daily Telegraph* writer evidently *meant* his second coordinate to do the work of a defining clause; he has merely failed to make the necessary connexion, which we supply, as above, either by turning the words into a second defining clause, or by embodying them, adverbially, in the first. Burke's intention is different, and would not be represented by our proposed alteration in the order. All that a defining clause can do in his sentence is to tell us *what* idea is going to be the subject. If we were to give a brief paraphrase of the whole, italicizing the words that represent the second coordinate, it would be, not 'mankind's *sole* idea of proportion is the suitableness . . .', but 'mankind's idea of proportion is the suitableness . . . , *and very little else*'; for the question answered is, not 'what is mankind's sole idea?' but 'what is mankind's idea?'. In other words, the second co-ordinate belongs in intention not, like the relative clause, to the subject, but to the predicate; to rectify it, we must either make it part of the predicate ('and is not concerned with . . .'), or, by inserting 'they', coordinate it with the main sentence. Obvious as the latter correction is, the sentence repays close examination, as illustrating the incoherence of thought that may underlie what seems a very trifling grammatical slip.

But in our third example the relative clause is non-defining; it is grammatically equivalent to, and could be replaced by, an independent sentence: 'Many persons are in the habit of using it'. There is nothing grammatically wrong in this type of co-ordination; it is objectionable only because it seems to promise what it does not fulfil. When the common subject of two co-ordinates is expressed only with the first, it is natural to assume that all words preceding it are also to be applied to both co-ordinates; and the violation of this principle, though not of course ungrammatical, is often felt to be undesirable in other than relative clauses.

(ii) In the sentences considered above, the antecedent of the relative did not belong to the second coordinate, and could not have been represented in it without the material alterations there proposed. But it may also happen that the antecedent, as in the following examples, belongs equally to both coordinates, being represented in the first by a relative, in the second by some other pronoun.

There were two or three *whose* accuracy was more scrupulous, *their* judgement more uniformly sober and cautious.—BRYCE.

He renewed the old proposal, *which* Pizarro treated as a piece of contemptible shuffling, and curtly rejected *it*.

Which she has it in her option either to do or to let *it* alone.—RICHARDSON.

In the pair of parallel coordinates from Mr Bryce, insert the suppressed 'was', and it becomes clear that 'whose', not 'their', is the right pronoun.

In the 'Pizarro' sentence, 'it' is not only superfluous, but disturbing to the reader, who assumes that 'which' is common to both clauses, and on reaching 'it' has to glance back and check the sentence. Here, as often, the pronoun seems to be added to restore an ill-balanced sentence; but that can be done in several other ways. In the Richardson sentence also the 'it' should go.

More commonly, the repetition of the antecedent in another form results from the superstitious avoidance of a preposition at the end:

A demand by Norway for political separation, to which Sweden will not assent, but will not go to war to prevent it.—*Times*.

'To (which)' is not common to both coordinates: accordingly the writer finds it necessary to give 'it' in the second. But, even if we respect our superstition, and exclude 'which Sweden will not assent to, but will not go to war to prevent', we have still the two possibilities of (1) complete relative coordination, 'to . . . , but which . . .'; (2) subordination, 'though she will not go to war to prevent it'.

In our next example, Lord Rosebery, again for fear of a preposition at the end, falls into the trap clumsily avoided by the *Times* writer:

That promised land for which he was to prepare, but scarcely to enter.

So perhaps Bagehot, though his verb may be *conceive of*:

English trade is carried on upon borrowed capital to an extent of which few foreigners have an idea, and none of our ancestors could have conceived.

(iii) When the relative is the subject of both coordinates, or the object of both, its repetition in the second is a matter of choice. But to omit the relative when it is in a different case from the first is a gross, though not uncommon, blunder. The following are instances:

A league which their posterity for many ages kept so inviolably, and proved so advantageous for both the kingdoms of France and Scotland. —LOCKHART.

Questions which we either do not put to ourselves, or are turned aside with traditional replies.—MARK RUTHERFORD.

It is just conceivable that in the last of these the subject of 'are' is 'we': if so, the sentence is to be referred to (i) above (wrong coordination of an independent sentence with a defining relative clause).

It is not easy to see why the relative more than other words should be mishandled in this way; few would write (but see p.70, No.5) 'This league we kept and has proved advantageous'.

The condensed antecedent-relative 'what' is only an apparent exception to this universal rule. In the sentence 'What I hold is mine', 'what' is only object to 'hold', not subject to 'is'; the subject to 'is' is the whole noun-clause 'what I hold'. Sentences of this type, so far from being exceptions, often give a double illustration of the rule, and leave a double possibility of error. For just as a single 'what' cannot stand in different relations to two coordinate verbs in its clause, so a single noun-clause cannot stand in different relations to two coordinate main verbs. We can say 'What I have and hold', where 'what' is object to both verbs, and 'what is mine and has been fairly earned by me', where it is subject to both; but we cannot say 'what I have and has been fairly earned by me'. Similarly, we can say 'What I have is mine and shall remain mine', where the noun-clause 'what I have' is subject to both verbs, and 'What I have I mean to keep, and will surrender to no man', where it is object to both; but not 'What I have is mine, and I will surrender to no man'. Of the various ways of avoiding this error (subordination, adaptation of verbs, insertion of a pronoun, relative or other), that chosen by Miss Brontë below is perhaps the least convenient. Her sentence is, however, correct; that from the *Spectator* is not.

Not mere empty ideas, but what were once realities, and that I long have thought decayed.—C. BRONTË.

Whatever we possessed in 1867 the British Empire possesses now, and is part of the Dominion of Canada.—*Spectator*.

'Things that were once realities, and that I long have thought decayed'; a pair of defining clauses.

The condensed 'what' must of course be distinguished from the 'what' of indirect questions, which is not relative but interrogative. In the following example, confusion of the two leads to an improper coordination.

What sums he made can only be conjectured, but must have been enormous.—MACAULAY.

In the first sentence, 'what' is an interrogative, in the second, a condensed antecedent-relative, standing for 'the sums that'. It is the sums that were enormous: it is the answer to the question 'What sums did he make?' that can only be conjectured. This mistake is possible only because 'can' and 'must' do not reveal their number: 'can' is singular, 'must' plural.

The differentiation between the two *what*s and their equivalents, is not, indeed, complete: just as the condensed antecedent-relative resembles in form, though not in treatment, the unresolved interrogative, so the interrogative, by resolution into 'the . . that (which)', not only resembles, but is grammatically identified with, the uncondensed relative and antecedent. The resolution is, no doubt, convenient: it should be noticed, however, that the verbs with which alone it can be employed (verbs that may denote either perception of a fact or other kinds of perception) are precisely those with which ambiguity may result. 'I know the house (that) you mean': it may (antecedent and relative) or may not (resolved interrogative) follow that I have ever seen it. 'We must first discover the scoundrel who did it'; antecedent and relative? then we must secure the scoundrel's person; resolved interrogative? then only information is needed.

'I can give a good guess at the problem that is puzzling you': and the solution?—I know nothing of the solution; I was resolving an interrogative.

This, however, does not affect sentences like the Macaulay one above: for although the resolved or uncondensed forms ('the . . . which') are grammatically identified, the condensed or unresolved forms ('what') are not.

(iv) The omission of the relative in isolated clauses (as opposed to coordinates) is a question not of correctness but of taste, so far as there is any question at all. A non-defining relative can never be omitted. The omission of a defining relative subject is often effective in verse, but in prose is either an archaism or a provincialism. It may, moreover, result in obscurity, as in the second of our examples, which may possibly puzzle the reader for a moment:

Now it would be some fresh insect won its way to a temporary fatal new development.—H. G. WELLS.

No one finds himself planted at last in so terribly foul a morass, as he would fain stand still for ever on dry ground.—TROLLOPE.

But when the defining relative is object, or has a preposition, there is no limit to the omission, unless euphony is allowed to be one. We give three instances in which the reader may or may not agree that the relative might have been retained with advantage:

We do that in our zeal our calmer moments would be afraid to answer.—SCOTT.

But did you ever see anything there you had never seen before?—BAGEHOT.

These ethical judgements we pass on self-regarding acts are ordinarily little emphasized.—SPENCER.

(v) When a defining relative has the same preposition as its antecedent, it is not uncommon, in the written as well as in the spoken language, to omit the preposition in the relative clause. There is something to be said for a licence that rids us of such cumbrous formulae as 'in the way in which', 'to the extent to which', and the like; in writing, however, it should be used with caution if at all.

In the first place, if the preposition is to go, the relative should go too, or if retained should certainly be 'that', not 'which'; and if the verb of the relative clause is the same as in the main sentence, it should be represented by 'do', or (in a compound tense) by its auxiliary component.

Because they found that it touched them in a way which no book in the world could touch them.—*Daily Telegraph*.

The man who cleaned the slate in the manner which Sir E. Satow has done both in Morocco and Japan might surely rank as a reflective diplomatist.—*Spectator*.

'In a way no other book in the world could': 'in the way (that) Sir E. Satow has done'.

A further limitation is suggested by our next example:

The Great Powers, after producing this absolutely certain result, are ending with what they ought to have begun,—coercion.—*Spectator*.

Here, of course, the relative cannot be omitted, since relative and antecedent are one. But that is not the principal fault, as will appear from a resolution of the antecedent-relative: 'they are ending with the very thing (that) they ought to have begun . . .' We are now at liberty to omit our relative or retain it, as we please; in either case, the omission of 'with' is unbearable. The reason is that 'with' does not, like the 'in' of our former examples, introduce a purely adverbial phrase: it is an inseparable component of the compound verbs 'end-with' and 'begin-with', of which the antecedent and relative are respectively the objects. Similarly, we cannot say, 'He has come to the precise conclusion (that) I thought he would come', because we should be mutilating the verb to 'come-to'; we can, however, say 'to the conclusion (that) I thought he would', 'come-to' being then represented by 'would'.

Finally, the omission is justifiable only when antecedent and relative have the same preposition. Sentences like the next may pass in conversation, but (except with the one noun *way*) are intolerable in writing:

One of the greatest dangers in London is the pace that the corners in the main streets are turned.—*Times*.

(vi) The use of 'such . . . who (which)', 'such . . . that (defining relative)', for 'such . . . as' is sometimes an archaism, sometimes a vulgarism.

Till such time when we shall throw aside our earthly garment.—*Daily Telegraph.*

Only such supplies were to be made which it would be inhuman to refuse to ships in distress.—*Times.*

The censorship of literature extends to such absurd prohibitions which it did not reach even during the worst period of the forties.—*Times.*

A God in such an abstract sense that, as I have pointed out before, does not signify.—*Daily Telegraph.*

They would find such faith, such belief, that would be a revelation to them.—*Daily Telegraph.*

Swift's plan was to offer to fulfil it on conditions so insulting that no one with a grain of self-respect could accept.—L. STEPHEN.

f. 'It . . . that.'

Two constructions, closely allied, but grammatically distinct, are often confused: (i) Antecedent 'it' followed by a defining relative clause with 'that' (who, which); (ii) 'it' followed by a clause in apposition, introduced by the conjunction 'that'. The various correct possibilities are represented in the set of examples given below. Relative clauses are marked R, conjunction clauses C. One impossible example is added in brackets, to mark the transition from relative to conjunction.

(1) It is money that I want.   R.
(2) It was you that told me.   R.
(3) It was you that I gave it to (or, to whom I gave it).   R.
(4) It was to you that I gave it.   C.
(5) It was the Romans that built this wall.   R.
(6) It is the Romans that we are indebted to for this.   R.
(7) It is to the Romans that we are indebted for this.   C.
(8) It was Jones whose hat I borrowed.   R.
(9) It was Jones's hat that I borrowed.   R.
(10) It was a knife that I cut it with.   R.
(11) It was with a knife that I cut it.   C.
(12) It was with difficulty that I cut it.   C.
(13) (It was difficulty that I cut it with.)   R.
(14) It was provisionally that I made the offer.   C.

(15) It was in this spring, too, that the plague broke out. C.

(16) Accordingly, it was with much concern that I presently received a note informing me of his departure. C.

In the relative construction, the antecedent 'it' is invariable, whatever the number and gender of the relative. The main verb is also invariable in number, but in tense is usually adapted to past, though not (for euphony's sake) to future circumstances: 'it was you that looked foolish', but 'it is you that will look foolish'.

In both constructions, the 'that' clause, supplemented or introduced by 'it', gives us the subject of a predication, the relative clause (with *it*) being equivalent to a pure noun, the conjunction clause to a verbal noun in apposition, partly retaining its verbal character. In both, also, the predication answers an imaginary question, recorded distinctly in the relative, less distinctly in the conjunction clause. 'What do you want?' 'It (the thing) that I want is money.' 'To whom did you give it?' 'It (the persons) that I gave it to was your friends.' 'As to your cutting it: give particulars.' 'It—that I cut it (my cutting it)—was with a knife.'

From the above examples it will be seen that the two constructions largely overlap. When (as in 1, 2, 5, 8) the relative is subject or direct object of the clause-verb, or is in the possessive case, it cannot be replaced by the conjunction; but when its relation to the clause-verb is marked by a preposition, the conjunction always may take its place, and sometimes must, as in 12 and 13. For the relative clause can only be used when the question reflected in it is calculated to secure the right kind of answer. Now the natural answer to the question 'What did you cut it with?' is not 'difficulty' but 'a knife'. The misleading 'with' is therefore removed from the relative clause in 13, and placed within the predicate, the definite question 'What did you cut it with?' giving place to the vague demand for particulars. 'With' being removed, the relative clause falls to pieces, for want of a word to govern the relative, and the conjunction clause takes its place. In the same way, 'it was *a cab* (but not *high indignation*) that he drove away in'; 'it was *a concert* (but not *curiosity*) that I was returning from'; 'it was a *beech-tree* (but not *unpleasant circumstances*) that I found him under'. And, generally, it will be found that a preposition is admissible in the relative clause only when used in the literal or the most obvious sense.

The conjunction clause is, as we have said, a verbal noun; so far a noun that things can be predicated of it, and so far a verb that the things predicated of it are verbal relations and verbal circumstances, indirect object, agent, instrument, means, manner, cause, attendant circumstances; anything but subject and direct object. 'My giving was to you'; 'my offering was provisionally'; 'my concealing it was because I was ashamed'.

The mistakes that constantly occur in careless writing result from hesitation between the two forms where both are possible. The confusion, however, ought not to arise; for always with a relative clause, and never with a conjunction, the complement of the main predicate (the answer to the suppressed question) is a noun or the grammatical equivalent of a noun. 'A knife', 'Jones', 'you', 'my friend in Chicago', 'the man who lives next door', are the answers that accompany the relative clause: 'with a knife', 'with difficulty', 'to you', 'occasionally', 'because I was ashamed', are those that accompany the conjunction.

Examples 15 and 16, though quite recognized types, are really artificial perversions. In 15 the true question and answer in the circumstances would be, not, as the sentence falsely implies, 'When did the plague break out?' 'That too happened in this same spring', but 'Were there any other notable events in this spring?' 'Yes: the plague broke out'. Impressiveness is given to the announcement by the fiction that the reader is wondering when the plague broke out; in fact, he is merely waiting for whatever may turn up in the history of this spring. In 16 we go still further: the implied question 'What were your feelings on receiving a (not *the*) note . . .?' could not possibly be asked; the information that alone could prompt it is only given in the 'that' clause.

It has been pointed out in b. that a relative clause with antecedent 'it' practically calls for the relative 'that', in preference to 'which', and even to 'who'. Even when the relative is in the possessive case, 'that', which has no possessive, is often retained by transferring to the main predicate the noun on which it depends; 8 thus gives place to 9, even at the risk of ambiguity; for the relative clause now supplies us with the question (not 'whose hat . . .?' but) 'what did you borrow?', leaving us theoretically in doubt whether Jones's hat is distinguished from his other property, from other people's hats, or from things in general.

On the other hand, the two blunders that are most frequently made almost invariably have the relative 'who' or 'which'.

And it is to me, the original promoter of the whole scheme, to whom they would deny my fair share in the profits!

'To me' implies a conjunction clause: 'to whom . . .' is a relative clause. 'It is to me that . .

It was *to Mrs.* Brent, the beetle-browed wife of Mr. Commissary Brent, *to whom* the General transferred his attentions now.—THACKERAY.

It is to you whom I address a history which may perhaps fall into very different hands.—SCOTT.

'To you that', or 'you to whom'.

It is not taste that is plentiful, but courage that is rare.—STEVENSON.

Again a common blunder; not, however, a confusion between the two constructions above, but between one of them (the relative) and a third. The sentence explains why every one seems to prefer Shakespeare to Ouida (they are afraid to say that they like Ouida best). 'What is the explanation of this?' 'It is not the plentifulness of taste, but the rarity of courage, that explains it.' Or, less clumsily, using the construction that Stevenson doubtless intended: 'It (the inference to be drawn) is not that taste is plentiful, but that courage is rare.'

Three more quotations, on which it will suffice to indicate by italics where the fault lies, and add an emendation in brackets:

The work of which it reminds us in a measure *is of that* once popular storehouse of anecdotes the 'Scottish . . .'—*Daily Telegraph.* (is that)

Is it in these circumstances of personal danger *in which* you expect me to overcome a resolution which is founded on . . .—SCOTT. (that)

And it is to them and to that doughty Surrey patriot, the Editor of the *Spectator*, *to whom belongs the credit* of . . . *Westminster Gazette.* (that the credit belongs)

PARTICIPLE AND GERUND

It is advisable to make a few remarks on the participle and gerund together before taking them separately. As the word *gerund* is variously used, we first define it. A gerund is the verbal noun identical in form with any participle, simple or compound, that contains the termination *-ing*. Thus the verb *write* has the active participles *writing, having written, being about to write, about to write*, and the passive participles *written, having been written, being written, about to be written, being about to be written*. Any of these except *written, about to write, about to be written*, may be a gerund also; but while the participle is an adjective, the gerund is a noun, differing from other nouns in retaining its power (if the active gerund of a transitive verb) of directly governing another noun.

Both these are of great importance for our purpose. The participle itself, even when confusion with the other cannot occur, is much abused; and the slovenly uses of it that were good enough in Burke's time are now recognized solecisms. Again, the identity between the two forms leads to loose and unaccountable gerund constructions that will probably be swept away, as so many other laxities have been, with the advance of grammatical consciousness. We shall have to deal with both these points at some length.

It is indeed no wonder that the forms in *-ing* should require close attention. Exactly how many old English terminations *-ing* is heir to is a question debated by historical grammarians, which we are not competent to answer. But we may point out that *writing* may now be (1) participle—I was writing; I saw him writing; writing piously, he acts profanely—, (2) gerund or full verbal noun—I object to your writing that—,

(3) hybrid between gerund and participle—I do not mind you writing it—, (4) detached verbal noun—Writing is an acquired art—, (5) concrete noun—This writing is illegible. Moreover, the verbal noun *writing* has the synonym *to write*, obligatory instead of it in some connexions, better in some, worse in some, and impossible in others; compare, for instance: I do not like the trouble of writing; I shall not take the trouble to write; the trouble of writing is too much for him; it is a trouble to write; writing is a trouble. The grammatical difficulties, that is, are complicated by considerations of idiom.

In these preliminary remarks, however, it is only with the distinction or want of distinction between participle and gerund that we are concerned. The participle is an adjective, and should be in agreement with a noun or pronoun; the gerund is a noun, of which it should be possible to say clearly whether, and why, it is in the subjective, objective, or possessive case, as we can of other nouns. That the distinction is often obscured, partly in consequence of the history of the language, will be clear from one or two facts and examples.

1. *The man is building* contains what we should all now call, whether it is so or not historically, a participle or verbal adjective: *the house is building* (older but still living and correct English for *the house is being built*) contains, as its remarkable difference of meaning prepares us to believe, a gerund or verbal noun, once governed by a now lost preposition.

2. In *He stopped, laughing* we have a participle; in *He stopped laughing*, a verbal noun governed directly by the verb; in *He burst out laughing*, a verbal noun governed by a vanished preposition.

3. Present usage does not bear out the definite modern ideas of the distinction between participle and gerund as respectively adjective and noun. So long as that usage continues, there are various degrees of ambiguity, illustrated by the three following examples. It would be impossible to say, whatever the context, whether the writer of the first intended a gerund or a participle. In the second, a previous sentence would pro-

bably have decided the question. In the third, though grammar (again as modified by present usage) leaves the question open, the meaning of the sentence is practically decisive by itself.

Can he conceive *Matthew Arnold permitting* such a book to be written and published about himself?—*Times*.

And no doubt that end will be secured by *the Commission sitting* in Paris.—*Times*.

Those who know least of them [the virtues] know very well how much they are concerned in *other people having* them.—MORLEY.

In the second of these, if *sitting* is a participle, the meaning is that the end will be secured by the Commission, which is described by way of identification as the one sitting in Paris. If *sitting* is gerund, the end will be secured by the wise choice of Paris and not another place for its scene. If *Commission's* were written, there could be no doubt the latter was the meaning. With *Commission*, there is, by present usage, absolutely no means of deciding between the two meanings apart from possible light in the context. In the third, common sense is able to tell us, though grammar gives the question up, that what is interesting is not the other people who have them, but the question whether other people have them.

We shall, in the section on the gerund, take up the decided position that all gerunds ought to be made distinguishable from participles. We are quite aware, however, that in the first place a language does not remodel itself to suit the grammarian's fancy for neat classification; that secondly the confusion is not merely wanton or ignorant, but the result of natural development; that thirdly the change involves some inconveniences, especially to hurried and careless writers. On the other hand it is certain that the permanent tendency in language is towards the correct and logical, not from it; it is merely hoped that the considerable number of instances here collected may attract the attention of some writers who have not been aware of the question, and perhaps convince them that the distinction is a useful one, that a writer ought to know and let us know whether he is using a participle or a gerund, and that to abandon the gerund when it cannot be distinguished without clumsiness need cause no difficulty to any but the very unskilful in handling words.

PARTICIPLES

The unattached or wrongly attached participle is one of the blunders most common with illiterate or careless writers. But there are degrees of heinousness in the offence; our examples are arranged from 1. to 8. in these degrees, starting with perfect innocence.

1. Participles that have passed into prepositions, conjunctions, or members of adverbial phrases.

Considering the circumstances, *you* may go.
Seeing that it was involuntary, *he* can hardly be blamed.
Roughly *speaking*, all *men* are liars.
Looking at it in a shortened perspective of time, those *years* of transition have the quality of a single consecutive occurrence.— H. G. WELLS.
The *Bill* . . . will bring about, *assuming* that it meets with good fortune in the remaining stages of its passage through Parliament, a very useful reform.—*Times*.

Regarded as participles, these are incorrect. It is not *you* that consider, but I; not *he* that sees, but we; not *men* that roughly speak, but the moralist; not *years* that look, but philosophic historians; not *the Bill* that assumes, but the newspaper prophet. The development into prepositions, &c., is a natural one, however; the only question about any particular word of the kind is whether the vox populi has yet declared for it; when it has, there is no more to be said; but when it has not, the process should be resisted as long as possible, writers acting as a suspensive House of Lords; an instance will be found in 4.

Three quotations from Burke will show that he, like others of his time, felt himself more at liberty than most good writers would now feel themselves.

Founding the appeal on this basis, *it was judged* proper to lay before Parliament . . .—BURKE.
Flattering themselves that their power is become necessary to the

support of all order and government, *everything* which tends to the support of that power *is sanctified.*—BURKE.

Having considered terror as producing an unnatural tension and certain violent emotions of the nerves; *it* easily *follows.*—BURKE.

Similar constructions may be found on almost every page of Smollett.

2. Participles half justified by attachment to a pronoun implied in *my, your, his, their.* These are perhaps better avoided.

Having thus *run* through the causes of the sublime with reference to all the senses, *my* first observation will be found very nearly true.— BURKE.

Being much *interested* in the correspondence bearing on the question 'Do we believe?', the first difficulty arising in *my* mind is . . .—*Daily Telegraph.*

My farm consisted of about twenty acres of excellent land, *having given* a hundred pounds for my predecessor's good will.—GOLDSMITH.

3. Mere unattached participles for which nothing can be said, except that they are sometimes inoffensive if the word to be supplied is very vague.

Doubling the point, and *running* along the southern shore of the little peninsula, the scene changes.—F. M. CRAWFORD.

The most trying . . . period was this one of enforced idleness *waiting* for the day of entry.—*Times.*

Having acquired so many tropical colonies there is the undoubted duty attached to such possession of . . .—*Times.*

4. Participles that may one day become prepositions, &c.

Sir—*Referring* to your correspondent's (the Bishop of Croydon's) letter in to-day's issue, *he* quotes at the close of it the following passage.—*Daily Telegraph.*

He must be the Bishop; for the immediately preceding *Sir*, marking the beginning of the letter, shows that no one else has been mentioned; but if we had given the sentence without this indication, no one could possibly have believed that this was so; *referring* is not yet unparticipled.

5. An unwary writer sometimes attaches a participle to the subject of a previous sentence, assuming that it will be the subject of the new sentence also, and then finds (or rather is

not awake enough to find) himself mistaken. This is a trap into which good writers sometimes fall, and so dangerous to bad writers that we shall give many examples. It is important for the tiro to realize that he has not satisfied the elementary requirements of grammar until he has attached the participle to the noun in the same sentence as itself, not in another. He must also remember that, for instance, *I went and he came*, though often spoken of loosely as a sentence, is in fact as fully two sentences as if each half of it were ten lines long, and the two were parted by a full stop and not connected by a conjunction.

They had now reached the airy dwelling where Mrs. Macshake resided, and *having rung*, *the door* was at length most deliberately opened.—S. FERRIER.

The lovers sought a shelter, and, mutually *charmed* with each other, *time* flew for a while on downy pinions.—S. FERRIER.

A molecular *change* is propagated to the muscles by which the body is retracted, and *causing* them to contract, *the act* of retraction is brought about.—HUXLEY.

Joseph, as they supposed, by tampering with Will, got all my secrets, and was acquainted with all my motions—; and *having* also *undertaken* to watch all those of his young lady, the wise *family* were secure.—RICHARDSON.

Miss Pinkerton . . . in vain . . . tried to overawe her. *Attempting* once to scold her in public, *Rebecca* hit upon the . . . plan of answering her in French, which quite routed the old woman.—THACKERAY.

But *he* thought it derogatory to a brave knight passively to await the assault, and *ordering* his own men to charge, the hostile *squadrons*, rapidly advancing against each other, met midway on the plain.—PRESCOTT.

Alvarado, roused by the noise of the attack on this quarter, hastened to the support of his officer, when *Almagro*, seizing the occasion, pushed across the bridge, dispersed the small body left to defend it, and, *falling* on Alvarado's rear, *that general* saw himself hemmed in on all sides.—PRESCOTT.

Murtagh, without a word of reply, went to the door, and *shouting* into the passage something in Irish, *the room* was instantly filled with bog-trotters.—BORROW.

But, as before, *Anne* once more made me smart, and *having equipped* herself in a gown and bonnet of mine—not of the newest—off *we* set.—CROCKETT.

At this I was silent for a little, and then *I* resolved to speak plainly to Anne. But not *being* ready with my words, *she* got in first.—
CROCKETT.

For many years *I* had to contend with much opposition in the nature of scepticism; but *having had* hundreds of successful cases and proofs *it* has become such an established fact in the eastern counties that many landowners, &c., would not think of sinking a well without first seeking the aid of a water diviner.—*Times*.

6. A more obvious trap, and consequently less fatal, is a change from the active construction that may have been intended to a passive, without corresponding alterations. If the writers of the next two had used *we must admit* instead of *it must be admitted*, *a policy that they put forward*, instead of *a policy put forward*, the participles *hesitating* and *believing* would have had owners.

While *hesitating* to accept this terrible indictment of French infancy, *it must be admitted* that French literature in all its strength and wealth is a grown-up literature.—*Spectator*.

He and those with whom he acted were responsible for the policy promulgated—*a policy* put forward in all seriousness and honesty *believing* it to be essential to the obtaining of the better government of Ireland.—*Times*.

7. Participles that seem to belong to a noun, but do not.

Letters on the constant stopping of omnibuses, thus *causing* considerable suffering to the horses.

Does *causing* agree with *letters*? Then the letters annoy the horses. With *stopping*? Then stopping causes suffering by stopping (*thus*). With *omnibuses*? The horses possibly blame those innocents, but we can hardly suppose a human being, even the writer of this sentence, so illogical. The word *thus*, however, is often considered to have a kind of dispensing power, freeing its participle from all obligations; so:

The Prince was, by the special command of his Majesty the Emperor, made the guardian of H.I.H. the Crown Prince, *thus necessitating* the Prince's constant presence in the capital of Japan.—*Times*.

A very wealthy man can never be sure even of friendship,—while the highest, strongest and noblest kind of love is nearly always denied to him, in this way *carrying out* the fulfilment of those strange but true words:—'How hardly shall he that is a rich man enter the Kingdom of Heaven!'—CORELLI.

It is not *love* that carries out, but the power that denies love, which is not mentioned.

8. Really bad unattached or wrongly attached participles. The reader will generally find no difficulty in seeing what has led to the blunder, and if he will take the trouble to do this, will be less likely to make similar blunders himself.

And then *stooping* to take up the key to let *myself* into the garden, *he* started and looked as if he heard somebody near the door.—RICHARDSON.

Sir—With reference to this question 'Do we believe?', while *recognizing* the vastness of the subject, its modern aspect has some definite features.—*Daily Telegraph*.

Taken in conjunction with the splendid white and brown trout-fishing of the Rosses lakes and rivers, anglers have now the opportunity of fishing one of the best, if not the best, fishery to be obtained in Ireland.—ADVT.

Sir—*Having read* with much interest the letters re 'Believe only' now appearing in the *Daily Telegraph*, perhaps some of your readers might be interested to know the following texts which have led some great men to 'believe only'.—*Daily Telegraph*.

Being pushed unceremoniously to one side—which was precisely what I wished—he usurped my place.—C. BRONTË.

The higher forms of speech acquire a secondary strength from association. *Having*, in actual life, habitually *heard* them in connexion with mental impressions, and *having been accustomed* to meet with them in the most powerful writing, they come to have in themselves a species of force.—SPENCER.

Standing over one of the sluices of the Aswan dam last January, not only was the vibration evident to the senses . . .—*Times*.

Being the actual lender, there are no fees or commissions charged.—Money-lender's circular.

The following passage may be commended for use in examination papers. 'Always *beloved* by the Imperial couple who are to-day the Sovereign lord and lady of Great Britain, their Majesties have, on many occasions since the Devonshire houses rejoiced in a mistress once more, honoured them by visits extending over some days.'—*Times*.

The last, as the *Times* reviewer has noticed, will repay analysis in several ways.

9. **The absolute construction** is not much to be recommended, having generally an alien air in English; but it is sometimes useful. It must be observed, first, that the case used should now invariably be the subjective, though it was otherwise in old English. Secondly, it is very seldom advisable to make an absolute construction and insert a pronoun for the purpose when the participle might simply be attached in ordinary agreement to a noun already to hand. Thirdly, it is very bad to use the construction, but omit to give the participle a noun or pronoun to itself. These three transgressions will be illustrated, in the same order, by the next three examples. But many of the wrong sentences in 5 above may be regarded as absolute constructions with the subject omitted.

I, with whom that Impulse was the most intractable, the most capricious, the most maddening of masters (*him* before me always excepted) . . .—C. BRONTË.

'Special' is a much overworked word, *it* being loosely used to mean great in degree, also peculiar in kind.—R. G. WHITE.

This is said now because, *having been said* before, I have been judged as if I had made the pretensions which were then and which are now again disclaimed.—R. G. WHITE.

THE GERUND

There are three questions to be considered: whether a writer ought to let us know that he is using a gerund and not a participle; when a gerund may be used without its subject's being expressed; when a gerund with preposition is to be preferred to the infinitive.

1. **Is the gerund to be made recognizable?** And, in the circumstances that make it possible, that is, when its subject is expressed, is this to be done sometimes, or always?

It is done by putting what we call for shortness' sake the subject of the gerund (i.e., the word *me* or *my* in *me doing* or *my doing*) in the possessive instead of in the objective or subjective case.

Take the typical sentence: I dislike my best friend('s) violating my privacy. It cannot be a true account of the matter to say that *friend* is the object of *I dislike*, and has a participle *violating* attached to it. For (a) we can substitute *resent*, which never takes a personal object, for *dislike*, without changing the sense. (b) If we substitute a passive construction, also without changing the sense, we find that *dislike* has quite a different object—*privacy*.—I dislike my privacy being violated by my friend. (c) Many of us would be willing to adopt the sentiment conveyed who yet would not admit for a moment that they disliked their best friend even when he intruded; they condemn the sin, but not the sinner.

Violating then is not an ordinary participle. It does not follow yet that it is a gerund. It may be an extraordinary participle, fused into one notion with the noun, so that *a friend violating* means *the-violation-by-a-friend*. The Latin scholar here at once puts in the idiom of *occisus Caesar*, which does not generally mean *Caesar after he was killed*, as it naturally should, but the killing of Caesar, or the fact that Caesar had been killed. The parallel is close (though the use is practically confined to the passive in Latin), and familiar to all who know any Latin at all. But it shows not so much what the English construction is as how educated people have been able to reconcile themselves to an ambiguous and not very reasonable idiom—not very reasonable, that is, after language has thrown off its early limitations, and got over the first difficulty of accomplishing abstract expression of any kind. The sort of fusion assumed is further illustrated for the Latinist, though not so closely, by the Latin accusative and infinitive. This theory then takes *violating* for a participle fused into one notion with *friend*. There are two difficulties.

I. The construction in English is, though in the nature of things not as common, yet as easy in the passive as in the active. Now the passive of *violating* is either *violated* or *being violated*. It is quite natural to say, Privacy violated once is no longer inviolable. Why then should it be most unnatural to say, The worst of privacy violated once is that it is no longer inviolable? No one, not purposely seeking the unusual for some

reason or other, would omit *being* before *violated* in the second.
Yet as participles *violated* and *being violated* are equally good—
not indeed always, but in this context, as the simpler Privacy
sentence shows. The only difference between the two participles (except that in brevity, which tells against *being violated*)
is that the longer form can also be the gerund, and the shorter
cannot. The almost invariable choice of it is due to the instinctive feeling that what we are using is or ought to be the
gerund. A more convincing instance than this mere adaptation
of our original example may be added:

Many years ago I became impressed with the necessity for *our
infantry being taught and practised* in the skilful use of their rifle.—
LORD ROBERTS.

The necessity for our infantry taught and practised is absolutely
impossible. But why, if *being taught* is participle, and not
gerund?

II. Assuming that the fused-participle theory is satisfactory
and recognized, whence comes the general, though not universal
impression among those who, without being well versed in
grammar, are habitually careful how they speak and write,
that constructions like the following are ignorant vulgarisms?
—It is no use he (his) doing it; it is no use him (his) doing it;
that need not prevent us (our) believing; excuse me (my)
interrupting you; a thing (thing's) existing does not prove that
it ought to exist; I was annoyed by Tom (Tom's) hesitating;
the Tsar (Tsar's) leaving Russia is significant; it failed through
the King (King's) refusing his signature; without us (our)
hearing the man, the facts cannot be got at; without the man
(man's) telling us himself, we can never know. With a single
exception for one (not both) of the first two, none of these ought
to cause a moment's uneasiness to any one who was consciously
or unconsciously in the fused-participle frame of mind; and if
they do cause uneasiness it shows that that frame of mind is not
effectively present.

The Fused-Participle Theory, having no sufficient answer
to these objections, but seeing that the gerund's case is also

weak, naturally tries a counter-attack:—If on the other hand the gerund theory is satisfactory and recognized, how is it conceivable that people should leave out the possessive *'s* in the reckless way they do? To which, however, the Gerund makes reply:—I regret that they do leave it out, but at least we can see how they come to; it is the combined result of a mistake and an inconvenience. The mistake is caused by certain types of sentence in which a real, not a fused participle is so used that the noun and its (unfused) participle give a sense hardly distinguishable from a possessive noun and a gerund. Examples are:

This plan has now been abandoned owing to *circumstances requiring* the convocation of representatives of the people at the earliest possible moment.—*Times*.

. . . by imposing as great difficulty as possible on *parents and publicans using* child messengers.—*Times*.

Of course no obstacles should be put in the way of *charitable people providing* free or other meals if they think fit.—*Times*.

The notion of *the Czar being addressed* in such terms by the nobility of his capital would have been regarded as an absolute impossibility.—*Spectator*.

There is of course a difference. For instance, in the example about the Czar, as in a previous one about *conceiving Matthew Arnold permitting*, the participle has a pictorial effect; it invites us to imagine the physical appearance of these two great men under indignity instead of merely thinking of the abstract indignity, as we should have done if *Czar's* and *Arnold's* had shown that we had a gerund; but the difference is very fine; the possessive sign might be inserted without practical effect in all these four, and in hundreds like them. And unlearned people may be excused for deducing that the subject of the gerund can be used at pleasure without the possessive sign, while the learned comfort themselves with the fused-participle theory. That is the mistake. The inconvenience is this: it is easy enough to use the possessive adjectives (*my*, &c.,) and to add the possessive sign to most names and many single nouns; but the subject of a gerund is often a long phrase, after which the sign is intolerable. So the mistake (that the gerund may have a subject not marked by the possessive) is eagerly applied to obviating the inconvenience (that long gerund subjects must be avoided). And that is why people drop their possessive *'s*, and why you, the Fused Participle, flourish, defrauding both me, the Gerund, and the honest participle. Thus answered, the Fused Participle does not continue the argument, but pleads only that there is room for all three forms.

Before giving some examples to help in the decision, we shall summarize our own opinion. (1) It is not a matter to be decided by appeal to historical grammar. All three constructions may have separate legitimate descents, and yet in the interests of clear thought and expression it may be better for one of them to be abandoned. (2) There are two opposite tendencies at present: among careful writers, to avoid the fused participle[1] (this, being negative, can naturally not be illustrated) and to put possessive signs in slightly uncomfortable places by way of compensation; among slovenly writers, to throw off all limits of length for the subject of the fused participle. (3) Long fused-participle phrases are a variety of abstract expression, and as such to be deprecated. Among the resources of civilization is the power of choosing between different ways of saying the same thing; and literary skill is very much a matter of exercising that power; a writer should recognize that if he cannot get round an ugly fused participle there is still much for him to learn. (4) Opportunities for ambiguity are so abundant in English, owing to the number of words whose parsing depends on context, that all aids to precision are valuable; and it is not too much to expect a writer to know and let us know whether he means a participle or a gerund.

a. That the possessive of all pronouns that have the form

---

[1] The present (1930) re-setting of the text gives me the opportunity of affirming again my belief in this tendency, in spite of the formidable criticism directed against its reality by Professor Jespersen. That criticism and my comments upon it appeared in numbers xxv, xxvi, of the *S.P.E. Tracts*, the reading of which I venture to recommend to any one seriously concerned over the fate of the Fused Participle.—H. W. F.

should be used instead of the objective or subjective is hardly disputed. Correct accordingly:

You may rely upon *me* doing all in my power.—SIR W. HARCOURT.

The confounded fetterlock clapped on my movements by old Griffiths prevents *me* repairing to England in person.—SCOTT.

But when it comes to *us* following his life and example . . .—*Daily Telegraph.*

Nothing can prevent *it* being the main issue at the General Election. —*Spectator.*

One of them, if you will pardon *me* reminding you, is that no discussion is to pass between us.—E. F. BENSON.

Frederick had already accepted the crown, lest James should object to *him* doing so.—*Times.*

. . . notwithstanding the fact that their suspicions of ease-loving, ear-tickling, parsons prevent *them* supporting the commercial churches of our time.—*Daily Telegraph.*

b. Examples in which the possessive of nouns might be written without a qualm.

Nearly a week passed over without *Mr. Fairford* hearing a word directly from his son.—SCOTT.

Mrs. Downe Wright had not forgiven the indignity of *her son* having been refused by Mary.—S. FERRIER.

In no other religion is there a thought of *man* being saved by grace and not by merit.—*Daily Telegraph.*

And it is said that, on *a visitor* once asking to see his library, Descartes led him . . .—HUXLEY.

It is true that one of our objects was to prevent[1] *children* 'sipping' the liquor they were sent for.—*Times.*

Orders were sometimes issued to prohibit[1] *soldiers* buying and eating cucumbers.—*Times.*

Renewed efforts at a settlement in 1891 failed through the *Swedish Government* leading off with a flippant and offensive suggestion.— NANSEN.

Hurried reading results in *the learner* forgetting half of what he reads, or in *his* forming vague conceptions.—SWEET.

c. All the last set involved what were either actual or virtual names of persons; there is more difficulty with abstract nouns,

---

[1] The reason why many who as a rule use the possessive are willing to do without it after verbs like *prevent* is perhaps this: in *I prevented him going* they consciously or unconsciously regard both *him* and *going* as nouns, one the indirect, one the direct object, as in *I refused him leave.*

compound subjects, and words of which the possessive is ugly.
Those that may perhaps bear the possessive mark will be put
first, and alterations suggested for the others.

We look forward to *much attention* being given.—*Times*.

He affirmed that such increases were the rule in that city on *the
change* being made.—*Times*.

I live in hopes of *this discussion* resulting in some modification in
our form of belief.—*Daily Telegraph*. (that this discussion may
result)

The real objection to the possessive here is merely the addition
to the crowd of sibilants.

In the event of *the passage* being found, he will estem it a favour . . .
(if the passage is found)

Conceive my vexation at being told by Papa this morning that he had
not the least objection to *Edward and me* marrying whenever we
pleased.—S. FERRIER. (our)

Or, if the names are essential, *did not in the least mind how soon
Edward and I married*.

It has been replied to the absurd taunt about *the French* inventing
nothing, that at least Descartes invented German philosophy.—MORLEY.
(Frenchmen's)

d. A modern construction called the compound possessive
was mentioned at the end of the section on Cases. It is sometimes ugly, sometimes inoffensive; that is a matter of degree
and of knowing where to draw the line; there is no objection to
it in principle. And the application of it will sometimes help
out a gerund. The first quotation gives a compound possessive
simply; the second, a gerund construction to which it ought
to be applicable; the third and fourth, two to which it can be
applied; and the last, one to which it cannot.

A protestation, read at Edinburgh, was followed, on *Archibald
Johnston of Warriston's* suggestion, by . . .—J. R. GREEN.

The retirement of Judge Stonor was made the subject of special
reference yesterday on the occasion of *Sir W. L. Selfe, his successor*,
taking his seat in Marylebone County Court.—*Times*.

The mere fact of *such a premier* being endured shows . . .—BAGEHOT.

There is no possibility of *the dissolution of the legislative union*
becoming a vital question.—*Spectator*.

If some means could be devised for . . . insisting upon *many English guardians of the poor* making themselves more acquainted . . .—*Times*.

The only objection to a possessive mark after *successor* is that the two commas cannot be dispensed with; we must say *when* . . . *took* for *on the occasion of* . . . *taking. Such a premier's* will certainly pass. In the *Spectator* sentence, we should ourselves allow *union's*; opinions will differ. But to put the *'s* after *poor* in the last sentence would be ridiculous; that sentence must be rewritten—insisting that many English guardians of the poor should make—or else *poor-law Guardians'* must be used.

e. Sometimes we can get over the difficulty without abandoning the gerund, by some slight change of order.

This incentive can only be supplied by *the nation itself* taking the matter up seriously.—LORD ROBERTS.

If *itself's* is objected to, omit *itself* (or shift it to the end), and write *nation's*.

f. But many types of sentence remain that will have to be completely changed if the gerund is to be recognizable. It will be admitted about most of our examples that the change is not to be regretted. The subject of the gerund is italicized in each, to emphasize its length.

We have to account for *the collision of two great fleets, so equal in material strength that the issue was thought doubtful by many careful statisticians*, ending in the total destruction of one of them and in the immunity of the other from damage greater than might well be incurred in a mere skirmish.—*Times*.

For *account for* . . . *ending* write *ascertain why* . . . *ended*. The sentence is radically bad, because the essential construction seems complete at *collision*—a false scent. That, which is one of the worst literary sins, is the frequent result of long fused participles. It is quite practically possible here for readers to have supposed that they were going to be told why the fleets met, and not why the meeting ended as it did. In the remaining sentences, we shall say when there is a false scent, but leave the reader to examine it.

The success of the negotiations depends on *the Russian Minister at Tokio* being allowed to convince Japan that . . .—*Times.*

The compound possessive—Tokio's—is tempting, but perhaps overbold. Insert *whether* after *depends on*, and write *is* for *being.*

So far from *this* being the case, the policy . . . was actually decided upon before . . . the question . . . was raised.—*Times.*

Omit *being the case.*

We are not without tokens of *an openness for this higher truth also, of a keen though uncultivated sense for it,* having existed in Burns.— CARLYLE.

For the first *of* write *that,* omit the second *of,* and omit *having.* False scent.

There is no apparent evidence of *an early peace* being necessitated by the pecuniary exigencies of the Russian Government.—SIR HOWARD VINCENT.

For *of . . . being* write *that . . . will be,* if *peace's* cannot be endured.

The general effect of his words was to show the absurdity of *the Secretary of State for War, and our military authorities generally,* denouncing the Militia as useless or redundant.—*Spectator.*

For *the absurdity of . . . denouncing* write *how absurd it was for . . . to denounce.* False scent, though less deceptive.

Apparently his mission was decided upon without *that of the British and Spanish Ministers* having been taken into account, or, at all events, without their having been sufficiently reckoned with.—*Times.*

Without regard (at all events without sufficient regard) to that of . . .

. . . capital seeking employment in foreign protected countries, in consequence of *manufacturing business in many branches in which it might be employed at home* being rendered unprofitable by our system of free trade.—LORD GOSCHEN.

For *in consequence of . . . being* write *because . . . has been.* Bad false scent again.

So far from *the relief given to agriculture by the State paying one-half of the rates* being inequitable, it is but a bare act of justice.—*Spectator.*

Observe the fused participle within fused participle here; and read thus: So far from its being inequitable that the state should relieve, &c.

After these specimens, chosen not as exceptional ones, but merely as not admitting of simple correction by insertion of the possessive mark, the reader will perhaps agree that the long gerund subject—or rather noun phrase of the fused participle—is a monstrosity, the abolition of which would be a relief to him, and good discipline for the writer.

Two sentences are added to show the chaotic state of present practice. Noticing the bold use of the strict gerund in the first, we conclude that the author is a sound gerundite, faithful in spite of all temptations; but a few pages later comes the needless relapse into fused participle.

I remember old *Colney's* once, in old days, *calling* that kind of marriage a sarcophagus.—MEREDITH.

She had thought in her heart that *Mr. Barmby espousing* the girl would smoothe a troubled prospect.—MEREDITH.

The following looks like a deliberate avoidance of both constructions by a writer who is undecided between the two. *Its being* is what should have been written.

I do not say that the advice is not sound, or complain that it is given. I do deprecate *that it should be* taken.—*Times.*

And perhaps a shyness of *something's being shown* accounts for the next odd arrangement; it is true that entire recasting is what is called for.

There being shown to be something radically defective in the management of the Bank *led* to the appointment of a Committee.—H. D. MACLEOD.

2. **When must the subject of the gerund (or infinitive) be expressed, and when omitted ?**

This is not a controversial matter like the last; the principles are quite simple, and will be accepted; but it is necessary to state and illustrate them because they are often forgotten. As the same mistakes are sometimes made with the infinitive, that is to be considered as included.

Roughly, the subject of the gerund (or infinitive) should be expressed if it is different from the subject of the sentence, but omitted if it is the same. To omit it when different is positively wrong, and may produce actual ambiguity or worse, though sometimes there is only a slipshod effect; to insert it when the same is generally clumsy.

No one would say 'I succeeded to his property upon dying', because *I* being the subject of the sentence, *my* is naturally suggested instead of the necessary *his* as subject of the gerund; the *his* must be inserted before *dying*, even though the nature of the case obviates ambiguity. To take an instance that will show both sides, the following is correct.

> I shut the door and stood with my back to it. Then, instead of *his philandering* with Bess, I, Clementina MacTaggart, had some plain speech with John Barnaby.—CROCKETT.

Subject of the sentence, I; subject of the gerund, he; they are different; therefore the *he* must be expressed, in the shape of *his*. Now rewrite the main sentence as—John Barnaby heard some plain speech from me, Clementina MacTaggart. The sense is the same; but the *his* before *philandering* at once becomes superfluous; it is not yet seriously in the way, because we do not know what is the subject of *philandering*, the name only coming later. Now rewrite it again as—Then John Barnaby heard some plain speech from . . . instead of . . . The *his* is now so clumsy as to be almost impossible.

The insertion of superfluous subjects is much less common than the omission of necessary ones; but three examples follow. The first is a rare and precious variety; the second has no apparent justification; for the third it may be said that the unusual *his* has the same effect as the insertion of the parenthetic words *as he actually does* after *limiting* would have had.

> You took food to him, but instead of *he reaching* out his hand and taking it, he kept asking for food.—*Daily Telegraph.*
> Harsh facts: sure as she was of *her* never *losing* her filial hold of the beloved.—MEREDITH.

I have said that Mr. Chamberlain has no warrant for *his limiting* the phrase . . . to the competitive manufacture of goods.—LORD GOSCHEN.

In giving the rule summarily, we used the phrase *subject of the sentence*. That phrase is not to be confined to the subject of the main sentence, but to be referred instead, when necessary, to the subject of the subordinate clause in which the gerund may stand. For instance:

The good, the illuminated, sit apart from the rest, censuring their dullness and vices, as if they thought that, *by sitting* very grand in their chairs, the very brokers, attorneys, and congressmen would see the error of their ways, and flock to them.—EMERSON.

Here *by sitting* breaks the rule, though the subject of *sitting* is the same as that of the main verb *sit*, because the subject of the clause in which *sitting* comes is not *the good*, but *brokers*, *&c.* The right way to mend this is not to insert *their* before *sitting*—which after all is clumsy, though correct—but to make *the good* the subject of the clause also, by writing *as if they thought that by sitting . . . they would make the brokers . . . see the error*.

And sometimes *subject of the sentence* is to be interpreted still more freely as the word grammatically dominant in the part of the sentence that contains the gerund. For instance:

From the Bible alone was she taught the duties of morality, but familiarized to her taste *by hearing* its stories and precepts from the lips she best loved.—S. FERRIER.

Here the dominant word is *Bible*, to which *familiarized* belongs. So, though *she* does happen to be the main subject, *her* must be inserted because the *familiarized* phrase removes the gerund from the reach of the main subject.

After these explanations we add miscellaneous instances. It will be seen that transgression of the rule, though it seldom makes a sentence ambiguous enough to deceive, easily makes it ambiguous enough to amuse the reader at wrong moments, or gives an impression of amateurish work. Mistakes are mended, sometimes by inserting the subject of the gerund (or infinitive), sometimes by changing the main subject to make it the same as that of the gerund, sometimes by other recasting.

... an excellent arrangement for a breeching, which, when released, remains with the carriage, so that lead or centre horses can be put in the wheel *without having* to affix a new breeching.—*Times*.

Lucky, reflects the reader, since horses are not good at affixing breechings. Write *the drivers can put . . . horses . . . without having to affix*.

I cultivated a passionless and cold exterior, for I discovered that *by assuming* such a character, certain otherwise crafty persons would talk more readily before me.—CORELLI.

Write *if I assumed*; or else *I should induce certain . . . persons to talk*. It will be noticed that the mistake here, and often, is analogous to the most frequent form of wrongly attached participle (participle 5); the writer does not observe that he has practically passed from the sphere of the sentence whose subject was the word that he still allows to operate.

After following a country Church of England clergyman for a period of half a century, a newly-appointed, youthful vicar, totally unacquainted with rural life, comes into the parish, and at once commences to alter the services of the Church, believed in by the parishioners for generations.—*Daily Telegraph*.

Grammar gives *his*, i.e., the new vicar's, as subject of *following*; it is really either *my* or *the parishioners'*. Insert *my* or *our*, or write *After we (I) have followed*.

I am sensible that *by conniving* at it it will take too deep root ever to be eradicated.—*Times*.

Insert *our*, or write *if connived at*.

This was experienced by certain sensitive temperaments, either by sensations which produced shivering, or *by seeing* at night a peculiar light in the air.—*Times*.

Who or what sees? Certainly not *this*, the main subject. Not even *temperaments*, which have no eyes. Write *Persons of sensitive temperament experienced this*, &c.

But the commercial interests of both Great Britain and the United

States were too closely affected by the terms of the Russo-Chinese agreement *to let* it pass unnoticed.—*Times*.

It is not the interests that cannot let it pass, but the countries. Insert *for those countries* before *to let*; or write *Both Great Britain and the United States were too closely affected in their interests to let* . . .

And it would be well for all concerned, for motor drivers and the public alike, if this were made law, instead of *fixing* a maximum speed. —*Times*.

Write *if the law required this* . . .

And *in order to bring* her to a right understanding, she underwent a system of persecution.—S. FERRIER.

Write *they subjected her to* for *she underwent*.

Her friendship is too precious to me, not *to doubt* my own merits on the one hand, and not to be anxious for the preservation of it on the other.—RICHARDSON.

Write *I value her friendship too highly not to* . . .

One cannot do good to a man whose mouth has been gagged *in order not to hear* what he desires for his welfare.—*Times*.

Grammar suggests that his mouth—or, if indulgent, that he— is not to hear; but the person meant is *one*. Write *one has gagged* for *has been gagged*.

Germany has, alas! victories enough *not to add* one of the kind which would have been implied in the retirement of M. Delcassé.—*Times*.

It is France, not Germany, that should not add. Write *without France's adding*.

In order to obtain peace, ordinary battles followed by ordinary victories and ordinary results will only lead to a useless prolongation of the struggle.—*Times*.

This is a triumph of inconsequence. Write *If peace is the object, it should be remembered that ordinary* . . .

It will have occurred to the reader that, while most of the sentences quoted are to be condemned, objection to a few of them might be called pedantic. The fact is that every writer probably breaks the rule often, and escapes notice, other

people's, his own, or both. Different readers, however, will be
critical in different degrees; and whoever breaks the rule does
so at his own risk; if his offence is noticed, that is hanging
evidence against him by itself; if it is not noticed, it is not an
offence. Having ourselves said, a page or two back, *Mistakes
are mended sometimes by inserting the subject*, we plead Guilty
if we were caught in the act, but otherwise Not Guilty. A form
of licence may perhaps be drawn up to cover the common type:
'A good cake may be made by taking 1 lb. best flour, &c.'.
When the subject of the sentence is inanimate and the main
verb passive, no ambiguity can result from omission of the
personal but indefinite subject of an active gerund.

3. **Choice between the gerund with preposition and the
infinitive.**

The differentiation between the infinitive and the gerund
with various prepositions is a modern but very valuable refinement, and should be rather developed than neglected.
Shakespeare uses the infinitive in many passages that we should
clear of serious ambiguity by substituting gerund and preposition. Thus (*M.N.D.* II. i. 215) You do impeach your modesty
too much *To leave* the city and *commit* yourself Into the hands of
. . . (mod. *by* or *in leaving and committing*).

It was said in the preliminary section on the Participle and
Gerund that *writing*—the verbal noun or gerund—and *to
write*—the infinitive—are in some sense synonyms; but
phrases were given showing that it is by no means always indifferent which of the two is used. It is matter of idiom rather
than of grammar; but this seems the most convenient place for
drawing attention to it. To give satisfactory rules would require
many more examples and much more space than can be afforded.
But something will be gained if students are convinced (1) that
many of the mistakes made give sentences the appearance
of having been written by a foreigner or one who is not at home
with the literary language; (2) that the mistakes are nearly
always on one side, the infinitive being the form that should

only be used with caution; (3) that a slight change in arrangement may require a change from infinitive to gerund or vice versa.

a. When the infinitive or gerund is attached to a noun, defining or answering the question *what* (hope, &c.) about it, it is almost always better to use the gerund with *of*; not quite always, however; for instance, *an intention to return*, usually, and *a tendency to think* always.

The vain *hope to be understood* by everybody possessed of a ballot makes us in the United States perhaps guiltier than public men in Great Britain in the use of that monstrous muddled dichotomy 'capital and labour'.—*Times*.

What hope?—That of being understood. Write it so, and treat all the following similarly:

The habitual *necessity to amass* [of amassing] matter for the weekly sermon, set him noting . . .—MEREDITH.

We wish to be among the first to felicitate Mr. Whitelaw Reid upon his *opportunity to exercise* [of exercising] again the distinguished talents which . . .—*Times*.

Men lie twenty times in as many hours in the *hope to propitiate* [of propitiating] you.—CORELLI.

We left the mound in the twilight, with the *design to return* [of returning] the next morning.—EMERSON.

The main duties of government were omitted—the *duty to instruct* [of instructing] the ignorant, *to supply* [of supplying] the poor with work and good guidance.—EMERSON.

Mr. Hay's *purpose to preserve or restore* [of preserving or restoring] the integrity of the administrative entity of China has never been abandoned.—*Times*.

My *custom to be dressed* [of being dressed] for the day, as soon as breakfast is over, . . . will make such a step less suspected.—RICHARDSON.

He points out ,that if Russia accepted the agreement, she would not attain her *object to clear* [of clearing] the situation, inasmuch as . . .—*Times*.

What accounts for these mistakes is the analogy of forms like: Our design was to return; it is a duty to instruct; man has power to interpret (but *the* power of interpreting); it is my custom to be dressed.

When, however, the noun thus defined is more or less closely fused into a single idea with the verb that governs it, the infinitive becomes legitimate, though seldom necessary.

The menace *to have secreted* Solmes, and that other, that I *had thoughts to run away* with her foolish brother, . . . so much terrified the dear creature . . .—RICHARDSON.

I passed my childhood here, and *had a weakness here to close* my life.—BEACONSFIELD.

Before ten o'clock in the evening, Gasca *had the satisfaction to see* the bridge so well secured that . . .—PRESCOTT.

Almagro's followers *made as little scruple to appropriate* to their own use such horses and arms as they could find.—PRESCOTT.

Had thoughts means *was planning*; *had a weakness* means *desired*; *had the satisfaction*, *was pleased*; *made as little scruple*, *scrupled as little*.

Again, an interval between the noun defined and the infinitive or gerund makes the former more tolerable.

The necessity which has confronted the Tokio War Office, *to enlarge* their views of the requirements of the situation.—*Times*.

Or the infinitive is used to avoid a multiplication of *of*.

He had as much as any man ever had that *gift* of a great preacher *to make* the oratorical fervour which persuades himself while it lasts into the abiding conviction of his hearers.—LOWELL.

The pastures of Tartary were still remembered by the tenacious *practice* of the Norsemen *to eat* horseflesh at religious feasts.—EMERSON.

If the noun has the indefinite article the infinitive is better sometimes.

But our recognition of it implies *a* corresponding *duty to make* the most of such advantages.—*Times*.

A duty to make: *the* duty of making. Compare *power* and *the power* above.

The following is probably an adaptation (not to be commended) of *it is necessary for Russia to secure—for Russia to secure* being regarded as a fused infinitive like the Latin accusative and infinitive.

His views on the *necessity* for Russia *to secure* the command of the sea . . .—*Times*.

b. Though the gerund with *of* is the usual construction after nouns, they sometimes prefer the gerund with other prepositions also to the infinitive. The gerund with *in* should be used, for instance, in the following. But euphony operates again in the first.

. . . the extraordinary *remissness* of the English commanders *to utilize* their preponderat*ing* strength against the Boers.—*Times*.

Lord Kenyon reminded the House of the resistance met with to vaccination, to [of?] the possible *effect* of the proposal *to increase* that resistance. . . .—*Times*.

I think sculpture and painting have an *effect to teach* us manners and abolish hurry.—EMERSON.

Such a capitulation would be inconsistent with the position of any Great Power, independently of the *humiliation* there would be for England and France *to submit* their agreement for approval and perhaps modification to Germany.—*Times*.

The humiliation there would be in submitting; or the humiliation it would be to submit.

c. After verbs and adjectives the infinitive is much more common; but no one will use a gerund where an infinitive is required, while many will do the reverse.

But history *accords* with the Japanese practice *to show* [in showing] that . . .—*Times*.

We must necessarily appeal to the intuition, and *aim* much more *to suggest* than *to describe* [at suggesting than at describing].—EMERSON.

But they can only highly serve us, when they *aim* not *to drill*, but *to create* [at drilling, but at creating].—EMERSON.

So far from *aiming to be* mistress of Europe, she was rapidly sinking into the almost helpless prey of France.—J. R. GREEN.

This is to avoid *aim*ing *at be*ing; compare the avoidance of double *of* above.

Lose no time, I pray you, to advise.—RICHARDSON.

In advising may have been avoided as ambiguous.

Egotism has its root in the cardinal necessity by which each individual *persists to be* [in being] what he is.—EMERSON.

Ï do not *despair to see* [of seeing] a motor public service.—*Guernsey Advertiser*.

Their journeymen are far too declamatory, and too much *addicted to substitute* [substituting] vague and puerile dissertations for solid instruction.—MORLEY.

In the common phrase *addicted to drink*, drink is a noun, not a verb.

His blackguard countrymen, always *averse*, as their descendants are, *to give* [giving] credit to anybody, for any valuable quality.—BORROW.

Is he *to be blamed*, if he thinks a person would make a wife worth having, *to endeavour* [for endeavouring] to obtain her?—RICHARDSON.

d. If a deferred subject, anticipated by *it*, is to be verbal, it must of course be either the infinitive or a gerund without preposition.

Fortune, who has generally been ready to gratify my inclinations, provided *it* cost her very little *by so doing* . . .—BORROW.

SHALL AND WILL

It is unfortunate that the idiomatic use, while it comes by nature to southern Englishmen (who will find most of this section superfluous), is so complicated that those who are not to the manner born can hardly acquire it; and for them the section is in danger of being useless. In apology for the length of these remarks it must be said that the short and simple directions often given are worse than useless. The observant reader soon loses faith in them from their constant failure to take him right; and the unobservant is the victim of false security.

Roughly speaking, *should* follows the same rules as *shall*, and *would* as *will*; in what follows, Sh. may be taken as an abbreviation for *shall*, *should*, and *should have*, and W. for *will*, *would*, and *would have*.

In our usage of the Sh. and W. forms, as seen in principal sentences, there are elements belonging to three systems. The first of these, in which each form retains its full original meaning, and the two are not used to give different persons of the same tense, we shall call the pure system: the other two, both hybrids, will be called, one the coloured-future, the other the plain-future system. In Old English there was no separate future; present and future were one. *Shall* and *will* were the presents of two verbs, to which belong also the pasts *should* and *would*, the conditionals *should* and *would*, and the past conditionals *should have* and *would have*. *Shall* had the meaning of command or obligation, and *will* of wish. But as commands and wishes are concerned mainly with the future, it was natural that a future tense auxiliary should be developed out of these two verbs. The coloured future results from the application to future time of those forms that were practically useful in the pure system; they consequently retain in the coloured future, with some modifications, the ideas of command and wish proper to the original verbs. The plain future results from the taking of those forms that were practically out of work in the pure system to make what had not before existed, a simple future tense; these have accordingly not retained the ideas of command and wish. Which were the practically useful and which the superfluous forms in the pure system must now be explained.

Thou shalt not steal is the type of *shall* in the pure system. We do not ordinarily issue commands to ourselves; consequently *I shall* is hardly required; but we often ask for orders, and therefore *shall I?* is required. The form of the *shall* present in the pure system is accordingly:

Shall I? You shall. He shall. Shall we? They shall.

As to the past tense, orders cannot be given, but may be asked about, so that, for instance, *What should I do?* (i.e., What was I to do?) can be done all through interrogatively.

In the conditionals, both statement and question can be done all through. I can give orders to my imaginary, though not to my actual self. I cannot say (as a command) *I shall do it*; but I can say, as a conditional command, *I should do it*.

I shall and *we shall* are accordingly the superfluous forms of the present *shall* in the pure system.

Again, with *will*, *I will* meaning *it is my will*, it is obvious that we can generally state this only of ourselves; we do not know the inside of other people's minds, but we can ask about it. The present runs, then,

I will. Will you? Will he? We will. Will they?

The past tense can here be done all through, both positively and interrogatively. For though we cannot tell other people's present will, we can often infer their past will from their actions. So (I was asked, but) *I would not*, and *Why would I do it?* all through. And similarly in the conditionals, *I would not* (if I could), &c.

The spare forms supplied by the present *will*, then, are *you will*, *he will*, *they will*; and these, with *I shall*, *we shall*, are ready, when the simple future is required, to construct it out of. We can now give

Rule 1. The Pure System

When Sh. and W. retain the full original meanings of command and wish, each of them is used in all three persons, so far as it is required.

The following examples show most of what we inherit directly from the pure system.

Thou shalt not steal. Not required in first person.
Shall I open the door? Not required in second.
You should not say such things. In all persons.
And shall Trelawny die? Hardly required in second.
Whom should he meet but Jones? (. . . was it his fate . . .) In all.
Why should you suspect me? In all.
It should seem so. (It would apparently be incumbent on us to believe.) Isolated idiom with third.
I will have my way. Not required in second and third; but see below.
I (he) asked him (me) to do it, but he (I) would not. In all.
I would not have done it for the world. In all.
I would be told to wait a while (Habitual). In all.
Will you come with me? Not required in first.
I would I were dead. Not required in second and third.
He will bite his nails, whatever I say. In all.
He will often stand on his head. In all.
You will still be talking (i.e., you always are). Not required in first.
A coat will last two years with care.

It will be noticed that the last four forms are among those that were omitted as not required by the pure system. *Will* would rarely be required in second and third person statements, but would of course be possible in favourable circumstances, as in describing habitual action, where the will of another may be inferred from past experience. The last of all is a natural extension of the idiom even to things that have no will. All these 'habitual' uses are quite different from *I will have my way*; and though *you will have your way* is possible, it always has the 'habitual' meaning, which *I will have my way* is usually without.

All the forms in the above list, and others like them, have three peculiarities—that they are not practically futures as distinguished from presents; that they use Sh. for all persons, or W. for all persons, if the idea is appropriate to all persons; and that the ideas are simply, or with very little extension, those of command or obligation and wish.

The coloured-future system is so called because, while the future sense is more distinct, it is still coloured with the speaker's mood; command and wish receive extensions and include promise, permission, menace, consent, assurance, intention, refusal, offer, &c.; and the forms used are invariably those —from both Sh. and W.—that we called the practically useful ones in the pure system. That is, we have always:

I will, shall I? You shall, will you? He shall, will he? We will, shall we? They shall, will they?

And the conditionals, *should* and *would*, *should have* and *would have*, are used with exactly the same variations. It will be borne in mind, however, that no clear line of division can be drawn between the pure system and the coloured-future system, since the latter is developed naturally (whereas the plain-future system is rather developed artificially) out of the former. And especially the questions of the coloured future are simply those of the pure system without any sort of modification.

Rule 2. The Coloured-Future System.

In future and conditional statements that include (without the use of special words for the purpose) an expression of the speaker's (not necessarily of the subject's) wish, intention, menace, assurance, consent, refusal, promise, offer, permission, command, &c.—in such sentences the first person has W., the second and third persons Sh.

I will tell you presently. My promise.
You shall repent it before long. My menace.
He shall not have any. My refusal.
We would go if we could. Our conditional intention.
You should do it if we could make you. Our conditional command.
They should have had it if they had asked. My conditional consent.

The only questions possible here are the asking for orders and the requests already disposed of under Rule 1.

Observe that *I would like* (which is not English[1]) is not justified by this rule, because the speaker's mood is expressed by *like*, and does not need double expression; it ought to be *I should like*, under Rule 3.

Observe also that *I sha'n't, You will go to your room and stay there*, are only apparent exceptions, which will be explained under Rule 3.

The archaic literary forms *You shall find, A rogue shall often pass for an honest man*, though now affected and pretentious, are grammatically defensible. The speaker asks us to take the fact on his personal assurance.

The forms little required in the pure system, and therefore ready to hand for making the new plain future, were *I*, and *we*, *shall*; *you*, *he*, and *they*, *will*. These accordingly constitute the plain future, and the corresponding forms of the plain conditional are used analogously. Questions follow the same

[1] Exceptis excipiendis. That sweeping statement is for the 99 per cent. of instances in which *I would like* precedes an infinitive (*I would like to mention* &c.), and not for such rarities as *I would like him if I could* ('my conditional intention', see above), and *When I was a child I would like and dislike people for foolish reasons* ('Habitual', see under Rule 1).

rule, with one very important exception, which will be given a separate rule (4). We now give

Rule 3. The Plain-Future System.

In plain statements about the future, and in the principal clause, result, or apodosis, of plain conditional sentences (whether the subordinate clause, condition, or *if*-clause, is expressed or not), the first person has Sh., the second and third persons W. Questions conform, except those of the second person, for which see Rule 4.

> I shall, you will, die some day.
> Shall I, will they, be here to-morrow?
> We should, he would, have consented if you had asked.
> Should we, would he, have missed you if you had been there?
> I should, you would, like a bathe.
> Should I, would he, like it myself, himself?

Some apparent exceptions, already anticipated, must here be explained. It may be said that *I shall execute your orders* being the speaker's promise, *You will go to your room* being the speaker's command, and *Sha'n't* (the nursery abbreviation for *I shall not do it*) being the speaker's refusal, these are all coloured futures, so that Sh. and W. should be reversed in each. They are such in effect, but they are not in form. In each, the other form would be possible and correct. The first is a promise only so far as the hearer chooses to take as a promise the plain future or impersonal prophecy; but the speaker emphasizes his obedience by implying that of course, since the order has been given, it will be executed; the matter is settled without his unimportant consent. The other two gain force by the opposite assumption that the speaker's will and the future are absolutely identical, so that what he intends may be confidently stated as a future fact. In the first example the desired submissiveness, in the other two the desired imperiousness, supercilious or passionate, are attained by the same impersonality.

Before giving the rule for second-person questions, we

observe that questions generally follow the rule of the class of statement they correspond to. This was shown in the pure system (Rule 1). There are no questions (apart from those already accounted for by the pure system) belonging to the coloured future (Rule 2). In the plain future (Rule 3), first and third person questions are like the plain-future statements. But second-person questions under the plain future invariably use Sh. or W. according as the answer for which the speaker is prepared has Sh. or W. Care is necessary, however, in deciding what that answer is. In *Should (would) you like a bathe?* *should* is almost always right, because the answer expected is almost always either *Yes, I should,* or *No, I should not,* the question being asked for real information. It is true that *Would you like?* is very commonly used, like the equally wrong *I would like*; but it is only correct when the answer is intended to be given by the asker:—*No, of course you would not.* A clearer illustration of this is the following sentence, which requires Sh. or W. according to circumstances: *Will (shall) you, now so fresh and fair, be in a hundred years nothing but mouldering dust?* This might possibly be asked in expectation of an answer from the person apostrophized—*Yes, I shall.* Much more probably it would be asked in expectation of the answer from the speaker himself to his own question—*Alas! yes, you will.* And *shall* ought to be used for the question only in the first case, *will* in the second case. Similarly, *Ah, yes, that is all very well; but will (shall) you be able to do it?* Use *will* if the answer is meant to be *No, of course you will not*; *shall*, if the answer expected is *Yes, I shall,* or *No, I shall not.*

In practice, Sh. is more commonly required, because questions asked for information are commoner than rhetorical ones. But observe the common *Would you believe it?,* Answer, *No, of course you would not. Should you believe it?,* also possible, would indicate real curiosity about the other person's state of mind, which is hardly ever felt. *Would you believe it?,* however, might also be accounted for on the ground that the answer would be *No, I would not*, which would be a coloured-future form, meaning *I should never consent to believe*.

Rule 4. Second-person Questions.

Second-person questions invariably have Sh. or W. by assimilation to the answer expected.

It may be added, since it makes the application of the rule easier, that the second-person questions belonging not to the plain future but to the pure system are also, though not because of assimilation, the same in regard to Sh. and W. as their answers. Thus *Will you come? Yes, I will* (each on its merits), as well as *Shall you be there? Yes, I shall* (assimilation). *Should you not have known? Yes, I should* (each on its merits; *should* means *ought*), as well as *What should you think? I should think you were right* (assimilation). The true form for all second-person questions, then, can be ascertained by deciding what the expected answer is.

This completes what need be said about principal sentences, with the exception of one important usage that might cause perplexity. If some one says to me 'You would think so yourself if you were in my position', I may either answer 'No, I should not' regularly, or may catch up his word, and retain the W., though the alteration of person requires Sh. Thus— 'Would I, though? No, I wouldn't'. Accordingly,

Rule 5. Echoes.

A speaker repeating and adapting another's words may neglect to make the alteration from Sh. to W., or from W. to Sh., that an alteration of the person strictly requires.

We have now all the necessary rules for principal sentences, and can put down a few examples of the right usage, note-worthy for various reasons, and some blunders, the latter being illustrated in proportion to their commonness. The number of the rule observed or broken will be added in brackets for reference. The passage from Johnson with which the correct examples begin is instructive.

Right.

I would (2) injure no man, and should (3) provoke no resentment; I would (2) relieve every distress, and should (3) enjoy the benedictions of gratitude. I would (2) choose my friends among the wise, and my wife among the virtuous; and therefore should (3) be in no danger from treachery or unkindness. My children should (2) by my care be learned and pious, and would (3) repay to my age what their childhood had received.—JOHNSON.

Chatham, it should (1) seem, ought to have taken the same side.—MACAULAY.

For instance, when we allege, that it is against reason to tax a people under so many restraints in trade as the Americans, the noble lord in the blue riband shall (2) tell you . . .—BURKE.

The 'critic fly', if it do but alight on any plinth or single cornice of a brave stately building, shall (2) be able to declare, with its half-inch vision, that here is a speck, and there an inequality.—CARLYLE.

John, why should you waste yourself (1) upon those ugly giggling girls?—R. G. WHITE.

It wouldn't be quite proper to take her alone, would it? What should (4) you say?—R. G. WHITE.

Whether I have attained this, the future shall decide (2. I consent to accept the verdict of the future).—*Times*.

Wrong.

We give first many examples of the mistake that is out of all proportion the commonest—using the coloured future when the speaker's mood is sufficiently given by a separate word. In the second example, for instance, *I would ask the favour* would be quite right, and would mean *I should like to ask.* As it stands, it means *I should like to like to ask.* The same applies to the other instances, which are only multiplied to show how dangerous this particular form is.

Among these . . . I would be inclined to place (3) those who acquiesce in the phenomenalism of Mr. Herbert Spencer.—*Daily Telegraph.*

As one of the founders of the Navy League, I would like (3) to ask the favour of your well-known courtesy . . .—*Times.*

I would be glad (3) to have some account of his behaviour.—RICHARDSON.

I would like (3) also to talk with you about the thing which has come to pass.—JOWETT.

But give your definition of romance. I would like to hear it (3).—
F. M. CRAWFORD.

These are typical of thousands of paragraphs in the newspaper. . . .
We would (3) wish for brighter news.—*Westminster Gazette.*

I have already had some offers of assistance, and I would be glad (3)
to receive any amount towards the object.—*Times.*

Some examples follow that have not this excuse; and the
first two deserve comment—the first because it results in
serious ambiguity, the second because it is possibly not wrong.

The two fleets present seven Russian battleships against four
Japanese—less than two to one; two Russian armoured cruisers
against eight, and seven Russian torpedo-boat destroyers against an
indefinite number of the enemy. Here we will (3) not exaggerate in
attributing to the Japanese three or four to one.—MAHAN.

With *will*, the meaning must be: We won't call them three
or four to one, because that would be exaggeration. But the
meaning is intended to be: We will call them that, and it will
be no exaggeration. *Shall* is absolutely necessary, however, to
make it bear that interpretation.

This character who delights us may commit murder like Macbeth,
or fly the battle for his sweetheart as did Antony, or betray his country
like Coriolanus, and yet we will rejoice (3) in every happiness that comes
to him.—W. B. YEATS.

It is possible that this is the use of *will* described as the 'habitual'
use—he will often stand on his head—under Rule 1. But this
is very rare, though admissible, in the first person of the present.
We shall rejoice, or simply *we rejoice*, would be the plain way
of saying it.

If this passion was simply painful, we would (3) shun with the
greatest care all persons and places that could excite such a passion.—
BURKE.

What would (3) we be without our appetites?—S. FERRIER.

If I was ever to be detected, I would (3) have nothing for it but to
drown myself.—S. FERRIER.

I will (3) never forget, in the year 1858, one notorious revivalist.—
Daily Telegraph.

As long as I am free from all resentment, hardness, and scorn, I
would (3) be able to face the life with much more calm and confidence
than I would . . .—WILDE.

In the next two, if 'I think', and the *if*-clause, were removed, the *shall* and *will* would stand, expressing resolve according to Rule 2. But with those additions it is clear that prophecy or pure future is meant; and *shall* and *will* should be *will* and *shall*.

Nothing, I think, shall ever make me (3) forgive him.—RICHARDSON.

We were victorious in 1812, and we will (3) be victorious now at any cost, if we are strong in an alliance between the governing class and the governed.—*Times*.

We now proceed to Subordinate Clauses, and first to the Substantival. The word 'reported' will mean 'made indirect' or 'subordinated substantivally', not always actually reported.

Reported statement is quite simple when it is of the pure system or the coloured future; the Sh. or W. of the original statement is retained in the reported form, unaffected by any change of person that the reporting involves. Thus: (Pure system) *He forgave me (you,* or *her), though he said I (you,* or *she) should not have left him in the lurch like that.* (Coloured future) *You said I (or he) should repent it*; either of these is a report of either *You shall repent it* or *He shall repent it.* (Coloured future) *You said you (or I said I) would apologize;* both are reports of *I will apologize.*

But with the plain-future system there is difficulty and some inconsistency. The change of person sometimes required by reported speech has almost always the effect here of introducing Sh. if *I* or *we* appears in the words as reported, and usually the effect of introducing W. if *you, he,* or *they,* appears. The following are all the types in which doubt can arise, except that each of these may occur in either number, and in past or present. The form that would be required by analogy (keeping the original Sh. or W.) is given first, and the one generally used instead is added in brackets. Reporting *I shall never succeed*, we get

You said you should (would) never succeed.
He says he shall (will) never succeed.

Reporting *you will* (or *he will*) *never succeed*, we get

You say I will (shall) never succeed.
He said I would (should) never succeed.

Even those persons who have generally a just confidence in their own correctness about Sh. and W. will allow that they have some doubt about the first pair; and nearly every one will find W. in the second pair, however reasonable and consistent, intolerable.

If the reader will now go through the four sentences again, and substitute for *succeed* the phrase *do it* (which may or may not mean *succeed*), he will see that the orthodox *should* and *shall* of the first pair become actually more natural than the commoner *would* and *will*; and that even in the second pair *will* and *would* are now tolerable. The reason is that with *do it* there is risk of confusion with the reported forms of *I will never do it* and *you shall never do it*, which are not plain futures, but coloured futures meaning something quite different.

Reported questions present the same difficulties. Again those only are doubtful that belong to the plain future. There, for instance, reporting *Shall you do it?* we can say by the correct analogy *I asked him whether he should*; and we generally do so if the verb, as here, lends itself to ambiguity: *I asked him whether he would do it* is liable to be mistaken for the report of *Will you do it?*—a request. If on the other hand (as in reporting *Shall you be there?*) there is little risk of misunderstanding, *I asked him whether he would* is commoner. And again it is only in extreme cases, if even then, that the original W. can be kept when the report introduces *I* in place of the original question's *you* or *he*. For instance, the original question being *How will he be treated?*, it may be just possible to say *You had made up your mind how I would be treated*, because *You had made up your mind how I should be treated* almost inevitably suggests (assisted by the ambiguity of *making up your mind*, which may imply either resolve or inference) that the original question was *How shall he be treated?*

It would be well, perhaps, if writers who take their responsibilities seriously would stretch a point sometimes to keep the more consistent and less ambiguous usage alive; but for practical purposes the rule must run:

Rule 6. Substantival Clauses.

In these (whether 'reported' strictly or otherwise subordinated) pure-system or coloured-future forms invariably keep the
Sh. or W. of the original statement or question, unaffected by
any change of person. Reports of plain-future forms do this
also, if there would be serious danger of ambiguity, but almost
always have Sh. in the first person, and usually W. in the second
and third persons.

As the division of substantival clauses into indirect (or reported or subordinate or oblique) statements, questions, *and
commands*, is familiar, it may be well to explain that in English
the reported command strictly so called hardly exists. In what
has the force of a reported command it is in fact a statement
that is reported. For instance, *He said I was to go*, though used
as the indirect form of *Go*, is really the indirect of the statement *You are to go*. *He ordered that they should be released*
(though the actual words were *Be they*, or *Let them be, released*)
is formed on the coloured-future statement, *They shall be released*. It is therefore unnecessary to give special rules for
reported command. But there are one or two types of apparent
indirect command about which, though there is no danger of
error, the reader may feel curious.

a. *I stipulate that I shall, you shall, he shall, do it.* Why
shall in all persons? because the original form is: *I (you, he)
shall do it, I stipulate that*, where *shall* means *am to, are to, is to*;
that is, it is a pure-system form.

b. *I beg that you* (or *he*) *will do it. He begs that I will do it.*
Again the original is pure-system: *You* (or *he*) *will* (i.e., you
consent to) *do it: that is what I beg. I will* (i.e., I consent to)
do it: that is what he begs.

c. *I beg that I* (or *he*) *shall not suffer for it. You begged that I
should not suffer for it.* Observe that b. has *will* and a. and c.
shall, because it is only in b. that the volition of the subject of
shall or *will* is concerned.

d. *I wish you would not sneeze.* Before subordination this

is: *You will not sneeze: that is what I wish.* W. remains, but *will* becomes *would* to give the remoteness always connected with wish, which is seen also, for instance, in *I wish I were* instead of *I wish I be*.

Before going on to examples of substantival clauses, we also register, again rather for the curious than for the practical reader, the peculiar but common use of *should* contained in the following:

It is not strange that his admiration for those writers should have been unbounded.—MACAULAY.

In this use *should* goes through all persons and is equivalent to a gerund with possessive: *that a man should be* is the same as *a man's being*. We can only guess at its origin; our guess is that (1) *should* is the remote form for *shall*, as *would* for *will* in d. above, substituted in order to give an effect of generality; and (2) the use of *shall* is the archaic one seen in *You shall find*, &c. So: a man shall be afraid of his shadow; that a man should be afraid (as a generally observed fact) is strange.

After each of the substantival clauses, of which examples now follow, we shall say whether it is a reported (subordinated) statement, or question, and give what we take to be the original form of the essential words, even when further comment is unnecessary.

Examples of Sh. and W. in Substantival clauses.
Right.

You, my dear, believe you shall be unhappy, if you have Mr. Solmes: your parents think the contrary; and that you will be undoubtedly so, were you to have Mr. Lovelace.—RICHARDSON.

Statement. The original of the first is *I shall be*; of the second, *she will be*. In this and the next three the strictly analogical form that we recommended is kept.

I have heard the Princess declare that she should not willingly die in a crowd.—JOHNSON.

Statement. I should not.

People imagine they should be happy in circumstances which they would find insupportably burthensome in less than a week.—COWPER.

Statement. We should. *They would* is not 'reported'.

Do you really fancy you should be more beholden to your correspondent, if he had been damning you all the time for your importunity?—STEVENSON.

Statement. I should be.

The nation had settled the question that it would not have conscription.—*Times*.

Statement. We will not. The blundering insertion of *the question*—perhaps due to some hazy notion of 'putting the question'—may be disregarded.

When the war will end still depends on Japan.—*Times*.

Question. When will it end?

Shaftesbury's anger vented itself in threats that the advisers of this dissolution should pay for it with their heads.—J. R. GREEN.

Statement. You shall pay.

He [i.e., James II] regarded his ecclesiastical supremacy as a weapon. . . . Under Henry and Elizabeth it had been used to turn the Church of England from Catholic to Protestant. Under James it should be used to turn it back again.—J. R. GREEN.

Statement. Under me it shall be. The reporting word not expressed.

She could not bear the sight of all these things that reminded her of Anthony and of her sin. Perhaps she should die soon; she felt very feeble.—ELIOT.

Statement. I shall. Again the reporting word absent.

There will never perhaps be a time when every question between London and Washington shall be laid at rest.—*Times*.

This is not properly speaking reported speech. But the *shall* is accounted for by a sort of allusion to a supposed prophecy—*every question shall one day be laid at rest*. In that prophecy, *shall* would convey that the prophet gave his personal guarantee for it, and would come under Rule 2. This is not to be confused with the use of *shall* in indefinite clauses that will be noticed later.

Wrong.

The four began their descent, not knowing at what step they should meet death nor which of them should reach the shore alive.—F. M. CRAWFORD.

Questions. At what step shall we meet? Which of us will reach? The first is accordingly right, the second wrong. The modern writer—who has been at the pains to use the strictly correct *should* in the first place rather than the now common *would*—has not seen, as Richardson did in the first of the right examples, that his two clauses are dissimilar.

I hope that our sympathy shall survive these little revolutions undiminished.—STEVENSON.

Statement. Will survive. It is possible, however, that the original was thought of, or rather felt, as Our sympathy shall survive. But as the effect of that is to give the speaker's personal guarantee for the truth of the thing, it is clearly not a proper statement to make dependent on the doubtful word *hope*.

After mentioning the advance made in reforms of the military force of the country he [Lord Lansdowne] announced that the Government should not oppose the motion, readily availing themselves of Lord Wemyss's suggestion that . . .—*Times*.

Statement. We shall not, or the Government will not. Probably Lord Lansdowne said *we*, and that accounts for *should*. But if *The Times* chooses to represent *we* by *the Government*, it must also represent *shall* by *would*.

It came with a strange stunning effect upon us all—the consciousness that never again would we hear the grind of those positive boot-heels on the gravel.—CROCKETT.

Statement. We shall never.

I think that if the matter were handed over to the parish councils . . . we would within a twelvemonth have exactly such a network of rifle clubs as is needed.—CONAN DOYLE.

Statement. We should. Of these two instances it may be thought that the writers would have made the mistake in the original unsubordinated sentence, instead of its arising in the process of subordination; our experience is, however, that many people do in fact go wrong in subordinate clauses who are alive to the danger in simple sentences.

> The Prime Minister ... would at once have asked the Opposition if they could suggest any further means for making the inquiry more drastic and complete, with the assurance that if they could suggest any such means, they would at once be incorporated in the Government scheme.—*Spectator.*

Statement. They shall be incorporated. We have classed this as wrong on the assumption, supported by the word *assurance*, that the Prime Minister gave a promise, and therefore used the coloured future, and did not state a fact and use the plain future.

Another type of subordinate clause important for Sh. and W. is **the conditional protasis or if-clause.** It is not necessary, nor with modern writers usual, to mark the future or conditional force of this separately, since it is sufficiently indicated by the apodosis. For instance, *If you come I shall be glad*; *if you came I should be glad*; *if you had come I should have been glad.* But in formal style or with a slight difference of meaning, it is often superfluously done in the protasis too. Sh. is then used for all persons, as, *If he should come, you would learn how the matter stands.* So

> Japan will adhere to her pledge of neutrality unless Russia shall first violate hers.—*Times.*

But to the rule that the protasis takes *shall* there are three exceptions, real or apparent; W. is found under the following circumstances:

(1.) An original pure-system or coloured-future W. is not changed to Sh. by being used in subordination to *if* (or *unless*). It is retained with its full original force instead of some verb like *wish* or *choose.* In *If we would believe we might move mountains*, the meaning is *If we chose to believe*, different from that of *If we believed* or *should believe.* So

It would be much better if you would not be so hypocritical, Captain Wybrow.—ELIOT.

If you consented not to be, or did not insist on being.

It would be valuable if he would somewhat expand his ideas regarding local defence by Volunteers.—*Times*.

If he consented to.

(2.) When the *if*-clause (though a genuine condition) is incorrectly expressed for the sake of brevity and compresses two verbs into one, the W. proper to the retained verb is sometimes necessarily used instead of the Sh. proper to the verb that, though it contains in strict logic the essential protasis, has been crushed out. Thus: *If it will be useless I shall prefer not to do it.* It is not the uselessness that is the condition of the preference; for the use or uselessness is subsequent to the decision; it is my conviction of the uselessness; so that the full form would be *If I shall be* (or *am* in ordinary speech) *convinced that it will be useless, I shall prefer*, &c. The following example can be defended on this ground, *if never again will he* standing for *if he shall realize that he will never*; the feebleness that decides his not wishing is subsequent to it, and can only condition it if taken in the sense of his anticipation of feebleness.

And if there is to be no recovery, *if never again will he* be young and strong and passionate, if the actual present shall be to him always like a thing read in a book or remembered out of the far-away past; he will not greatly wish for the continuance of a twilight that . . .—STEVENSON.

The next is more difficult only because, besides the compression, the *if*-clause is protasis not to the expressed main sentence, but to another that is suppressed.

I shall wait for fine weather, if that will ever come.—R. G. WHITE.

Given fully, this would run: I shall wait for fine weather; (at least I should say so) if (I were sure that) that will ever come.

(3.) When an *if*-clause is not a condition at all, as for instance where it expresses contrast, and is almost equivalent to *although*, the ordinary plain-future use prevails. Thus: *If annihilation will end our joys it will also end our griefs.* Contrast with this the real condition, in: *If annihilation shall end* (or *ends*) *our joys, we shall never regret the loss of them.*

Indefinite clauses, relative or other, bearing the same relation to a conditional or future principal sentence that a conditional protasis bears to its apodosis follow the same rules. Thus *Whoever compares the two will find* is equivalent to *If any one compares*; *When we have won the battle we can decide that question* is equivalent to *If ever we have won.* Accordingly we can if we choose write *Whoever shall compare,* and *When we shall have won*; but we cannot write *When we will have won,* and must only write *Whoever will compare* if we distinctly mean *Whoever chooses to compare.* As there is sometimes difficulty in analysing indefinite clauses of this sort, one or two instances had better be considered.

The candidate who should have distinguished himself most was to be chosen.

This is clear enough; it is equivalent to *if any one should have . . . he was . . .*

We must ask ourselves what victory will cost the Russian people when at length it will become possible to conclude the peace so ardently desired.—*Times.*

Equivalent to *If ever it at length becomes. Will* is therefore wrong; either *becomes,* or *shall become.*

Nothing can now prevent it from continuing to distil upwards until there shall be no member of the legislature who shall not know . . .—HUXLEY.

This is a complicated example. The *shall*s will be right if it appears that each *shall*-clause is equivalent to a conditional protasis. We may show it by starting at the end as with the house that Jack built and constructing the sentence backwards, subordinating by stages, and changing *will* to *shall* as the protases come in; it will be allowed that *until* means *to the time when,* and that *when* may be resolved into *if ever.* Thus we get: *a.* One will know. *b.* None will be a member of the legislature unless one shall know. *c*. It will distil to the time if ever none shall be a member unless one shall know.

Think what I will about them, I must take them for politeness' sake.—R. G. WHITE.

Although *think what I will* is an indefinite relative clause, meaning practically *whatever I think*, *will* here is right, the strict sense being *whatever I choose to think*. Indeed the time of *think* is probably not, at any rate need not be, future at all; compare *Think what I will, I do not tell my thoughts*.

We now give

Rule 7. Conditional protasis and Indefinite Clauses.

In the protasis or *if*-clause of conditional sentences Sh. may be used with all persons. Generally neither Sh. nor W. is used. W. is only used (1) when the full meaning of *wish* is intended; it may then be used with all persons; (2) when the protasis is elliptically expressed; W. may then be necessary with the second and third persons; (3) when the *if*-clause is not a real conditional protasis; there is then no reason for Sh. with second and third persons. Indefinite clauses of similar character follow the same rules.

A few right but exceptional, and some wrong subordinate clauses may now be added.

Examples of Sh. and W. in Subordinate Clauses.
Right.

As an opiate, or spirituous liquors, shall suspend the operation of grief . . .—BURKE.

We may conceive Mr. Worldly Wiseman accosting such an one, and the conversation that should thereupon ensue.—STEVENSON.

She is such a spare, straight, dry old lady—such a pew of a woman—that you should find as many individual sympathies in a chip.—DICKENS.

In these three we have the archaic *shall* of personal assurance that comes under Rule 2, and its corresponding conditional, appearing in subordinate clauses. There is no objection to it except that, in modern writers, its context must be such as to exonerate it from the charge of affectation.

The longing of the army for a fresh struggle which should restore its glory.—J. R. GREEN.

This use of Sh. after final relatives is seen, if the compound sentence is resolved, to point to an original coloured future; We long for a fresh struggle; a fresh struggle shall restore (that is, we intend it to restore) our glory.

He was tormented by that restless jealousy which should seem to belong only to minds burning with the desire of fame.—MACAULAY.

This is the *should seem* explained under Rule 1 appearing also as subordinate.

Wrong.

It should never be, but often is, forgotten that when the apodosis of a conditional sentence (with or without expressed protasis) is subordinate it is nevertheless still an apodosis, and has still Sh. in the first, W. in the second and third persons.

In 'he struck him a blow', we do not feel the first object to be datival, as we would in 'he gave him a blow'.—H. SWEET.

I cannot let the moment pass at which I would have been enjoying a visit to you after your severe illness without one word of sympathy.—GLADSTONE.

It would mean that I would always be haunted by an intolerable sense of disgrace.—WILDE.

But though I would not willingly part with such scraps of science, I do not set the same store by them.—STEVENSON.

We must reconcile what we would like to do with what we can do.—*Times.*

All these are wrong; in the last two the mistake is perhaps accounted for by the presence of *willingly* and *like*. *I would not willingly* can indeed be defended at the cost of admitting that *willingly* is mere tautology, and saying that *I would not* means *I should not consent to*, according to Rule 2.

It may be worth while to add that the subordinate apodosis still follows the rule even if it is subordinated to *if*, so that it is part of the protasis of another conditional sentence. The following, which is of course quite correct, seems, but only seems, to break the rules for both protasis and apodosis: If you would be patient for yourself, you should be patient for

me. But we have W. with second person in the protasis
because *would be patient* is also apodosis to the implied protasis
if occasion should arise; and the *should* with second person in
the apodosis is not a conditional *should* at all, but a pure-
system *should*, which would be the same with any person; it
means simply *you ought*, or *it would be your duty*.

The result in part of a genuine anxiety lest the Chinese would
gradually grow until they monopolized the country.—*Times*.

We have purposely refrained until now from invoking the
subjunctive, because the word is almost meaningless to Englishmen, the thing having so nearly perished. But on this instance
it must be remarked that when conjunctions like *lest*, which
could once or still can take a subjunctive (as *lest he die*), use
a compound form instead, they use the Sh. forms for all persons. It is a matter of little importance, since hardly any one
would go wrong in such a sentence.

THE PERFECT INFINITIVE

This has its right and its wrong uses. The right are obvious,
and can be left alone. Even of the wrong some are serviceable,
if not strictly logical. *I hoped to have succeeded*, for instance,
means *I hoped to succeed, but I did not succeed*, and has the
advantage of it in brevity; it is an idiom that it would be a
pity to sacrifice on the altar of Reason. So:

Philosophy began to congratulate herself upon such a proselyte from
the world of business, and hoped to have extended her power under the
auspices of such a leader.—BURKE.

And here he cannot forbear observing, that it was the duty of that
publisher to have rebutted a statement which he knew to be a calumny.
—BORROW.

I was going to have asked, when . . .—SLADEN.

But other perfects, while they are still more illogical than
these, differ as little in meaning from the present as the *deposuisse*, dear to the hearts of elegiac writers ancient and modern,
differs from *deponere*. And whereas there is at least metre,
and very useful metre, in *deposuisse*, there is in our corresponding
perfect infinitive neither rhyme nor reason. Thus,

With whom on those golden summer evenings I should have liked to have taken a stroll in the hayfield.—THACKERAY.

To have taken means simply to take; the implication of non-fulfilment that justified the perfects above is here needless, being already given in *I should have liked*; and the doubled *have* is ugly in sound. Similar are

If my point had not been this, I should not have endeavoured to have shown the connexion.—*Times*.

The author can only wish it had been her province to have raised plants of nobler growth.—S. FERRIER.

Had you given your advice in any determined or positive manner, I had been ready to have been concluded by it.—RICHARDSON.

Jim Scudamore would have been the first man to have acknowledged the anomaly.—CROCKETT.

Though certainly before she commenced her mystic charms she would have liked to have known who he was.—BEACONSFIELD.

Peggy would have liked to have shown her turban and bird of paradise at the ball.—THACKERAY.

It might have been thought to be a question of bare alternatives, and to have been susceptible of no compromise.—BAGEHOT.

The less excusable that Bagehot has started with the correct *to be*.

Another very common form, still worse, occurs especially after *seem* and *appear*, and results from the writer's being too lazy to decide whether he means *He seems to have been*, or *He seemed to be*. The mistake may be in either verb or both.

[Repudiating the report of an interview] I warned him when he spoke to me that I could not speak to him at all if I was to be quoted as an authority. He *seemed to have taken* this as applying only to the first question he asked me.—*Westminster Gazette*. (seems)

They, as it has been said of Sterne, seemed to have wished, every now and then, to have thrown their wigs into the faces of their auditors. —I. DISRAELI. (seem to have wished . . . to throw)

Lady Austen's fashionable friends occasioned no embarrassment; they *seemed to have preferred* some more fashionable place for summering in, for they *are* not again spoken of.—SOUTHEY. (seem)

Sometimes *have* is even transferred from the verb with which it would make sense to the other with which it makes nonsense.

On the point of church James was obdurate . . . He would like to have insisted on the other grudging items.—SLADEN.

In the next the perfect is wanting; for a child that has been flogged cannot be left unflogged—not, that is, in the past; and the future is not meant.

A child flogged left-handedly had better be left unflogged.—POE.

We add, for the reader's refreshment rather than for practical purposes, an illustration of where careless treatment of *have* may end:

Oh, Burgo, hadst thou not have been a very child, thou shouldst have known that now, at this time of day—after all that thy gallant steed had done for thee—it was impossible for thee or him.—TROLLOPE.

CONDITIONALS

These, which cost the schoolboy at his Latin and Greek some weary hours, need not detain us long. The reader passes lightly and unconsciously in his own language over mixtures that might have caused him searchings of heart in a dead one.

But there is one corrupt and meaningless form, apparently gaining ground, that calls for protest. When a clause begins with *as if*, it must be remembered that there is an ellipse. *I treat her as tenderly as if she were my daughter* would be in full *I treat her as tenderly as I should if she were*, &c. If this is forgotten, there is danger in some sentences, though not in this one, of using a present indicative in the place where the verb *were* stands. So:

We will not appear like fools in this matter, and as if we *have* no authority over our own daughter.—RICHARDSON.

This may be accounted for, but not justified, as an attempt to express what should be merely implied, our actual possession of authority.

As if the fruit or the flower not only *depends* on a root as one of the conditions among others of its development, but *is* itself actually the root.—MORLEY.

This is absolutely indefensible so far as *is* is concerned; *depends* has the same motive as *have* in the Richardson.

But this looks as if he *has* included the original 30,000 men.—*Times*.

There have been rumours lately, as if the present state of the nation *may* seem to this species of agitators a favourable period for recommencing their intrigues.—SCOTT.

This is a place where *as if* should not have been used at all. If it is used, the verb should be *seemed*, not *may seem*, the full form being *as there would be* (*rumours*). Read *suggesting. that* for *as if*, and *seems* for *may seem*.

General Linevitch reports that the army is concentrating as if it *intends* to make a stand.—*Times*.

A mixture between *it apparently intends* and *as if it intended*.

As if the same end *may* not, and must not, be compassed, according to its circumstances, by a great diversity of ways.—BURKE.

May should be *might*. *As if it may not* is made to do the work of *as if it might not, as of course it may*.

The same rule applies to *as though*.

The use of true subjunctive forms (if he be, though it happen) in conditional sentences is for various reasons not recommended. These forms, with the single exception of *were*, are perishing so rapidly that an experienced word-actuary[1] puts their expectation of life at one generation. As a matter of style, they should be avoided, being certain to give a pretentious air when handled by any one except the skilful and practised writers who need no advice from us. And as matter of grammar, the instinct for using subjunctives rightly is dying with the subjunctive, so that even the still surviving *were* is often used where it is completely wrong. So

It would be advisable to wait for fuller details before making any attempt to appraise the significance of the raid from the military point of view, if, indeed, the whole expedition *were* not planned with an eye to effect.—*Times*.

Here the last clause means *though perhaps it was only planned with an eye to effect* (*and therefore has no military significance*). But *if* followed by *were not* necessarily means that it certainly is. The mistake here results in making the clause look as if

[1] Dr. Henry Bradley, *The Making of English*, p. 53.

it were the protasis to *It would be advisable*, with which it has in fact nothing whatever to do; it is a note on the words *military significance*. Write *was* for *were*.

> . . . and who, taking my offered hand, bade me 'Good morning'—nightfall though it *were*.—*Times*.

The sentence describes a meeting with a person who knew hardly any English; he said good morning, though it *was* nightfall. A single example may be added of the intrusion of *were* for *was* in a sentence that is not conditional.

> Dr. Chalmers was a believer in an Establishment as he conceived an Establishment should be. Whether such an Establishment *were* possible or not it is not for me now to discuss.—LORD ROSEBERY.

Were, however, is often right and almost necessary: other subjunctives are never necessary, often dangerous, and in most writers unpleasantly formal. The tiro had much better eschew them.

'DOUBT THAT' AND 'DOUBT WHETHER'

Instances will be found in Part II of verbs constructed with wrong prepositions or conjunctions. Most mistakes of this kind are self-evident; but the verb 'doubt', which is constructed with 'that' or 'whether' according to the circumstances under which the doubt is expressed, requires special notice. The broad distinction is between the positive, 'I doubt whether (that)' and the negative, 'I do not doubt that (whether)'; and the rule, in order to include implied as well as expressed negatives, questions as wells as statements, will run thus:

The word used depends upon the writer's or speaker's opinion as to the reasonableness of the doubt, no matter in whose mind it is said to exist or not to exist.

1. If there is nothing to show that the writer considers the doubt an unreasonable one, the word is always 'whether', which reminds us that there is a suppressed alternative:

> I doubt whether this is true (or not).
> Every one is at liberty to doubt whether . . . (or not).

To this part of the rule there is no exception.

2. If it is evident that the writer disapproves of the doubt, the words introducing it amount to an affirmation on his part that the thing doubted is undoubtedly true; the alternative is no longer offered; 'that' is therefore the word:

> I do not doubt that (i.e., I am sure that) . . .
> Who can doubt that . . . ?

This, however, is modified by 3.

3. The 'vivid' use of 'whether'. When the writer's point is rather the extravagance of the doubt than the truth of the thing doubted, 'whether' is often retained:

> It is as if a man should doubt whether he has a head on his shoulders.
> Can we imagine any man seriously doubting whether . . . ?

Here, according to 2, we ought to have 'that', since the writer evidently regards the doubt as absurd. But in the first sentence it is necessary for the force of the illustration that the deplorable condition of the doubter's mind should be vividly portrayed: accordingly, he is represented to us as actually handling the two alternatives. Similarly, in the second, we are invited to picture to ourselves, if we can, a hesitation so ludicrous in the writer's opinion. We shall illustrate this point further by a couple of sentences in which again the state of mind of the doubter, not the truth of the thing doubted, is clearly the point, but in which 'that' has been improperly substituted for the vivid 'whether':

> She found herself wondering at the breath she drew, doubting that another would follow.—MEREDITH.
> I am afraid that you will become so afraid of men's motives as to doubt that any one can be honest.—TROLLOPE.

The mistake commonly made is to use 'that' for 'whether' in violation of 1. 'Whether' is seldom used in place of 'that', and apparent violations of 2 often prove to be legitimate exceptions of the 'vivid' kind. Some of our examples may suggest that when the dependent clause is placed before the verb, 'that' appears because the writer had not decided what verb of doubt or denial to use. This is probably the true explanation of many incorrect *that*s, but is not a sufficient defence. It supplies, on the contrary, an additional reason for adhering to 'whether': the reader is either actually misled or at any rate kept in needless suspense as to what is going to be said, because the writer did not make up his mind at the right time how to say it. 'Whether' at the beginning at once proclaims an open question: after 'that' we expect (or ought to expect) 'I have *no* reason to doubt'.

In all the following, 'whether' should have been used.

There is nothing for it but to doubt such diseases exist.—H. G. WELLS.

'Whether' is never suppressed.

I do not think it would have pleased Mr. Thackeray; and to doubt that he would have wished to see it carried out determines my view of the matter.—GREENWOOD.

That the movement is as purely industrial as the leaders of the strike claim may be doubted.—*Times.*

And I must be allowed to doubt that there is any class who deliberately omit . . .—*Times.*

He may doubt that his policy will be any more popular in England a year or two hence than it is now.—GREENWOOD.

I doubt the correctness of the assertion . . . I doubt, I say, that Becky would have selected either of these young men.—THACKERAY.

But that his army, if it retreats, will carry with it all its guns . . . we are inclined to doubt.—*Times.*

It was generally doubted that France would permit the use of her port.—*Times.*

The undeniable avoidance, by most idiomatic speakers and writers, of *I doubt that* in the sense 'I hardly think' or 'I do not believe' is remarkable, and seems to invite attempts at explanation. Ours would be that it is the abiding effect of a vanished cause. The meaning of *I doubt* before a clause was in older English much oftener I incline to believe (the thing said) than I disbelieve (it); Shakespeare is full of sentences like 'I doubt they will be too hard for us' (*H. IV* A, i. ii. 204). That use is now obsolete or archaic, but the following quotation brings it down to the nineteenth century: *Nicky doubted, from his appearance, that he would be nice* [=expected he would be

fastidious], *and she had no patience with nice men.*—SUSAN
FERRIER. The general abstinence from *I doubt that* meaning *I
do not believe* may well have been originally established in the
days, not so very long ago, when its usual meaning was *I
believe* or *fear* or *expect*.

PREPOSITIONS

In an uninflected language like ours these are ubiquitous,
and it is quite impossible to write tolerably without a full
knowledge, conscious or unconscious, of their uses. Misuse of
them, however, mostly results not in what may be called in the
fullest sense blunders of syntax, but in offences against idiom.
It is often impossible to convince a writer that the preposition
he has used is a wrong one, because there is no reason in the
nature of things, in logic, or in the principles of universal
grammar (whichever way it may be put), why that preposition
should not give the desired meaning as clearly as the one that
we tell him he should have used. Idioms are special forms of
speech that for some reason, often inscrutable, have proved
congenial to the instinct of a particular language. To neglect
them shows a writer, however good a logician he may be, to
be no linguist—condemns him, from that point of view, more
clearly than grammatical blunders themselves. But though the
subject of prepositions is thus very important, the idioms in
which they appear are so multitudinous that it is hopeless to
attempt giving more than the scantiest selection; this may at
least put writers on their guard. Usages of this sort cannot be
acquired from dictionaries and grammars, still less from a
treatise like the present, not pretending to be exhaustive;
good reading with the idiomatic eye open is essential. We
give a few examples of what to avoid.

1. After adjectives and adverbs.

Another stroke of palsy soon rendered Sir Sampson *unconscious* even
to the charms of Grizzy's conversation.—S. FERRIER.
Being *oblivious to* the ill feeling it would be certain to engender.—
Cheltenham Examiner.

To me it is incredible that the British people, who own one-half of the world's sea-going ships, should be so *oblivious to* the manner in which . . .—*Times*.

Insensible to, but unconscious of; indifferent to, but oblivious of.

The adjectives *different* and *averse*, with their adverbs or nouns, *differently*, *difference*, *aversion*, *averseness*, call for a few words of comment. There is no essential reason whatever why either set should not be as well followed by *to* as by *from*. But *different to* is regarded by many newspaper editors and others in authority as a solecism, and is therefore better avoided by those to whom the approval of such authorities is important. It is undoubtedly gaining ground, and will probably displace *different from* in no long time; perhaps, however, the conservatism that still prefers *from* is not yet to be named pedantry. It is at any rate defensive, and not offensive pedantry, *different to* (though 'found in writers of all ages'—*Oxford Dictionary*) being on the whole the aggressor. With *averse*, on the other hand, though the *Oxford Dictionary* gives a long roll of good names on each side, the use of *from* may perhaps be said to strike most readers as a distinct protest against the more natural *to*, so that *from* is here the aggressor, and the pedantry, if it is pedantry, is offensive. Our advice is to write *different from* and *averse to*. We shall give a few examples, and add to them two sentences in which the incorrect use of *from* with other words looks like the result of insisting on the slightly artificial use of it after *different* and *averse*.

My experience caused me to make quite *different* conclusions *to* those of the Coroner for Westminster.—*Times*.

It will be noticed that *to* is more than usually uncomfortable when it does not come next to *different*.

We must feel charitably towards those who think *differently to* ourselves.—*Daily Telegraph*.

Why should these profits be employed *differently to* the profits made by capitalists at home?—LORD GOSCHEN.

Ah, how *different* were my feelings as I sat proudly there on the box *to* those I had the last time I mounted that coach!—THACKERAY.

What is the great *difference* of the one *to* the other?—*Daily Telegraph*.

From would in this last be clearly better than *to*; but *between the two* would be better than either.

> The Queen and the cabinet, however, were entirely *averse to* meddling with the council.—MORLEY.

> Perhaps he is not *averse from* seeing democrats on this, as on railway rates, range themselves with him.—*Times*.

> In all democratic circles *aversion from* the Empire of the Tsar may be intensified by the events of the last few days.—*Times*.

> *To* no kind of begging are people so *averse* as *to* begging pardon.—*Guesses at Truth*.

> This *averseness* in the dissenting churches *from* all that looks like absolute government.—BURKE.

> I deeply regret the *aversion to* 'conscience clauses'.—GLADSTONE.

> But she had no sort of *aversion for* either Puritan or Papist.—J. R. GREEN.

Disagree from (for *with*), and *adverse from* (for *to*), seem to have resulted from the superstition against *averse* and *different to*.

> A general proposition, which applies just as much to those who *disagree from* me as to those who agree with me.—LORD ROSEBERY.

> There were politicians in this country who had been very *adverse from* the Suez Canal scheme altogether.—F. GREENWOOD.

2. After verbs.

> I *derive* an unholy pleasure *in* noting.—*Guernsey Evening Press*.

> We must *content ourselves* for the moment *by* observing that from the juridical standpoint the question is a doubtful one.—*Times*.

> The petition which now reaches us from Bloemfontein . . . *contents itself by* begging that the isolation laws may be carried out nearer to the homes of the patients.—*Times*.

I content you *by* submitting: I content myself *with* saying.

> 'Doing one's duty' generally *consists of* being moral, kind and charitable.—*Daily Telegraph*.

> The external world which is dealt with by natural science *consisted*, according to Berkeley, *in* ideas. According to Mr. Mill it *consists of* sensations and permanent possibilities of sensation.—BALFOUR.

The moon consists *of* green cheese: virtue consists *in* being good. *Consist of* gives a material, *consist in* a definition. Mr. Balfour's 'elegant variation' (see *Airs and Graces*) is certainly wrong, though nominalists and realists will perhaps differ about which should have been used in both sentences, and no one below the degree of a metaphysician can pretend to decide between them.

A scholar *endowed by* [with] an ample knowledge and persuasive eloquence to cite and instance.—MEREDITH.

I say to you plainly there is no end *to* [at] which your practical faculty can *aim* . . .—EMERSON.

He urged that it was an undesirable thing to be always *tinkering with* this particular trade.—*Times*.

We tamper *with*, but tinker *at*, the thing that is to be operated on.

You may hunt the alien from his overcrowded tenement, you may *forbid* him, if you like, *from toiling* ten hours a day for a wage of a few shillings.—*Times*.

His toiling, or *him to toil*.

His readiness, not only at catching a point, but at making the most of it *on a moment's notice*, was amazing.—BRYCE.

On the spur of the moment, but *at* a moment's notice. The motive was, no doubt, to avoid repeating *at*; but such devices are sins if they are detected.

Nataly had her sense of safety in *acquiescing to* such a voice.—MEREDITH.

We acquiesce *in*, not *to*, though either phrase is awkward enough with *a voice*; *to* is probably accounted for again by the desire to avoid repeating *in*.

3. After nouns.

There can be no *fault found to* her manners or sentiments.—SCOTT.

I find fault *with*: I find a fault *in*. Write *in* or *with*, as one or the other phrase is meant.

The Diet should leave to the Tsar *the initiative of* taking such measures as may be necessary.—*Times*.

M. Delcassé took *the initiative of* turning the conversation to Moroccan affairs.—*Times*.

We assume the *right of* turning, we take the *initiative in* turning.

Those, who are urging with most ardour what are called the greatest *benefits of* mankind.—EMERSON.

Benefits *of* the benefactor, but *to* the beneficiary.

A power to marshal and adjust particulars, which can only come from an *insight of* [into] their whole connection.—EMERSON.

From its driving energy, its personal weight, its invincible *oblivion to* [of] certain things, there sprang up in Redwood's mind the most grotesque and strange of images.—H. G. WELLS.

4. Superfluous prepositions, whether due to ignorance of idiom, negligence, or mistaken zeal for accuracy.

As to Mr. Lovelace's approbation of your assumption-scheme, I wonder not *at*.—RICHARDSON.

That the American attitude towards both property and democracy is changing we can neither doubt nor wonder *at*.—*Outlook*.

A something *of* which the sense can in no way assist the mind to form a conception *of*.—*Daily Telegraph*.

The Congress could occupy itself with no more important question than *with* this.—HUXLEY.

This is due to confusion with 'could occupy itself with no question more profitably than with this'.

5. Necessary prepositions omitted.

The Lady Henrietta . . . *wrote him* regularly through his bankers, and once in a while he *wrote her*.—BARONESS VON HUTTEN.

Write without *to* will now pass in commercial letters only; elsewhere, we can say 'I write you a report, a letter', but neither 'I will write you' simply, nor 'I wrote you that there was danger'. That is, we must only omit the *to* when *you* not only is the indirect object, but is unmistakably so at first sight. It may be said that *I write you* is good old English. So is *he was a-doing of it*; *I guess* is good Chaucerian. But in neither case can the appeal to a dead usage—dead in polite society or in England—justify what is a modern vulgarism.

6. Compound prepositions and conjunctions.

The increasing use of these is much to be regretted. They, and the love for abstract expression with which they are closely allied, are responsible for much of what is flaccid, diffuse, and nerveless, in modern writing. They are generally, no doubt, invented by persons who want to express a more precise shade of meaning than they can find in anything already existing; but they are soon caught up by others who not only do not need the new delicate instrument, but do not understand it. *Inasmuch as,* for instance, originally expressed that the truth of its clause gave the exact measure of the truth that belonged to the main sentence. So (from the *Oxford Dictionary*):

God is only God inasmuch as he is the Moral Governor of the world. —SIR W. HAMILTON.

But long before Hamilton's day the word passed, very naturally, into the meaning, for which it need never have been invented, of *since* or *because.* Consequently most people who need the original idea have not the courage to use *inasmuch as* for it, like Sir W. Hamilton, but resort to new combinations with *far.* Those new combinations, however, as will be shown, fluctuate and are confused with one another. The best thing we can now do with *inasmuch as* is to get it decently buried; when it means *since, since* is better; when it means what it once meant, no one understands it. The moral we wish to draw is that these compounds should be left altogether alone except in passages where great precision is wanted. Just as a word like *save* (except) is ruined for the poet by being used on every page of ordinary prose (which it disfigures in revenge for its own degradation), so *inasmuch as* is spoilt for the logician.

We shall first illustrate the absurd prevailing abuse of the compound preposition *as to.* In each of the following sentences, if *as to* is simply left out, no difference whatever is made in the meaning. It is only familiarity with unnecessary circumlocution that makes such a state of things tolerable to any one with a glimmering of literary discernment. *As to* flows from the pen now at every possible opportunity, till many writers seem quite unaware that such words as *question* or *doubt* can bear the weight of a *whether*-clause without help from this offensive parasite.

With the idea of endeavouring to ascertain as to this, I invited . . .—
Times.

Confronted with the simple question as to in what way other people's
sisters, wives and daughters differ from theirs . . .—*Daily Telegraph*.

It is not quite clear as to what happened.—*Westminster Gazette*.

Doubt is expressed as to whether the fall of Port Arthur will materi-
ally affect the situation.—*Times*.

I feel tempted to narrate one that occurred to me, leaving it to your
judgment as to whether it is worthy of notice in your paper.—*Spectator*.

I was entirely indifferent as to the results of the game, caring nothing
at all *as to* whether I had losses or gains.—CORELLI.

The first *as to* in this may pass, though plain *to* is better.

German anticipations with regard to the future are apparently based
upon the question as to how far the Sultan will . . .—*Times*.

But you are dying to know what brings me here, and even if you find
nothing new in it you will perhaps think *it* makes some difference *as to*
who says a thing.—GREENWOOD.

This is the worst of all. The subject of *makes* (anticipated
in the ordinary way by *it*) is *who says a thing*; but the construction is obscured by the insertion of *as to*. We are forced
to suppose, wrongly, that *it* means *what brings me here*. Worse
than the worst, however, at least more aggressively wrong, is
an instance that we find while correcting this sheet for the press:

. . . Although it is open to doubt as to what extent individual saving
through more than one provident institution prevails.—*Westminster
Gazette*.

Another objection to the compound prepositions and conjunctions is that they are frequently confused with one another
or miswritten. We illustrate from two sets. (*a*) The word
view is common in the forms *in view of*, *with a view to*, *with the
view of*. The first expresses external circumstances, existing
or likely to occur, that must be taken into account; as, *In view
of these doubts about the next dividend, we do not recommend* . . .
The other two both express the object aimed at, but must not
have the correspondence, *a* view *to*, *the* view *of*, upset.

A Resolution was moved and carried *in favour of* giving facilities to
the public vaccination officers of the Metropolis to enter the schools
of the Board *for the purpose of* examining the arms of the children *with*

a view to advising the parents to allow their children to be vaccinated.
—*Spectator*.

The Sultan . . . will seek to obtain money by contracting loans with private firms *in view of* beginning for himself the preliminary reforms. —*Times*.

If Germany has anything to propose *in view of* the safeguarding of her own interests, it will certainly meet with that courteous consideration which is traditional in French diplomacy.—*Times*.

Its execution is being carefully prepared *with a view of* avoiding any collision with the natives.—*Times*.

My company has been approached by several firms *with a view of* overcoming the difficulty.—*Times*.

Of these the first is correct; but the sentence it comes in is so typical of the compound-prepositional style that no one who reads it will be surprised that its patrons should sometimes get mixed; how should people who write like that keep their ideas clear? The second should have *with a view to*. Still more should the third, which is ambiguous as well as unidiomatic; the words used ought to mean *seeing that her interests are safeguarded already*. The fourth and fifth should again have *with a view to* (or *with the view of*).

(*b*) The combinations with *far—as far as, so far as, so far that, in so far as, in so far that*, of which the last is certainly, and the last but one probably needless—have some distinctions and limitations often neglected. For instance, *as far as* must not be followed by a mere noun except in the literal sense, *as far as London*. *So far as* and *so far that* are distinguished by good writers in being applied, the first to clauses that contain a doubtful or varying fact, the other to clauses containing an ascertained or positive fact. *So far as* (and *in so far as*), that is, means *to whatever extent*, and *so far that* means *to this extent, namely that*.

The question of the Capitulations and of the Mixed Tribunals is not in any way essentially British, save *in so far as* the position of Great Britain in Egypt makes her primarily responsible.—*Times*.

Correct; but *except that* would be much better than *save in so far as*.

Previous to 1895, when a separate constitution existed for the Bombay and Madras armies, possibly a military department and a military member were necessary in order to focus at the seat of government the general military situation in India, but in the judgment of many officers well qualified to form an opinion, no such department under present conditions is really requisite, *in so far as* the action of the Commander-in-Chief is thwarted in cases where he should be the best judge of what is necessary.—*Times*.

Entirely wrong. It is confused with *inasmuch as*, and *since* should be written.

The officials have done their utmost to enforce neutrality, and have *in so far* succeeded *as* the Baltic fleet keeps outside the three-mile limit.—*Times*.

Should be *so far succeeded that*; we are meant to understand that the fleet does keep outside, though it does not go right away as might be wished.

The previous appeal made by M. Delcassé was *so far* successful *as* the Tsar himself sent orders to Admiral Rozhdestvensky to comply with the injunctions of the French colonial authorities.—*Times*.

As should be *that*. It is not doubtful to what extent or whether the Tsar sent. He did send; that is the only point.

They are exceptional in character, *in so far as* they do not appear to be modifications of the epidermis.—HUXLEY.

Should probably be *so far exceptional that*. The point is that there *is* this amount of the exceptional in them, not that their irregularity depends on the doubtful fact of their not being modifications; the word *appear* ought otherwise to have been parenthetically arranged.

This influence was *so far* indirect *in that* it was greatly furthered by Le Sage, who borrowed the form of his Spanish contemporaries.—*Times*.

A mixture of *was so far indirect that* and *was indirect in that*.

He seemed quickly to give up first-hand observation and to be content to reproduce and re-reproduce his early impressions, always trusting to his own invention, and the reading public's inveterate preference for symmetry and satisfaction, to pull him through. They have pulled him through *in so far as* they have made his name popular; but an artist and a realist—possibly even a humourist—have been lost.—*Times*.

In so far as leaves the popularity and the pulling through doubtful, which they are clearly not meant to be. It should be *so far that*.

A man can get help from above to do what *as far as* human possibility has proved out of his power.—*Daily Telegraph*.

This is a whole sentence, not a fragment, as might be supposed. But *as far as* (except in the local sense) must have a verb, finite or infinite. Supply *goes*.

The large majority would reply in the affirmative, *in so far as* to admit that there is a God.—*Daily Telegraph*.

So far as to admit, or *in so far as they would admit*; not the mixture. And this distinction is perhaps the only justification for the existence of *in so far as* by the side of *so far as*; the first is only conjunction, the second can be preposition as well.

[*Note*, 1930. Mention has been made here and there of the 'superstition' against ending clause or sentence with a preposition; but in 1906 it had not occurred to us to examine seriously the validity of what, superstition or no, is a widespread belief. It was indeed *spretae injuria formae* that brought home to us the need for such examination, a reviewer having condemned our book out of hand on the ground that the first paragraph of its preface ended in a preposition. I may perhaps be allowed to refer readers, for the result of our inquiry, to the article PREPOSITION AT END in *Modern English Usage*. H.W.F.]

CHAPTER III

AIRS AND GRACES

Certain types of humour—Elegant variation—Inversion—Archaism—
Metaphor—Repetition—Miscellaneous.

CERTAIN TYPES OF HUMOUR

Some of the more obvious devices of humorous writers, being fatally easy to imitate, tend to outlive their natural term, and to become a part of the injudicious novice's stock-in-trade. *Olfactory organ*, once no doubt an agreeable substitute for 'nose', has ceased to be legal tender in literature, and is felt to mark a low level in conversation. No amount of classical authority can redeem a phrase that has once reached this stage. The warmest of George Eliot's admirers, called upon to swallow some tough morsel of polysyllabic humour in a twentieth century novel, will refuse to be comforted with parallel passages from *Adam Bede*. Loyalty may smother the ejaculation that 'George Eliot knew no better': it is none the less clear to him that we know better now. A few well-worn types are illustrated below.

a. Polysyllabic humour.

He was a boy whom Mrs. Hackit had pronounced stocky (a word that etymologically, in all probability, conveys some allusion to an instrument of punishment for the refractory).—ELIOT.

Tommy was a saucy boy, impervious to all impressions of reverence, and excessively addicted to humming-tops and marbles, with which recreative resources he was in the habit of immoderately distending the pockets of his corduroys.—ELIOT.

No one save an individual not in a condition to distinguish a hawk from a handsaw . . .—*Times*.

And an observer of Miss Tox's proceedings might have inferred so much without declaratory confirmation.—DICKENS.

But it had its little inconveniences at other times, among which may be enumerated the occasional appearance of the river in the drawing-room, and the contemporaneous disappearance of the lawn and shrubbery.—DICKENS.

They might be better employed in composing their quarrels and preparing a policy than in following the rather lugubrious occupations indicated by Mr. Asquith.—*Times*.

Or perhaps, from a presentiment of calves' brains, you refrain from any lacteal addition, and rasp your tongue with unmitigated bohea.—ELIOT.

The rooks were cawing with many-voiced monotony, apparently—by a remarkable approximation to human intelligence—finding great conversational resources in the change of weather.—ELIOT.

I had been terribly shaken by my fall, and had subsequently, owing to the incision of the surgeon's lancet, been deprived of much of the vital fluid.—BORROW.

An elderly man stood near me, and a still more elderly female was holding a phial of very pungent salts to my olfactory organ.—BORROW.

The minister, honest man, was getting on his boots in the kitchen to see us home . . . Well, this preparation ministerial being finished, we stepped briskly out.—CROCKETT.

We have ourselves been reminded of the deficiencies of our femoral habiliments, and exhorted upon that score to fit ourselves more beseemingly.—SCOTT.

b. Playful repetition.

When she had banged out the tune slowly, she began a different manner of 'Gettin' up Stairs', and did so with a fury and swiftness quite incredible. She spun up stairs; she whirled up stairs; she galloped up stairs; she rattled up stairs . . . Then Miss Wirt played the 'Gettin' up Stairs' with the most pathetic and ravishing solemnity . . . Miss Wirt's hands seemed to faint and wail and die in variations: again, and she went up with a savage clang and rush of trumpets, as if Miss Wirt was storming a breach.—THACKERAY.

My mind was, to a certain extent, occupied with the marks on the teapot; it is true that the mournful idea strove hard with the marks on the teapot for the mastery in my mind, and at last the painful idea drove the marks of the teapot out.—BORROW.

The pastrycook is hard at work in the funereal room in Brook Street, and the very tall young men are busy looking on. One of the very tall young men already smells of sherry, and his eyes have a tendency to become fixed in his head, and to stare at objects without seeing them. The very tall young man is conscious of this failing in himself; and informs his comrade that it 's his 'exciseman'. The very tall young man would say excitement, but his speech is hazy.—DICKENS.

Busy is Mrs. Miff this morning at the church-door, beating and dusting the altar-cloth, the carpet and the cushions; and much has

Mrs. Miff to say about the wedding they are going to have. Mrs. Miff is told that the new furniture and alterations in the house cost full five thousand pound, if they cost a penny; and Mrs. Miff has heard, upon the best authority, that the lady hasn't got a sixpence wherewithal to bless herself. Mrs. Miff remembers, likewise, as if it had happened yesterday, the first wife's funeral, and then the christening, and then the other funeral; and Mrs. Miff says, By-the-bye, she'll soap-and-water that 'ere tablet presently, against the company arrive.—DICKENS.

Mr. Dombey was a grave sight, behind the decanters, in a state of dignity; and the East India Director was a forlorn sight, near the unoccupied end of the table, in a state of solitude; and the major was a military sight, relating stories of the Duke of York to six of the seven mild men (the ambitious one was utterly quenched); and the Bank Director was a lowly sight, making a plan of his little attempt at a pinery, with dessert knives, for a group of admirers; and Cousin Feenix was a thoughtful sight, as he smoothed his long wristbands and stealthily adjusted his wig.—DICKENS.

The author is very much at his ease in the last example; the novice who should yawn in our faces with such engaging candour would render himself liable to misinterpretation.

c. The well-worn 'flood-of-tears-and-sedan-chair' pleasantry.

Phib Cook left her evening wash-tub and appeared at her door in soap-suds, a bonnet-poke, and general dampness.—ELIOT.

Sir Charles, of course, rescues her from the clutches of the Italian, and they return together in triumph and a motor-car.—*Times*.

Miss Nipper . . . shook her head and a tin-canister, and began unasked to make the tea.—DICKENS.

And for the rest it is not hard to be a stoic in eight-syllable metre and a travelling-carriage.—LOWELL.

But what the bare-legged men were doing baffled conjecture and the best glasses.—E. F. BENSON.

d. Other worn-out phrases of humorous tendency.

For, tell it not in Gath, the Bishop had arrived on a bicycle.—D. SLADEN.

Tell it not in Smith-st., but . . .—*Guernsey Evening Press*.

Sleeping the sleep of the just.

The gallant sons of Mars.—*Times*.

Mr. Mackenzie, with a white hat . . . and long brown leather gaiters buttoned upon his nether anatomy.—LOCKHART.

Looking for all the world like . . .—D. SLADEN.

Too funny for words.

These two phrases are commonly employed to carry off a humorous description of which the success is doubted. They are equivalents, in light literature, of the encouragement sometimes offered by the story-teller whose joke from *Punch* has fallen flat: 'You should have seen the illustration'. *Worthy* and *gallant* are similarly used:

To hear the worthy and gallant Major resume his favourite topic is like law-business, or a person who has a suit in Chancery going on.— HAZLITT.

Home.—I would implore God to survey with an eye of mercy their unoffending bairns. *Hume.*—And would not you be disposed to behold them with an eye *of the same materials*?—LANDOR.

Two or three haggard, ragged drawers ran to and fro . . . Guided by one of these blinking *Ganymedes*, they entered . . .—SCOTT.

The ancient *Hebe* who acted as Lord Glenvarloch's cup-bearer took his part against the intrusion of the still more antiquated *Ganymede*, and insisted on old Trapbois leaving the room instantly.—SCOTT.

It may be doubted whether any resemblance or contrast, however striking, can make it worth a modern writer's while to call waiters Ganymedes, waitresses Hebes, postmen Mercuries, cabmen Automedons or Jehus. In Scott's time, possibly, these phrases had still an agreeable novelty: they are now so hackneyed as to have fallen into the hands of writers who are not quite certain who Ganymede and Hebe were. Thus, there are persons who evidently think that it is rather complimentary to one's host than otherwise to call him an Amphitryon; and others who are fond of using the phrase 'l'Amphitryon où l'on dîne' altogether without point, apparently under the impression that 'où l'on dîne' is an alternative version for the use of the uninitiated ('Amphitryon', that is to say, 'one's host').

Japan, says M. Balet, can always borrow money so long as she can provide two things—guarantees and victories. She has guarantees enough and victories *galore.—Times.*

The English people has insisted on its preference for a married clergy, and Dr. Ingram's successor may have 'arrows in the hand of a giant'.—*Times.*

The inverted commas seem to implore the reader's acceptance of this very battered ornament. One could forgive it more easily, if there were the slightest occasion for its appearance here.

Hats of the cartwheel persuasion.—*Times.*

The only change ever known in his outward man was . . .—DICKENS.

Rob the Grinder, thus transformed as to his outer man . . .—DICKENS.

One hundred parishioners and friends partaking of tea.—*Guernsey Advertiser.*

But that's another story.—KIPLING.

But that is 'another story'.—*Times.*

It was all that Anne could do to keep from braining him with the poker for daring to call her 'Little One',—and Anne's arm is no joke when she hits to hurt. Once John Barnaby—but the tale of John Barnaby can wait.—CROCKETT.

Nevertheless, some folk like it so, and even now the Captain, when his pipe draws well and his grog is to his liking, says—But there is no use in bringing the Captain into the story.—CROCKETT.

The notion that Mr. Kipling, left to himself, is not competent to bring out all the latent possibilities of another story is a mistaken one, and argues an imperfect acquaintance with his works.

Many heads in England, I find, are shaken doubtfully over the politics, or what are thought to be the politics, of Australia. They—the politics, not the heads—are tangled, they are unsatisfactory in a high degree.—W. H. FITCHETT.

ELEGANT VARIATION

We include under this head all substitutions of one word for another for the sake of variety, and some miscellaneous examples will be found at the end of the section. But we are chiefly concerned with what may be called pronominal variation, in which the word avoided is either a noun or its obvious pronoun substitute. The use of pronouns is itself a form of variation, designed to avoid ungainly repetition; and we are only going one step further when, instead of either the original noun or the pronoun, we use some new equivalent. 'Mr Gladstone', for instance, having already become 'he', presently appears as 'that statesman'. Variation of this kind is often necessary in practice; so often, that it should never be admitted except when it is necessary. Many writers of the present day abound in types of variation that are not justified by expediency, and have consequently the air of cheap ornament. It is impossible to lay down hard and fast rules, but two general principles may be suggested: (1) Variation should take place only when there is some awkwardness, such as ambiguity or noticeable monotony, in the word avoided. (2) The substitute should be of a purely pronominal character, a substitute and nothing more; there should be no killing of two birds with one stone. Even when these two requirements are satisfied, the variation is often worse, because more noticeable, than the monotony it is designed to avoid.

The examples in our first group do not offend against (2): how far they offend against (1), and how far they are objectionable on other grounds, we shall consider in detail.

Mr. Wolff, the well-known mining engineer, yesterday paid a visit to the scene of the disaster. *The expert* gave it as his opinion that no blame attached . . .

The expert is gratuitous: *He* would have done quite well.

None the less Mrs. Scott [Sir Walter's mother] was a motherly comfortable woman, with much tenderness of heart, and a well stored, vivid memory. Sir Walter, writing of her, after *his mother's* death, to Lady Louisa Stewart, says . . .—HUTTON.

His mother's is not only unnecessary, but misleading: there is a difficulty in realizing that *her* and *his mother*, so placed, can be meant to refer to the same person.

Mr. J. Hays Hammond, a friend of President Roosevelt, lecturing before the American Political Science Association, quoted a recent utterance of the President of the Japanese House of Peers. *That dignitary* said: . . .—*Spectator*.

That dignitary said might have been omitted, with the full stop before it.

Mr. Sidney Lee's study of the Elizabethan Sonnets, the late Mr. Charles Elton's book on Shakespeare's Family and Friends, and Professor Bradley's on Shakespearean Tragedy—a work which may be instructively read with Professor Campbell's 'Tragic Drama in Aeschylus, Sophocles and Shakespeare'—remind us that *the dramatist* still holds his own with the publishers. The last two or three weeks have seen two new editions of him.—*Times*.

The writer has thoroughly puzzled himself. He cannot call Shakespeare Shakespeare, because there is a Shakespeare just before: he cannot call him *he*, because six other persons in the sentence have claims upon *he*: and he ought not to call him *the dramatist*, because Aeschylus and Sophocles were dramatists too. We know, of course, which dramatist is meant, just as we should have known which *he* was meant; but the appropriation is awkward in either case. *The dramatist* is no doubt the best thing under the circumstances; but when matters are brought to such a pass that we can neither call a man by his own name, nor use a pronoun, nor identify him by means of his profession, it is time to remodel the sentence.

If Mr. Chamberlain has been injured by the fact that till now Mr. Balfour has clung to him, Mr. Balfour has been equally injured by the fact that Mr. Chamberlain has persistently locked his arm in *that of the Prime Minister.—Spectator*.

Elegant variation is the last thing we should expect here. For what is the writer's principal object? Clearly, to emphasize the idea of reciprocity by the repetition of names, and by their arrangement. Mr. Chamberlain, Mr. Balfour: Mr. Balfour, Mr. Chamberlain. It is easy enough, so far: 'If Mr. Chamberlain has been injured by the persistent attachment of Mr. Balfour, Mr. Balfour has been equally injured by that of Mr. Chamberlain'. But that is not all that is required: there is to be the graphic touch; arm is to be locked in arm. Now comes the difficulty: in whose arm are we to lock Mr. Chamberlain's? in 'his'? in '*his*'? in 'his own'? in 'Mr. Balfour's'? in 'that of the Prime Minister'? As the locking of arms is perhaps after all only an elegant variation for clinging, remodelling seems again to be the best way out of the difficulty. Perhaps our simplified form above might serve.

On Thursday evening last, as a horse and cart were standing at Mr. Brown's shop, the animal bolted.

'The horse'.—An unconscious satirist, of tender years but ripe discernment, parsed 'animal' in this sentence as a personal pronoun; 'it replaced the subject of the sentence'. Journalists (it was explained to her) are equipped with many more personal pronouns than ever get into the grammars.

The King yesterday morning made a close inspection of the Cruiser Drake at Portsmouth, and afterwards made a tour of the harbour on board the Admiral's launch. His Majesty then landed and drove to Southsea, where he inspected the Royal Garrison Artillery at Clarence Barracks. The King returned to London in the course of the afternoon. —Times.

This is, no doubt, a difficult case. The royal pronoun (His Majesty) does not lend itself to repetition: on the other hand, it is felt that hes, if indulged in at all, must be kept a respectful distance apart; hence The King in the third sentence. We can get rid of it by reading '. . . at Clarence Barracks; returning . . .'. But of course that solution would not always be possible.

The Emperor received yesterday and to-day General Baron von Beck . . . It may therefore be assumed with some confidence that the terms of a feasible solution are maturing themselves in His Majesty's mind and may form the basis of further negotiations with Hungarian party leaders when the Monarch goes again to Budapest.—Times.

If the Emperor of Austria should disappear from the scene, war, according to this authority, is to be feared, as the Emperor Francis Joseph alone controls . . .—Times.

There is no excuse either for the Monarch or for the Emperor Francis Joseph. 'He' could scarcely have been misinterpreted even in the latter sentence.

Sir Charles Edward Bernard had a long and distinguished career in the Indian Civil Service . . . Five years later Sir Charles Bernard was appointed Commissioner of Nagpur . . . In 1876 Sir Edward Bernard returned to Nagpur.—Times.

It is natural that Sir Charles Edward Bernard should be introduced to us under his full name; natural, also, that an abbreviation should be chosen for working purposes. But why two abbreviations? If *Sir Charles* and *he* are judiciously employed, they will last out to the end of the longest article, without any assistance from *Sir Edward*.

Among the instances here given, there is scarcely one in which variation might not have been avoided with a little trouble. There are some, indeed, in which it is not gratuitous; and if in these the effect upon the reader were as negative as the writer's intention, there would be nothing to complain of. But it is not; the artistic concealment of art is invariably wanting. These elephantine shifts distract our attention from the matter in hand; we cannot follow His Majesty's movements, for wondering what the King will be called next time; will it be plain Edward VII? or will something be done, perhaps, with 'the Emperor of India'? When the choice lies between monotonous repetition on the one hand and clumsy variation on the other, it may fairly be laid down that of two undesirable alternatives the natural is to be preferred to the artificial.

But variation of this kind is, at the worst, less offensive than that which, in violation of our second principle above, is employed as a medium for the conveyance of sprightly allusion, mild humour, or (commonest of all) parenthetic information.

When people looked at his head, they felt he ought to have been a giant, but he was far from *rivalling the children of Anak*.—H. CAINE.

'Far from it', in fact.

He never fuddled himself with rum-and-water in his son's presence, and only talked to his servants in a very reserved and polite manner; and *those persons* remarked . . .—THACKERAY.

'What made ye sae late?' said Mr. Jarvie, as I entered the dining-parlour of *that honest gentleman*.—SCOTT.

The parlour was Mr Jarvie's.

At the sixth round, there were almost as many *fellows shouting out* 'Go it, Figs', as there were *youths exclaiming* 'Go it, Cuff'.—THACKERAY.

Great advances in the education of women . . . are likely, perhaps, to find more congenial soil in Universities less bound by time-honoured traditions and by social conventions than Oxford or Cambridge. Whatever may be the case *by Isis or Cam*, . . .—*Times*.

Our representative yesterday ran down to Brighton to interview the Cambridge Captain. *The weight-putter and high-jumper* received him with his usual cordiality.

This is a favourite newspaper type.

The miscellaneous examples given below (except 'the former of the last two') are connected with pronominal variation only so far as they illustrate the same principle of false elegance.

. . . hardly calculated to impress *at this juncture* more than *upon any former occasion* the audience . . .—*Times*.

His mother *possessed* a good development of benevolence, but he *owned* a better and larger.—C. BRONTË.

In the subjoined official record of 'business done', transactions *marked* thus * relate to small bonds, those *signalized* thus † to small bonds free of stamp and fee, and those *distinguished* thus + to an exceptional amount at special rates. Stocks and shares marked thus †† have paid no dividend for the last two half-years and upwards.— *Times*.

The return to *marked* is humiliating; we would respectfully suggest *characterized*.

One might be more intelligible in such moods if one wrote in *waving lines*, and accordingly the question 'Why do you not ask Alfred Tennyson to your home?' is written in *undulating script.—Spectator*.

Eighty-three volumes are *required for* letter "M," seventy-seven are *demanded by* "L," and seventy-six are perforce *conceded to* "B"; but *the former of the last two* . . .—*Westminster Gazette*.

I must *ask* the reader to *use* the same twofold procedure that I before *requested* him to *employ* in considering . . .—H. SIDGWICK.

We have not room to record at length, from the *Westminster Gazette*, the elegant variety of fortune that attended certain pictures, which (within twenty lines) made, fetched, changed hands for, went for, produced, elicited, drew, fell at, accounted for, realized, and were knocked down for, various sums.

INVERSION

Of all the types of inversion (or abnormal placing of the subject after its verb) used by modern writers, there is perhaps not one that could not be shown to exist in older English.

Ordinary modern usage, however, has retained those forms only in which ancient authority combines with practical convenience; and not all of those. To set aside the verdict of time in this respect is to prove archaic. Before using inversion, therefore, the novice should ask himself two questions: is there any solid, practical reason (ornamental reasons will not do) for tampering with the normal order of subject and verb? and does the inversion sound natural?

Throughout this section it must be borne in mind that in all questions of right and wrong inversion the final appeal is not to history, but to the reader's perception: what sounds right to most modern ears is right for modern purposes. When, under balance inversion, we speak of a true and a false principle, we do not mean to imply that the 'true' principle was, historically, the origin of this kind of inversion, or that the 'false' is a mistaken analogy from-it: all that is meant is that, if we examine a collection of instances, those that sound natural will prove to be based upon the 'true' principle, and those that do not on the 'false'.

a. Exclamatory inversion.

This may be regarded as an abbreviated form of exclamation, as if the word 'How' had dropped out at the beginning, and a note of exclamation at the end. The inverted order, which is normal in the complete exclamation, sounds natural also in the abbreviated form. The requirements for this kind of inversion are these: (1) The intention must be genuinely exclamatory, so that the full form of exclamation could be substituted without extravagance. (2) The word placed first must be that which would bear the chief emphasis in the uninverted form. It should be observed that this is the only kind of inversion in which the emphatic word, as such, stands at the beginning.

Our first three examples satisfy these conditions, and are unobjectionable. The fourth does not: we could not substitute 'With what difficulty ... !'; nor are the first words emphatic; the emphasis is on 'conceive'. Yet the inversion is inoffensive, being in fact not exclamatory at all, but a licensed extension of negative inversion, which is treated below.

> Bitterly did I regret the perverse, superstitious folly that had induced me to neglect so obvious a precaution.
>
> But in these later times, with so many disillusions, with fresh problems confronting science as it advances, rare must be the spirit of faith with which Haeckel regards his work.—*Times*.
>
> Gladly would he now have consented to the terms . . .
>
> With difficulty can I conceive of a mental condition in which . . .

Exclamatory inversion, like everything else that is exclamatory, should of course be used sparingly.

b. Balance inversion.

The following are familiar and legitimate types:

> First on our list stands the question of local option.
>
> On these two commandments hang all the law and the prophets.
>
> To this cause may be attributed . . .
>
> Among the guests were A, B, C, . . . Z.

We give the name of 'balance' to this kind of inversion because, although the writer, in inverting the sentence, may not be distinctly conscious of rectifying its balance, the fact that it was ill-balanced before is the true cause of inversion. It is a mistake to say that the words placed first in the above examples are so placed for the sake of emphasis; that is a very common impression, and is responsible for many unlawful inversions. It is not emphasis that is given to these words, it is protection; they are placed there to protect them from being virtually annihilated, as they would have been if left at the end. Look at the last of our examples: how can we call the words 'Among the guests were' emphatic, or say that they were placed there for emphasis? They are essential words, they show the connexion, nor could the sentence be a sentence without them; but they are as unemphatic as words could well be.—Why, then (it may be asked), are they put at the beginning? is not this an emphatic position? and does not any unusual position give emphasis?—No: it gives not emphasis but prominence, which is another thing.

Put the sentence back into its original form, and we shall see why inversion was desirable. 'A, B, C, D, E, F . . . Z were among the guests.' Observe how miserably the sentence tails off; it has no balance. By inverting it, we introduce several improvements. First, we give prominence to the unemphatic predicate, and enable it to discharge its humble office, that of a sign-post, indicating the connexion with what has gone before. Secondly, by giving prominence to the predicate, we give balance to the sentence, which before was top-heavy. Thirdly, we give prominence to the subject, by placing it in an unusual position.

Next take the 'local option' sentence. Are the words 'First on our list' emphatic? Not if the inverter knows his business. How did it run originally? 'The question of local option stands first on our list.' These words might be meant to tell us either of two things: what stood first on the list, or where local option stood. If the inversion is right, they are meant to tell us what stood first. If the other had been meant, then 'First on our list' would have been emphatic, and the writer would have left it in its place; but as it is not emphatic, and the other words are, the sentence is top-heavy; he therefore inverts it, thus balancing the sentence, and placing the unemphatic words in a prominent position, where they continue to be unemphatic, but are sure to be noticed. In spoken language, the relative importance of the different parts of a sentence can be indicated merely by the inflexion of the voice; but the balance of the sentence is best maintained, even then, by means of inversion.

It is the same with the other examples. If we restore the St Matthew quotation to the uninverted form, again we have an answer to either of two questions: What is the basis of the law?, and What is the importance of these two commandments?. Obviously it is meant as an answer to the latter, and therefore the words that convey that answer are the emphatic words; the others are not emphatic, but merely essential to the connexion; the general importance of the 'two commandments', as forming the subject-matter of the whole context, does not in the slightest degree affect their relation to the other words in this particular sentence.

It follows from what has been said that true balance inversion is employed not for the sake of impressiveness, but with the purely negative object of avoiding a bad balance. The data required for its justification are (i) An emphatic subject, carrying in itself the point of the sentence. (ii) Unemphatic 'sign-post' words, essential to the connexion, standing originally at the end of the sentence, and there felt to be inadequately placed. The results of the inversion must be (iii) That the sign-post stands at the beginning, (iv) That the subject stands absolutely at the end.

When these four conditions are fulfilled, the inversion, far from being objectionable, may tend greatly to vigour and lucidity. It is liable, of course, to be overdone, but there are several ways of avoiding that: sometimes it is possible to place the sign-post at the beginning without inversion; or the uninverted sentence may be reconstructed, so that the subject no longer carries the emphasis; and, as often as not, a sentence of which the accentuation is theoretically doubtful may in practice be left to the reader's discernment.

One occasional limitation remains to be mentioned, before we proceed to instances. It applies to those sentences only that have a compound verb: if the compound verb cannot be represented simply by its auxiliary component, the inversion may have to be abandoned, on account of the clumsiness of compound verbs in the middle of an inverted sentence, for to carry the other component to the end would be to violate our fourth rule. Take the type sentence 'To these causes may be attributed . . .', and first let the subject be 'our disasters'. The clumsiness of the verb is then distinctly felt; and 'To these causes may our disasters be attributed' is ugly enough to show the importance of the rule it violates. But next let the subject be 'every one of the disasters that have come upon us'. This time the inversion is satisfactory; whence we conclude that if the verb is compound, the subject must be long as well as emphatic, or the inversion will not do.

On the answer to this question depends entirely every decision concerning the goodness or badness of conduct.—SPENCER.

Just as, after contact, some molecules of a mass of food are absorbed by the part touched, and excite the act of prehension, so are absorbed such of its molecules as, spreading through the water, reach the organism.—SPENCER.

These are both formed on the right principle, but the second suffers from the awkwardness of the auxiliary.

Still more when considered in the concrete than when considered in the abstract do the views of Hobbes and his disciples prove to be inconsistent.—SPENCER.

Here we have neither the data that justify balance inversion, nor the results that should follow from it. It is due to the false principle of 'emphasis' dealt with below in d (p. 199) and reads as awkwardly as such inversions usually read. The sentence is, no doubt, cumbrous in the uninverted form; but it wants reconstruction, not inversion.

Much deeper down than the history of the human race must we go to find the beginnings of these connections.—SPENCER.

Wrong again, for the same reasons, but not with the same excuse; for the original form is unobjectionable. The emphasis is not on the problem (*to find* . . .), but on the clue to it (*much deeper down*), which, being emphatic, can maintain its position at the end of the sentence. The compound verb is only a secondary objection: we do not mend matters much by substituting *lie* for *must we go to find*.

You say he is selfish. Well, so is every one.
You say he is selfish. Well, so is every one selfish.

So is every one is a correct inversion: *so* is too weak to stand at the end, and at the beginning it is a good enough sign-post to tell us that selfishness is going to be defended. But *so is every one selfish* is wrong: for if *selfish* is repeated at all, it is repeated with rhetorical effect, and is strong enough to take

care of itself. Our second rule is thus violated; and so is our
fourth—the subject does not come at the end.

All three methods had their charm. So may have Mr. Yeats's notion
of . . .—*Times*.

This time, the compound verb is fatal. 'So, perhaps, has . . .
would do.

The arrival of the Hartmanns created no little excitement in the
Falconet family, both among the sons and the daughters. Especially
was there no lack of speculation as to the character and appearance of
Miss Hartmann.—BEACONSFIELD.

Right or wrong in principle, this does not read comfortably;
but that may seem to be due to the cumbrous phrase 'was
there no lack of', which for practical purposes is a compound
verb. That difficulty we can remove without disturbing the
accentuation of the sentence: 'Especially numerous were the
speculations as to the character of Miss Hartmann'. This
resembles in form our old type 'Among the guests were . . .',
but with the important difference that 'especially numerous'
is emphatic, and can therefore stand at the end. The inversion
is rather explained than justified by the still stronger emphasis on
'Miss Hartmann'. Sentences in which both subject and predicate
are independently emphatic should be avoided, quite apart from
the question of inversion: italics are more or less necessary to secure
the inferior emphasis, and italics are a confession of weakness.

Somewhat lightened was the *provincial* panic by this proof that the
murderer had not condescended to sneak into the country, or to
abandon for a moment, under any motion of caution or fear, the great
metropolitan *castra stativa* of gigantic crime seated for ever on the
Thames.—DE QUINCEY (the italics are his).

Not a happy attempt. We notice, for one thing, that the
subject does not come at the end; the inversion is not complete. Let us complete it. To do so, we must convey our
huge sign-post to the beginning: 'By this proof . . . Thames,
was somewhat lightened the *provincial* panic.' Worse than
ever; is the compound verb to blame? Remove it, and see:
'In consequence of this proof . . . Thames, subsided in some

degree the *provincial* panic'. This is not much better. There is another and a worse flaw: condition number one is not satisfied; we want 'an emphatic subject that carries in itself the point of the sentence'. Now we must not assume that because 'provincial' is italicized, therefore the subject (however emphatic) carries in itself the point of the sentence. What is that point? what imaginary question does the sentence answer? can it be meant to answer the question 'What limitations were there upon the comfort derived from the intelligence that the murderer was still in London?'? No; that question could not be asked; we have not yet been told that any comfort at all was derived. The question it answers is 'What effect did this intelligence produce upon the general panic?' This question can be asked; for the reader evidently knows that a panic had prevailed, and that the intelligence had come. If, then, we are to use balance inversion, we must so reconstruct the sentence that the words containing the essential answer to this question become the subject; we must change 'somewhat lightened' into 'some alleviation'. 'From this proof ... Thames, resulted some alleviation of the *provincial* panic.' That is the best that inversion will do for us; it is not quite satisfactory, and the reason is that the sentence is made to do too much. When the essential point is subject to an emphatic limitation (an unemphatic one like 'somewhat' does not matter), the limitation ought to be conveyed in a separate sentence; otherwise the sentence is overworked, and either shirks its work, with the result of obscurity, or protests by means of italics. We ought therefore to have: 'From ... resulted some alleviation of the general panic; this, however, was confined to the provinces'. But, except for this incidental fault, the sentence can be mended without inversion: 'By this proof ... Thames, the *provincial* panic was somewhat lightened'.

c. Inversion in syntactic clauses.

In clauses introduced by *as*, *than*, or a relative (pronoun or adverb), we have only a special case of balance inversion.

They differ from the instances considered above in this important respect, that their relation to the preceding words is no longer paratactic, but syntactic, with the result that the sign-post indicating this relation is necessarily placed at the beginning. This will be seen from a comparison of the paratactic and syntactic forms in the following pairs of examples:

> He was quick-tempered: so are most Irishmen. (Paratactic.)
> He was quick-tempered, as are most Irishmen. (Syntactic.)
> Several difficulties now arose: among them was . . .
> Several difficulties now arose, among which was . . .

Now in each of these sentences there are the same inducements to inversion in the syntactic form as in the paratactic; and added to these is the necessity for placing the sign-post at the beginning. We might expect, therefore, that inversion of syntactic clauses would be particularly common. But (i) we have already seen that inversion does not necessarily follow from the fact that the sign-post is placed at the beginning; and (ii) the verb in *as* and *than* clauses will probably, from the nature of the case, be the same as in the preceding clause. If it is in the same mood and tense, it can usually be omitted, unless effective repetition is required, in which case it will go to the end: a change of mood or tense, on the other hand, will often be marked by an auxiliary (itself perhaps compound), which again will usually preclude inversion.

The result is this:

i. Relative clauses, uninfluenced by the position of the sign-post, remain subject to precisely the same conditions as the corresponding paratactic sentences. Thus 'Among whom were . . .' is right, just as 'Among the guests were . . .' was right; 'Among which would I mention . . .' is of course impossible, because the subject does not carry the point; and 'To which may be attributed . . .' is right or wrong, according as the subject is or is not long enough to balance the compound verb.

ii. Inversion of an *as* or *than* clause, having become unusual for the reason mentioned above, is almost certain to

look either archaic or clumsy; clumsy when the reason for it
is apparent, archaic when it is not. The practical rule is this:
if you cannot omit the verb, put it at the end; and if you can
neither omit it nor put it at the end, reconstruct the sentence.

> The German government was as anxious to upset M. Delcassé as
> have been his bitterest opponents in France.—*Times*.

The verb is preserved to avoid ambiguity. But it should go
to the end, especially as it is compound.

> Relishing humour more than does any other people, the Americans
> could not be seriously angry.—BRYCE.

Ambiguity cannot fairly be pleaded here; the verb should be
omitted.

> If France remains as firm as did England at that time, she will
> probably have as much reason as had England to congratulate herself.
> —*Times*.

Either 'as England did', or, since the parallel is significant,
'as England then remained'. Also, 'as England had'.

> St. Paul's writings are as full of apparent paradoxes as sometimes
> seems the Sermon on the Mount.—*Spectator*.

The verb must be retained, for the sake of *sometimes*; but it
should go to the end.

> But he has performed as have few, if any, in offices similar to his the
> larger, benigner functions of an Ambassador.—*Times*.

'As few . . . have performed them.'

> Her impropriety was no more improper than is the natural instinct
> of a bird or animal improper.—E. F. BENSON.

This is like the case considered in b 'so is every one selfish'.
If *improper* is repeated with rhetorical effect, there is no need
of inversion: if not, it should be left out.

> There had been from time to time a good deal of interest over
> Mrs. Emsworth's career, the sort of interest which does more for a time
> in filling a theatre than would acting of a finer quality than hers have
> done.—E. F. BENSON.

Either 'would have done' at the end, or (perhaps better) no
verb at all.

All must join with me in the hope you express—that . . . as also must all hope that some good will come of . . .—*Times*.

Like the indiscriminate use of *while*, this ungainly *as* connexion is popular with slovenly writers, and is always aggravated by inversion. 'All, too, must hope . . .'

d. Negative inversion, and false 'emphasis' inversion.

The connexion here suggested between certain forms of inversion must be taken to represent, not by any means the historical order of development, with which we are not directly concerned, but the order in which a modern writer may be supposed, more or less unconsciously, to adopt them. Starting from an isolated case of necessary inversion, we proceed to extensions of it that seem natural and are sanctioned by modern usage; and from these to other extensions, based probably on a misunderstanding, and producing in modern writers the effect of archaism.

Nor, except when used in conjunction with *neither*, always stands first; and if the subject appears at all, the sentence is always inverted. This requires no illustration.

On the analogy of *nor*, many other negative words and phrases are thrown to the beginning of the sentence, and again inversion is the result.

Never had the Cardinal's policy been more triumphantly vindicated.
Nowhere is this so noticeable as in the South of France.
In no case can such a course be justified merely by success.
Systems, neither of which can be regarded as philosophically established, but neither of which can we consent to surrender.—BALFOUR.
Two sorts of judgments, neither of which can be deduced from the other, and of neither of which can any proof be given.—BALFOUR.

It is at this stage that misconception creeps in. Most of these negative phrases are in themselves emphatic; and from their being placed first (really on the analogy of *nor*) comes the mistaken idea that they derive emphasis from their position. This paves the way for wholesale inversion: any words, other than the subject, are placed at the beginning; and this not always in order to emphasize the words so placed, but merely to give an impressive effect to the whole. The various steps are marked by the instances that follow. In the first two, inversion may be on the analogy of negatives, or may be designed for emphasis; in the third, emphasis is clearly the motive; and in the rest we have mere impressiveness—not to say mere mannerism.

With difficulty could he be persuaded . . .

Disputes were rife in both cases, but in both cases have the disputes been arranged.—*Times*.

Almost unanimously do Americans assume that . . .—*Times*.

They hardly resembled real ships, so twisted and burnt were the funnels and superstructure; rather did they resemble the ghosts of a long departed squadron . . . *Times*.

His love of romantic literature was as far as possible from that of a mind which only feeds on romantic excitements. Rather was it that of one who was so moulded . . .—HUTTON.

There is nothing to show that the Asclepiads took any prominent share in the work of founding anatomy, physiology, zoology, and botany. Rather do these seem to have sprung from the early philosophers.—HUXLEY.

His works were ordered to be burnt by the common hangman. Yet was the multitude still true to him.—MACAULAY.

Henry Fox, or nobody, could weather the storm which was about to burst. Yet was he a person to whom the court, even in that extremity, was unwilling to have recourse.—MACAULAY.

A book of 'levities and gravities', it would seem from the author's dedication, is this set of twelve essays, named after the twelve months. —*Westminister Gazette*.

The set epistolary pieces, one might say, were discharged before the day of Elia. Yet is there certainly no general diminution of sparkle or interest . . .—*Times*.

Futile were the endeavor to trace back to Pheidias' varied originals, as we are tempted to do, many of the later statues . . .—L. M. MITCHELL.

Inevitably critical was the attitude that he adopted towards religion . . . Odious to him were, on the one hand, . . .—*Journal of Education*.

Finely conceived is this poem, and not less admirable in execution. —*Westminster Gazette*.

'The Rainbow and the Rose', by E. Nisbet, is a little book that will not disappoint those who know the writer's 'Lays and Legends'. Facile and musical, sincere and spontaneous, are these lyrics.—*Westminster Gazette*.

Then to the resident Medical Officer at the Brompton Hospital for Consumption for an authoritative opinion on the subject went the enquirer.—*Westminster Gazette.*

In view of the rapidly increasing tendency to causeless inversion of all kinds, it is far from certain that this last is intentional satire.

e. Miscellaneous.

(i) In narrated dialogue, the demand for variations of 'he said', &c., excuses considerable freedom in the matter of inversion. One or two points, however, may be noticed.

When the subject is a personal pronoun, *say* is perhaps the only verb with which inversion is advisable. 'Said I, he, they', and 'retorted Jones': but not 'enquired I', 'rejoined he', 'suggested they'.

Compound verbs, as usual, do not lend themselves to inversion:

'I won't plot anything extra against Tom,' had said Isaac.— M. MAARTENS.

'At any rate, then,' may rejoin our critic, 'it is clearly useless . . .'— SPENCER.

'I am the lover of a queen,' had often sung the steward in his pantry below.—R. ELLIOT.

'The cook and the steward are always quarrelling, it is quite unbearable,' had explained Mrs. Tuggy to the chief mate.—R. ELLIOT.

Still less do elaborate Meredithian phrases:

'Next door to the Last Trump', Colney Durance assisted her to describe the soundest of sleep.—MEREDITH.

'He may happen to be in the humour for a shaking!' Colney's poor consolation it was to say.—MEREDITH.

Inverted *said* at the beginning is one of the first pitfalls that await the novice who affects sprightliness. It is tolerable, if anywhere, only in light playful verse.

Said a friend to me the other day, 'I should like to be able to run well across country, but have never taken part in a paper-chase, for I have always been beaten so easily when trying a hundred yards or so against my acquaintances . . .'—S. THOMAS.

Mr. Takahira and Count Cassini continue to exchange repartees through friends or through the public press. Said the Japanese Minister yesterday evening: . . .—*Times*.

It is inferred here officially and unofficially that neutral rights are unlikely to suffer from any derangement in Morocco to which England is a consenting party. Said a Minister:—'American interests are not large enough in Morocco to induce us to . . .'—*Times*.

With verbs other than *said*, this form of inversion is still more decidedly a thing to be left to the poets. 'Appears Verona'; 'Rose a nurse of ninety years'; but not

Comes a new translation . . . in four neat olive-green volumes.—*Journal of Education*.

(ii) The inverted conditionals *should, had, could, would, were, did*, being recommended by brevity and a certain neatness, are all more or less licensed by modern usage. It is worth while, however, to name them in what seems to be their order of merit. *Should I*, from its frequency, is without taint of archaism; but *could* and *would*, and, in a less degree, *had*, are apt to betray their archaic character by the addition of *but* ('would he but consent'); and *were* and *did* are felt to be slightly out of date, even without this hint.

I should be, therefore, worse than a fool, did I object.—SCOTT.

Did space allow, I could give you startling proof of this.—*Times*.

(iii) Always, after performing inversion of any kind, the novice should go his rounds, and see that all is shipshape. For want of this precaution, a writer who was no novice, particularly in the matter of inversion, produces such curiosities as these:

Be this a difference of inertia, of bulk or of form, matters not to the argument.—SPENCER.

It is true that, disagreeing with M. Comte, though I do, in all those fundamental views that are peculiar to him, I agree with him in sundry minor views.—SPENCER.

We shall venture on removing the comma before 'though'; but must leave it to connoisseurs in inversion to decide between the rival attractions of 'disagree with M. Comte though I do' and 'disagreeing . . . though I am'. 'Though I do', in spite of the commas, can scarcely be meant to be parenthetic; that would give (by resolution of the participle) 'though I disagree with M. Comte, though I do, . . .'

a. Occasional.

We have implied in former sections, and shall here take it for granted, that occasional archaism is always a fault, conscious or unconscious. There are, indeed, a few writers—Lamb is one of them—whose uncompromising terms, 'Love me, love my archaisms', are generally accepted; but they are taking risks that a novice will do well not to take.

As to unconscious archaism, it might be thought that such a thing could scarcely exist: to employ unconsciously a word that has been familiar, and is so no longer, can happen to few. Yet charitable readers will believe that in the following sentence *demiss* has slipped unconsciously from a learned pen:

He perceived that the Liberal ministry had offended certain influential sections by appearing too demiss or too unenterprising in foreign affairs.—BRYCE.

The guilt of such peccadilloes as this may be said to vary inversely as the writer's erudition; for in this matter the learned may plead ignorance, where the novice knows too well what he is doing. It is conscious archaism that offends, above all the conscious archaisms of the illiterate: the historian's *It should seem*, even the essayist's *You shall find*, is less odious, though not less deliberate, than the *ere, oft, aught, thereanent, I wot, I trow*, and similar ornaments, with which amateurs are fond of tricking out their sentences. This is only natural. An educated writer's choice falls upon archaisms less hackneyed than the amateur's; he uses them, too, with more discretion, limiting his favourites to a strict allowance, say, of once in three essays. The amateur indulges us with his whole repertoire in a single newspaper letter of twenty or thirty lines, and—what is worse—cannot live up to the splendours of which he is so lavish: charmed with the discovery of some antique order of words, he selects a modern slang phrase to operate upon; he begins a sentence with *ofttimes*, and ends it with a grammatical blunder; aspires to *albeit*, and achieves *howbeit*. Our list begins with the educated specimens, but lower down the reader will find several instances of this fatal incongruity of style; fatal, because the culprit proves himself unworthy of what is worthless. For the vilest of trite archaisms has this latent virtue, that it might be worse; to use it, and by using it to make it worse, is to court derision.

A coiner or a smuggler *shall* get off tolerably well.—LAMB.

The same circumstance may make one person laugh, which *shall* render another very serious.—LAMB.

You *shall* hear the same persons say that George Barnwell is very natural, and Othello is very natural.—LAMB.

Don Quixote *shall* last you a month for breakfast reading.—*Spectator*.

Take them as they come, you *shall* find in the common people a surly indifference.—EMERSON.

The worst of making a mannerism of this *shall* is that, after the first two or three times, the reader is certain to see it coming; for its function is nearly always the same—to bring in illustrations of a point already laid down.

Some of us, like Mr. Andrew Lang for instance, *cannot away with* a person who does not care for Scott or Dickens.—*Spectator*.

One *needs* not praise their courage.—EMERSON.

What turn things are likely to take if this version *be* persisted in is a matter for speculation.—*Times*.

If Mr. Hobhouse's analysis of the vices of popular government *be* correct, much more would seem to be needed.—*Times*.

Mr. Bowen has been, not recalled, but ordered to Washington, and will be expected to produce proof, if any he *have*, of his charges against Mr. Loomis.—*Times*.

It *were* futile to attempt to deprive it of its real meaning.—*Times*.

It *were* idle to deny that the revolutionary movement in Russia is nowhere followed with keener interest than in this country.—*Times*.

It *were* idle to deny that coming immediately after the Tangier demonstration it assumes special and unmistakable significance.—*Times*.

He is putting poetic 'frills', if the phrase *be* not too mean, on what is better stated in the prose summary of the argument.—*Times*.

Regarded as a counter-irritant to slang, archaism is a failure. *Frills* is ten times more noticeable for the prim and pompous *be*.

Under them the land is being rapidly frivolled away, and, unless immediate action *be* taken, the country will be so tied that . . .—*Times*.

That will depend a good deal on whether he *be* shocked by the cynicism of the most veracious of all possible representations . . .— H. JAMES.

We *may* not quote the lengthy passage here: it is probably familiar to many readers.—*Times*.

'We must not'. Similarly, the modern prose English for *if I be, it were*, is *if I am, it would be*.

'I have no particular business at L.,' said he; 'I was merely going *thither* to pass a day or two.'—BORROW.

I am afraid you will hardly be able to ride your horse *thither* in time to dispose of him.—BORROW.

It will necessitate my recurring *thereto* in the House of Commons.— *Spectator*.

The Scottish Free Church had *theretofore* prided itself upon the rigidity of its orthodoxy.—BRYCE.

The special interests of France in Morocco, *whereof* the recognition by Great Britain and Spain forms the basis of the international agreements concluded last year by the French Government.—*Times*.

To what extent has any philosophy or any revelation assured us *hereof* till now?—F. W. H. MYERS.

On the concert I need not dwell; the reader would not care to have my impressions *thereanent*.—C. BRONTË.

There, not *thither*, is the modern form; *to it*, not *thereto*; *of which*, *of this*, not *whereof*, *hereof*; *till then*, or *up to that time*, not *theretofore*. So, in the following examples, *except*, *perhaps*, *before*, *though*; not *save*, *perchance*, *ere*, *albeit*.

Nobody *save* an individual in no condition to distinguish a hawk from a handsaw . . .—*Times*.

My ignorance as to 'figure of merit' is of no moment *save* to myself.— *Times*.

This we obtain by allowing imports to go untaxed *save* only for revenue purposes.—*Spectator*.

Who now reads Barry Cornwall or Talfourd *save* only in connexion with their memorials of the rusty little man in black?—*Times*.

In my opinion the movements may be attributed to unconscious cerebration, *save* in those cases in which it is provoked wilfully.— *Times*.

When Mr. Roosevelt was but barely elected Governor of New York, when Mr. Bryan was once and again by mounting majorities excused from service at the White House, *perchance* neither correctly forecasted the actual result.—*Times*.

Dr. Bretton was a cicerone after my own heart; he would take me betimes *ere* the galleries were filled.—C. BRONTË.

He is certainly not cruising on a trade route, or his presence would long *ere* this have been reported.—*Times*.

Mr. Shaynor unlocked a drawer, and *ere* he began to write, took out a meagre bundle of letters.—KIPLING.

Fortifications are fixed, immobile defences, and, in time of war, must await the coming of an enemy *ere* they can exercise their powers of offence.—*Times*.

'It is something in this fashion', she cried out *ere* long; 'the man is too romantic and devoted.'—C. BRONTË.

Ere departing, however, I determined to stroll about and examine the town.—BORROW.

The use of *ere* with a gerund is particularly to be avoided.

And that she should force me, by the magic of her pen to mentally acknowledge, *albeit* with wrath and shame, my own inferiority!— CORELLI.

Such things as our modern newspapers chronicle, *albeit* in different form.—CORELLI.

It is thought by experts that there could be no better use of the money, *albeit* the best American colleges, with perhaps one exception, have very strong staffs of professors at incredibly low salaries.—*Times*.

'Oxoniensis' approaches them with courage, his thoughts are expressed in plain, unmistakable language, *howbeit* with the touch of a master hand.—*Daily Telegraph*.

The writer means *albeit*; he would have been safer with *though*.

Living in a coterie, he seems to have read the laudations and not to have noticed *aught* else.—*Times*.

Hence, if higher criticism, or *aught* besides, compels any man to question, say, the historic accuracy of the fall . . .—*Daily Telegraph*.

Many a true believer *owned not up* to his faith.—*Daily Telegraph*.

The controversy now going on in your columns *anent* 'Do we believe?' throws a somewhat strange light upon the religion of to-day. —*Daily Telegraph*.

It is because the world has not accepted the religion of Jesus Christ
our Lord, that the world is *in the parlous state we see it still.—Daily
Telegraph.*

A discussion in which *well nigh* every trade, profession and calling
have been represented.—*Daily Telegraph.*

Why not? Because we have *well-nigh bordering on* 300 different
interpretations of the message Christ bequeathed us.—*Daily Telegraph.*

It is quite a common thing to see ladies with their hymn-books in
their hands, *ere* returning home from church enter shops and make
purchases which might *every whit* as well have been effected on the
Saturday.—*Daily Telegraph.*

How *oft* do those who train young minds need to urge the necessity
of being in earnest . . .—*Daily Telegraph.*

I *trow* not.—*Daily Telegraph.*

The clerk, as I conjectured him to be from his appearance, was also
commoved; for, sitting opposite to Mr. Morris, that honest gentleman's terror communicated itself to him, though he *wotted* not why.—
SCOTT.

I should be *right* glad if the substance could be made known to
clergy and ministers of all denominations.—*Daily Telegraph.*

So sordid are the lives of such natures, who are not only not heroic
to their valets and waiting-women, but have neither valets nor waiting-
women to be heroic to *withal.*—DICKENS.

b. Sustained archaism in narrative and dialogue.

A novelist who places his story in some former age may
do so for the sake of a purely superficial variety, without any
intention of troubling himself or his readers with temporal
colour more than is necessary to avoid glaring absurdities;
he is then not concerned with archaism at all. More commonly, however, it is part of his plan to present a living picture
of the time of which he writes. When this is the case, he
naturally feels bound to shun anachronism not only in externals,
but in thought and the expression of thought. Now with regard
to the language of his characters, it would be absurd for him
to pretend anything like consistent realism: he probably has
no accurate knowledge of the language as his characters would
speak it; and if he had this knowledge, and used it, he would
be unintelligible to most of his readers, and burdensome to
the rest. Accordingly, if he is wise, he will content himself

with keeping clear of such modes of expression as are essentially
modern and have only modern associations, such as would jar
upon the reader's sense of fitness and destroy the time illusion.
He will aim, that is to say, at a certain archaic directness and
simplicity; but with the archaic vocabulary, which instead of
preserving the illusion only reminds us that there is an illusion
to be preserved, he will have little to do. This we may call
negative archaism. *Esmond* is an admirable example of it, and
the 'Dame Gossip' part of Mr Meredith's *Amazing Marriage*
is another. It hardly occurs to us in these books that the
language is archaic; it is appropriate, that is all. The same
may be said, on the whole, of *Treasure Island*, and of one or
two novels of Besant's.

Only the novelist who is not wise indulges in positive
archaism. He is actuated by the determination to have everything in character at all costs. He does not know very much
about old English of any period; very few people do, and those
who know most of it would be the last to attempt to write a
narrative in it. He gives us, however, all that he knows,
without much reference to particular periods; it may not be
good ancient English, but, come what may, it shall not be good
modern. This, it need scarcely be said, is not fair play: the
recreation is all on the writer's side. Archaism is, no doubt,
very seductive to the archaist. Well done (that is, negatively
done), it looks easy; and to do it badly is perhaps even easier
than it looks. No very considerable stock-in-trade is required;
the following will do quite well: Prithee—quotha—perchance
—peradventure—i' faith—sirrah—beshrew me—look ye—
sith that—look to it—leave prating—it shall go hard but—I
tell you, but—the more part—fair cold water—to me-ward—I
am shrewdly afeared—it is like to go stiff with me—y' are—y'
have—it irks me sorely—benison—staunch—gyves—yarely—
this same villain—drink me this—you were better go; to these
may be added the indiscriminate use of 'Nay' and 'Now (by the
rood, &c.)'; free inversion; and verb terminations in -*st* and -*th*.
Our list is largely drawn from Stevenson, who, having tried

negative archaism with success in *Treasure Island*, chose to give us a positive specimen in *The Black Arrow*. How vexatious these reach-me-down archaisms can become, even in the hands of an able writer, will be seen from the following examples of a single trick, all taken from *The Black Arrow*.

An I had not been a thief, I could not have painted *me* your face.
Put *me* your hand into the corner, and see what ye find there.
Bring *me* him down like a ripe apple. And keep ever forward, Master Shelton; turn *me* not back again, an ye love your life.
Selden, take *me* this old shrew softly to the nearest elm, and hang *me* him tenderly by the neck, where I may see him at my riding.
Mark *me* this old villain on the piebald.
'Sirrah, no more words,' said Dick. 'Bend *me* your back.'
'Here is a piece of forest that I know not,' Dick remarked. 'Where goeth *me* this track?'
'I slew him fair. I ran *me* in upon his bow,' he cried.
'Swallow *me* a good draught of this,' said the knight.

It is like a child with a new toy.

But there is the opposite fault. The judicious archaist, as we have said, will abstain from palpable modernisms, especially from modern slang. The following extracts are taken from an old woman's reminiscences of days in which a 'faultless attire' included 'half high boots, knee-breeches very tight above the calf (as the fashion was then), a long-tailed cutaway coat, . . .':

But the Captain, who, of course, lacks bowels of mercy for this kind of thing, says that if he had been Caesar, 'Caius would have *got the great chuck*. Yes, madam, I would have broke Mister Caius on the spot'.—CROCKETT.

But if you once go in for *having a good time* (as Miss Anne in her innocence used to remark) you must be prepared to . . .—CROCKETT.

. . . as all girls love to do when they are content with the way they have *put in their time*.—CROCKETT.

METAPHOR

Strictly speaking, metaphor occurs as often as we take a word out of its original sphere and apply it to new circumstances. In this sense almost all words can be shown to be metaphorical when they do not bear a physical meaning; for the original meaning of almost all words can be traced back to something physical; in our first sentence above, for instance, there are eight different metaphors. Words had to be found to express mental perceptions, abstract ideas, and complex relations, for which a primitive vocabulary did not provide; and the obvious course was to convey the new idea by means of the nearest physical parallel. The commonest Latin verb for *think* is a metaphor from vine-pruning; 'seeing' of the mind is borrowed from literal sight; 'pondering' is metaphorical 'weighing'. Evidently these metaphors differ in intention and effect from such a phrase as 'smouldering' discontent; the former we may call, for want of a better word, 'natural' metaphor, as opposed to the latter, which is artificial. The word metaphor as ordinarily used suggests only the artificial kind: but in deciding on the merits or demerits of a metaphorical phrase we are concerned as much with the one class as the other; for in all doubtful cases our first questions will be, what was the writer's intention in using the mataphor? is it his own, or is it common property? if the latter, did he use it consciously or unconsciously?

This distinction, however, is useful only as leading up to another. We cannot use it directly as a practical test: artificial metaphors, as well as natural ones, often end by becoming a part of ordinary language; when this has happened, there is no telling to which class they belong, and in English the question is complicated by the fact that our metaphorical vocabulary is largely borrowed from Latin in the metaphorical state. Take such a word as *explain*: its literal meaning is 'spread out flat': how are we to say now whether necessity or picturesqueness first prompted its metaphorical use? And the same doubt might arise centuries hence as to the origin of a phrase so obviously artificial to us as 'glaring inconsistency'.

Our practical distinction will therefore be between conscious or 'living' and unconscious or 'dead' metaphor, whether natural or artificial in origin: and again, among living metaphors, we shall distinguish between the intentional, which are designed for effect, and the unintentional, which, though still felt to be metaphors, are used merely as a part of the ordinary vocabulary. It may seem at first sight that this classification leaves us where we were: how can we know whether a writer uses a particular metaphor consciously or unconsciously? We cannot know for certain: it is enough if we think that he used it consciously, and know that we should have used it consciously ourselves; experience will tell us how far our perceptions in this respect differ from other people's. Most readers, we think, will agree in the main with our classification of the following instances; they are taken at random from a couple of pages of the *Spectator*.

These we should call dead: 'his *views* were personal'; '*carry out* his policy'; 'not *acceptable* to his *colleagues*'; 'the Chancellor *proposed*'; 'some *grounds* for *complaint*'; '*refrain* from talking about them'; 'the *remission* of the Tea-duty'; '*sound* policy'; 'a speech almost entirely *composed* of *extracts*'; '*reduction* of taxation'; '*discussion*'; 'the *low* price of Consols'; '*falls* due'; '*succeeded*'; 'will *approach* their task'; '*delivered* a speech'; '*postponing* to a future year'. The next are living, but not intentional metaphor; the writer is aware that his phrase is still picturesque in effect, but has not chosen it for that reason: 'a Protestant *atmosphere*'; 'this would leave a *margin* of £122,000'; 'the loss of *elasticity*' in the Fund; '*recasting* our whole Fiscal system'; 'to *uphold* the unity of the Empire'; 'to *strengthen* the Exchequer balances'; 'all *dwelt* on the grave injury'; 'his somewhat *shattered* authority'; 'the policy of evasion now *pursued*'; '*throws* new *light* on the situation'; 'a *gap* in our fiscal system'. Intentional metaphors are of course less plentiful: 'the home-rule motion designed to "*draw*" Sir Henry'; 'a *dissolving view* of General Elections'; 'this reassuring declaration *knocks the bottom out of* the plea of urgency'; 'the *scattered remnants* of that party might *rally after the disastrous defeat*'.

One or two general remarks may be made before we proceed to instances. It is scarcely necessary to warn any one against

over-indulgence in intentional metaphor; its effects are too
apparent. The danger lies rather in the use of live metaphor
that is not intentional. The many words and phrases that
fall under this class are all convenient; as often as not they
are the first that occur, and it is laborious, sometimes impossible, to hit upon an equivalent; the novice will find it
worth while, however, to get one whenever he can. We may
read a newspaper through without coming upon a single
metaphor of this kind that is at all offensive in itself; it is in
the aggregate that they offend. 'Cries aloud for', 'drop the
curtain on', 'goes hand in hand with', 'a note of warning',
'leaves its impress', 'paves the way for', 'heralds the advent
of', 'opens the door to', are not themselves particularly noisy
phrases; but writers who indulge in them generally end by
being noisy.

Unintentional metaphor is the source, too, of most actual
blunders. Every one is on his guard when his metaphor is intentional; the nonsense that is talked about mixed metaphor,
and the celebrity of one or two genuine instances of it that
come down to us from the eighteenth century, have had that
good effect. There are few obvious faults a novice is more afraid
of committing than this of mixed metaphor. His fears are often
groundless; many a sentence that might have stood has been
altered from a misconception of what mixed metaphor really
is. The following points should be observed.

1. If only one of the metaphors is a live one, the confusion
is not a confusion for practical purposes.

2. Confusion can only exist between metaphors that are
grammatically inseparable; parallel metaphors between which
there is no grammatical dependence cannot result in confusion. The novice must beware, however, of being misled
either by punctuation or by a parallelism that does not secure
grammatical independence. Thus, no amount of punctuation
can save the time-honoured example 'I smell a rat: I see him
hovering in the air: . . . I will nip him in the bud'. *Him* is
inseparable from the later metaphors, and refers to the rat.

But there is no confusion in the following passage; any one of the metaphors can be removed without affecting the grammar:

> This royal throne of kings, this sceptred isle,
> This earth of majesty, this seat of Mars, . . .
> This fortress built by Nature for herself . . .
> This happy breed of men, this little world,
> This precious stone set in the silver sea, . . .
> This blessed plot, this earth, this realm, this England,
> This nurse, this teeming womb of royal kings, . . .

3. Metaphor within metaphor is dangerous. Here there is a grammatical dependence between the metaphors, and if the combination is unsuitable confusion will result. But combination is one thing, and confusion is another: if the internal metaphor is not inconsistent with the external, there is no confusion, though there may be ugliness. To adapt one of our examples below, 'The Empire's butcher (i.e. New Zealand) has not all his eggs in one basket' is not a confusion, because a metaphorical butcher can have his eggs in one basket as well as any one else. What does lead to confusion is the choice of an internal metaphor applicable not to the words of the external metaphor, but to the literal words for which it is substituted. In the following example, the confusion is doubtless intended.

> This pillar of the state
> Hath swallowed hook and bait.

The swallowing is applicable only to the person metaphorically called a pillar.

4. Confusion of metaphor is sometimes alleged against sentences that contain only one metaphor—a manifest absurdity. These are really cases of a clash between the metaphorical and the non-metaphorical. A striking or original metaphor is apt to appear violent, and a commonplace one impertinent, if not adequately borne out by the rest of the sentence. This we may label 'unsustained metaphor'. It sometimes produces much the same effect as mixed metaphor; but the remedy for it, as well as the cause, is different. Mixed metaphor is the result of negligence, and can generally be put right by a simple adapta-

tion of the language to whichever metaphor is to be retained. Unsustained metaphor is rather an error of judgement: it is unsustained either because it was difficult to sustain, or because it was not worth sustaining; in either case abandonment is the simplest course.

This diverting incident contributed in a high degree to the general merriment.

Here we have four different metaphors; but as they are all dead, there is no real confusion.

This, as you know, was a burning question; and its unseasonable introduction threw a chill on the spirits of all our party.

Burning and *chill* are both live metaphors, they are grammatically connected by *its*, and they are inconsistent; there is therefore confusion.

The uncertainty which hangs over every battle extends in a special degree to battles at sea.—*Spectator*.

Extends is usually dead; and if in this case it is living, it is also suitable.

A centre and nucleus round which the scattered remnants of that party might rally after the disastrous defeat.—*Spectator*.

The main or external metaphor is that of an army. Now any metaphor that is applicable to a literal army is also applicable to a metaphorical one: but 'rally round a nucleus' is a confusion of metaphor, to whichever it is applied; it requires us to conceive of the army at the same time as animal and vegetable, *nucleus* being literally the kernel of a nut, and metaphorically a centre about which growth takes place. An army can have a nucleus, but cannot rally round it.

Sir W. Laurier had claimed for Canada that she would be the granary and baker of the Empire, and Sir Edmund Barton had claimed for Australia that she would be the Empire's butcher; but in New Zealand they had not all their eggs in one basket, and they could claim a combination of the three.

This is quoted in a newspaper as an example of mixed metaphor. It is nothing of the kind: *they* in New Zealand are detached from the metaphor.

We move slowly and cautiously from old moorings in our English life, that is our laudable constitutional habit; but my belief is that the great majority of moderate churchmen, to whatever political party they may belong, desirous as they are to lift this question of popular education out of the party rut, . . .

'A rut', says the same newspaper, 'is about the very last thing we should expect to find at sea, despite the fact that it is ploughed.' There is no mention of ruts at sea; the two metaphors are independent. If the speaker had said 'Moderate churchmen, moving at length from their old moorings, are beginning to lift this question out of the party rut', we should have had a genuine confusion, the *moorings* and the *rut* being then inseparable. Both this sentence and the preceding one, the reader may think, would have been better without the second metaphor; we agree, but it is a question of taste, not of correctness.

. . . the keenest incentive man can feel to remedy ignorance and abolish guilt. It is under the impelling force of this incentive that civilization progresses.—*Spectator*.

This illustrates the danger of deciding hastily on the deadness of a metaphor, however common it may be. Probably any one would have said that the musical idea in *incentive* had entirely vanished: but the successive attributes *keenness* and *impelling force* are too severe a test; the dead metaphor is resuscitated, and a perceptible confusion results.

Her forehand drive—her most trenchant asset.—*Daily Mail*.

Another case of resuscitation. *Trenchant* turns in its grave; and *asset*, ready to succumb under the violence of athletic reporters, has yet life enough to resent the imputation of a keen edge. As the critic of 'ruts at sea' might have observed, the more blunt, the better the assets.

And the very fact that the past is beyond recall imposes upon the present generation a continual stimulus to strive for the prevention of such woes.—*Spectator*.

We *impose* a burden, we apply a *stimulus*. It looks as if the writer had meant by a short cut to give us both ideas; if so, his guilt is clear; and if we call *impose* a mere slip in idiom, the confusion is none the less apparent.

Sword of the devil, running with the blood of saints, poisoned adder, thy work is done.

These are independent metaphors; and, as *thy work is done* is applicable to each of them, there is no confusion.

In the hope that something might be done, even at the eleventh hour, to stave off the brand of failure from the hide of our military administration.—*Times.*

To *stave off* a *brand* is not, perhaps, impossible; but we suspect that it would be a waste of energy. The idea of bulk is inseparable from the process of staving off. The metaphor is usually applied to literal abstract nouns, not to metaphorical concretes: ruin and disaster one can suppose to be of a tolerable size; but a metaphorical brand does not present itself to the imagination as any larger than a literal one. We assume that by *brand* the instrument is meant: the eleventh hour is all too early to set about staving off the mark.

This is a good example of mixed metaphor of the more pronounced type; it differs only in degree from some of those considered above. We suggested that *impose a stimulus* was perhaps a short cut to the expression of two different metaphors, and the same might be said of *staving off the brand.* But we shall get a clearer idea of the nature of mixed metaphor if we regard all these as violations of the following simple rule: When a live metaphor (intentional or unintentional) has once been chosen, the words grammatically connected with it must be either (a) recognizable parts of the same metaphorical idea, or one consistent with it, or (b) unmetaphorical, or dead metaphor; literal abstract nouns, for instance, instead of metaphorical concretes. Thus, we shall impose not the stimulus, but either (a) the burden of resistance, or (b) the duty of resistance; and we shall stave off not the 'brand' but the 'ignominy of failure from our military administration'.

But from our remarks in 4 above, it will be clear that (b),

though it cannot result in confusion of metaphor, may often leave the metaphor unsustained. Our examples illustrate several common types.

Is it not a little difficult to ask for Liberal votes for Unionist Free-traders, if we put party interests in the front of the consideration?—*Spectator*.

May I be allowed to add a mite of experience of an original Volunteer in a good City regiment?—*Spectator*.

But also in Italy many ancient edifices have been recently coated with stucco and masked by superfluous repairs.—*Spectator*.

The elementary schools are hardly to be blamed for this failure. Their aim and their achievement have to content themselves chiefly with moral rather than with mental success.—*Spectator*.

The scourge of tyranny had breathed his last.

The means of education at the disposal of the Protestants and Presbyterians of the North were stunted and sterilized.—BALFOUR.

I once heard a Spaniard shake his head over the present Queen of Spain.—(Quoted by *Spectator*.)

But, apart from all that, we see two pinching dilemmas even in this opium case—dilemmas that screw like a vice—which tell powerfully in favour of our Tory views.—DE QUINCEY.

The reader who is uncharitable enough to insist upon the natural history of dilemmas will call this not unsustained metaphor, but a gross confusion; horns cannot be said to *screw*. We prefer to believe that De Quincey was not thinking of the horns at all; they are a gratuitous metaphorical ornament; *dilemma*, in English at any rate, is a literal word, and means an argument that presents two undesirable alternatives. The circumstances of a dilemma are, indeed, such as to prompt metaphorical language, but the word itself is incorrigibly literal; we confess as much by clapping horns on its head and making them do the metaphorical work.

These remarks have been dictated in order that the importance of recognizing the difference and the value of soils may be understood.—J. LONG.

This metaphor always requires that the dictator—usually a personified abstract—should be mentioned. 'Dictated by the importance.'

The opposite fault of over-conscientiousness must also be noticed. Elaborate poetical metaphor has perhaps gone out of fashion; but technical metaphor is apt to be overdone, and something of the same tendency appears in the inexorable working-out of popular catchword metaphors:

> Tost to and fro by the high winds of passionate control, I behold the desired port, the single state, into which I would fain steer; but am kept off by the foaming billows of a brother's and sister's envy, and by the raging winds of a supposed invaded authority; while I see in Lovelace, the rocks on the one hand, and in Solmes, the sands on the other; and tremble, lest I should split upon the former or strike upon the latter. But you, my better pilot, . . .—RICHARDSON.

> Such phases of it as we did succeed in mentally kodaking are hardly to be 'developed' in cold print.—*Times*.

We are not photographers enough to hazard a comment on *cold* print.

> The leading planks of the Opposition policy are declared to be the proper audit of public accounts, . . .—*Times*.

REPETITION

'Rhetorical' or—to use at once a wider and a more intelligible term—'significant' repetition is a valuable element in modern style; used with judgement, it is as truly a good thing as clumsy repetition, the result of negligence, is bad. But there are some writers who, from the fact that all good repetition is intentional, rashly infer that all intentional repetition is good; and others who may be suspected of making repetitions from negligence, and retaining them from a misty idea that to be aware of a thing is to have intended it. Even when the repetition is a part of the writer's original plan, consideration is necessary before it can be allowed to pass: it is implied in the terms 'rhetorical' or significant repetition that the words repeated would ordinarily be either varied or left out; the repetition, that is to say, is more or less abnormal, and whatever is abnormal may be objectionable in a single instance, and is likely to become so if it occurs frequently.

The writers who have most need of repetition, and are most justified in using it, are those whose chief business it is to appeal not to the reader's emotions, but to his understanding; for, in spite of the term 'rhetorical', the object ordinarily is not impressiveness for impressiveness' sake, but emphasis for the sake of clearness. It may seem, indeed, that a broad distinction ought to be drawn between the rhetorical and the non-rhetorical: they differ in origin and in aim, one being an ancient device to secure impressiveness, the other a modern development, called forth by the requirements of popular writers on subjects that demand lucidity; and there is the further difference, that rhetorical repetition often dictates the whole structure of the sentence, whereas the non-rhetorical, in its commonest form, is merely the completion of a sentence that need not have been completed. But in practice the two things become inseparable, and we shall treat them together; only pointing out to the novice that of the two motives, impressiveness and lucidity, the latter is far the more likely to seem justifiable in the reader's eyes.

We shall illustrate both the good and bad points of repetition almost exclusively from a few pages of Bagehot, one of its most successful exponents, in whom nevertheless it degenerates into mannerism. To a writer who has so much to say that is worth hearing, almost anything can be forgiven that makes for clearness; and in him clearness, vigour, and a certain pleasant rapidity, all result from the free use of repetition. It will be seen that his repetitions are not of the kind properly called rhetorical; it is the spontaneous fullness of a writer who, having a clear point to make, is determined to make it clearly, elegance or no elegance. Yet the growth of mannerism is easily seen in him; the justifiable repetitions are too frequent, and he has some that do not seem justifiable.

He analysed not a particular government, but what is common to all governments; not one law, but what is common to all laws; not political communities in their features of diversity, but political communities in their features of necessary resemblance. He gave politics not an interesting aspect, but a new aspect: for by giving men a steady view of what political communities must be, he nipped in the bud many questions as to what they ought to be. As a gymnastic of the intellect, and as a purifier, Mr. Austin's philosophy is to this day admirable— even in its imperfect remains; a young man who will study it will find that he has gained something which he wanted, but something which he did nòt know that he wanted: he has clarified a part of his mind which he did not know needed clarifying.

All these powers were states of some magnitude, and some were states of great magnitude. They would be able to go on as they had always gone on—to shift for themselves as they had always shifted.

Without Spanish and without French, Walpole would have made a good peace; Bolingbroke could not do so with both.

Cold men may be wild in life and not wild in mind. But warm and eager men, fit to be the favourites of society, and fit to be great orators, will be erratic not only in conduct but in judgement.

A man like Walpole, or a man like Louis Napoleon, is protected by an unsensitive nature from intellectual destruction.

After a war which everyone was proud of, we concluded a peace which nobody was proud of, in a manner that everyone was ashamed of.

He hated the City because they were Whigs, and he hated the Dutch because he had deserted them.

But he professed to know nothing of commerce, and did know nothing.

The fierce warlike disposition of the English people would not have endured such dishonour. We may doubt if it would have endured any peace. It certainly would not have endured the best peace, unless it were made with dignity and with honesty.

Using the press without reluctance and without cessation.

He ought to have been able to bear anything, yet he could bear nothing. He prosecuted many more persons than it was usual to prosecute then, and far more than have been prosecuted since . . . He thought that everything should be said for him, and that nothing should be said against him.

Between these fluctuated the great mass of the Tory party, who did not like the House of Hanover because it had no hereditary right, who did not like the Pretender because he was a Roman Catholic.

He had no popularity; little wish for popularity; little respect for popular judgement.

Here is a writer who, at any rate, has not the vice of 'elegant variation'. Most of the possibilities of repetition, for good and for evil, are here represented. As Bagehot himself might have said, 'we have instances of repetition that are good in themselves; we have instances of repetition that are bad in themselves; and we have instances of repetition that are neither particularly good nor particularly bad in themselves, but that offend simply by recurrence'. The ludicrous appearance presented by our collection as a whole necessarily obscures the merit of individual cases; but if the reader will consider each sentence by itself, he will see that repetition is often a distinct improvement. The point best illustrated here, no doubt, is that it is possible to have too much of a good thing; but it is a good thing for all that. As instances of unjustifiable mannerism, we may select 'fit to be the favourites . . ., and fit to be great orators'; 'not political communities . . ., but political communities . . .'; 'something which he wanted, but something which he did not know he wanted'; 'a man like Walpole, or a man like Louis Napoleon'; 'without reluctance and without cessation'; 'who did not like . . ., who did not like . . .'; and 'without Spanish and without French'. We have mentioned clearness as the ultimate motive for repetition of this kind: in this last sentence, we get not clearness, but obscurity. Any one would suppose that there was some point in the distinction between Spanish and French: there is none; the point is, simply, that languages do not make a statesman. Again, there is sometimes virtue in half-measures: from 'something which he did not know that he wanted' remove the first three words, and there remains quite repetition enough. 'Wild in life and not wild in mind' is a repetition that is clearly called for; but it is followed by the wholly gratuitous 'fit . . . and fit . . .', and the result is disastrous. Finally, in 'who did not like . . . , who did not like . . .', mannerism gets the upper hand altogether: instead of the appearance of natural vigour that ordinarily characterizes the writer, we have stiff, lumbering artificiality.

Writers like Bagehot do not tend at all to impressive repetition: their motive is always the business-like one of lucidity, though it is sometimes lucidity run mad. Repetition of this kind, not being designed to draw the reader's attention to itself, wears much better in practice than the more pronounced types of rhetorical repetition. The latter should be used very sparingly. As the spontaneous expression of strong feeling in the writer, it is sometimes justified by circumstances: employed as a deliberate artifice to impress the reader, it is likely to be frigid, and to fail in its object; and the term 'rhetorical' should remind us in either case that what may be spoken effectively will not always bear the test of writing.

Rhetorical repetition, when it is clearly distinguishable from the non-rhetorical, is too obvious to require much illustration. Of the three instances given, the last is an excellent test case for the principle that 'whatever is intentional is good'.

I have summoned you here to witness your own work. I have summoned you here to witness it, because I know it will be gall and wormwood to you. I have summoned you here to witness it, because I know the sight of everybody here must be a dagger in your mean false heart!—DICKENS.

As the lark rose higher, he sank deeper into thought. As the lark poured out her melody clearer and stronger, he fell into a graver and profounder silence. At length, when the lark came headlong down . . . he sprang up from his reverie.—DICKENS.

Russia may split into fragments, or Russia may become a volcano.—Spectator.

MISCELLANEOUS

a. Some more trite phrases.

The worn-out phrases considered in a former section were of a humorous tendency: we may add here some expressions of another kind, all of them calculated in one way or another to save the writer trouble; the trouble of description, or of producing statistics, or of thinking what he means. Such phrases naturally die hard; even 'more easily imagined than described' still survives the rough handling it has met with, and flourishes in writers of a certain class. 'Depend upon it', 'you may take my word for it', 'in a vast majority of cases', 'no thinking man will believe', 'all candid judges must surely agree', 'it would be a slaying of the slain', 'I am old-fashioned enough to think', are all apt to damage the cause they advocate.

No thinking man can believe that, without fairer conditions of international competition, without a broader basis of revenue, without a league of commerce and defence, between the Mother country and her colonies, the Imperial State can continue to exist.—*Outlook*.

But of course a formula that enables one to rule out the whole Liberal Party from rational humanity in one sentence *is* a thing not to be lightly abandoned.

The shrill formula 'It stands to reason' is one of the worst offenders. Originally harmless, and still no doubt often used in quite rational contexts, the phrase has somehow got a bad name for prefacing fallacies and for begging questions; it lacks the delicious candour of its feminine equivalent— 'Kindly allow me to know best'—, but appeals perhaps not less irresistibly to the generosity of an opponent. Apart from this, there is a correct and an incorrect use of the words. It is of course the conclusion drawn from certain premisses that stands to reason; the premisses do not stand to reason; they are assumed to be a matter of common knowledge, and ought to be distinguished from the conclusion by *if* or a causal participle, not co-ordinated with it by *and*.

My dear fellow, it stands to reason that if the square of a is a squared, and the square of b is b squared, then the square of a minus b is a squared minus b squared. You may argue till we are both tired, you will never alter that.

It stands to reason that a thick tumbler, having a larger body of cold matter for the heat to distribute itself over, is less liable to crack when boiling water is poured into it than a thin one would be.

It stands to reason that my men have their own work to attend to, and cannot be running about London all day rectifying other people's mistakes.

It stands to reason that Russia, though vast, is a poor country, that the war must cost immense sums, and that there must come a time . . . —*Spectator*.

Just as 'stands to reason' is not an argument, but an invitation to believe, 'the worthy Major' not amusing, but an invitation to smile, so the sentimental or sensational novelist has his special vocabulary of the impressive, the tender, the tragic, and the horrible. One or two of the more obvious catch-phrases may be quoted. In the 'strong man' of fiction the reader may have observed a growing tendency to 'sob like a child'; the right-minded hero to whom temptation comes decides, with archaic rectitude, that he 'will not do *this thing*'; the villain, taught by incessant ridicule to abstain from 'muffled curses', finds a vent in 'discordant laughs, that somehow jarred unpleasantly upon my nerves'; this laugh, *mutátis mutandis* ('cruel little laugh, that somehow . . .'), he shares with the heroine, who for her exclusive perquisite has 'this man who had somehow come into her life'. *Somehow* and *half-dazed* are invaluable for throwing a mysterious glamour over situations and characters that shun the broad daylight of common sense.

b. Elementary irony.

A well-known novelist speaks of the resentment that children feel against those elders who insist upon addressing them in a jocular tone, as if serious conversation between the two were out of the question. Irony is largely open to the same objection: the writer who uses it is taking our intellectual measure; he forgets our *ex officio* perfection in wisdom. Theoretically, indeed, the reader is admitted to the author's confidence; *he* is not the *corpus vile* on which experiment is made: that, however, is scarcely more convincing than the two-edged formula 'present company excepted'. For minute, detailed illustration of truths that have had the misfortune to become commonplaces without making their due impression, sustained irony has its legitimate use: tired of being told, and shown by direct methods, that only the virtuous man is admirable, we are glad enough to go off with Fielding on a brisk *reductio ad absurdum*: 'for if not, let some other kind of man be admirable; as Jonathan Wild'. But the *reductio* process should be kept for emergencies, as Euclid kept it, with whom it is a confession that direct methods are not available. The isolated snatches of irony quoted below have no such justification: they are for ornament, not for utility; and it is a kind of ornament that is peculiarly un-English—a way of shrugging one's shoulders in print.

He had also the comfortable reflection that, by the violent quarrel with Lord Dalgarno, he must now forfeit the friendship and good offices of that nobleman's father and sister.—SCOTT.

Naturally that reference was received with laughter by the Opposition, who are, or profess to be, convinced that our countrymen in the Transvaal do not intend to keep faith with us. They are very welcome to the monopoly of that unworthy estimate, which must greatly endear them to all our kindred beyond seas.—*Times*.

The whole of these proceedings were so agreeable to Mr. Pecksniff, that he stood with his eyes fixed upon the floor . . ., as if a host of penal sentences were being passed upon him.—DICKENS.

The time comes when the banker thinks it prudent to contract some of his accounts, and this may be one which he thinks it expedient to reduce: and then perhaps he makes the pleasant discovery, that there are no such persons at all as the acceptors, and that the funds for meeting all these bills have been got from himself!—H. D. MACLEOD.

Pleasant is put for *unpleasant* because the latter seemed dull and unnecessary; the writer should have taken the hint, and put nothing at all.

The climax is reached by those pessimists who, regarding the reader's case as desperate, assist him with punctuation, italics, and the like:

And this honourable (?) proposal was actually made in the presence of two at least of the parties to the former transaction!

These so-called *gentlemen* seem to forget . . .

I was content to be snubbed and harassed and worried a hundred times a day by one or other of the 'great' personages who wandered at will all over my house and grounds, and accepted my lavish hospitality. Many people imagine that it must be an 'honour' to entertain a select party of aristocrats, but I . . .—CORELLI.

The much-prated-of 'kindness of heart' and 'generosity' possessed by millionaires, generally amounts to this kind of thing.—CORELLI.

Was I about to discover that the supposed 'woman-hater' had been tamed and caught at last?—CORELLI.

That should undoubtedly have been your 'great' career—you were born for it—made for it! You would have been as brute-souled as you are now . . .—CORELLI.

c. Superlatives without *the*.

The omission of *the* with superlatives is limited by ordinary prose usage to (1) Superlatives after a possessive: 'Your best plan'. (2) Superlatives with *most*: 'in most distressing circumstances', but not 'in saddest circumstances'. (3) Superlatives in apposition, followed by *of*: 'I took refuge with X., kindliest of hosts'; 'We are now at Scarmouth, dingiest of decayed watering-places'. Many writers of the present day affect the omission of *the* in all cases where the superlative only means *very*. No harm will be done if they eventually have their way: in the meantime, the omission of *the* with inflected superlatives has the appearance of gross mannerism.

Our enveloping movements since some days proved successful, and fiercest battle is now proceeding.—*Times*.

In which, too, so many noblest men have . . . both made and been what will be venerated to all time.—CARLYLE.

Struggling with objects which, though it cannot master them, are essentially of richest significance.—CARLYLE.

The request was urged with every kind suggestion, and every assurance of aid and comfort, by friendliest parties in Manchester, who, in the sequel, amply redeemed their word.—EMERSON.

In Darkest Africa.—STANLEY.

Delos furnishes, not only quaintest tripods, crude bronze oxen and horses like those found at Olympia, but . . .—L. M. MITCHELL.

The scene represents in crudest forms the combat of gods and giants, a subject which should attain long afterwards fullest expression in the powerful frieze of the Great Altar at Pergamon.—L. M. MITCHELL.

A world of highest and noblest thought in dramas of perfect form.—L. M. MITCHELL.

From earliest times such competitive games had been celebrated.—L. M. MITCHELL.

When fullest, freest forms had not yet been developed.—L. M. MITCHELL.

d. Cheap originality.

Just as 'elegant variation' is generally a worse fault than monotony, so the avoidance of trite phrases is sometimes worse than triteness itself. Children have been known to satisfy an early thirst for notoriety by merely turning their coats inside out; and 'distinction' of style has been secured by some writers on the still easier terms of writing a common expression backwards. By this simplest of all possible expedients, English 'wear and tear' becomes Carlylese 'tear and wear',[1] and Emerson acquires an exclusive property (so at least one hopes) in 'nothing or little'. The novice need scarcely be warned against infringing these writers' patents; it would be as unpardonable as stealing the idea of a machine for converting clean knives into dirty ones. Hackneyed phrases become hackneyed because they are useful, in the first instance; but they derive a new efficiency from the very fact that they are hackneyed. Their precise form grows to be an essential part of the idea they convey, and all that a writer effects by turning such a phrase backwards, or otherwise tampering with it, is to give us our triteness at second-hand; we are put to the trouble of translating 'tear and wear', only to arrive at our old friend 'wear and tear', hackneyed as ever.

How beautiful is noble-sentiment; like gossamer-gauze beautiful and cheap, which will stand no *tear and wear*.—CARLYLE.

Bloated promises, which end in *nothing or little*.—EMERSON.

The universities also are *parcel* of the ecclesiastical system.—EMERSON.

Fox, Burke, Pitt, Erskine, Wilberforce, Sheridan, Romilly, or *whatever national man*, were by this means sent to Parliament.—EMERSON.

And the stronger these are, the individual is so much weaker.—EMERSON.

The faster the ball falls to the sun, the force to fly off is by so much augmented.—EMERSON.

The friction in nature is so enormous that we cannot spare any power. *It is not question* to express our thought, to elect our way, but to overcome resistances.—EMERSON.

[1] Now that the *O.E.D.* is available for T, I find that 'tear and wear', though much the rarer form, is not, as we supposed, peculiar to Carlyle, and is rather a national (Scottish) than a personal variant.—H. W. F.

CHAPTER IV

PUNCTUATION

What a sight it is to see writers committed together by the ears for ceremonies, syllables, points, colons, commas, hyphens, and the like!—
BEN JONSON.

IN this chapter we shall adhere generally to our plan of not giving systematic positive directions, or attempting to cover all ground familiar and unfamiliar, important or not, but drawing attention only to the most prevalent mistakes. On so technical a subject, however, a few preliminary remarks may be made; and to those readers who would prefer a systematic treatise Beadnell's *Spelling and Punctuation* (Wyman's Technical Series, Menken, 2s. 6d.) may be recommended. We shall refer to it occasionally in what follows; and the examples to which —B. is attached instead of an author's name are taken from it; these are all given in Beadnell (unless the contrary is stated) as examples of correct punctuation. It should be added that the book is written rather from the compositor's than from the author's point of view, and illustrates the compositor's natural weaknesses; it is more important to him, for instance, that a page should not be unsightly (the unsightliness being quite imaginary, and the result of professional conservatism) than that quotation marks and stops, or dashes and stops, should be arranged in their true significant order; but, as the right and unsightly is candidly given as well as the wrong and beautiful, this does not matter; the student can take his choice.

We shall begin by explaining how it is that punctuation is a difficult matter, and worth a writer's serious attention. There are only six stops, comma, semicolon, colon, full stop, question mark, exclamation mark; or, with the dash, seven. The work of three of them, full stop, question, exclamation, is so clear that mistakes about their use can hardly occur without gross carelessness; and it might be thought that with the four thus left it ought to be a very simple matter to exhaust all possibilities in a brief code of rules. It is not so, however. Apart from temporary disturbing causes—of which two now operative are (1) the gradual disappearance of the colon in its old use with the decay of formal periodic arrangement, and (2) the encroachments of the dash as a saver of trouble and an exponent of emotion—there are also permanent difficulties.

Before mentioning these we observe that the four stops in the strictest acceptance of the word (,) (;) (:) (.)—for (!) and (?) are tones rather than stops—form a series (it might be expressed also by 1, 2, 3, 4), each member of which directs us to pause for so many units of time before proceeding. There is essentially nothing but a quantitative time relation between them.

The first difficulty is that this single distinction has to convey to the reader differences of more than one kind, and not commensurable; it has to do both logical and rhetorical work. Its logical work is helping to make clear the grammatical relations between parts of a sentence or paragraph and the whole or other parts; its rhetorical work is contributing to emphasis, heightening effect, and regulating pace. It is in vain that Beadnell lays it down: 'The variation of pause between the words of the same thought is a matter of rhetoric and feeling, but punctuation depends entirely upon the variation of relations— upon logical and grammatical principles'. The difference between these two:

> The master beat the scholar with a strap.—B.
> The master beat the scholar, with a strap.

is in logic nothing; but in rhetoric it is the difference between matter-of-fact statement and indignant statement: a strap, we are to understand from the comma, is a barbarous instrument.

Again, in the two following examples, so far as logic goes, commas would be used in both, or semicolons in both. But the writer of the second desires to be slow, staccato, and impressive: the writer of the first desires to be rapid and flowing, or rather, perhaps, does not desire to be anything other than natural.

Mathematicians have sought knowledge in figures, philosophers in systems, logicians in subtilties, and metaphysicians in sounds.—B.

In the eclogue there must be nothing rude or vulgar; nothing fanciful or affected; nothing subtle or abstruse.—B.

The difference is rhetorical, not logical. It is true, however, that modern printers make an effort to be guided by logic or grammar alone; it is impossible for them to succeed entirely; but any one who will look at an Elizabethan book with the original stopping will see how far they have moved: the old stopping was frankly to guide the voice in reading aloud, while the modern is mainly to guide the mind in seeing through the grammatical construction.

A perfect system of punctuation, then, that should be exact and uniform, would require separate rhetorical and logical notations in the first place. Such a system is not to be desired; the point is only that, without it, usage must fluctuate according as one element is allowed to interfere with the other. But a second difficulty remains, even if we assume that rhetoric could be eliminated altogether. Our stop series, as explained above, provides us with four degrees; but the degrees of closeness and remoteness between the members of sentence or paragraph are at the least ten times as many. It is easy to show that the comma, even in its purely logical function, has not one, but many tasks to do, which differ greatly in importance. Take three examples:

His method of handling the subject was ornate, learned, and perspicuous.—B.

The removal of the comma after *learned* makes so little difference that it is an open question among compositors whether it should be used or not.

The criminal, who had betrayed his associates, was a prey to remorse.

With the commas, the criminal is necessarily a certain person already known to us: without them, we can only suppose a past state of society to be described, in which all traitors were ashamed of themselves—a difference of some importance.

Colonel Hutchinson, the Governor whom the King had now appointed, having hardened his heart, resolved on sterner measures.

Omission of the comma after *appointed* gives us two persons instead of one, and entirely changes the meaning, making the central words into, what they could not possibly be with the comma, an absolute construction.

These commas, that is, have very different values; many intermediate degrees might be added. Similarly the semicolon often separates grammatically complete sentences, but often also the mere items of a list, and between these extremes it marks other degrees of separation. A perfect system for the merely logical part of punctuation, then, would require some scores of stops instead of four. This again is not a thing to be desired; how little, is clear from the fact that one of our scanty supply, the colon, is now practically disused as a member of the series, and turned on to useful work at certain odd jobs that will be mentioned later. A series of stops that should really represent all gradations might perhaps be worked by here and there a writer consistently with himself; but to persuade all writers to observe the same distinctions would be hopeless.

A third difficulty is this: not only must many tasks be performed by one stop; the same task is necessarily performed by different stops according to circumstances; as if polygamy were not bad enough, it is complicated by an admixture of polyandry. We have already given two sentences of nearly similar pattern, one of which had its parts separated by commas, the other by semicolons, and we remarked that the difference was there accounted for by the intrusion of rhetoric. But the same thing occurs even when logic or grammar (it should be explained that grammar is sometimes defined as logic applied to speech, so that for our purposes the two are synonymous) is free from the disturbing influence; or when that influence acts directly, not on the stop itself that is in question, but only on one of its neighbours. To illustrate the first case, when the stops are not affected by rhetoric, but depend on grammar alone, we may take a short sentence as a nucleus, elaborate it by successive additions, and observe how a particular stop has to go on increasing its power, though it continues to serve only the same purpose, because it must keep its predominance.

When ambition asserts the monstrous doctrine of millions made for individuals, is not the good man indignant?

The function of the comma is to mark the division between the subordinate and the main clauses.

When ambition asserts the monstrous doctrine of millions made for individuals, their playthings, to be demolished at their caprice; is not the good man indignant?

The semicolon is doing now exactly what the comma did before; but, as commas have intruded into the clause to do the humble yet necessary work of marking two appositions, the original comma has to dignify its relatively more important office by converting itself into a semicolon.

When ambition asserts the monstrous doctrine of millions made for individuals, their playthings, to be demolished at their caprice; sporting wantonly with the rights, the peace, the comforts, the existence, of nations, as if their intoxicated pride would, if possible, make God's earth their football: is not the good man indignant?—B.

The new insertion is also an apposition, like the former ones; but, as it contains commas within itself, it must be raised above their level by being allowed a semicolon to part it from them. The previous semicolon, still having the same supreme task to do, and challenged by an upstart rival, has nothing for it but to change the regal for the imperial crown, and become a colon. A careful observer will now object that, on these principles, our new insertion ought to have had an internal semicolon, to differentiate the subordinate clause, *as if*, &c., from the mere enumeration commas that precede; in which case the semicolon after *caprice* should be raised to a colon; and then what is the newly created emperor to do? there is no papal tiara for him to assume, the full stop being confined to the independent sentence. The objection is quite just, and shows how soon the powers of the four stops are exhausted if relentlessly worked. But we are concerned only to notice that the effect of stops, even logically considered, is relative, not absolute. It is also true that many modern writers, if they put down a sentence like this, would be satisfied with using commas throughout; the old-fashioned air of the colon will hardly escape notice. But the whole arrangement is according to the compositor's art in its severer form.

A specimen of the merely indirect action of rhetoric may be more shortly disposed of. In a sentence already quoted—

Mathematicians have sought knowledge in figures, philosophers in systems, logicians in subtilties, and metaphysicians in sounds—

suppose the writer to have preferred for impressive effect, as we said he might have, to use semicolons instead of commas. The immediate result of that would be that what before could be left to the reader to do for himself (i.e., the supplying of the words *have sought knowledge* in each member) will in presence of the semicolon require to be done to the eye by commas, and the sentence will run:

Mathematicians have sought knowledge in figures; philosophers, in systems; logicians, in subtilties; and metaphysicians, in sounds.

But, lest we should be thought too faithful followers of the logicians, we will now assume that our point has been sufficiently proved: the difficulties of punctuation, owing to the interaction of different purposes, and the inadequacy of the instruments, are formidable enough to be worth grappling with.

We shall now only make three general remarks before proceeding to details. The first is implied in what has been already said: the work of punctuation is mainly to show, or hint at, the grammatical relation between words, phrases, clauses, and sentences; but it must not be forgotten that

stops also serve to regulate pace, to throw emphasis on particular words and give them significance, and to indicate tone.
These effects are subordinate, and must not be allowed to
conflict with the main object; but as the grammatical relation
may often be shown in more than one way, that way can be
chosen which serves another purpose best.

Secondly, it is a sound principle that as few stops should be
used as will do the work. There is a theory that scientific or
philosophic matter should be punctuated very fully and
exactly, whereas mere literary work can do with a much looser
system. This is a mistake, except so far as scientific and
philosophic writers may desire to give an impressive effect by
retarding the pace; that is legitimate; but otherwise, all that
is printed should have as many stops as help the reader, and
not more. A resolution to put in all the stops that can be
correctly used is very apt to result in the appearance of some
that can only be used incorrectly; some of our quotations from
Huxley and Mr Balfour may be thought to illustrate this.
And whereas slight stopping may venture on small irregularities,
full stopping that is incorrect is also unpardonable. The
objection to full stopping that is correct is the discomfort
inflicted upon readers, who are perpetually being checked
like a horse with a fidgety driver.

Thirdly, every one should make up his mind not to depend
on his stops. They are to be regarded as devices, not for
saving him the trouble of putting his words into the order
that naturally gives the required meaning, but for saving his
reader the moment or two that would sometimes, without
them, be necessarily spent on reading the sentence twice over,
once to catch the general arrangement, and again for the
details. It may almost be said that what reads wrongly if
the stops are removed is radically bad; stops are not to alter
meaning, but merely to show it up. Those who are learning
to write should make a practice of putting down all they want
to say without stops first. What then, on reading over, naturally
arranges itself contrary to the intention should be not punctu-

ated, but altered; and the stops should be as few as possible, consistently with the recognized rules. At this point those rules should follow; but adequately explained and illustrated they would require a volume; and we can only speak of common abuses and transgressions of them.

First comes what may be called for short the spot-plague— the tendency to make full stops do all the work. The comma, most important, if slightest, of all stops, cannot indeed be got rid of, though even for that the full stop is substituted when possible; but the semicolon is now as much avoided by many writers as the colon (in its old use) by most. With the semicolon go most of the conjunctions. Now there is something to be said for the change, or the two changes: the old-fashioned period, or long complex sentence, carefully worked out with a view to symmetry, balance, and degrees of subordination, though it has a dignity of its own, is formal, stiff, and sometimes frigid; the modern newspaper vice of long sentences either rambling or involved (far commoner in newspapers than the spot-plague) is inexpressibly wearisome and exasperating. Simplification is therefore desirable. But journalists now and then, and writers with more literary ambition than ability generally, overdo the thing till it becomes an affectation; it is then little different from Victor Hugo's device of making every sentence a paragraph, and our last state is worse than our first. Patronizing archness, sham ingenuousness, spasmodic interruption, scrappy argument, dry monotony, are some of the resulting impressions. We shall have to trouble the reader with at least one rather long specimen; the spot-plague in its less virulent form, that is, when it is caused not by pretentiousness or bad taste, but merely by desire to escape from the period, does not declare itself very rapidly. What follows is a third or so of a literary review, of which the whole is in exactly the same style, and which might have been quoted entire for the same purpose. It will be seen that it shows twenty full stops to one semicolon and no colons. Further, between no two of the twenty sentences is there a conjunction.

The life of Lord Chatham, which has just appeared in three volumes, by Dr. Albert v. Ruville of the University of Halle deserves special notice. It is much the most complete life which has yet appeared of one of the most commanding figures in English history. It exhibits that thoroughness of method which characterized German historical writings of other days, and which has not lately been conspicuous. It is learned without being dull, and is free from that uncritical spirit of hostility to England which impairs the value of so many recent German histories. That portion which deals with the closing years of George II and with events following the accession of George III is exceptionally interesting. One of the greatest misfortunes that ever happened to England was the resignation of Pitt in 1761. It was caused, as we all know, by difference of opinion with his colleagues on the Spanish question. Ferdinand VI of Spain died in 1759, and was succeeded by King Charles III, one of the most remarkable princes of the House of Bourbon. This sovereign was an enthusiastic adherent of the policy which found expression in the celebrated family compact. On August 15, 1761, a secret convention was concluded between France and Spain, under which Spain engaged to declare war against England in May, 1762. Pitt quite understood the situation. He saw that instant steps should be taken to meet the danger, and proposed at a Cabinet held on October 2 that war should be declared against Spain. Newcastle, Hardwicke, Anson, Bute, and Mansfield combated this proposal, which was rejected, and two days afterwards Pitt resigned. His scheme was neither immature nor ill-considered. He had made his preparations to strike a heavy blow at the enemy, to seize the Isthmus of Panama, thereby securing a port in the Pacific, and separating the Spanish provinces of Mexico and Peru. He had planned an expedition against Havana and the Philippine Islands, where no adequate resistance could have been made; and, had he remained in office, there is but little doubt that the most precious possessions of Spain in the New World would have been incorporated in the British Empire. When he left the Cabinet all virility seems to have gone out of it with him. As he had foreseen, Spain declared war on England at a suitable moment for herself, and the unfortunate negotiations were opened leading to the Peace of Paris in 1763, which was pregnant with many disastrous results for England. The circumstances which led to the resignation of Pitt are dealt with by Dr. v. Ruville much more lucidly than by most historians. This portion of his work is the more interesting because of the pains he takes to clear George III from the charge of conspiring against his great Minister.—*Times*.

The reader's experience has probably been that the constant

fresh starts are at first inspiriting, that about half-way he has had quite enough of the novelty, and that he is intensely grateful, when the solitary semicolon comes into sight, for a momentary lapse into ordinary gentle progress. Writers like this may almost be suspected of taking literally a summary piece of advice that we have lately seen in a book on English composition: *Never use a semicolon when you can employ a full stop*. Beadnell lays down a law that at first sight seems to amount to the same thing: *The notion of parting short independent sentences otherwise than by a full-stop, rests upon no rational foundation, and leads to endless perplexities*. But his practice clears him of the imputation: he is saved by the ambiguity of the word *independent*. There are grammatical dependence, and dependence of thought. Of all those 'little hard round unconnected things', in the *Times* review, that 'seem to come upon one as shot would descend from a shot-making tower' (Sir Arthur Helps), hardly one is not dependent on its neighbours in the more liberal sense, though each is a complete sentence and independent in grammar. Now one important use of stops is to express the degrees of thought-dependence. A style that groups several complete sentences together by the use of semicolons, because they are more closely connected in thought, is far more restful and easy—for the reader, that is—than the style that leaves him to do the grouping for himself; and yet it is free from the formality of the period, which consists, not of grammatically independent sentences, but of a main sentence with many subordinate clauses. We have not space for a long example of the group system rightly applied; most good modern writers free from the craving to be up to date will supply them on every page; but a very short quotation may serve to emphasize the difference between group and spot-plague principles. The essence of the latter is that almost the only stops used are full stops and commas, that conjunctions are rare, and that when a conjunction does occur the comma is generally used, not the full stop. What naturally follows is an arrangement of this kind:

The sheil of Ravensnuik was, for the present at least, at his disposal. The foreman or 'grieve' at the Home Farm was anxious to be friendly, but even if he lost that place, Dan Weir knew that there was plenty of others.—CROCKETT.

(To save trouble, let it be stated that the sheil is a dependency of the Home Farm, and not contrasted with or opposed to it.) Here there are three grammatically independent sentences, between the two latter of which the conjunction *but* is inserted. It follows from spot-plague principles that there will be a full stop at the end of the first, and a comma at the end of the second. With the group system it is not so simple a matter; before we can place the stops, we have to inquire how the three sentences are connected in thought. It then appears that the friendliness of the grieve is mentioned to account for the sheil's being at disposal; that is, there is a close connexion, though no conjunction, betwen the first and the second sentences. Further, the birds in the bush of the third sentence are contrasted, not with the second sentence's friendliness, but with the first sentence's bird in the hand (which, however, is accounted for by the second sentence's friendliness). To group rightly, then, we must take care, quite reversing the author's punctuation, that the first and second are separated by a stop of less power than that which separates the third from them. Comma, semicolon, would do it, if the former were sufficient between two grammatically independent sentences not joined by a conjunction; it is obviously not sufficient there (though in some such pairs it might be); so, instead of comma, semicolon, we must use semicolon, full stop; and the sentence will run, with its true meaning much more clearly given:

The sheil of Ravensnuik was, for the present at least, at his disposal; the foreman or 'grieve' at the Home Farm was anxious to be friendly. But even if he lost that place, Dan Weir knew that there was plenty of others.

The group system gives more trouble to the writer or compositor, and less to the reader; the compositor cannot be expected to like it, if the burden falls on him; inferior writers cannot be expected to choose it either, perhaps; but the good writers who do choose it no doubt find that after a short time the work comes to do itself by instinct.

We need now only add two or three short specimens, worse, though from their shortness less remarkable, than the *Times* extract. They are not specially selected as bad; but it may be hoped that by their juxtaposition they may have some deterrent effect.

So Dan opened the door a little and the dog came out as if nothing had happened. It was now clear. The light was that of late evening. The air hardly more than cool. A gentle fanning breeze came from the North and . . .—CROCKETT.

Allies must have common sentiments, a common policy, common interests. Russia's disposition is aggressive. Her policy is the closed door. Her interests lie in monopoly. With our country it is precisely the opposite. Japan may conquer, but she will not aggress. Russia may be defeated, but she will not abandon her aggression. With such a country an alliance is beyond the conception even of a dream.—*Times*.

Upon a hillside, a great swelling hillside, high up near the clouds, lay a herd lad. Little more than a boy he was. He did not know much, but he wanted to know more. He was not very good, but he wanted to be better. He was lonely, but of that he was not aware. On the whole he was content up there on his great hillside.—CROCKETT.

To be popular you have to be interested, or appear to be interested, in other people. And there are so many in this world in whom it is impossible to be interested. So many for whom the most skilful hypocrisy cannot help us to maintain a semblance of interest.—*Daily Telegraph*.

Of course a girl so pretty as my Miss Anne could not escape having many suitors, especially as all over the countryside Sir Tempest had the name of being something of a skinflint. And skinflints are always rich, as is well known.—CROCKETT.

The last sentence here is a mere comment on what is itself only an appendage, the clause introduced by *especially*; it has therefore no right to the dignity of a separate sentence. But it can hardly be mended without some alteration of words as well as stops; for instance, put a semicolon after suitors, write *moreover* for *especially as*, and put only a comma after *skinflint*; the right proportion would then be secured.

The spot-plague, as we have shown, sometimes results in illogicality; it need not do so, however; when it does, the fault lies with the person who, accepting its principles, does not arrange his sentences to suit them. It is a new-fashioned and, in our opinion, unpleasant system, but quite compatible with correctness.

Over-stopping, to which we now proceed, is on the contrary old-fashioned; but it is equally compatible with correctness. Though old-fashioned, it still lingers obstinately enough to make some slight protest desirable; the superstition that every possible stop should be inserted in scientific and other such writing misleads compositors, and their example affects literary authors who have not much ear. Any one who finds himself putting down several commas close to one another should reflect that he is making himself disagreeable, and question his conscience, as severely as we ought to do about disagreeable conduct in real life, whether it is necessary. He will find that the parenthetic or emphatic effect given to an adverbial phrase by putting a comma at each end of it is often of no value whatever to his meaning; in other words, that he can make himself agreeable by merely putting off a certain pompous solemnity; erasing a pair of commas may make the difference in writing that is made in conversation by a change of tone from the didactic to the courteous. Sometimes the abundance of commas is not so easily reduced; a change in the order of words, the omission of a needless adverb or conjunction, even the recasting of a sentence, may be necessary. But it is a safe statement that a gathering of commas (except on certain lawful occasions, as in a list) is a suspicious circumstance. The sentence should at least be read aloud, and if it halts or jolts some change or other should be made.

The smallest portion possible of curious interest had been awakened within me, and, at last, I asked myself, within my own mind . . .—
BORROW.

None of the last three commas is wanted; those round *at last* are very unpleasant, and they at least should be omitted.

In questions of trade and finance, questions which, owing, perhaps, to their increasing intricacy, seem . . .—BRYCE.

Perhaps can do very well without commas.

It is, however, already plain enough that, unless, indeed, some great catastrophe should upset all their calculations, the authorities have very little intention . . .—*Times*.

Indeed can do without commas, if it cannot itself be done without.

Jeannie, too, is, just occasionally, like a good girl out of a book by a sentimental lady-novelist.—*Times*.

If *just* is omitted, there need be no commas round *occasionally*. There may be a value in *just*; but hardly enough to compensate for the cruel jerking at the bit to which the poor reader is subjected by a remorseless driver.

Thus, their work, however imperfect and faulty, judged by modern lights, it may have been, brought them face to face with . . .—HUXLEY.

The comma after *thus* is nothing if not pompous. And another can be got rid of by putting *it may have been* before *judged by modern lights*.

Lilias suggested the advice which, of all others, seemed most suited to the occasion, that, yielding, namely, to the circumstances of their situation, they should watch . . .—SCOTT.

Omit *namely* and its commas.

Shakespeare, it is true, had, as I have said, as respects England, the privilege which only first-comers enjoy.—LOWELL.

A good example of the warning value of commas. None of these can be dispensed with, since there are no less than three parenthetic qualifications to the sentence. But the crowd of commas ought to have told the writer how bad his sentence was; it is like an obstacle race. It should begin, It is true that . . ., which disposes of one obstacle. *As I have said* can be given a separate sentence afterwards—So much has been said before.

Private banks and capitalists constitute the main bulk of the subscribers, and, apparently, they are prepared to go on subscribing indefinitely.—*Times*.

Putting commas round *apparently* amounts to the insertion of a further clause, such as, Though you would not think they could be such fools. But what the precise contents of the further clause may be is problematic. At any rate, a writer should not invite us to read between the lines unless he is sure of two things: what he wants to be read there; and that we are likely to be willing and able readers of it. The same is true of many words that are half adverbs and half conjunctions, like *therefore*. We have the right to comma them off if we like; but, unless it is done with a definite purpose, it produces perplexity as well as heaviness. In the first of the next two examples, there is no need whatever for the commas. In the second, the motive is clear: having the choice between commas and no commas, the reporter uses them because he so secures a pause after *he*, and gives the word that emphasis which in the speech delivered doubtless made the *I* that it represents equivalent to *I for my part*.

Both Tom and John knew this; and, therefore, John—the soft-hearted one—kept out of the way.—TROLLOPE.

It would not be possible to sanction an absolutely unlimited expenditure on the Volunteers; the burden on the tax-payers would be too great. He, therefore, wished that those who knew most about the Volunteers would make up their minds as to the direction in which there should be development.—*Times*.

After *for* and *and* beginning a sentence commas are often used that are hardly even correct. It may be suspected that writers allow themselves to be deceived by the false analogy of sentences in which the *and* or *for* is immediately followed by a subordinate clause or phrase that has a right to its two commas. When there is no such interruption, the only possible plea for the comma is that it is not logical but rhetorical, and conveys some archness or other special significance such as is hardly to be found in our two examples:

The lawn, the soft, smooth slope, the . . . bespeak an amount of elegant comfort within, that would serve for a palace. This indication is not without warrant; for, within it is a house of refinement and luxury.—DICKENS.

And, it is true that these were the days of mental and moral fermentation.—HUTTON.

We shall class here also, assuming for the present that the rhetorical plea may be allowed even when there is no logical justification for a stop, two sentences in which the copula *is*, standing between subject and complement, has commas on each side of it. Impressiveness is what is aimed at; it seems to us a tawdry device for giving one's sentence an *ex cathedra* air.

The reason why the world lacks unity, is, because man is disunited with himself.—EMERSON.
The charm in Nelson's history, is, the unselfish greatness.—EMERSON.

Many other kinds of over-stopping might be illustrated; but we have intentionally confined ourselves here to specimens in which grammatical considerations do not arise, and the sentence is equally correct whether the stops are inserted or not. Sentences in which over-stopping outrages grammar more or less decidedly will be incidentally treated later on. Meanwhile we make the general remark that ungrammatical insertion of stops is a high crime and misdemeanour, whereas ungrammatical omission of them is often venial, and in some cases even desirable. Nevertheless the over-stopping that offends against nothing but taste has its counterpart in under-stopping of the same sort. And it must be added that nothing so easily exposes a writer to the suspicion of being uneducated as omission of commas against nearly universal custom. In the examples that follow, every one will see at the first glance where commas are wanting. When it is remembered that, as we have implied, an author has the right to select the degree of intensity, or scale, of his punctuation, it can hardly be said that grammar actually demands any stops in these sentences taken by themselves. Yet the effect, unless we choose to assume misprints, as we naturally do in isolated cases, is horrible.

It may be asked can further depreciation be afforded.—*Times*.
I believe you used to live in Warwickshire at Willowsmere Court did you not?—CORELLI.

The hills slope gently to the cliffs which overhang the bay of Naples and they seem to bear on their outstretched arms a rich offering of Nature's fairest gifts for the queen city of the south.—F. M. CRAWFORD.

'You made a veritable sensation Lucio!' 'Did I?' He laughed. 'You flatter me Geoffrey.'—CORELLI.

I like your swiftness of action Geoffrey.—CORELLI.

Good heavens man, there are no end of lords and ladies who will . . . —CORELLI.

Although we are, when we turn from taste to grammar, on slightly firmer ground, it will be seen that there are many debatable questions; and we shall have to use some technical terms. As usual, only those points will be attended to which our observation has shown to be important.

1. The substantival clause.

Subordinate clauses are sentences containing a subject and predicate, but serving the purpose in the main sentence (to which they are joined sometimes by a subordinating conjunction or relative pronoun, but sometimes without any separate and visible link) of single words, namely, of noun, adjective, or adverb; they are called respectively substantival, adjectival, or adverbial clauses. Examples:

Substantival. He asked *what I should do*. (*my plan*, noun)
Adjectival. The man *who acts honestly* is respected. (*honest*, adjective)
Adverbial. I shall see you *when the sun next rises*. (*to-morrow*, adverb)

Now there is no rule that subordinate clauses must be separated from the main sentence by a stop; that depends on whether they are essential parts of the proposition (when stops are generally wrong), or more or less separable accidents (when commas are more or less required). But what we wish to draw attention to is a distinction in this respect, very generally disregarded, between the substantival clause and the two other kinds. When the others are omitted, though the desired meaning may be spoilt, the grammar generally remains uninjured; a complete, though not perhaps valuable sentence is left. *The man is respected, I shall see you*, are as much sentences alone as they were with the adjectival and adverbial clauses. With substantival clauses this is seldom true; they are usually the subjects, objects, or complements, of the verbs, that is, are grammatically essential. *He asked* is meaningless by itself. (Even if the point is that he asked and did not answer, *things*, or *something*, has to be supplied in thought.) Now it is a principle, not without exceptions, but generally sound, that the subject, object, or complement, is not to be separated from its verb even by a comma (though *two* commas belonging to an inserted parenthetic clause or phrase or word may intervene). It follows that there is no logical or grammatical justification, though there may be a rhetorical one, for the comma so frequently placed before the *that* of an indirect statement. Our own opinion (which is, however, contrary to the practice of most compositors) is that this should always be omitted except when the writer has a very distinct reason for producing rhetorical impressiveness by an unusual pause. Some very ugly overstopping would thus be avoided.

Yet there, too, we find, that character has its problems to solve.— MEREDITH.

We know, that, in the individual man, consciousness grows.— HUXLEY.

And it is said, that, on a visitor once asking to see his library, Descartes led him . . .—HUXLEY.

The general opinion however was, that, if Bute had been early practised in debate, he might have become an impressive speaker.— MACAULAY.

The comma before *whether* in the next is actually misleading; we are tempted to take as adverbial what is really a substantival clause, object to the verbal noun *indifference*:

The book . . . had merits due to the author's indifference, whether he showed bad taste or not, provided he got nearer to the impression he wished to convey.—*Speaker*.

Grammar, however, would afford some justification for distinguishing between the substantival clause as subject, object, or complement, and the substantival clause in apposition with one of these. Though there should decidedly be no

comma in *He said that* . . ., it is strictly defensible in *It is said,
that* . . . The *that*-clause in the latter is explanatory of, and in
apposition with, *it*; and the ordinary sign of apposition is a
comma. Similarly, *My opinion is that*: *It is my opinion, that*.
But as there seems to be no value whatever in the distinction,
our advice is to do without the comma in all ordinary cases of
either kind. A useful and reasonable exception is made in some
manuals; for instance, in Bigelow's *Manual of Punctuation* we
read: 'Clauses like "It is said", introducing several propositions
or quotations, each preceded by the word *that*, should have a
comma before the first *that*. But if a single proposition or
quotation only is given, no comma is necessary. Example:

> Philosophers assert, that Nature is unlimited in her operations, that
> she has inexhaustible treasures in reserve, that . . .'

Anything that shows the reader what he is to expect, and so
saves him the trouble of coming back to revise his first impressions, is desirable if there is no strong reason against it.

A more important distinction is this : *He said*, &c., may
have for its object, and *It is said*, &c., for its (virtual) subject,
either the actual words said, or a slight rearrangement of
them (not necessarily to the eye, but at least to the mind),
which makes them more clearly part of the grammatical
construction, and turns them into true subordinate clauses.
Thus *He told her, You are in danger* may be kept, but is usually
altered to *He told her that she was in danger*, or to *He told her
she was in danger*. In the first, *You are in danger* is not properly
a subordinate clause, but a sentence, which may be said to be
in apposition with *these words* understood. In the second and
third alike, the altered words are a subordinate substantival
clause, the object to *told*. It follows that when the actual words
are given as such (this is sometimes only to be known by the
tone: compare *I tell you, I will come*, and *I tell you I will come*),
a comma should be inserted; whereas, when they are meant
as mere reported or indirect speech, it should be omitted. Actual
words given as such should also be begun with a capital letter;

and if they consist of a compound sentence, or of several sentences, a comma will not suffice for their introduction; a colon, a colon and dash, or a full stop, with quotation marks always in the last case, and usually in the others, will be necessary; but these are distinctions that need not be considered here in detail.

Further, it must be remembered that substantival clauses include indirect questions as well as indirect statements, and that the same rules will apply to them. The two following examples are very badly stopped:

(a) Add to all this that he died in his thirty-seventh year: and then ask, If it be strange that his poems are imperfect?—CARLYLE.

Accommodation of the stops to the words would give:

and then ask if it be strange that his poems are imperfect.

And accommodation of the words to the stops would give:

and then ask, Is it strange that his poems are imperfect?

(b) It may be asked can further depreciation be afforded.—*Times.*

The two correct alternatives here are similarly:

It may be asked, Can further depreciation be afforded?
It may be asked whether further depreciation can be afforded.

As the sentences stood originally, we get in the Carlyle a most theatrical, and in the *Times* a most slovenly effect.

2. The verb and its subject, object, or complement.

Our argument against the common practice of placing a comma before substantival *that*-clauses and others like them was, in brief: This sort of *that*-clause is simply equivalent to a noun; that noun is, with few exceptions, the subject, object, or complement, to a verb; and between things so closely and essentially connected as the verb and any of these no stop should intervene (unless for very strong and special rhetorical reasons). This last principle, that the verb and its essential belongings must not be parted, was merely assumed. We think it will be granted by any one who reads the next two examples. It is felt at once that a writer who will break the principle with so little excuse as here will shrink from nothing.

So poor Byron was dethroned, as I had prophesied he would be, though I had little idea that his humiliation, would be brought about by one, whose sole strength consists in setting people to sleep.—BORROW.

He was, moreover, not an unkind man; but the crew of the *Bounty*, mutinied against him, and set him half naked in an open boat.—BORROW.

Very little better than these, but each with some perceptible motive, are the next six:

Depreciation of him, fetched up at a stroke the glittering armies of her enthusiasm.—MEREDITH.

Opposition to him, was comparable to the stand of blocks of timber before a flame.—MEREDITH.

In each of these the comma acts as an accent upon *him*, and is purely rhetorical and illogical.

Such women as you, are seldom troubled with remorse.—CORELLI.

Here the comma guards us from taking *you are* together. We have already said that this device is illegitimate. Such sentences should be recast; for instance, Women like you are seldom, &c.

The thick foliage of the branching oaks and elms in my grounds afforded grateful shade and repose to the tired body, while the tranquil loveliness of the woodland and meadow scenery, comforted and soothed the equally tired mind.—CORELLI.

With them came young boys and little children, while on either side, maidens white-veiled and rose-wreathed, paced demurely, swinging silver censers to and fro.—CORELLI.

Swift's view of human nature, is too black to admit of any hopes of their millennium.—L. STEPHEN.

Loveliness, *maidens*, *view*, the strict subjects, have adjectival phrases attached after them. The temptation to insert the comma is comprehensible, but slight, and should have been resisted.

In the three that come next, the considerable length of the subject, it must be admitted, makes a comma comforting; it gives us a sort of assurance that we have kept our hold on the sentence. It is illogical, however, and, owing to the importance of not dividing subject from verb, unpleasantly illogical. In each case the comfort would be equally effective if it were legitimized by the insertion of a comma before as well as after the clause or phrase at the end of which the present comma stands. The extra commas would be after *earth, victims, Schleiden.*

To see so many thousand wretches burdening the earth when such as her die, makes me think God did never intend life for a blessing.—SWIFT.

An order of the day expressing sympathy with the families of the victims and confidence in the Government, was adopted.—*Times.*

The famous researches of Schwann and Schleiden in 1837 and the following years, founded the modern science of histology.—HUXLEY.

It may be said that it is 'fudging' to find an excuse, as we have proposed to do, for a stop that we mean really to do something different from its ostensible work. But the answer is that with few tools and many tasks to do much fudging is in fact necessary.

A special form of this, in protest against which we shall give five examples, each from a different well-known author, is when the subject includes and ends with a defining relative clause, after which an illogical comma is placed. As the relative clause is of the defining kind (a phrase that has been explained[1]), it is practically impossible to fudge in these sentences by putting a comma before the relative pronoun. Even in the first sentence the length of the relative clause is no sufficient excuse; and in all the others we should abolish the comma without hesitation.

The same quickness of sympathy which had served him well in his work among the East End poor, enabled him to pour feeling into the figures of a bygone age.—BRYCE.

One of its agents is our will, but that which expresses itself in our will, is stronger than our will.—EMERSON.

The very interesting class of objects to which these belong, do not differ from the rest of the material universe.—BALFOUR.

And thus, the great men who were identified with the war, began slowly to edge over to the party . . .—L. STEPHEN.

In becoming a merchant-gild the body of citizens who formed the 'town', enlarged their powers of civic legislation.—J. R. GREEN.

[1] See chapter *Syntax*, section *Relatives*.

In the two sentences that now follow from Mr Morley, the offending comma of the first parts *centre*, which is what grammarians call the oblique complement, from its verb *made*; the offending comma of the second parts the direct object *groups* from its verb *drew*. Every one will allow that the sentences are clumsy; most people will allow that the commas are illogical. As for us, we do not say that, if the words are to be kept as they are, the commas should be omitted; but we do say that a good writer, when he found himself reduced to illogical commas, should have taken the trouble to rearrange his words.

De Maistre was never more clear-sighted than when he made a vigorous and deliberate onslaught upon Bacon, the centre of his movement against revolutionary principles.—MORLEY.

In saying that the Encyclopaedists began a political work, what is meant is that they drew into the light of new ideas, groups of institutions, usages, and arrangements which affected the well-being of France, as closely as nutrition affected the health and strength of an individual Frenchman.—MORLEY.

It may be added, by way of concluding this section, that the insertion of a comma in the middle of an absolute construction, which is capable, as was shown in the sentence about Colonel Hutchinson and the governor, of having very bad results indeed, is only a particular instance and *reductio ad absurdum* of inserting a comma between subject and verb. The comma in the absolute construction is so recognized a trap that it might have been thought needless to mention it; the following instances, however, will show that a warning is even now necessary.

Sir E. Seymour, having replied for the Navy, the Duke of Connaught, in replying for the Army, said . . .—*Times*.

Thus *got*, having been by custom poorly substituted for *gat*, so that we say He got away, instead of He gat away, many persons abbreviate *gotten* into *got*, saying He had got, for He had gotten.—R. G. WHITE.

The garrison, having been driven from the outer line of defences on July 30, Admiral Witoft considered it high time to make a sortie.—*Times*.

But that didn't last long; for Dr. Blimber, happening to change the position of his tight plump legs, as if he were going to get up, Toots swiftly vanished.—DICKENS.

3. The adjectival clause.

This, strictly speaking, does the work of an adjective in the sentence. It usually begins with a relative pronoun, but sometimes with a relative adverb. The man *who does not breathe* dies, is equivalent to The *unbreathing* man dies. The place *where we stand* is holy ground, is equivalent to *This* place is holy ground. But we shall include under the phrase all clauses that begin with a relative, though some relative clauses are not adjectival, because a division of all into defining clauses on the one hand, and non-defining or commenting on the other, is more easily intelligible than the division into adjectival and non-adjectival. This distinction is more fully gone into in the chapter on Syntax, where it is suggested that *that*, when possible, is the appropriate relative for defining, and *which* for non-defining clauses. That, however, is a debatable point, and quite apart from the question of stopping that arises here. Examples of the two types are:

(Defining) The river that (which) runs through London is turbid.

(Commenting) The Thames, which runs through London, is turbid.

It will be seen that in the first the relative clause is an answer to the imaginary question, 'Which river?'; that is, it defines the noun to which it belongs. In the second, such a question as 'Which Thames?' is hardly conceivable; the relative clause gives us a piece of extra and non-essential information, an independent comment. The two types are not always so easily distinguished as in these examples constructed for the purpose. What we wish here to say is that it would contribute much to clearness of style if writers would always make up their minds whether they intend a definition or a comment, and would invariably use no commas with a defining clause, and two commas with a non-defining. All the examples that

follow are in our opinion wrong. The first three are of defining
relative clauses wrongly preceded by commas; the second three
of commenting relative clauses wrongly not preceded by commas.
The last of all there may be a doubt about. If the long clause
beginning with *which* is intended merely to show how great
the weariness is, and *which* is practically equivalent to *so great
that*, it may be called a defining clause, and the omission of the
comma is right. But if the *which* really acts as a mere connexion
to introduce a new fact that the correspondent wishes to record,
the clause is non-defining, and the comma ought according
to our rule to be inserted before it.

The man, *who* thinketh in his heart and hath the power straightway
(very straightway) to go and do it, is not so common in any country.—
CROCKETT.

Now everyone must do after his kind, be he asp or angel, and these
must. The question, *which* a wise man and a student of modern history
will ask, is, what that kind is.—EMERSON.

Those, *who* are urging with most ardour what are called the greatest
benefits of mankind, are narrow, self-pleasing, conceited men.—
EMERSON.

A reminder is being sent to all absent members of the Nationalist
party that their attendance at Westminster is urgently required next
week *when* the Budget will be taken on Monday.—*Times*.

The Marshall Islands will pass from the control of the Jaluit Company under that of the German colonial authorities *who* will bear the
cost of administration and will therefore collect all taxes.—*Times*.

The causes of this popularity are, no doubt, in part, the extreme
simplicity of the reasoning on which the theory rests, in part its
extreme plausibility, in part, perhaps, the nature of the result *which* is
commonly thought to be speculatively interesting without being
practically inconvenient.—BALFOUR.

Naval critics . . . are showing signs of weariness *which* even the
reported appearance of Admiral Nebogatoff in the Malacca Strait is
unable to remove.—*Times*.

4. The adverb, adverbial phrase, and adverbial clause.

In writing of substantival and adjectival clauses, our appeal
was for more logical precision than is usual. We said that
the comma habitual before substantival clauses was in most
cases unjustifiable, and should be omitted even at the cost

of occasional slight discomfort. We said that with one division of adjectival, or rather relative clauses, commas should always be used, and with another they should always be omitted. With the adverbial clauses, phrases, and words, on the other hand, our appeal is on the whole for less precision; we recommend that less precision should be aimed at, at least, though more attained, than at present. Certain kinds of laxity here are not merely venial, but laudable: certain other kinds are damning evidence of carelessness or bad taste or bad education. It is not here a mere matter of choosing between one right and one wrong way; there are many degrees.

Now is an adverb; *in the house* is usually an adverbial phrase; *if I know it* is an adverbial clause. Logic and grammar never prohibit the separating of any such expressions from the rest of their sentence—by two commas if they stand in the middle of it, by one if they begin or end it. But use of the commas tends, especially with a single word, but also with a phrase or clause, though in inverse proportion to its length, to modify the meaning. *I cannot do it now* means no more than it says: *I cannot do it, now* conveys a further assurance that the speaker would have been delighted to do it yesterday or will be quite willing tomorrow. This distinction, generally recognized with the single word, applies also to clauses; and writers of judgement should take the fullest freedom in such matters, allowing no superstition about 'subordinate clauses' to force upon them commas that they feel to be needless, but inclining always when in doubt to spare readers the jerkiness of overstopping. It is a question for rhetoric alone, not for logic, so long as the proper allowance of commas, if any, is given; what the proper allowance is, has been explained a few lines back. We need not waste time on exemplifying this simple principle; there is so far no real laxity; the writer is simply free.

Laxity comes in when we choose, guided by nothing more authoritative than euphony, to stop an adverbial phrase or adverbial clause, but not to stop it at both ends, though it stands in the middle of its sentence. This is an unmistakable offence against logic, and lays one open to the condemnation of examiners and precisians. But the point we wish to make is that in a very large class of sentences the injury to meaning is so infinitesimal, and the benefit to sound so considerable, that we do well to offend. The class is so large that only one example need be given:

But with their triumph over the revolt, Cranmer and his colleagues advanced yet more boldly.—J. R. GREEN.

The adverbial phrase is *with their triumph over the revolt*. *But* does not belong to it, but to the whole sentence. The writer has no defence whatever as against the logician; nevertheless, his reader will be grateful to him. The familiar intrusion of a comma after initial *And* and *For* where there is no intervening clause to justify it, of which we gave examples when we spoke of overstopping, comes probably by false analogy from the unpleasant pause that rigid punctuation has made common in sentences of this type.

Laxity once introduced, however, has to be carefully kept within bounds. It may be first laid down absolutely that when an adverbial clause is to be stopped, but incompletely stopped, the omitted stop must always be the one at the beginning, and never the one at the end. Transgression of this is quite intolerable; we shall give several instances at the end of the section to impress the fact. But it is also true that even the omission of the beginning comma looks more and more slovenly the further we get from the type of our above cited sentence. The quotations immediately following are arranged from the less to the more slovenly.

His health gave way, and *at the age of fifty-six*, he died prematurely in harness at Quetta.—*Times*.

If mankind was in the condition of believing nothing, and *without a bias in any particular direction*, was merely on the look-out for some legitimate creed, it would not, I conceive, be possible . . . .—BALFOUR.

The party *then*, consisted of a man and his wife, of his mother-in-law and his sister.—F. M. CRAWFORD.

These men *in their honorary capacity*, already have sufficient work to perform.—*Guernsey Evening Press*.

It will be observed that in the sentence from Mr. Balfour the chief objection to omitting the comma between *and* and *without* is that we are taken off on a false scent, it being natural at first to suppose that we are to supply *was* again; this can only happen when we are in the middle of a sentence, and not at the beginning as in the pattern Cranmer sentence.

The gross negligence or ignorance betrayed by giving the first and omitting the second comma will be convincingly shown by this array of sentences from authors of all degrees.

It is not strange that the sentiment of loyalty should, *from the day of his accession* have begun to revive.—MACAULAY.

Was it possible that having loved she should not so rejoice, or that, *rejoicing* she should not be proud of her love?—TROLLOPE.

I venture to suggest that, *had Lord Hugh himself been better informed in the matter* he would scarcely have placed himself . . .—*Times.*

The necessary consequence being that the law, *to uphold the restraints of which such unusual devices are employed* is in practice destitute of the customary sanctions.—*Times.*

The view held . . . is that, *owing to the constant absence of the Commander-in-Chief on tour* it is necessary that . . .—*Times.*

The master of the house, to whom, *as in duty bound* I communicated my intention . . .—BORROW.

After this victory, Hunyadi, *with his army* entered Belgrade, to the great joy of the Magyars.—BORROW.

M. Kossuth declares that, *until the King calls on the majority to take office with its own programme* chaos will prevail.—*Times.*

A love-affair, *to be conducted with spirit and enterprise* should always bristle with opposition and difficulty.—CORELLI.

And that she should force me, *by the magic of her pen* to mentally acknowledge . . ., albeit with wrath and shame, my own inferiority!—CORELLI.

She is a hard-working woman dependant on her literary success for a livelihood, and you, *rolling in wealth* do your best to deprive her of the means of existence.—CORELLI.

Although three trainings of the local militia have been conducted under the new regime, Alderney, *despite the fact that it is a portion of the same military command* has not as yet been affected.—*Guernsey Evening Press.*

5. Parenthesis.

In one sense, everything that is adverbial is parenthetic:

it can be inserted or removed, that is, without damaging the grammar, though not always without damaging the meaning, of the sentence. But the adverbial parenthesis, when once inserted, forms a part of the sentence; we have sufficiently dealt with the stops it requires in the last section; the use of commas emphasizes its parenthetic character, and is therefore sometimes desirable, sometimes not; no more need be said about it.

Another kind of parenthesis is that whose meaning practically governs the sentence in the middle of which it is nevertheless inserted as an alien element that does not coalesce in grammar with the rest. The type is—But, you will say, Caesar is not an aristocrat. This kind is important for our purpose because of the muddles often made, chiefly by careless punctuation, between the real parenthesis and words that give the same meaning, but are not, like it, grammatically separable. We shall start with an indisputable example of this muddle:

Where, do you imagine, she would lay it?—MEREDITH.

These commas cannot possibly indicate anything but parenthesis; but, if the comma'd words were really a parenthesis, we ought to have *would she* instead of *she would*. The four sentences that now follow are all of one pattern. The bad stopping is probably due to this same confusion between the parenthetic and the non-parenthetic. But it is possible that in each the two commas are independent, the first being one of those that are half rhetorical and half caused by false analogy, which have been mentioned as common after initial *And* and *For*; and the second being the comma wrongly used, as we have maintained, before substantival *that*-clauses.

Whence, it would appear, that he considers that all deliverances of consciousness are original judgments.—BALFOUR.

Hence, he reflected, that if he could but use his literary instinct to feed some commercial undertaking, he might gain a considerable . . .—HUTTON.

But, depend upon it, that no Eastern difficulty needs our intervention so seriously as . . .—HUXLEY.

And yet, it has been often said, that the party issues were hopelessly confused.—L. STEPHEN.

A less familiar form of this mistake, and one not likely to occur except in good writers, since inferior ones seldom attempt the construction that leads to it, is sometimes found when a subordinating conjunction is placed late in its clause, after the object or other member. In the Thackeray sentence, it will be observed that the first comma would be right (1) if *them* had stood after *discovered* instead of where it does, (2) if *them* had been omitted, and *any* had served as the common object to both verbs.

And to things of great dimensions, if we annex an adventitious idea of terror, they become without comparison greater.—BURKE.

Any of which peccadilloes, if Miss Sharp discovered, she did not tell them to Lady Crawley.—THACKERAY.

6. The misplaced comma.

Some authors would seem to have an occasional feeling that here or hereabouts is the place for a comma, just as in handwriting some persons are well content if they get a dot in somewhere within measurable distance of its *i*. The dot is generally over the right word at any rate, and the comma is seldom more than one word off its true place.

All true science begins with empiricism—though all true science is such exactly, in so far as it strives to pass out of the empirical stage.—HUXLEY.

Exactly qualifies and belongs to *in so far*, &c., not *such*. The comma should be before it.

This, they for the most part, throw away as worthless.—CORELLI.

For the most part, alone, is the adverbial parenthesis.

But this fault occurs, perhaps nine times out of ten, in combination with the *that*-clause comma so often mentioned. It may be said, when our instances have been looked into, that in each of them, apart from the *that*-clause comma, which is recognized by many authorities, there is merely the licence that we have ourselves allowed, omission of the first, without omission of the last, comma of an adverbial parenthesis.

But we must point out that Huxley, Green, and Mr Balfour, man of science, historian, and philosopher, all belong to that dignified class of writers which is supposed to, and in most respects does, insist on full logical stopping; they, in view of their general practice, are not entitled to our slovenly and merely literary licences.

And the second is, that for the purpose of attaining culture, an exclusively scientific education is at least as effectual as . . .—HUXLEY.

But the full discussion which followed over the various claims showed, that while exacting to the full what he believed to be his right, Edward desired to do justice to the country.—J. R. GREEN.

The one difference between these gilds in country and town was, that in the latter case, from their close local neighbourhood, they tended to coalesce.—J. R. GREEN.

It follows directly from this definition, that however restricted the range of possible knowledge may be, philosophy can never be excluded from it.—BALFOUR.

But the difficulty here, as it seems to me, is, that if you start from your idea of evolution, these assumptions are . . .—BALFOUR.

He begged me to give over all unlawful pursuits, saying, that if persisted in, they were sure of bringing a person to destruction.—BORROW.

7. Enumeration.

This name, liberally interpreted, is meant to include several more or less distinct questions. They are difficult, and much debated by authorities on punctuation, but are of no great importance. We shall take the liberty of partly leaving them undecided, and partly giving arbitrary opinions; to argue them out would take more space than it is worth while to give. But it *is* worth while to draw attention to them, so that each writer may be aware that they exist, and at least be consistent with himself. Typical sentences (from Beadnell) are:

a. Industry, honesty, and temperance, are essential to happiness.—B.

b. Let us freely drink in the soul of love and beauty and wisdom, from all nature and art and history.—B.

c. Plain honest truth wants no colouring.—B.

d. Many states are in alliance with, and under the protection of France.—B.

Common variants for (*a*) are (1) Industry, honesty and temperance are essential . . . (2) Industry, honesty and temperance,
are essential . . . (3) Industry, honesty, and temperance are
essential . . . We unhesitatingly recommend the original
and fully stopped form, which should be used irrespective of
style, and not be interfered with by rhetorical considerations;
it is the only one to which there is never any objection. Of
the examples that follow, the first conforms to the correct
type, but no serious harm would be done if it did not. The
second also conforms; and, if this had followed variant (1) or
(2), here indistinguishable, we should have been in danger of
supposing that Education and Police were one department
instead of two. The third, having no comma after *interests*,
follows variant (3), and, as it happens, with no bad effect on
the meaning. All three variants, however, may under different
conditions produce ambiguity or worse.

But those that remain, the women, the youths, the children, and the
elders, work all the harder.—*Times*.

Japanese advisers are now attached to the departments of the
Household, War, Finance, Education, and Police.—*Times*.

An American, whose patience, tact, and ability in reconciling conflicting interests have won the praise of all nationalities.—*Times*.

Sometimes enumerations are arranged in pairs; it is then
most unpleasant to have the comma after the last pair omitted,
as in:

The orange and the lemon, the olive and the walnut elbow each other
for a footing in the fat dark earth.—F. M. CRAWFORD.

There is a bastard form of enumeration against which
warning is seriously needed. It is viewed as, but is not really,
a legitimate case of type (*a*); and a quite unnecessary objection
to the repetition of *and* no doubt supplies the motive. Examples
are:

He kept manœuvring upon Neipperg, who counter-manœuvred with
vigilance, good judgment, and would not come to action.—CARLYLE.

Moltke had recruited, trained, and knew by heart all the men under
him.—*Times*.

Hence loss of time, of money, and sore trial of patience.—R. G. WHITE.

The principle is this: in an enumeration given by means of a comma or commas, the last comma being replaced by or combined with *and*—our type (*a*), that is—, there must not be anything that is common to two members (as here, *counter-manœuvred with, had, loss*) without being common to all. We may say, Moltke had recruited and trained and knew, Moltke had recruited, had trained, and knew, or, Moltke had recruited, trained, and known; but we must not say what the *Times* says. The third sentence may run, Loss of time and money, and sore trial, or, Loss of time, of money, and of patience; but not as it does.

So much for type (*a*). Type (*b*) can be very shortly disposed of. It differs in that the conjunction (*and, or, nor*, &c.) is expressed every time, instead of being represented except in the last place by a comma. It is logically quite unnecessary, but rhetorically quite allowable, to use commas as well as conjunctions. The only caution needed is that, if commas are used at all, and if the enumeration does not end the sentence, and is not concluded by a stronger stop, a comma must be inserted after the last member as well as after the others. In the type sentence, which contains two enumerations, it would be legitimate to use commas as well as *and*s with one set and not with the other, if it were desired either to avoid monotony or to give one list special emphasis. The three examples now to be added transgress the rule about the final comma. We arrange them from bad to worse; in the last of them, the apparently needless though not necessarily wrong comma after *fall* suggests that the writer has really felt a comma to be wanting to the enumeration, but has taken a bad shot with it, as in the examples of section 6 on the misplaced comma.

Neither the Court, nor society, nor Parliament, nor the older men in the Army have yet recognized the fundamental truth that . . .—*Times*.

A subordinate whose past conduct in the post he fills, and whose known political sympathies make him wholly unfitted, however loyal his intentions may be, to give that . . .—*Times*.

But there are uninstructed ears on whom the constant abuse, and imputation of low motives may fall, with a mischievous and misleading effect.—*Times*.

Of type (*c*) the characteristic is that we have two or more adjectives attached to a following noun; are there to be commas between the adjectives, or not? The rule usually given is that there should be, unless the last adjective is more intimately connected with the noun, so that the earlier one qualifies, not the noun, but the last adjective and the noun together; it will be noticed that we strictly have no enumeration then at all. This is sometimes useful; and so is the more practical and less theoretic direction to ask whether *and* could be inserted, and if so use the comma, but not otherwise. These both sound sufficient in the abstract. But that there are doubts left in practice is shown by the type sentence, which Beadnell gives as correct, though either test would rather require the comma. He gives also as correct, Can flattery soothe the dull, cold ear of death?— which is not very clearly distinguishable from the other. Our advice is to use these tests when in doubt, but with a leaning to the omission of the comma. If it happens that a comma of this particular class is the only stop in a sentence, it has a false appearance of dividing the sentence into two parts that is very unpleasant, and may make the reader go through it twice to make sure that all is right—an inconvenience that should by all means be spared him.

Type (*d*) is one in which the final word or phrase of a sentence has two previous expressions standing in the same grammatical relation to it, but their ending with different prepositions, or the fact that one is to be substituted for the other, or the length of the expressions, or some other cause, obscures this identity of relation. Add to the type sentence the following:

His eloquence was the main, one might almost say the sole, source of his influence.—BRYCE.

To dazzle people more, he learned or pretended to learn, the Spanish language.—BAGEHOT.

. . . apart from philosophical and sometimes from theological, theories.—BALFOUR.

The rules we lay down are: (1) If possible use no stops at all. (2) Never use the second comma and omit the first. (3) Even when the first is necessary, the second may often be dispensed with. (4) Both commas may be necessary if the phrases are long.

We should correct all the examples, including the type: the type under rule (1); the Bryce (which is strictly correct) under rule (3); the Bagehot under rules (2) and (1); and the Balfour under rules (2) and (3); the last two are clearly wrong. The four would then stand as follows:

> Many states are in alliance with and under the protection of France.
> His eloquence was the main, one might almost say the sole source of his influence.
> To dazzle people more, he learned or pretended to learn the Spanish language.
> . . . apart from philosophical, and sometimes from theological theories.

Learners will be inclined to say: all this is very indefinite; do give us a clear rule that will apply to all cases. Such was the view with which, on a matter of even greater importance than punctuation, Procrustes identified himself; but it brought him to a bad end. The clear rule, Use all logical commas, would give us:

> He was born, in, or near, London, on December 24th, 1900.

No one would write this who was not suffering from bad hypertrophy of the grammatical conscience. The clear rule, Use no commas in this sort of enumeration, would give:

> If I have the queer ways you accuse me of, that is because but I should have thought a man of your perspicacity might have been expected to see that it was also why I live in a hermitage all by myself.

No one would write this without both commas (after *because* and *why*) who was not deeply committed to an anti-comma crusade. Between the two extremes lie cases calling for various treatment; the ruling principle should be freedom within certain limits.

8. The comma between independent sentences.

Among the signs that more particularly betray the uneducated writer is inability to see when a comma is not a sufficient stop. Unfortunately little more can be done than to warn beginners that any serious slip here is much worse than they will probably suppose, and recommend them to observe the practice of good writers.

It is roughly true that grammatically independent sentences should be parted by at least a semicolon; but in the first place there are very large exceptions to this; and secondly, the writer who really knows a grammatically independent sentence when he sees it is hardly in need of instruction; this must be our excuse for entering here into what may be thought too elementary an explanation. Let us take the second point first; it may be of some assistance to remark that a sentence joined to the previous one by a coordinating conjunction is grammatically independent, as well as one not joined to it at all. But the difference between a coordinating and a subordinating conjunction is itself in English rather fine. Every one can see that 'I will not try; it is dangerous' is two independent sentences—independent in grammar, though not in thought. But it is a harder saying that 'I will not try, for it is dangerous' is also two sentences, while 'I will not try, because it is dangerous' is one only. The reason is that *for* coordinates, and *because* subordinates; instead of giving lists, which would probably be incomplete, of the two kinds of conjunction, we mention that a subordinating conjunction may be known from the other kind by its being possible to place it and its clause before the previous sentence instead of after, without destroying the sense: we can say 'Because it is dangerous, I will not try', but not 'For it is dangerous, I will not try'. This test cannot always be applied in complicated sentences; simple ones must be constructed for testing the conjunction in question.

Assuming that it is now understood (1) what a subordinating and what a coordinating conjunction is, (2) that a member joined on by no more than a coordinating conjunction is a grammatically independent sentence, or simply a sentence in the proper meaning of the word, and not a subordinate clause, we return to the first point. This was that, though independent sentences are regularly parted by at least a semicolon, there are large exceptions to the rule. These we shall only be able to indicate very loosely. There are three conditions that may favour the reduction of the semicolon to a comma: (1) Those coordinating conjunctions which are most common tend in the order of their commonness to be humble, and to recognize a comma as sufficient for their dignity. The order may perhaps be given as: *and, or, but, so, nor, for*; conjunctions less common than these should scarcely ever be used with less than a semicolon; and many good writers would refuse to put a mere comma before *for*. (2) Shortness and lightness of the sentence joined on helps to lessen the need for a heavy stop. (3) Intimate connexion in thought with the preceding sentence has the same effect. Before giving our examples, which are all of undesirable commas, we point out that in the first two there are independent signs of the writers' being uneducated; and such signs will often be discoverable. It will be clear from what we have said why the others are bad—except perhaps the third; it is particularly disagreeable to have two successive independent sentences tagged on with commas, as those beginning with *nor* and *for* are in that example.

No peace at night he enjoys, *for* he lays awake.—*Guernsey Advertiser*.

Now accepted, nominal Christendom believes this, and strives to attain unto it, *then* why the inconsistency of creed and deed?—*Daily Telegraph*.

But who is responsible to Government for the efficiency of the Army? The Commander-in-Chief and no one else, *nor* has anyone questioned the fact, *for* it is patent.—*Times*.

But even on this theory the formula above stated holds good, *for* such systems, so far from being self-contained (as it were) and sufficient evidence for themselves, are really . . .—BALFOUR.

Some banks on the Nevsky Prospect are having iron shutters fitted, *otherwise* there is nothing apparently to justify General Trepoff's proclamation.—*Times*.

Everybody knows where his own shoe pinches, and, if people find drawbacks in the places they inhabit, they must also find advantages, *otherwise* they would not be there.—*Times*.

We have suffered many things at the hands of the Russian Navy during the war, *nevertheless* the news that Admiral Rozhdestvensky . . . will send a thrill of admiration . . .—*Times*.

, I think that on the whole we may be thankful for the architectural merits of the Gaiety block, it has breadth and dignity of design and groups well on the angular site.—*Times*.

It will not be irrelevant to add here, though the point has been touched upon in Under-stopping, that though a light *and*-clause may be introduced by no more than a comma, it does not follow that it need not be separated by any stop at all, as in:

When the Motor Cars Act was before the House it was suggested that these authorities should be given the right to make recommendations to the central authorities and that right was conceded.—*Times*.

9. The semicolon between subordinate members.

Just as the tiro will be safer if he avoids commas before independent sentences, so he will generally be wise not to use a semicolon before a mere subordinate member. We have explained, indeed, that it is sometimes quite legitimate for rhetorical reasons, and is under certain circumstances almost required by proportion. This is when the sentence contains commas doing less important work than the one about which the question arises. But the tiro's true way out of the difficulty is to simplify his sentences so that they do not need such differentiation. Even skilful writers, as the following two quotations will show, sometimes come to grief over this.

One view called me to another; one hill to its fellow, half across the country, and since I could answer at no more trouble than the snapping forward of a lever, I let the country flow under my wheels.—KIPLING.

Nay, do not the elements of all human virtues and all human vices; the passions at once of a Borgia and of a Luther, lie written, in stronger or fainter lines, in the consciousness of every individual bosom?—CARLYLE.

In the first of these the second comma and the semicolon clearly ought to change places. In the second it looks as if Carlyle had thought it dull to have so many commas about; but the remedy was much worse than dullness. Avoidance of what a correspondent supposes to be dull, but what would in fact be natural and right, accounts also for the following piece of vicarious rhetoric; the writer is not nearly so excited, it may be suspected, as his semicolons would make him out. The ordinary sensible man would have (1) used commas, and (2) either omitted the third and fourth *denies* (reminding us of Zola's famous *j'accuse*, not vicarious, and on an adequate occasion), or else inserted an *and* before the last repetition.

Mr. Loomis denies all three categorically. He denies that the Asphalt Company paid him £2,000 or any other sum; denies that he purchased a claim against the Venezuelan Government and then used his influence when Minister at Caracas to collect the claim; denies that he agreed with Mr. Meyers or anybody else to use his influence for money.—*Times*.

A particular use of the semicolon experimented upon by Dickens may be here mentioned. When he had occasion to interrupt a sentence with a parenthesis of some length, he would enclose this not between commas, brackets, or dashes (see DASHES, *m*.), but between a pair of semicolons:

Such was the account; rapidly furnished in whispers, and interrupted, brief as it was, by many false alarms of Mr. Pecksniff's return; which Martin received of his godfather's decline.—DICKENS.

The double dash would clearly have been less upsetting to the reader.

10. The exclamation-mark when there is no exclamation.

My friend! this conduct amazes me!—B.

We must differ altogether from Beadnell's rule that 'This point is used to denote any sudden emotion of the mind, whether of joy, grief, surprise, fear, or any other sensation'— at least as it is exemplified in his first instance, given above. The exclamation-mark after *friend* is justifiable, not the other. The stop should be used, with one exception, only after real exclamations. Real exclamations include (1) the words recog-

nized as interjections, as *alas*, (2) fragmentary expressions that
are not complete sentences, as *My friend* in the example, and
(3) complete statements that contain an exclamatory word, as:

> What a piece of work is man!—B.

The exception mentioned above is this: when the writer
wishes to express his own incredulity or other feeling about
what is not his own statement, but practically a quotation
from some one else, he is at liberty to do it with a mark of
exclamation; in the following example, the epitaph writer
expresses either his wonder or his incredulity about what
Fame says.

> Entomb'd within this vault a lawyer lies
> Who, Fame assureth us, was just and wise!—B.

The exclamation-mark is a neat and concise sneer at the legal
profession.

Outside these narrow limits the exclamation-mark must not
be used. We shall quote a very instructive saying of Landor's:
'I read warily; and whenever I find the writings of a lady,
the first thing I do is to cast my eye along her pages, to see
whether I am likely to be annoyed by the traps and spring-guns
of interjections; and if I happen to espy them I do not leap the
paling'. To this we add that when the exclamation-mark is
used after mere statements it deserves the name, by which it is
sometimes called, mark of admiration; we feel that the writer
is indeed lost in admiration of his own wit or impressiveness.
But this use is mainly confined to lower-class authors; when a
grave historian stoops to it, he gives us quite a different sort of
shock from what he designed.

> The unfortunate commander was in the situation of some bold,
> high-mettled cavalier, rushing to battle on a warhorse whose tottering
> joints threaten to give way at every step, and leave his rider to the
> mercy of his enemies!—PRESCOTT.

> The road now struck into the heart of a mountain region, where
> woods, precipices, and ravines were mingled together in a sort of
> chaotic confusion, with here and there a green and sheltered valley,
> glittering like an island of verdure amidst the wild breakers of a troubled
> ocean!—PRESCOTT.

11. Confusion between question and exclamation.

Fortunate man!—who would not envy you! Love!—who would, who could exist without it—save me!—CORELLI.

What wonder that the most docile of Russians should be crying out 'how long'!—*Times*.

We have started with three indisputable instances of the exclamation-mark used for the question-mark. It is worth notice that the correct stopping for the end of the second quotation (though such accuracy is seldom attempted) would be:—long?'? To have fused two questions into an exclamation is an achievement. But these are mere indefensible blunders, not needing to be thought twice about, such as author and compositor incline to put off each on the other's shoulders.

The case is not always so clear. In the six sentences lettered for reference, *a-d* have the wrong stop; in *e* the stop implied by *he exclaims* is also wrong; in *f*, though the stop is right assuming that the form of the sentence is what was really meant, we venture to question this point, as we do also in some of the earlier sentences. Any one who agrees with the details of this summary can save himself the trouble of reading the subsequent discussion.

a. In that interval what had I not lost!—LAMB.

b. And what will not the discontinuance cost me!—RICHARDSON.

c. A streak of blue below the hanging alders is certainly a characteristic introduction to the kingfisher. How many people first see him so?—*Times*.

d. Does the reading of history make us fatalists? What courage does not the opposite opinion show!—EMERSON.

e. What economy of life and money, he exclaims, would not have been spared the empire of the Tsars had it not rendered war certain by devoting itself so largely to the works of peace.—*Times*.

f. How many, who think no otherwise than the young painter, have we not heard disbursing secondhand hyperboles?—STEVENSON.

It will be noticed that in all these sentences except *c* there is a negative, which puts them, except *f*, wrong; while in *c* it is the absence of the negative that makes the question wrong. It will be simplest to start with *c*. The writer clearly means to let us know that many people see the kingfisher first as a blue streak. He might give this simply so, as a statement. He might (artificially) give it as an exclamation—*How many first see him so!* Or he might (very artificially) give it as a question—*How many do not first see him so?*—a 'rhetorical question' in which *How many* interrogative is understood to be equivalent to *Few* positive. He has rejected the simple statement; vaulting ambition has o'erleapt, and he has ended in a confusion between the two artificial ways of saying the thing, taking the words of the possible exclamation and the stop of the possible question. In *a, b, d,* and implicitly in *e,* we have the converse arrangement, or derangement. But as a little more clear thinking is required for them, we point out that the origin of the confusion (though the careless printing of fifty or a hundred years ago no doubt helped to establish it) lies in the identity between the words used for questions and for exclamations. It will be enough to suggest the process that accounts for *a*; the ambiguity is easily got rid of by inserting a noun with *what.*

> *Question*: What amount had I lost?
> *Exclamation*: What an amount I had lost!

That is the first stage; the resemblance is next increased by inverting subject and verb in the exclamation, which is both natural enough in that kind of sentence, and particularly easy after *In that interval.* So we get

> *Question*: In that interval, what (amount) had I lost?
> *Exclamation*: In that interval, what (an amount) had I lost!

The words, when the bracketed part of each sentence is left out, are now the same; but the question is of course incapable of giving the required meaning. The writer, seeing this, but deceived by the order of words into thinking the exclamation a question, tries to mend it by inserting *not*; *what . . . not,* in rhetorical questions, being equivalent to *everything.* At this stage some writers stick, as Stevenson in *f.* Others try to make a right out of two wrongs by restoring to the quondam exclamation, which has been wrongly converted with the help of *not* into a question, the exclamation-mark to which it has after conversion no right. Such is the genesis of *a*, *b*, *d*. The proper method, when the simple statement is rejected, as it often reasonably may be, is to use the exclamation, not the Stevensonian question,[1] to give the exclamation its right mark, and not to insert the illogical negative.

12. Internal question and exclamation marks.

By this name we do not mean that insertion of a bracketed stop of which we shall nevertheless give one example. That is indeed a confession of weakness and infallible sign of the prentice hand, and further examples will be found in *Airs and Graces*, *miscellaneous*; but it is outside grammar, with which these sections are concerned.

Under these circumstances, it would be interesting to ascertain the exact position of landlords whose tenants decline to pay rent, and whose only asset (!) from their property is the income-tax now claimed. —*Times*.

What is meant is the ugly stop in the middle of a sentence, unbracketed and undefended by quotation-marks, of which examples follow. To novelists, as in the first example, it may be necessary for the purpose of avoiding the nuisance of perpetual quotation-marks. But elsewhere it should be got rid of by use of the indirect question or otherwise. Excessive indulgence in direct questions or exclamations where there is no need for them whatever is one of the sensational tendencies of modern newspapers.

Why be scheming? Victor asked.—MEREDITH.
What will Japan do? is thought the most pressing question of all.— *Times*. (What Japan will do is thought, &c.)
What next? is the next question which the American Press discusses. —*Times*. ('What next?' is, &c. Or, What will come next is, &c.)

Amusing efforts are shown below at escaping the ugliness

---

[1] Of course, however, the rhetorical question is often not, as here, the result of a confusion, nor to be described as 'very artificial'. E.g., *What would I not give to be there? To what subterfuge has he not resorted?*

of the internal question-mark. Observe that the third quotation has a worse blunder, since we have here two independent sentences.

Can it be that the Government will still persist in continuing the now hopeless struggle is the question on every lip?—*Times*.

Men are disenchanted.. They have got what they wanted in the days of their youth, yet what of it, they ask?—MORLEY.

Yet we remember seeing l'Abbé Constantin some sixteen years ago or more at the Royalty, with that fine old actor Lafontaine in the principal part, and seeing it with lively interest. Was it distinctly 'dates', for nothing wears so badly as the namby-pamby?—*Times*.

13. The unaccountable comma.

We shall now conclude these grammatical sections with a single example of those commas about which it is only possible to say that they are repugnant to grammar. It is as difficult to decide what principle they offend against as what impulse can possibly have dictated them. They are commonest in the least educated writers of all; and, next to these, in the men of science whose overpowering conscientiousness has made the mechanical putting in of commas so habitual that it perhaps becomes with them a sort of reflex action, and does itself at wrong moments without their volition.

The Rector, lineal representative of the ancient monarchs of the University, though now, little more than a 'king of shreds and patches'. —HUXLEY.

THE COLON

It was said in the general remarks at the beginning of this chapter that the systematic use of the colon as one of the series (,), (;), (:), (.), had died out with the decay of formal periods. Many people continue to use it, but few, if we can trust our observation, with any nice regard to its value. Some think it a prettier or more impressive stop than the semicolon, and use it instead of that; some like variety, and use the two indifferently, or resort to one when they are tired of the other. As the abandonment of periodic arrangement really makes the colon useless, it would be well (though of course any one who still writes in formal periods should retain his rights over it) if ordinary writers would give it up altogether except in the special uses, independent of its quantitative value, to which it is being more and more applied by common consent. These are (1) between two sentences that are in clear antithesis, but not connected by an adversative conjunction; (2) introducing a short quotation; (3) introducing a list; (4) introducing a sentence that comes as fulfilment of a promise expressed or implied in the previous sentence; (5) introducing an explanation or proof that is not connected with the previous sentence by *for* or the like. Examples are:

(1) Man proposes: God disposes.
(2) Always remember the ancient maxim: Know thyself.—B.
(3) Chief rivers: Thames, Severn, Humber . . .
(4) Some things we can, and others we cannot do: we can walk, but we cannot fly.—BIGELOW.
(5) Rebuke thy son in private: public rebuke hardens the heart.—B.

In the following clear case of antithesis a colon would have been more according to modern usage than the semicolon.

As apart from our requirements Mr. Arnold-Forster's schemes have many merits; in relation to them they have very few.—*Times*.

It now only remains, before leaving actual stops for the dash, hyphen, quotation mark, and bracket, to comment on a few stray cases of ambiguity, false scent, and ill-judged stopping. We have not hunted up, and shall not manufacture, any of the patent absurdities that are amusing but unprofitable. The sort of ambiguity that most needs guarding against is that which allows a sleepy reader to take the words wrong when the omission or insertion of a stop would have saved him.

The chief agitators of the League, who have—not unnaturally considering the favours showered upon them in the past—a high sense of their own importance . . .—*Times*.

With no comma after *unnaturally* the first thought is that the agitators not unnaturally consider; second thoughts put it right; but second thoughts should never be expected from a reader.

Simultaneously extensive reclamation of land and harbour improvements are in progress at Chemulpo and Fusan.—*Times.*

With no comma after the first word, the sleepy reader is set wondering what *simultaneously extensive* means, and whether it is journalese for *equally extensive.*

But Anne and I did, for we had played there all our lives—at least, all the years we had spent together and the rest do not count in the story. When Anne and I came together we began to live.—CROCKETT.

A comma after *together* would save us from adding the two sets of years to each other. In the next piece, on the other hand, the uncomfortable comma after *gold* is apparently meant to warn us quite unnecessarily that *here and there* belongs to the verb.

Flecks of straw-coloured gold, here and there lay upon it, where the sunshine touched the bent of last year.—CROCKETT.

After that, having once fallen off from their course, they at length succeeded in crossing the Aegean, and beating up in the teeth of the Etesian winds, only yesterday, seventy days out from Egypt, put in at the Piraeus.—S. T. IRWIN.

The omission of the comma between *and* and *beating* would ordinarily be quite legitimate. Here, it puts us off on a false scent, because it allows *beating* to seem parallel with *crossing* and object to *succeeded in*; we have to go back again when we get to the end, and work it out.

The French demurring to the conditions which the English commander offered, again commenced the action.—B.

The want of a comma between *French* and *demurring* makes us assume an absolute construction and expect another subject, of which we are disappointed.

The next two pairs of examples illustrate the effect of mere accidental position on stopping. This is one of the numberless small disturbing elements that make cast-iron rules impossible in punctuation.

I must leave you to discover what the answer is.
What the answer is, I must leave you to discover.

That is, a substantival clause out of its place is generally allowed the comma that all but the straitest sect of punctuators would refuse it in its place.

In the present dispute, therefore, the local politicians have had to choose between defence of the principle of authority and espousing the cause of the local police.—*Times*.

Of its forty-four commissioners however few actually took any part in its proceedings; and the powers of the Commission . . .—J. R. GREEN.

The half adverbs half conjunctions of which *therefore* and *however* are instances occupy usually the second place in the sentence. When there, it is of little importance whether they are stopped or not, though we have indicated our preference for no stops. But when it happens that they come later (or earlier), the commas are generally wanted. *Therefore* in the first of these sentences would be as uncomfortable if stripped as *however* actually is in the second.

DASHES

Moved beyond his wont by our English ill-treatment of the dash, Beadnell permits himself a wail as just as it is pathetic.

'The dash is frequently employed in a very capricious and arbitrary manner, as a substitute for all sorts of points, by writers whose thoughts, although, it may be, sometimes striking and profound, are thrown together without order or dependence; also by some others, who think that they thereby give prominence and emphasis to expressions which in themselves are very commonplace, and would, without this fictitious assistance, escape the observation of the reader, or be deemed by him hardly worthy of notice.'

It is all only too true; these are the realms of chaos, and the lord of them is Sterne, from whom modern writers of the purely literary kind have so many of their characteristics. Wishing for an example, we merely opened the first volume of *Tristram Shandy* at a venture, and 'thus the Anarch old With faltering speech and visage incomposed Answered':

—Observe, I determine nothing upon this.—My way is ever to point out to the curious, different tracts of investigation, to come at the first springs of the events I tell:—not with a pedantic fescue,—or in the decisive manner of Tacitus, who outwits himself and his reader;—but with the officious humility of a heart devoted to the assistance merely of the inquisitive;—to them I write,—and by them I shall be read,—if any such reading as this could be supposed to hold out so long,—to the very end of the world.—STERNE.

The modern newspaper writer who overdoes the use of dashes is seldom as incorrect as Sterne, but is perhaps more irritating:

There are also a great number of people—many of them not in the least tainted by militarism—who go further and who feel that a man in order to be a complete man—that is, one capable of protecting his life, his country, and his civil and political rights—should acquire as a boy and youth the elements of military training,—that is, should be given a physical training of a military character, including . . .—*Spectator.*

It must be added, however, that Beadnell himself helps to make things worse, by countenancing the strange printer's superstition that (,—) is beautiful to look upon, and (—,) ugly.

Under these circumstances we shall have to abandon our usual practice of attending only to common mistakes, and deal with the matter a little more systematically. We shall first catalogue, with examples, the chief uses of the dash; next state the debatable questions that arise; and end with the more definite misuses. It will be convenient to number all examples for reference; and, as many or most of the quotations contain some minor violation of what we consider the true principles, these will be corrected in brackets.

1. Chief common uses.

a. Adding to a phrase already used an explanation, example, or preferable substitute.

1. Nicholas Copernicus was instructed in that seminary where it is always happy when any one can be well taught,—the family circle.—B. (Omit the comma)

2. Anybody might be an accuser,—a personal enemy, an infamous person, a child, parent, brother, or sister.—LOWELL. (Omit the comma)

3. That the girls were really possessed seemed to Stoughton and his colleagues the most rational theory,—a theory in harmony with the rest of their creed.—LOWELL. (Omit the comma)

b. Inviting the reader to pause and collect his forces against the shock of an unexpected word that is to close the sentence.

It is generally, but not always, better to abstain from this device; the unexpected, if not drawn attention to, is often more effective because less theatrical.

4. To write imaginatively a man should have—imagination.—LOWELL.

We have talked about it for years; speeches have been made, and articles and even books written, printed, and published; dozens of schemes have been brought forward; and the upshot of it all is—nothing.—*Speaker*.

c. Assuring the reader that what is coming, even if not unexpected, is witty. Writers should be exceedingly sparing of this use; good wine needs no bush.

5. Misfortune in various forms had overtaken the country families, from high farming to a taste for the junior stage, and—the proprietors lived anywhere else except on their own proper estates.—CROCKETT.

d. Marking arrival at the principal sentence or the predicate after a subordinate clause or a subject that is long or compound.

6. As soon as the queen shall come to London, and the houses of Parliament shall be opened, and the speech from the throne be delivered,—then will begin the great struggle of the contending factions.—B.

e. Resuming after a parenthesis or long phrase, generally with repetition of some previous words in danger of being forgotten.

7. It is now idle to attempt to hide the fact that never was the Russian lack of science, of the modern spirit, or, to speak frankly, of intelligence—never was the absence of training or of enthusiasm which retards the efforts of the whole Empire displayed in a more melancholy fashion than in the Sea of Japan.—*Times*. (Add a comma after *intelligence*)

f. Giving the air of an afterthought to a final comment that would spoil the balance of the sentence if preceded only by an ordinary stop. Justifiable when really wanted, that is, when it is important to keep the comment till the end; otherwise it is slightly insulting to the reader implying that he was not worth working out the sentence for before it was put down.

8. As they parted, she insisted on his giving the most solemn promises that he would not expose himself to danger—which was quite unnecessary.

g. Marking a change of speakers when quotation marks and 'he said', &c., are not used; or, in a single speech, a change of subject or person addressed.

9. Who created you?—God.—B.
10. . . . And lose the name of action.—Soft you now!
    The fair Ophelia!

h. With colon or other stop before a quotation.

11. Hear Milton:—How charming is divine Philosophy!
12. What says Bacon?—Revenge is a kind of wild justice.

i. Introducing a list.

13. The four greatest names in English literature are almost the first we come to,—Chaucer, Spenser, Shakespeare, and Milton.—B. (Omit the comma before the dash)

k. Confessing an anacoluthon, or substitution of a new construction for the one started with.

14. Then the eye of a child,—who can look unmoved into that well undefiled, in which heaven itself seems to be reflected?—BIGELOW. (Omit the comma)

l. Breaking off a sentence altogether.

15. Oh, how I wish—! But what is the use of wishing?

m. Doubled to serve the purpose of brackets. It gives a medium between the light comma parenthesis and the heavy bracket parenthesis. It also has the advantage over brackets that when the parenthesis ends only with the sentence the second dash need not be given; this advantage, however, may involve ambiguity, as will be shown.

16. In every well regulated community—such as that of England,— the laws own no superior.—B. (The comma should either be omitted or placed after instead of before the second dash)

These are a dozen distinct uses of more or less value or importance, to which others might no doubt be added; but they will suffice both to show that the dash is a hard-worked symbol, and to base our remarks upon.

2. Debatable questions.

There are several questions that must be answered before we can use the dash with confidence. First, is the dash to supersede stops at the place where it is inserted, or to be added to them? Secondly, what is its relation to the stops in the part of the sentence (or group of sentences) that follows it? does its authority, that is, extend to the end of the sentence or group, or where does it cease? Thirdly, assuming that it is or can be combined with stops, what is the right order as between the two?

Beadnell's answer to the first question is: *The dash does not dispense with the use of the ordinary points at the same time, when the grammatical construction of the sentence requires them.* But inasmuch as the dash implies some sort of break, irregular pause, or change of intention, it seems quite needless to insert the stop that would have been used if it had not been decided that a stop was inadequate. The dash is a confession that the stop will not do; then let the stop go. The reader, who is the person to be considered, generally neither knows nor cares to know how the sentence might, with inferior effect, have been written; he only feels that the stop is otiose, and that his author had better have been off with the old love before he was on with the new. There are exceptions to this: obviously in examples 9, 10, 11, 12, and 15, where the dash is at the end or beginning of a sentence; and perhaps also in sentences of which the reader can clearly foresee the grammatical development. In example 7, for instance, it is clear that a participle (*displayed* or another) is due after *never was* &c.; a comma after *intelligence* is therefore definitely expected. So in example 6 we are expecting either another continuation of *as soon as*, or the principal sentence, before either of which a comma is looked for. In examples 2 and 3, on the other hand, the sentence may for all we know be complete at the place where the dash stands, so that no expectation is disappointed by omitting the comma. The rule, then, should be that a dash is a substitute for any internal stop, and not an addition to it, except when, from the reader's point of view, a particular stop seemed inevitable.

It must be admitted that that conclusion is not very certain, and also that the matter is of no great importance, provided that the stops, if inserted, are the right ones. More certainty is possible about the combination of stops with the double dash, which we have not yet considered. The probable origin of the double dash will be touched upon when we come to the second question; but whatever its origin, it is now simply equivalent to a pair of brackets, except that it is slightly less conspicuous, and sometimes preferred on that account. Consequently, the same rule about stops will apply to both, and as there is no occasion to treat of brackets separately, it may here be stated for both. The use of a parenthesis being to insert, without damage to the rest of the sentence, something that is of theoretically minor importance, it is necessary that we should be able simply to remove the two dashes or brackets with everything enclosed by them, and after their removal find the sentence complete and rightly punctuated. Further, there is no reason for using inside the parenthesis any stop that has not an internal value; that is, no stop can possibly be needed just before the second dash except an exclamation or question mark, and none at all just after the first; but stops may be necessary to divide up the parenthesis itself if it is compound. Three examples follow, with the proper corrections in brackets:

17. Garinet cites the case of a girl near Amiens possessed by three demons,—Mimi, Zozo, and Crapoulet,—in 1816.—LOWELL. (Omit both commas; the first is indeed just possible, though not required, in the principal sentence; the last is absolutely meaningless in the parenthesis)

18. Its visions and its delights are too penetrating,—too living,—for any white-washed object or shallow fountain long to endure or to supply.—RUSKIN. (Omit both commas; this time the first is as impossible in the principal sentence as the second is meaningless in the parenthesis)

19. The second carries us on from 1625 to 1714—less than a century —yet the walls of the big hall in the Examination Schools are not only well covered . . .—*Times*. (Insert a comma, as necessary to the principal sentence, outside the dashes; whether before the first or after the last will be explained in our answer to the third question)

The second question is, how far the authority of the dash extends. There is no reason, in the nature of things, why we should not on the one hand be relieved of it by the next stop, or on the other be subject to it till the paragraph ends. The three following examples, which we shall correct in brackets by anticipation, but which we shall also assume not to be mere careless blunders, seem to go on the first hypothesis.

20. The Moral Nature, that Law of laws, whose revelations introduce greatness—yea, God himself, into the open soul, is not explored. —EMERSON. (Substitute a dash for the comma after *himself*. Here, however, Emerson expects us to terminate the authority at the right comma rather than at the first that comes, making things worse)

21. I . . . there complained of the common notions of the special virtues—justice, &c., as too vague to furnish exact determinations of the actions enjoined under them.—H. SIDGWICK. (Substitute a dash for the comma after *&c.*)

22. There are vicars and vicars, and of all sorts I love an innovating vicar—a piebald progressive professional reactionary, the least.—H. G. WELLS. (Substitute a dash for the comma after *reactionary*)

It needs no further demonstration, however, that commas are frequently used after a dash without putting an end to its influence; and if they are to be sometimes taken, nevertheless, as doing so, confusion is sure to result. Unless the author of the next example is blind to the danger that two neighbouring but independent dashes may be mistaken for a parenthetic pair, he must have assumed that the authority of a dash is terminated at any rate by a semicolon; that, if true, would obviate the danger.

23. It is a forlorn hope, however excellent the translation—and Mr. Hankin's could not be bettered; or however careful the playing—

and the playing at the Stage Society performance was meticulously
careful.—*Times*.   (Insert a dash between *bettered* and the semicolon,
which then need not be more than a comma)

But that it is not true will probably be admitted on the
strength of sentences like:

24. There may be differences of opinion on the degrees—no one
takes white for black: most people sometimes take blackish for black—,
but that is not fatal to my argument.

On the other hand, we doubt whether a full stop is ever
allowed to stand in the middle of a dash parenthesis, as it of
course may in a bracket parenthesis. The reason for the distinction is clear. When we have had a left-hand bracket we
know for certain that a right-hand one is due, full stops or no
full stops; but when we have had a dash, we very seldom know
for certain that it is one of a pair; and the appearance of a
full stop would be too severe a trial of our faith. It seems
natural to suppose that the double-dash parenthesis is thus
accounted for: the construction started with a single dash;
but as it was often necessary to revert to the main construction, the second dash was resorted to as a declaration that the
close time, or state of siege, was over. The rule we deduce is:
All that follows a dash is to be taken as under its influence
until either a second dash terminates it, or a full stop is reached.

Our answer to the third question has already been given by
implication; but it may be better to give it again explicitly.
We first refer to examples 1, 2, 3, 6, 13, 14, 24, in all of which
the stop, if one is to be used, though our view is that in most
of these sentences it should not, is in the right place; and to
example 16, in which it is in the wrong place. We next add
two new examples of wrong order, with corrections as usual; the
rules for stops with brackets are the same as with double dashes.

25. Throughout the parts which they are intended to make most
personally their own, (the Psalms,) it is always the Law which is
spoken of with chief joy.—RUSKIN. (Remove both commas, and use
according to taste either none at all, or one after the second
bracket)

26. What is the difference, whether land and sea interact, and worlds revolve and intermingle without number or end,—deep yawning under deep, and galaxy balancing galaxy, throughout absolute space,—or, whether . . .—EMERSON. (Remove both commas, and place one after the second dash)

A protest must next be made against the compositor's superstition embodied in Beadnell's words: *As the dash in this case supplies the place of the parenthesis, strictly speaking, the grammatical point should follow the last dash; but as this would have an unsightly appearance, it is always placed before it.* This unsightliness is either imaginary or at most purely conventional, and should be entirely disregarded. The rules will be (1) For the single dash: Since the dash is on any view either a correction of or an addition to the stop that would have been used if dashes had not existed, the dash will always stand after the stop. (2) For the double dash or brackets: There will be one stop or none according to the requirements of the principal sentence only; there will never be two stops (apart, of course, from internal ones); if there is one, it will stand before the first or after the last dash or bracket according as the parenthesis belongs to the following or the preceding part of the principal sentence. It may be added that it is extremely rare for the parenthesis to belong to the last part, and therefore for the stop to be rightly placed before it. In the following example constructed for the occasion it does so belong; but for practical purposes the rule might be that if a stop is required it stands after the second dash or bracket.

27. When I last saw him, (a singular fact) his nose was pea-green.

3. Common misuses.

a. If two single independent dashes are placed near each other, still more if they are in the same sentence, the reader naturally takes them for a pair constituting a parenthesis, and has to reconsider the sentence when he finds that his first reading gives nonsense. We refer back to example 23. But this indiscretion is so common that it is well to add some more. The sentences should be read over without the two dashes and what they enclose.

Then there is also Miss Euphemia, long deposed from her office of governess, but pensioned and so driven to good works and the manufacture of the most wonderful crazy quilts—for which, to her credit be it said, she shows a remarkable aptitude—as I should have supposed.—CROCKETT.

The English came mainly from the Germans, whom Rome found hard to conquer in 210 years—say, impossible to conquer—when one remembers the long sequel.—EMERSON.

As for Anne—well, Anne was Anne—never more calm than when others were tempestuous.—CROCKETT.

b. The first dash is inserted and the second forgotten. It will suffice to refer back to examples 20, 21, 22.

c. Brackets and dashes are combined. It is a pity from the collector's point of view that Carlyle, being in the mood, did not realize the full possibilities, and add a pair of commas, closing up the parenthesis in *robur et aes triplex.*

How much would I give to have my mother—(though both my wife and I have of late times lived wholly for her, and had much to endure on her account)—how much would I give to have her back to me.—CARLYLE.

d. Like the comma, the dash is sometimes misplaced by a word or two. In the first example, the first dash should be one place later; and in the second, unless we misread the sentence, and this is another case of two single dashes, the second dash should be two places earlier, and itself be replaced by a comma.

Here she is perhaps at her best—and in the best sense—her most feminine, as a woman sympathizing with the sorrows peculiar to women.—*Times.*

The girl he had dreamed about—the girl with the smile was there—near him, in his hut.—CROCKETT.

e. Dashes are sometimes used when an ordinary stop would serve quite well. In the Lowell sentences, the reason why a comma is not used is that the members are themselves broken up by commas, and therefore demand a heavier stop to divide them from each other; this, as explained in the early part of the chapter, is the place for a semicolon. In the Corelli sentence, it is a question between comma and semicolon, either of which would do quite well.

Shakespeare found a language already to a certain extent established, but not yet fetlocked by dictionary and grammar mongers,—a versification harmonized, but which had not yet . . .—LOWELL.

While I believe that our language had two periods of culmination in poetic beauty,—one of nature, simplicity, and truth, in the ballads, which deal only with narrative and feeling,—another of Art . . .—LOWELL.

We were shown in,—and Mavis, who had expected our visit did not keep us waiting long.—CORELLI.

HYPHENS

We return here to our usual practice of disregarding everything not necessary for dealing with common mistakes. But some general principles, most of which will probably find acceptance, will be useful to start from.

1. Hyphens are regrettable necessities, and to be done without when they reasonably may.

2. There are three degrees of intimacy between words, of which the first and loosest is expressed by their mere juxtaposition as separate words, the second by their being hyphened, and the third or closest by their being written continuously as one word. Thus, hand workers, hand-workers, handworkers.

3. It is good English usage to place a noun or other nonadjectival part of speech before a noun, printing it as a separate word, and to regard it as serving the purpose of an adjective in virtue of its position; for instance, *war expenditure*; but there are sometimes special objections to its being done. Thus, words in *-ing* may be actual adjectives (participles), or nouns (gerunds), used in virtue of their position as adjectives; and a visible distinction is needed. A *walking stick* is a stick that walks, and the phrase might occur as a metaphorical description of a stiffly behaved person: a *walking-stick* or *walkingstick* is a stick for walking; the difference may sometimes be important,

and consistency may be held to require that all compounds with gerunds should be hyphened or made into single words.

4. Not only can a single word in ordinary circumstances be thus treated as an adjective, but the same is true of a phrase; the words of the phrase, however, must then be hyphened, or ambiguity may result. Thus: Covent Garden; Covent-Garden Market; Covent-Garden-Market salesmen.

The prevailing method of giving railway and street names, besides its ungainliness, is often misleading and contrary to common sense. For one difficulty we suggest recurrence to the old-fashioned formula with commas, and *and*, as in *The London, Chatham, and Dover*. On another, it is to be observed that *New York-Street* should mean the new part of York Street, but *New-York Street* the street named after New York.[1] The set of examples includes some analogous cases, besides the railway and street names.

It is stated that the train service on the Hsin-min-tun-Kau-pan-tse-Yingkau section of the Imperial Chinese Railway will be restored within a few days.—*Times*.

Hsinmintun, Kaupantse, and Yingkau. These places can surely do without their internal hyphens in an English newspaper; and one almost suspects, from the absence of a hyphen between *Ying* and *kau*, that *The Times's* stock must have run short.

The Hendon-Mill Hill bypass.—*Times*.
Carriages are scarce on the Dalny-Port Arthur line.—*Times*.

[1] A correspondent has raised an interesting question—the hyphening of road and street names apart from context. It is remarkable that of such words as street, road, lane, terrace, avenue, crescent, place, and square, when preceded by a distinguishing word for use as names, one alone is treated in speech as enclitic, all the rest retaining their separate accents. The exception is street. If the reader will say aloud: Oxford Street, Edgware Road, Trafalgar Square, Marylebone Lane, Fleet Street, he will perceive at once that, while Road, Square, and Lane, keep their accent as separate words, that of Street is entirely swallowed up by Oxford and Fleet. The natural result should be the appearance of the names, whether at street-corners or in print, as Oxford-street, Edgware Road, Trafalgar Square, Marylebone Lane, Fleet-street. At present every one uses or rejects hyphens and capitals at random.

The Dalny and Port-Arthur line. By general principle 4,
though *Port Arthur* does not need a hyphen by itself, it does as
soon as it stands for an adjective with *line*: the Port-Arthur
line. Also, by 2, the *Times* version implies that *Dalny* is more
closely connected with *Port* than *Port* with *Arthur*. We do indeed most of us know at present that there is no Dalny Port
so called, and that there is a Port Arthur. But in the next
example, who would know that there was a Brest Litovski,[1]
but for the sentence that follows?

A general strike has been declared on the Warsaw-Brest Litovski
railway. The telegraph stations at Praga, Warsaw, and Brest Litovski
have been damaged.—*Times*.

The Warsaw and Brest-Litovski railway. By 4, the hyphen
between *Brest* and *Litovski* is necessary. If we write *Warsaw-
Brest-Litovski*, it is natural to suppose that three places are
meant; the *and* solution is accordingly the best.

At Bow-street, Robert Marsh, greengrocer, of Great Western-road,
Harrow-road, was charged . . .—*Times*.

Great-Western Road, Harrow Road. Bow-Street, as *at* (not
in) shows, is a compound epithet for *police-court* understood,
and has a right to its hyphen. By 3, there is no need for a
hyphen after *Harrow*, and by 1, if unnecessary, it is undesirable.
As to the other road, there are three possibilities. The *Times*
is right if there is a *Western Road* of which one section is called
Great, and the other *Little*. If the name means literally the
great road that runs west, there should be no hyphen at all.
If the road is named from the Great Western Railway, or from
the Great-Western Hotel, our version is right.

Cochin China waters.—*Times*.

By 4, *Cochin China* gives *Cochin-China* waters.

Within the last ten days two Anglo-South Americans have been in
my office arranging for passages to New Zealand.—*Times*.

Anglo-South-Americans is the best that can be done. What is
really wanted is *Anglo-SouthAmericans*, to show that *South*

---

[1] Since the War, many; but few in 1906, when this was written.

goes more closely with *America*. But it is too hopelessly contrary to usage at present.

> The proceeds of the recent London-New York loan.—*Times*. (London and New-York loan.)
> A good, generous, King Mark-like sort of man.—*Times*.

King-Mark-like, in default of *KingMark-like*. But the addition of *-like* to compound names should be avoided.

> The Fugitive Slave-law in America before the rebellion.—H. SIDGWICK. (Fugitive-Slave law)
> The steam-cars will have 16-horse power engines.—*Times*.

Steam cars is better, by 3, and 1. And 16-horsepower engines. We can do this time what the capitals of *American* and *Mark* prevented in the previous compounds.

Entirely gratuitous hyphens.

> One had a male-partner, who hopped his loutish burlesque.—MEREDITH.
> Gluttony is the least-generous of the vices.—MEREDITH.
> A little china-box, bearing the motto 'Though lost to sight, to memory dear,' which Dorcas sent her as a remembrance.—ELIOT.

This evidently means a box made of china. A box to hold china would have the hyphen properly, and there are many differentiations of this kind, of which *black bird*, as opposed to *black-bird* or *blackbird*, is the type.

> Bertie took up a quantity of waste-papers, and thrust them down into the basket.—E. F. BENSON.

This is probably formed by a mistaken step backwards from *waste-paper basket*, where the hyphen is correct, as explained in 3.

In phrases like *wet and dry fly fishing*, compounded of *wet-fly fishing* and *dry-fly fishing*, methods vary. For instance:

> A low door, leading through a moss and ivy-covered wall.—SCOTT.
> A language . . . not yet fetlocked by dictionary and grammar mongers.—LOWELL.
> Those who take human or womankind for their study.—THACKERAY.

The single phrases would have the hyphen for different reasons (*moss-covered*, &c.), all but *human kind*. The only

quite satisfactory plan is the Germans', who would write
moss- and *ivy-covered*. This is imitated in English, as:

> In old woods and on fern- and gorse-covered hilltops they do no
> harm whatever.—SPECTATOR.
> Refreshment-, boarding-, and lodging-house keepers have suffered
> severely too.—*Westminster Gazette.*

But imitations of foreign methods are not much to be recommended; failing that, Lowell's method seems the best—to
use no hyphens, and keep the second compound separate.

Adverbs that practically form compounds with verbs, but
stand after, and not necessarily next after them, need not be
hyphened unless they would be ambiguous in the particular
sentence if they were not hyphened. This may often happen,
since most of them are also prepositions; but even then it is
better to rearrange the sentence than to hyphen.

> He gratefully hands-over the establishment to his country.—
> MEREDITH.
> Thoughtful persons, unpledged to shore-up tottering dogmas.—
> HUXLEY.

It is a much commoner fault to over-hyphen than to under-
hyphen. But in the next example *malaria-infected* must be
written, by 3. And in the next again, one of the differentiations
we have spoken of is disregarded; *the fifty first* means the fifty
that come first: *the fifty-first* is the one after fifty. The ambiguity
in the third example is obvious.

> The demonstration that a malaria infected mosquito, transported a
> great distance to a non-malarial country, can . . .—*Times.*
> 'Nothing serious, I hope? How do cars break down?' 'In fifty
> different ways. Only mine has chosen the fifty first.'—KIPLING.
> The Cockney knew what the Lord of Session knew not, that the
> British public is gentility crazy.—BORROW.

There comes a time when compound words that have long
had a hyphen should drop it; this is when they have become
quite familiar. It seems absurd to keep any longer the division
in *to-day* and *to-morrow*; there are no words in the language
that are more definitely single and not double words; so much
so that the ordinary man can give no explanation of the *to.*

On the other hand, the word italicized in the next example may well puzzle a good many readers without its hyphen[1]; it has quite lately come into use in this country ('Chiefly U.S.' says the *Oxford Dictionary*, which prints the hyphen, whereas Webster does not), and is in danger of being taken at first sight for a foreign word and pronounced in strange ways.

> The soldiers . . . have been building *dugouts* throughout April.— *Times*.

There is a tendency to write certain familiar combinations irrationally, which may be mentioned here, though it does not necessarily involve the hyphen. With *in no wise* and *at any rate*, the only rational possibilities are to treat them like *nevertheless* as one word, or like *none the less* as three words (the right way, by usage), or give them two hyphens. *Nowise* and *anyrate* are not nouns that can be governed by *in* and *at*.

> Don McTaggart was the only man on his estate whom Sir Tempest could in nowise make afraid.—CROCKETT.
> French rules of neutrality are in nowise infringed by the squadron.— *Times*.
> At anyrate.—CORELLI, passim.

QUOTATION-MARKS

Quotation-marks, like hyphens, should be used only when necessary. The degree of necessity will vary slightly with the mental state of the audience for whom a book is intended. To an educated man it is an annoyance to find his author warning him that something written long ago, and quoted every day almost ever since, is not an original remark now first struck out. On the other hand, writers who address the uneducated may find their account in using all the quotation-marks they can; their readers may be gratified by seeing how well read the author is, or may think quotation-marks decorative. The following examples start with the least justifiable uses, and stop at the point where quotation-marks become more or less necessary.

[1] A pre-war apprehension; but the hyphen is still welcome.

John Smith, Esq., 'Chatsworth', Melton Road, Leamington.

The implication seems to be: living in the house that sensible people call 164 Melton Road, but one fool likes to call Chatsworth.

How is it that during the year in which that scheme has been, so to speak, 'in the pillory', no alternative has, at any rate, been made public?—*Times*.

Every metaphor ought to be treated as a quotation, if *in the pillory* is to be. Here, moreover, quotation-marks are a practical tautology, after *so to speak*.

Robert Brown and William Marshall, convicted of robbery with violence, were sentenced respectively to five years' penal servitude and eighteen strokes with the 'cat', and seven years' penal servitude.— *Times*.

There is by this time no danger whatever of confusion with the cat of one tail.

. . . not forgetful of how soon 'things Japanese' would be things of the past for her.—SLADEN.

This may be called the propitiatory use, analogous in print to the tentative air with which, in conversation, the Englishman not sure of his pronunciation offers a French word. So trifling a phrase is not worth using at the cost of quotation-marks. If it could pass without, well and good.

So that the prince and I were able to avoid that 'familiarity that breeds contempt' by keeping up our own separate establishments.— CORELLI.

. . . the Rector, lineal representative of the ancient monarchs of the University, though now, little more than a 'king of shreds and patches'. —HUXLEY.

We agree pretty well in our tastes and habits—yet so, as 'with a difference'.—LAMB.

With a difference (*Ophelia*: O, you must wear your rue with a difference) might escape notice as a quotation if attention were not drawn to it. A reader fit to appreciate Lamb, however, could scarcely fail to be sufficiently warned by the odd turn of the preceding words.

A question of some importance to writers who trouble themselves about accuracy, though no doubt the average reader is profoundly indifferent, is that of the right order as between quotation-marks and stops. Besides the conflict in which we shall again find ourselves with the aesthetic compositor, it is really difficult to arrive at a completely logical system. Before laying down what seems to be the best attainable, we must warn the reader that it is not the system now in fashion; but there are signs that printers are feeling their way towards better things, and this is an attempt to anticipate what they will ultimately come to. We shall make one or two postulates, deduce rules, and give examples. After the examples (in order that readers who are content either to go on with the present compromise or to accept our rules may be able to skip the discussion), we shall consider some possible objections.

No stop is ever required at the end of a quotation to separate the quotation, as such, from what follows; that is sufficiently done by the quotation-mark.

A stop is required to separate the containing sentence, which may go on beyond the quotation's end, but more commonly does not, from what follows.

An exclamation or question mark—which are not true stops, but tone symbols—may be an essential part of the quotation.

When a quotation is broken by such insertions as *he said*, any stop or tone symbol may be an essential part of the first fragment of quotation.

No stop is needed at either end of such insertions as *he said* to part them from the quotation, that being sufficiently done by the quotation-marks.

From these considerations we deduce the following rules:

1. The true stops should never stand before the second quotation-mark except

(*a*) when, as in dialogue given without framework, complete sentences entirely isolated and independent in grammar are printed as quotations. Even in these, it must be mentioned that the true stops are strictly unnecessary; but if the full stop (which alone can here be in question) is used in deference to universal custom, it should be before the quotation-mark.

(*b*) when a stop is necessary to divide the first fragment of an interrupted quotation from the second.

2. Words that interrupt quotations should never be allowed stops to part them from the quotation.

3. The tone symbols should be placed before or after the second quotation-mark according as they belong to the quotation or to the containing sentence. If both quotation and containing sentence need a tone symbol, both should be used, with the quotation-mark between them.

The bracketed numbers before the examples repeat the numbers of the rules.

(1) Views advocated by Dr Whately in his well-known 'Essays';
It is enough for us to reflect that 'Such shortlived wits do wither as they grow'.
We hear that 'whom the gods love die young', and thenceforth we collect the cases that illustrate it.
(1 *a*) 'You are breaking the rules.' 'Well, the rules are silly.'
(1 *b*) 'Certainly not;' he exclaimed 'I would have died rather'.
(2) 'I cannot guess' he retorted 'what you mean'.
(3) But 'why drag in Velasquez?'
But what is the use of saying 'Call no man happy till he dies'?
Is the question 'Where was he?' or 'What was he doing?'?
How absurd to ask 'Can a thing both be and not be?'!

If indignation is excited by the last two monstrosities, we can only say what has been implied many other times in this book, that the right substitute for correct ugliness is not incorrect prettiness, but correct prettiness. There is never any difficulty in rewriting sentences like these. (Is the question where he was, &c.?) ('Can a thing both be and not be?' The question is absurd.) But it should be recognized that, if such sentences are to be written, there is only one way to punctuate them.

It may be of interest to show how these sentences stand in the books. 1st sentence ('Essays;'); 2nd (grow.'); 3rd (young,');

4th, as here; 5th (not,' he exclaimed;) (rather.'); 6th (guess,'
he retorted,) (mean.'); 7th (Velasquez'?); 8th (saying,) (dies?').
The last two are fabricated.

The objections may now be considered.

'The passing crowd' is a phrase coined in the spirit of indifference.
Yet, to a man of what Plato calls 'universal sympathies,' and even to the
plain, ordinary denizens of this world, what can be more interesting
than 'the passing crowd'?—B.

After giving this example, Beadnell says:—'The reason is
clear: the words quoted are those of another, but the *question*
is the writer's own. Nevertheless, for the sake of neatness,
the ordinary points, such as the comma, semicolon, colon, and
full stop, *precede* the quotation-marks in instances analogous
to the one quoted; but the exclamation follows the same
rule as the interrogation'.

Singularly enough, the stops that are according to this
always to precede the quotation-mark (for the 'analogous
cases' are the only cases in which the outside position would
be so much as considered) are just the ones that by our rules
ought hardly ever to do so, whereas the two that are sometimes allowed the outside position are the two that we admit to
be as often necessary inside as outside. Neatness is the sole
consideration; just as the ears may be regarded as not hearing
organs, but 'handsome volutes of the human capital', so quotation-marks may be welcomed as giving a good picturesque finish
to a sentence; those who are of this way of thinking must feel
that, if they allowed outside them anything short of fine
handsome stops like the exclamation and question marks,
they would be countenancing an anticlimax. But they are
really mere conservatives, masquerading only as aesthetes;
and their conservatism will soon have to yield. Argument
on the subject is impossible; it is only a question whether the
printer's love for the old ways that seem to him so neat, or the
writer's and reader's desire to be understood and to understand fully, is to prevail.

Another objector takes a stronger position. He admits

that logic, and not beauty, must decide: 'but before we give up the old, let us be sure we are giving it up for a new that is logical'. He invites our attention to the recent paragraph containing Beadnell's views. 'Why, in the last sentence of that paragraph, is the full stop outside? "But the exclamation follows the same rule as the interrogation" is a complete sentence, quoted; why should its full stop be separated from it?' The answer is that the full stop is not *its* full stop; *it* needs no stop, having its communications forward absolutely cut off by the quotation-mark. It is a delusion to suppose that any sentence has proprietary rights in a stop, though it may have in a tone symbol; a stop is placed after it merely to separate it from what follows, if necessary.—'And the full stop after every last sentence (not a question or exclamation) of a paragraph, chapter, or book?'—Is illogical, and only to be allowed, like those in the isolated quotations mentioned in rule (1 *a*), in deference to universal custom. Our full stop belongs, not to the last sentence of the quotation, but to the paragraph, which is all one sentence, the whole quotation simply playing the part, helped by the quotation-marks, of object to *says*.— 'But *says* is followed by a colon, and a colon between verb and object breaks your own rules.'—No; (:—) is something different from a stop; it is an extra quotation-mark, as much a conventional symbol as the full stop in M.A. and other abbreviations.—'Well, then, instead of *says*, read *continues*, to which the quotation clearly cannot be object; will that affect our full stop?'—No; the quotation will still be part of the sentence; not indeed a noun, as before, and object to the verb; but an adverb, simply equivalent to *thus*, attached to the verb.

Satisfied on that point, the objector takes up our statement that the quotation-mark cuts communications; a similar statement was made in the *Dashes* section about brackets and double dashes. He submits a quotation:—Some people 'grunt and sweat under' very easy burdens indeed; and a pair of brackets:— It is (not a little learning, but) much conceit that is a dangerous thing. 'It is surely not true that either quotation-mark or bracket cuts the communications there; *under* in the quotation, *but* in the brackets, are in very active communication with *burdens* and *conceit*, outside'. The answer is that these are merely convenient misuses of quotation-marks and brackets. A quotation and a parenthesis should be complete in themselves, and instances that are not so may be neglected in arguing out principles. Special rules might indeed be required in consequence for the abnormal cases; but in practice this is not so with quotations.—'A last point. To adapt one of your instances, here are two sets of sentences, stopped as I gather you would stop them:—(1) He asked me "Can a thing both be and not be?" The question is absurd. (2) He said "A thing cannot both be and not be". I at once agreed. Now, if the full stop is required after the quotation-mark in the second, it must be required after that in the first, in each case to part, not the quotation, but the containing sentence, from the next sentence. What right have you to omit the full stop in the first?'—None whatever; it will not be omitted.—'So we have an addition of some importance to the monstrosities you said we should have to avoid.'—Well, sentences of this type are not common except in a style of affected simplicity.—'Or real simplicity. He saith unto him the third time, Simon, son of Jonas, lovest thou me? And is there any particular simplicity, real or affected, about this:—(Richmond looked at him with an odd smile for a moment or two before asking, as if it were the most natural question in the world, "But is it true?".)?'—In the Bible quotation there is, as you say, real simplicity—or rather there was. That sort of simplicity now would not be real, but artificial. Any one who has good reason to imitate primitive style may imitate primitive punctuation too. But one step forward in precision we have definitely taken from the biblical typography: we should insist on quotation-marks in such a sentence. They do not seem pedantic or needless now; nor will a further step in precision seem so when once it has been taken. And as to your Richmond sentence, and 'monstrosities' in general, it may be confessed here, as we are out of hearing in this discussion of all but those who are really interested, that the word was used for the benefit only of those who are indifferent. A sentence with two stops is not a monstrosity, if it wants them; and that will be realized, if once sensible punctuation gets the upper hand of neatness.

These are the most plausible objections on principle to a system of using quotation-marks with stops that would be in the main logical. It may be thought, however, that it was our business to be practical and opportunist, and suggest nothing that could not be acted on at once. But general usage, besides being illogical, is so inconsistent, different writers improving upon it in special details that appeal to them, that it seemed simpler to give our idea of what would be the best attainable, and trust to the tiro's adopting any parts of it that may not frighten him by their unaccustomed look.

There are single and double quotation-marks, and, apart from minor peculiarities, two ways of utilizing the variety. The prevailing one is to use double marks for most purposes, and single ones for quotations within quotations, as:—"Well, so he said to me 'What do you mean by it?' and I said 'I didn't mean anything' ". Some of those who follow this system also use the single marks for isolated words, short phrases, and anything that can hardly be called a formal quotation; this avoids giving much emphasis to such expressions, which is an advantage. The more logical method is that adopted, for instance, by the Oxford University Press, of reserving the double marks exclusively for quotations within quotations. Besides the loss of the useful degrees in emphasis (sure, however, to be inconsistently utilized), there is a certain lack of full-dress effect about important quotations when given this way; but that is probably a mere matter of habituation. It should be mentioned that most of the quoted quotations in this section had originally the double marks, but have been altered to suit the more logical method; and the unpleasantness of the needless quotation-marks with which we started has so been slightly toned down.

A common mistake, of no great importance, but resulting in more or less discomfort or perplexity to the reader, is the placing of the first quotation-mark earlier than the place where quotation really begins. The commonest form of it is the including of the quoter's introductory *that*, which it is often obvious that the original did not contain. Generally speaking, if *that* is used the quotation-marks may be dispensed with; not, however, if the exact phraseology is important; but at least the mark should be in the right place.

I remember an old scholastic aphorism, which says, 'that the man who lives wholly detached from others, must be either an angel or a devil.'—BURKE.

As the aphorism descends through Latin from Aristotle (ἢ θηρίον ἢ θεός), the precise English words are of no importance, and the quotation-marks might as well be away; at least the first should be after *that*.

Then, with 'a sarvant, sir' to me, he took himself into the kitchen.— BORROW.

Clearly *a* is not included in the quotation.

They make it perfectly clear and plain, he informed the House, that 'Sir Antony MacDonnell was invited by him, rather as a colleague than as a mere Under-Secretary, to register my will.'—*Times*.

The change from *him* to *my* would be quite legitimate if the first quotation-mark stood before *rather* instead of where it does; as it stands, it is absurd.

It is long since he partook of the Holy Communion, though there was an Easterday, of which he writes, when 'he might have remained quietly in (his) corner during the office, if . . .'.—*Times*.

The (*his*) is evidently bracketed to show that it is substituted for the original writer's *my*. This is very conscientious; but it follows that either the same should have been done for *he*, or the quotation-mark should be after *he*.

We began this section by saying that quotation-marks should be used only when necessary. A question that affects the decision to some extent is the difference between direct, indirect, and half-and-half quotation. We can say (1) He said 'I will go'. (2) He said he would go. (3) He said 'he would go'. The first variety is often necessary for the sake of vividness. The third is occasionally justified when, though there is no occasion for vividness, there is some turn of phrase that it is important for the reader to recognize as actually originating, not with the writer, but with the person quoted; otherwise, that variety is to be carefully avoided; how disagreeable it is will appear in the example below. For ordinary purposes the second variety, which involves no quotation-marks, is the best.

He then followed my example, declared he never felt more refreshed in his life, and, giving a bound, said, 'he would go and look after his horses.'—BORROW.

Further, there may be quotation, not of other people's words, but of one's own thoughts. In this case the method prevailing at present is that exemplified in the *Times* extract below. Taken by itself, there is no objection to it. We point out, however, that it is irreconcilable with the principles explained in this section, which demand the addition of a full stop (derived?.). That would be a worse monstrosity than the one in the first of the three legitimate alternatives that we add. We recommend that the *Times* method should be abandoned, and the first or second of the others used according to circumstances.

The next question is, Whence is this income derived?—*Times*.
The next question is 'Whence is this income derived?'. (Full direct quotation. Observe the 'monstrosity' stop)
The next question is whence this income is derived. (Indirect quotation)
The next question is 'Whence this income is derived'. (Indirect quotation with quotation-marks, or half-and-half quotation, like the Borrow sentence)

In concluding the chapter on Punctuation we may make the general remark that the effect of our recommendations, whether advocating as in the last section more strictness, or as in other parts more liberty, would be, certainly, a considerable reduction in the number of diacritical marks cutting up and disfiguring the text; and, as we think, a practice in most respects more logical and comprehensible.

PART II

Some less important chapters had been designed on Euphony, Ambiguity, Negligence, and other points. But as the book would with them have run to too great length, some of the examples have been simply grouped here in independent sections, with what seemed the minimum of comment.

I. JINGLES

To read his tales is a bapt*ism* of optim*ism*.—*Times.*

Sensation is the dir*ect* eff*ect* of the *mo*de of *mo*tion of the sensorium. —HUXLEY.

There have been no periodi*cal* gener*al* physi*cal* catastrophes. —HUXLEY.

It is con*tended*, indeed, that these preparations are in*tended* only . . . —*Times.*

It is in*tende*d to ex*tend* the system to this country.—*Times.*

M. Sphakianakis con*ducted* pro*tracted* negotiations.—*Times.*

Those inalienable rights of life, liber*ty* and proper*ty* upon which the safe*ty* of socie*ty* depends.—CHOATE.

He served his apprentice*ship* to statesman*ship*.—BRYCE.

Ap*par*ently pre*par*ed to hold its ground.—*Times.*

I aw*aited* a bel*ated* train.—R. G. WHITE.

Hand them on sil*ver* sal*ver*s to the ser*ver*.—E. F. BENSON.

. . . adjourned the discus*sion* of the ques*tion* of dela*tion* until to-day. —*Times.*

In this house of pover*ty* and digni*ty*, of past grandeur and present simplici*ty*, the brothers lived together in uni*ty*.—H. CAINE.

Their invalidi*ty* was caused by a technicali*ty*.—*Times.*

. . . had for consola*tion* the expan*sion* of its domin*ion*.—*Spectator.*

The essential found*ation* of all the organiz*ation* needed for the promo*tion* of educ*ation*.—HUXLEY.

The projects of M. Witte *rel*ative to the *regula*tion of the *rela*tions between capital and labour.—*Times.*

The remaining instances are of consecutive adverbs in *-ly*. Parallel adverbs, qualifying the same word simultaneously, do not result in a jingle; but in all our instances the two adverbs either qualify different words, or qualify the same word at different times. Thus, in the Huxley sentence, *unquestionably* either qualifies *is*, or qualifies *true* only after *largely* has qualified it: it is not the (universal) truth, but the partial truth, of the proposition that is unquestionable.

When the traffic in our streets becomes entirely mechanically propelled.—*Times*.

He lived practically exclusively on milk.—E. F. BENSON.

Critics would probably decidedly disagree.—HUTTON.

The children are functionally mentally defective.—*Times*.

What is practically wholly and entirely the British commerce and trade.—*Times*.

. . . who answered, usually monosyllabically, . . .—E. F. BENSON.

The policy of England towards Afghanistan is, as formerly, entirely friendly.—*Times*.

Money spent possibly unwisely, probably illegally, and certainly hastily.—*Times*.

The deer are necessarily closely confined to definite areas.—*Times*.

We find Hobbes's view . . . tolerably effectively combated.—MORLEY.

Great mental endowments do not, unhappily, necessarily involve a passion for obscurity.—H. G. WELLS.

The proposition of Descartes is unquestionably largely true.—HUXLEY.

2. ALLITERATION

Alliteration is not much affected by modern prose writers of any experience; it is a novice's toy. The antithetic variety has probably seen its best days, and the other instances quoted are doubtless to be attributed to negligence.

I must needs trudge at every old *beldam's bidding* and every young *minx's maggot*.—SCOTT.

Onward *gl*ided Dame Ursula, now in *gl*immer and now in *gl*oom.—SCOTT.

I have seen her in the same day as changeful as a *m*armozet, and as stubborn as a *m*ule.—SCOTT.

Thus, in *con*sequence of the *con*tinuance of that grievance, the means of education at the disposal of the *P*rotestants and *P*resbyterians were *st*unted and *st*erilized.—BALFOUR.

A gaunt well with a shattered pent-house *dw*arfed the *dw*elling.—H. G. WELLS.

It shall be lawful to *p*icket *p*remises for the *p*urpose of *p*eacefully *p*ersuading any *p*erson to . . .—*Times*.

3. REPEATED PREPOSITIONS

The founders *of* the study *of* the origin *of* human culture.—MORLEY.

After the manner *of* the author *of* the immortal speeches *of* Pericles.—MORLEY.

Togo's announcement *of* the destruction *of* the fighting power *of* Russia's Pacific squadron.—*Times*.

The necessity *of* the modification *of* the system *of* administration.—*Times*.

An exaggeration *of* the excesses *of* the epoch *of* sentimentalism.—MORLEY.

Hostile to the justice *of* the principle *of* the taxing *of* those values which . . .—LORD ROSEBERY.

The observation *of* the facts *of* the geological succession *of* the forms *of* life.—HUXLEY.

Devoid *of* any accurate knowledge *of* the mode *of* development *of* many groups *of* plants and animals.—HUXLEY.

One uniform note *of* cordial recognition *of* the complete success *of* the experiment.—*Times*.

The first fasciculus *of* the second volume *of* the Bishop *of* Salisbury's critical edition *of* St. Jerome's Revision *of* the Latin New Testament.—*Times*.

The appreciation *of* the House *of* the benefits derived *by* the encouragement afforded *by* the Government to the operations *of* . . .—*Times*.

The study *of* the perfectly human theme *of* the affection *of* a man *of* middle age.—*Times*.

His conviction *of* the impossibility *of* the proposal either *of* the creation *of* elective financial boards . . .—*Daily Express*.

Representative *of* the mind *of* the age *of* literature.—RUSKIN.

Indignation *against* the worst offenders *against* . . .—*Times*.

A belief *in* language *in* harmony with . . .—*Daily Telegraph*.

The opposition . . . *to* the submission *to* the claims.—*Times*.

Taken up *with* warfare *with* an enemy . . .—FREEMAN.

Palmerston wasted the strength derived *by* England *by* the great war *by* his brag.—GRANVILLE.

Unpropitious *for* any project *for* the reduction . . .—*Times*.

Called *upon* to decide *upon* the reduction . . .—*Times*.

4. SEQUENCE OF RELATIVES

A garret, in *which* were two small beds, in one of *which* she gave me to understand another gentleman slept.—BORROW.

Still no word of enlightenment had come *which* should pierce the thick clouds of doubt *which* hid the face of the future.—E. F. BENSON.

The ideal of a general alphabet . . . is one *which* gives a basis *which* is generally acceptable.—H. SWEET.

He enjoyed a lucrative practice, *which* enabled him to maintain and educate a family with all the advantages *which* money can give in this country.—TROLLOPE.

The clown *who* views the pandemonium of red brick *which* he has built on the estate *which* he has purchased.—BORROW.

The main thread of the book, *which* is a daring assault upon that serious kind of pedantry *which* utters itself in . . .—L. STEPHEN.

Practical reasons *which* combine to commend this architectural solution of a problem *which* so many of us dread . . .—*Times*.

The teachers, *who* took care that the weaker, *who* might otherwise be driven to the wall, had . . . their fair share.—*Times*.

Let the heads and rulers of free peoples tell this truth to a Tsar *who* seeks to dominate a people *who* will not and cannot . . .—*Times*.

He made a speech . . . *which* contained a passage on the conditions of modern diplomacy *which* attracted some attention.—*Times*.

There is of course no objection to the recurrence when the relatives are parallel.

5. SEQUENCE OF 'THAT' OR OTHER CONJUNCTIONS

Here, as with relatives, the recurrence is objectionable only when one of the clauses is subordinate to the other.

I do not forget *that* some writers have held *that* a system is to be inferred.—BALFOUR.

I say *that* there is a real danger *that* we may run to the other extreme. —HUXLEY.

It is clear . . . *that* the opinion was *that* it is not incompatible.— NANSEN.

I find *that* the view *that* Japan has now a splendid opportunity . . . is heartily endorsed.—*Times*.

I must point out *that* it is a blot on our national education *that* we have serving . . .—*Times*.

The Chairman replied to the allegation made by the Radical press to the effect *that* the statement *that* the British workman will not work as an unskilled labourer in the mines is inaccurate.—*Times*.

An official telegram states *that* General Nogi reports *that* . . .—*Times*.

The conviction *that* the Tsar must realize *that* the prestige of Russia is at stake.—*Times*.

He was so carried away by his discovery *that* he ventured on the assertion *that* the similarity between the two languages was so great *that* an educated German could understand whole strophes of Persian poetry.—H. SWEET.

I may fairly claim to have no personal interest in defending the council, *although* I believe, *though* I am not certain, that . . .—*Times.*

6. METRICAL PROSE

The novice who is conscious of a weakness for the high-flown and the inflated should watch narrowly for metrical snatches in his prose; they are a sure sign that the fit is on him.

Oh, moralists, who treat of happiness / and self-respect, innate in every sphere / of life, and shedding light on every grain / of dust in God's highway, so smooth below / your carriage-wheels, so rough beneath the tread / of naked feet, bethink yourselves /in looking on the swift descent / of men who *have* lived in their own esteem, / that there are scores of thousands breathing now, -/ and breathing thick with painful toil, who in / that high respect have never lived at all, / nor had a chance of life! Go ye, who rest / so placidly upon the sacred Bard / who had been young, and when he strung his harp / was old, . . . / go, Teachers of content and honest pride, / into the mine, the mill, the forge, / the squalid depths of deepest ignorance, / and uttermost abyss of man's neglect, / and say can any hopeful plant spring up / in air so foul that it extinguishes / the soul's bright torch as fast as it is kindled! / —DICKENS.

But now,—now I have resolved to stand alone,—/ fighting my battle as a man should fight, / seeking for neither help nor sympathy, / and trusting not in self . . .—CORELLI.

And the gathering orange stain / upon the edge of yonder western peak, / reflects the sunsets of a thousand years.—RUSKIN.

His veins were opened; but he talked on still / while life was slowly ebbing, and was calm / through all the agony of lingering death.— W. W. CAPES.

Can I then trust the evidence of sense? / And art thou really to my wish restored? / Never, oh never, did thy beauty shine / with such bewitching grace, as that which now / confounds and captivates my view! / . . . Where hast thou lived? where borrowed this perfection? / . . . Oh! I am all amazement, joy and fear! / Thou wilt not leave me! No! we must not part / again. By this warm kiss! a thousand times / more sweet than all the fragrance of the East! / we never more will part. O! this is rapture! / ecstasy! and what no language will explain!— SMOLLETT.

7. SENTENCE ACCENT

It is only necessary to read aloud any one of the sentences quoted below, to perceive at once that there is something wrong with its accentuation. To lay down rules on this point would be superfluous, even if it were practicable; for in all doubtful cases the ear can and should decide. A writer who cannot trust himself to balance his sentences properly should read aloud all that he writes. It is useless for him to argue that readers will not read his works aloud, and that therefore the fault of which we are speaking will escape notice. For, although the fault may appear to be exclusively one of sound, it is always in fact a fault of sense: unnatural accentuation is only the outward sign of an unnatural combination of thought. Thus, nine readers out of ten would detect in a moment, without reading aloud, the ill-judged structure in our first example: the writer has tried to do two incompatible things at the same time, to describe in some detail the appearance of his characters, and to begin a conversation; the result is that any one reading the sentence aloud is compelled to maintain, through several lines of new and essential information, the tone that is appropriate only to what is treated as a matter of course. The interrogative tone protests more loudly than any other against this kind of mismanagement; but our examples will show that other tones are liable to the same abuse.

The accentuation of each clause or principal member of a sentence is primarily fixed by its relation to the other members: when the internal claims of its own component parts clash with this fixed accentuation—when, for instance, what should be read with a uniformly declining accentuation requires for its own internal purposes a marked rise and fall of accent— reconstruction is necessary to avoid a badly balanced sentence. The passage from Peacock will illustrate this: after *pupils*, and still more after *counterpoint*, the accentuation should steadily decline to the end of the passage; but, conflicting with this requirement, we have the exorbitant claims of a complete anecdote, containing within itself an elaborately accented speech. To represent the anecdote as an insignificant appendage to *pupils* was a fault of sense; it is revealed to the few who would not have perceived it by the impossibility of reading the passage naturally.

'Are Japanese Aprils always as lovely as this?' asked the man in the light tweed suit of two others in immaculate flannels with crimson sashes round their waists and puggarees folded in cunning plaits round their broad Terai hats.—D. SLADEN.

'Here we are', he said presently, after they had turned off the main road for a while and rattled along a lane between high banks topped with English shrubs, and looking for all the world like an outskirt of Tunbridge Wells.—D. SLADEN.

I doubt if Haydn would have passed as a composer before a committee of lords like one of his own pupils, who insisted on demonstrating to him that he was continually sinning against the rules of counterpoint; on which Haydn said to him, 'I thought I was to teach you, but it seems you are to teach me, and I do not want a preceptor', and thereon he wished his lordship a good morning.—PEACOCK.

She wondered at having drifted into the neighbourhood of a person resembling in her repellent formal chill virtuousness a windy belfry tower, down among those districts of suburban London or appalling provincial towns passed now and then with a shudder, where the funereal square bricks-up the church, that Arctic hen-mother sits on the square, and the moving dead are summoned to their round of penitential exercise by a monosyllabic tribulation-bell.—MEREDITH.

The verb *wonder* presupposes the reader's familiarity with the circumstance wondered at; it will not do the double work of announcing both the wonder and the thing wondered at. 'I wondered at Smith's being there' implies that my hearer knew that Smith was there; if he did not, I should say, 'I was surprised to find . . .'. Accordingly, in this very artificial sentence, the writer presupposes the inconceivable question: 'What were her feelings on finding that she had drifted . . . tribulation-bell?'. To read a sentence of minute and striking description with the declining accentuation that necessarily follows the verb *wondered* is of course impossible.

How doth the earth terrifie and oppress us with terrible earthquakes, which are most frequent in China, Japan, and those eastern climes, swallowing up sometimes six cities at once!—BURTON.

Of the many possible violations of sentence accent, one—common in inferior writers—is illustrated in the next section.

8. CAUSAL 'AS' CLAUSES

There are two admissible kinds of causal 'as' clauses—the pure and the mixed. The pure clause assigns as a cause some fact that is already known to the reader and is sure to occur to him in the connexion: the mixed assigns as a cause what is not necessarily known to the reader or present in his mind; it has the double function of conveying a new fact, and indicating its relation to the main sentence. Context will usually decide whether an *as* clause is pure or mixed; in the following examples, it is clear from the nature of the two clauses that the first is pure, the second mixed:

I have an edition with German notes; but that is of no use, as you do not read German.

I caught the train, but afterwards wished I had not, as I presently discovered that my luggage was left behind.

The second of these, it will be noticed is unreadable, unless we slur the *as* to such an extent as practically to acknowledge that it ought not to be there. The reason is that, although a pure clause may stand at any point in the sentence, a mixed one must always precede the main statement. The pure clause, having only the subordinate function normally indicated by *as*, is subordinate in sense as well as in grammar; and the declining accentuation with which it is accordingly pronounced will not be interfered with wherever we may place it. But the mixed clause has another function, that of conveying a new fact, for which *as* does not prepare us, and which entitles it to an accentuation as full and as varied as that of the main statement. To neutralize the subordinating effect of *as*, and secure the proper accentuation, we must place the clause at the beginning; where this is not practicable, *as* should be removed, and a colon or semicolon used instead of a comma. Persistent usage tends of course to remove this objection by weakening the subordinating power of conjunctions: *because*, *while*, *whereas*, *since*, can be used where *as* still betrays a careless or illiterate writer. There is the same false ring in all the following sentences:

I myself saw in the estate office of a large landed proprietor a procession of peasant women begging for assistance, as owing to the departure of the bread-winners the families were literally starving.—*Times*.

Remove *as*, and use a heavier stop.

Very true, Jasper; but you really ought to learn to read, as, by so doing, you might learn your duty towards yourselves.—BORROW.

To read; by so doing, . . .

There was a barber and hairdresser, who had been at Paris, and talked French with a cockney accent, the French sounding all the better, as no accent is so melodious as the Cockney.—BORROW.

Use a semicolon and 'for'; the assertion requires all the support that vigorous accentuation can lend.

One of the very few institutions for which the Popish Church entertains any fear, and consequently respect, as it respects nothing which it does not fear.—BORROW.

For instead of *as* will best suit this illogical and falsely coordinated sentence.

Everybody likes to know that his advantages cannot be attributed to air, soil, sea, or to local wealth, as mines and quarries, . . . but to superior brain, as it makes the praise more personal to him.—EMERSON.

Again the clause is a mixed one. The point of view it suggests is, indeed, sufficiently obvious; but (unlike our typical pure clause above—'you do not know German') it depends for its existence upon the circumstances of the main sentence, which may or may not have occurred to the reader before. The full accentuation with which the clause must inevitably be read condemns it at once; use a colon, and remove *as*.

Pure clauses, being from their nature more or less otiose, belong rather to the spoken than to the written language.

It follows that a good writer will seldom have a causal *as* clause of any kind at the end of a sentence. Two further limitations remain to be noticed:

i. When the cause, not the effect, is obviously the whole point of the sentence, *because*, not *as*, should be used; the following is quite impossible English:

I make these remarks as quick shooting at short ranges has lately been so strongly recommended.—*Times*.

ii. *As* should be used only to give the cause of the thing asserted, not the cause of the assertion, nor an illustration of its truth, as in the following instances:

You refer me to the Encyclopaedia: you are mistaken, as I find the Encyclopaedia exactly confirms my view.

The Oxford Coxswain did not steer a very good course here, as he kept too close in to the Middlesex shore to obtain full advantage of the tide; it made little difference, however, as his crew continued to gain. —*Times*.

My finding the Encyclopaedia's confirmation was not the cause of mistake, nor the keeping too close the cause of bad steering.

9. WENS AND HYPERTROPHIED MEMBERS

No sentence is to be condemned for mere length; a really skilful writer can fill a page with one and not tire his reader, though a succession of long sentences without the relief of short ones interspersed is almost sure to be forbidding. But the tiro, and even the good writer who is not prepared to take the trouble of reading aloud what he has written, should confine himself to the easily manageable. The tendency is to allow some part of a sentence to develop unnatural proportions, or a half parenthetic insertion to separate too widely the essential parts. The cure, indispensable for every one who aims at a passable style, and infallible for any one who has a good ear, is reading aloud after writing.

1. Disproportionate insertions.

Some simple eloquence distinctly heard, though only uttered in her eyes, unconscious that he read them, as, 'By the death-beds I have tended, by the childhood I have suffered, by our meeting in this dreary house at midnight, by the cry wrung from me in the anguish of my heart, O father, turn to me and seek a refuge in my love before it is too late!' may have arrested them.—DICKENS.

Captain Cuttle, though no sluggard, did not turn so early on the morning after he had seen Sol Gills, through the shopwindow, writing in the parlour, with the Midshipman upon the counter, and Rob the Grinder making up his bed below it, but that the clocks struck six as he raised himself on his elbow, and took a survey of his little chamber. —DICKENS.

A perpetual consequent warfare of her spirit and the nature subject to the thousand sensational hypocrisies invoked for concealment of its reviled brutish baseness, held the woman suspended from her emotions. —MEREDITH.

Yesterday, before Dudley Sowerby's visit, Nataly would have been stirred where the tears which we shed for happiness or repress at a flattery dwell when seeing her friend Mrs. John Cormyn enter . . .— MEREDITH.

'It takes', it is said that Sir Robert Peel observed, 'three generations to make a gentleman'.—BAGEHOT.

Behind, round the windows of the lower story, clusters of clematis, like large purple sponges, blossomed, miraculously fed through their thin, dry stalks.—E. F. BENSON.

It is a striking exhibition of the power which the groups, hostile in different degrees to a democratic republic, have of Parliamentary combination.—Spectator.

Sir,—With reference to the custom among some auctioneers and surveyors of receiving secret commissions, which was recently brought to light in a case before the Lord Chief Justice and Justices Kennedy and Ridley (King's Bench Division), when the L. C. J. in giving judgment for the defendants said:—Unfortunately in commercial circles, in which prominent men played a part, extraordinary mistakes occurred. But a principal who employed an agent to do work for him employed him upon terms that the agent was not liable to get secret commissions. The sooner secret commissions were not approved by an honourable profession, the better it would be for commerce in all its branches. I desire to take this opportunity . . .—Times.

In the course of a conversation with a representative of the Gaulois, Captain Klado, after repeating his views on the necessity for Russia to secure the command of the sea which have already appeared in the Times, replied as follows to a question as to whether, after the new squadron in the course of formation at Libau has reinforced Admiral Rozhdestvensky's fleet, the Russian and Japanese naval forces will be evenly balanced: [here follows reply]—Times.

2. Sentences of which the end is allowed to trail on to unexpected length.

But though she could trust his word, the heart of the word went out of it when she heard herself thanked by Lady Blachington (who could so well excuse her at such a time for not returning her call, that she called in a friendly way a second time, warmly to thank her) for throwing open the Concert Room at Lakelands in August, to an entertainment in assistance of the funds for the purpose of erecting an East London Clubhouse, where the children of the poor by day could play, and their parents pass a disengaged evening.—MEREDITH.

How to commence the ceremony might have been a difficulty, but for the zeal of the American Minister, who, regardless of the fact that he was the representative of a sister Power, did not see any question of delicacy arise in his taking a prominent part in proceedings regarded as entirely irregular by the representatives of the Power to which the parties concerned belonged.—D. SLADEN.

The style holds the attention, but perhaps the most subtle charm of the work lies in the inextricable manner in which fact is interwoven with something else that is not exactly fiction, but rather fancy bred of the artist's talent in projecting upon his canvas his own view of things seen and felt and lived through by those whose thoughts, motives, and actions, he depicts.—Times.

The cock-bustard that, having preened himself, paces before the hen birds on the plains that he can scour when his wings, which are slow in the air, join with his strong legs to make nothing of grassy leagues on leagues.—Times.

I don't so much wonder at his going away, because, leaving out of consideration that spice of the marvellous which was always in his character, and his great affection for me, before which every other consideration of his life became nothing, as no one ought to know so well as I who had the best of fathers in him—leaving that out of consideration, I say, I have often read and heard of people who, having some near and dear relative, who was supposed to be shipwrecked at sea, have gone down to live on that part of the seashore where any tidings of the missing ship might be expected to arrive, though only an hour or two sooner than elsewhere, or have even gone upon her track to the place whither she was bound, as if their going would create intelligence.—DICKENS.

What he had to communicate was the contents of despatches from Tokio containing information received by the Japanese Government respecting infringements of neutrality by the Baltic Fleet in Indo-Chinese waters outside what are, strictly speaking, the territorial limits, and principally by obtaining provisions from the shore.— *Times*.

3. Decapitable sentences.

Perhaps the most exasperating form is that of the sentence that keeps on prolonging itself by additional phrases, each joint of which gives the reader hopes of a full stop.

It was only after the weight of evidence against the economic success of the endeavour became overwhelming that our firm withdrew its support /, and in conjunction with almost the entire British population of the country concentrated its efforts on endeavouring to obtain permission to increase the coloured unskilled labour supply of the mines / so as to be in a position to extend mining operations /, and thus assist towards re-establishing the prosperity of the country /, while at the same time attracting a number of skilled British artisans / who would receive not merely the bare living wage of the white unskilled labourer, but a wage sufficient to enable these artisans to bring their families to the country / and to make their permanent home there.— *Westminster Gazette*.

Here may still be seen by the watchful eye the Louisiana heron and smaller egret, all that rapacious plume-hunters have left of their race, tripping like timid fairies in and out the leafy screen / that hides the rank jungle of sawgrass and the grisly swamp where dwells the alligator /, which lies basking, its nostrils just level with the dirty water of its bath, or burrows swiftly in the soft earth to evade the pursuit of those who seek to dislodge it with rope and axe / that they may sell its hide to make souvenirs for the tourists / who, at the approach of summer, hie them north or east with grateful memories of that fruitful land.—F. G. AFLALO.

Running after milkmaids is by no means an ungenteel rural diversion; but let any one ask some respectable casuist (the Bishop of London, for instance), whether Lavengro was not far better employed, when in the country, at tinkering and smithery than he would have been in running after all the milkmaids in Cheshire /, though tinkering is in general considered a very ungenteel employment /, and smithery little better /, notwithstanding that an Orcadian poet, who wrote in Norse about 800 years ago, reckons the latter among nine noble arts which he possessed /, naming it along with playing at chess, on the harp, and ravelling runes /, or as the original has it, 'treading runes' / — that is, compressing them into small compass by mingling one letter with another /, even as the Turkish caligraphists ravel the Arabic letters /, more especially those who write talismans.—BORROW.

10. CARELESS REPETITION

Conscious repetition of a word or phrase has been discussed in Part I (Airs and Graces): in the following examples the repetition is unconscious, and proves only that the writer did not read over what he had written.

. . . a man. . . who directly *impresses* one with the *impression* . . .—*Times.*

For most *of them* get rid *of them* more or less completely.—H. SWEET.

The most important distinction between dialogue on the one hand and *purely* descriptive and narrative pieces on the other hand is a *purely* grammatical one.—H. SWEET.

And it *may* be that from a growing familiarity with Canadian winter amusements *may* in time spring an even warmer regard . . .—*Times.*

It *may* well induce the uncomfortable reflection that these historical words *may* prove . . .—*Times.*

The inclusion of *adherents* would be *adhered* to.—*Times.*

The *remainder remaining* loyal, fierce fighting commenced.—*Spectator.*

Every subordinate shortcoming, every incidental defect, will be *pardoned.* 'Save us' is the cry of the moment; and, in the confident hope of safety, any deficiency will be overlooked, and any frailty *pardoned.*—BAGEHOT.

They were *followed* by jinrikshas *containing* young girls with very carefully-dressed hair, *carrying* large bunches of real flowers on their laps, *followed* in turn by two more coolies *carrying* square white wooden jars, *containing* huge silver tinsel flowers.—D. SLADEN.

It can do so, in all reasonable probability, *provided* its militia character is maintained. But in any case it will *provide* us at home with the second line army of our needs.—*Times.*

Dressed in a subtly ill-*dressed*, expensive mode.—E. F. BENSON.

Toodle being the *family* name of the apple-faced *family.*—DICKENS.

Artillery firing *extends* along the whole front, *extending* for eighty miles.—*Times.*

I regard the action and conduct of the Ministry *as* a whole *as* of far greater importance.—*Times.*

The fleet passed the port *on its way* through the Straits *on the way* to the China Sea.—*Times.*

Much of his popularity he owed, we believe, to *that* very timidity *which* his friends lamented. *That* timidity often prevented him from exhibiting his talents to the best advantage. But it propitiated Nemesis. It averted *that* envy *which* would otherwise have been excited . . .—MACAULAY.

I will lay down *a pen* I am so little able to govern.—And I will try to subdue *an impatience which* . . . may otherwise lead me into still more punishable errors.—I will return to *a subject which* I cannot fly from for ten minutes together.—RICHARDSON.

At the same time it was largely *owing to* his careful training that so many great Etonian cricketers *owed* their success.—*Times*.

11. COMMON MISQUOTATIONS

These are excusable in talk, but not in print. A few pieces are given correctly, with the usual wrong words in brackets.

An *ill-favoured* thing, sir, but mine own. (poor)
Fine by degrees and beautifully less. (small)
That last infirmity of noble *mind*. (the: minds)
Make assurance *double* sure. (doubly)
To-morrow to fresh *woods* and pastures new. (fields)
The devil can *cite* Scripture for his purpose. (quote)
Chewing the *food* of sweet and bitter fancy. (cud)
When *Greeks joined Greeks*, then *was* the tug of war. (Greek meets Greek: comes)
A goodly apple rotten at the *heart*. (core)

12. UNCOMMON MISQUOTATIONS OF WELL-KNOWN PASSAGES
OR PHRASES

It is still worse to misquote what is usually given right, however informal the quotation. The true reading is here added in brackets.

Now for the trappings and the *weeds* of woe.—S. FERRIER. (suits)

She had an instinctive knowledge that she knew her, and she felt her genius *repressed* by her, as *Julius Caesar's* was by *Cassius*.—S. FERRIER. (My genius is *rebuked* as, it is said, *Mark Antony's* was by *Caesar*)

The new drama represented the very age and body of the time, his form and *feature*.—J. R. GREEN. (pressure)

He lifts the veil from the sanguinary affair at Kinchau, and we are allowed glimpses of blockade-running, train-wrecking and cavalry reconnaissance, and of many other moving *incidents* by flood and field.—*Times*. (accidents)

To him this *rough* world was but too literally a rack.—LOWELL. (who would, upon the rack of this *tough* world, stretch him out longer)

Having once begun, they found returning more tedious than *giving* o'er.—LOWELL. (returning were as tedious as *go* o'er)

Posthaec [*sic*] meminisse juvabit.—HAZLITT. (et haec olim)

Quid vult valde vult. What they do, they do with a will.—EMERSON. (quod) Quid is not translatable.

Then that wonderful esprit *du* corps, by which we adopt into our self-love everything we touch.—EMERSON. (de)

Let not him that *putteth* on his *armour boast* as *him* that *taketh* it off.— *Westminster Gazette.* (girdeth, harness, boast himself, he, putteth)

Elizabeth herself, says Spenser, 'to mine *open* pipe inclined her ear'. —J. R. GREEN. (oaten)

He could join the crew of Mirth, and look pleasantly on at a village fair, 'where the *jolly* rebecks sound to many a youth and many a maid, dancing in the chequered shade'.—J. R. GREEN. (jocund)

Heathen Kaffirs, et hoc genero, &c.: . . . *Daily Mail* . (genus omne)

If she takes her husband *au pied de lettre.*—*Westm. Gaz.* (de la lettre)

13. MISQUOTATION OF LESS FAMILIAR PASSAGES

But the greatest wrong is done to readers when a passage that may not improbably be unknown to them is altered.

It was at Dublin or in his castle of Kilcolman, two miles from Doneraile, 'under the *fall* of Mole, that mountain hoar', that he spent the memorable years in which . . .—J. R. GREEN. (foot)

Petty spites of the village *squire.*—*Spectator.* (pigmy: spire)

14. MISAPPLIED AND MISUNDERSTOOD QUOTATIONS
AND PHRASES

Before *leading question* or *the exception proves the rule* is written, a lawyer should be consulted; before *cui bono*, Cicero; before *more honoured in the breach than in the observance*, Hamlet. A leading question is one that unfairly helps a witness to the desired answer; *cui bono* has been explained on p. 44; *the exception*, &c., is not an absurdity when understood, but it is as generally used; *more honoured*, &c., means not that the rule is generally broken, but that it is better broken. A familiar line of Shakespeare, on the other hand, gains by being mis-understood: 'One touch of nature makes the whole world kin' merely means 'In one respect, all men are alike'.

But *cui bono* all this detail of our debt? Has the author given a single light towards any material reduction of it? Not a glimmering.—BURKE.

A rule dated March 3, 1801, which has never been abrogated, lays it

down that, to obtain formal leave of absence, a member must show
some sufficient cause, such as . . . but this rule is more honoured in the
breach than in the observance.—*Times*.

Every one knows that the Governor-General in Council is invested
by statute with the supreme command of the Army and that it would
be disastrous to subvert that power. But 'why drag in Velasquez'? If
any one wishes us to infer that Lord Kitchener has, directly or indirectly, proposed to subvert this unquestioned and unquestionable
authority, they are very much mistaken.—*Times*. (Why indeed? no
worse literary treason than to spoil other people's wit by dragging it in
where it is entirely pointless. Velasquez here outrages those who know
the story, and perplexes those who do not)

The Nationalist, M. Archdeacon, and M. Meslier put to the Prime
Minister several *leading questions*, such as, 'Why were you so willing
promptly to part with M. Delcassé, and why, by going to the conference, did you agree to revive the debate as to the unmistakable
rights . . .?' To these pertinent inquiries M. Rouvier did not reply.—
Times. (Leading questions are necessarily not hostile, as these clearly
were)

The happy phrase that an Ambassador is an honest man sent abroad
to lie for his country.—*Westminster Gazette*. (Happier when correctly
quoted: sent to lie abroad for the good of)[1]

14 *a*. PARVUM IN MULTO

The mere substitution, without blundering, of some famous
but longish phrase for the single word that would do the work
required should not go unnoticed; the obvious is at all costs
to be shunned. We have quoted elsewhere 'Dr. Ingram's
successor may have "arrows in the hand of a giant" ', inexcusable for 'children' or 'a family'; and here is the way to show

[1] A correspondent has pointed out to me that the play on 'lie' (lodge, tell
lies) does not appear in Wotton's original epigram, which was in Latin; and,
as this may be known to and confuse the reader, here is Walton's account of
the matter:—and Sir Henry Wotton . . . took an occasion . . . to write a
pleasant definition of an ambassador in these very words: 'Legatus est vir
bonus peregre missus ad mentiendum reipublicae causa.' Which Sir Henry
Wotton could have been content should have been thus Englished: 'An
ambassador is an honest man, sent to *lie* abroad for the good of his country.'
But the word for *lie* (being the hinge upon which the conceit was to turn)
was not so expressed in Latin, as would admit . . . so fair a construction as
Sir Henry thought in English.—*The Life of Sir Henry Wotton*. Since it is the
order of the words in the English version that has kept the definition alive
for 300 years, that order should be adhered to.

that, though one may have to write of such nastinesses as whale-oil and blubber, one's thoughts fly off naturally to higher things:

[The history of Spitzbergen] resolved itself into a struggle, firstly, for life; secondly, for the gratification of the lust which drove folk thither; the said lust being a lust for whale-oil, for 'the sovereign'st thing on earth for an inward bruise', or, in some cases, for the uncleanly blubber of the whale.—*Speaker*.

15. ALLUSION

A writer who abounds in literary allusions necessarily appeals to a small audience, to those acquainted with about the same set of books as himself; they like his allusions, others dislike them. Writers should decide whether it is not wise to make their allusions explain themselves. In the first two instances quoted, though the reader who knows the original context has a slight additional pleasure, any one can see what the point is. In the last two, those who have not the honour of the wetnurse's and Rosamund's acquaintance feel that the author and the other readers with whom he is talking aside are guilty of bad manners.

The select academy, into whose sacred precincts the audacious Becky Sharp flung back her leaving present of the 'Dixonary', survives here and there, but with a different curriculum and a much higher standard of efficiency.—*Times*.

Why can't they stay quietly at home till they marry, instead of trying to earn their living by unfeminine occupations? So croaks Mrs. Partington, twirling her mop; but the tide comes on.—*Times*.

Sir,—Were it not for M. Kokovtsoff's tetchiness in the matter of metaphors, I should feel inclined to see in his protest against my estimates of the decline in the Russian gold reserve and of the increase of the note issue a variant of the classic excuse of Mrs. Easy's wetnurse for the unlawfulness of her baby.—LUCIEN WOLF.

Three superb glass jars—red, green, and blue—of the sort that led Rosamund to parting with her shoes—blazed in the broad plate-glass windows.—KIPLING.

16. INCORRECT ALLUSION

Every one who detects a writer pretending to more knowledge than he has jumps to the conclusion that the detected must know less than the detective, and cannot be worth his reading. Incorrect allusion of this kind is therefore fatal.

Homer would have seemed arrogantly superior to his audience if he had not called Hebe 'white-armed' or 'ox-eyed'.—*Times*. (He seldom mentions her, and calls her neither)

My access to fortune had not, so far, brought me either much joy or distinction,—but it was not too late for me yet to pluck the golden apples of Hesperides.—CORELLI. (It is hardly possible for any one who knows what the Hesperides were to omit *the*)

My publisher, John Morgeson ... was not like Shakespeare's Cassio strictly 'an honourable man'.—CORELLI. (Cassio was an honourable man, but was never called so. Even Cassius has only his share in *So are they all, all honourable men*. Brutus, perhaps?)

A sturdy Benedict to propose a tax on bachelors.—*Westminster Gazette*. (Benedick. In spite of the *Oxford Dictionary*, the differentiation between the saint, Benedict, and the converted bachelor, Benedick, is surely not now to be given up)

But impound the car for a longer or shorter period according to the offence, and that, as the French say, 'will give them reason to think'.—*Times*. (The French do not say *give reason to think*; and if they did the phrase would hardly be worth treating as not English; they say *give to think*, which is often quoted because it is unlike English)

17. DOVETAILED AND ADAPTED QUOTATIONS AND PHRASES

The fitting into a sentence of refractory quotations, the making of facetious additions to them, and the constructing of Latin cases with English governing words, have often intolerably ponderous effects.

Though his denial of any steps in that direction may be true in his official capacity, *there is probably some smoke in the fire of comment* to which his personal relations with German statesmen have given rise.—*Times*. (The reversal of smoke and fire may be a slip of the pen or a joke; but the correction of it mends matters little)

It remains to be seen whether ... the pied à terre which Germany hopes she has won by her preliminary action in the Morocco question will form the starting-point for further achievements or will merely represent, like so many other German enterprises, *the end of the beginning*.—*Times*. (The reversal this time is clearly facetious)

But they had gone on adding misdeed to misdeed, they had *blundered after blunder.*—L. COURTNEY.

Germany has, it would appear, yet another card in her hand, a card *of the kind which is useful to players when in doubt.*—*Times.*

But the problem of inducing *a refractory camel* to squeeze himself through the eye of *an inconvenient needle* is and remains insoluble. —*Times.*

But these unsoldierlike recriminations among the Russian officers as well as their luxurious lives and their complete insouciance in the presence of their country's misfortunes, seems to have *set back the hand on the dial of Japanese rapprochement.*—*Times.*

Is there no spiritual purge to make the eye of the camel easier for a South-African millionaire?—*Times.*

And so it has come to pass that, not only *where invalids do congregate,* but in places hitherto reserved for the summer recreation of the tourist or the mountaineer there is a growing influx of winter pleasure-seekers.—*Times.*

Salmasius alone was not *unworthy sublimi flagello.*—LANDOR.

Even if a change were desirable *with Kitchener duce et auspice.*— *Times.*

The Leighton *qui savait vivre* perhaps better than did ever any other conspicuous, overworked servant of the public.—*Westminster Gazette.* (*Savoir vivre* is by this time English: *qui savait vivre* is an outrage on English readers)

It is not in the interests of the Japanese to close the book of the war, until they have placed themselves in the position of beati possidentes. —*Times.* (*Beati possidentes* is a sentence, meaning *Blessed are those who are in possession*; to fit it into another sentence is most awkward)

Resignation became a virtue of necessity for Sweden in hopes that a better understanding might in time grow out of the new order of things.—*Times.* (In the original phrase, *of necessity* does not depend on *virtue,* but on *make*; and it is intolerable without the word that gives it its meaning)

Many of the celebrities who in that most frivolous of watering-places do congregate.—BARONESS VON HUTTEN.

If misbehaviour be not checked in an effectual manner before long, there is every prospect that the whips of the existing Motor Act will be transformed into the scorpions of the Motor Act of the future.— *Times.*

A special protest should be made against the practice of introducing a quotation in two or three instalments of a word or two, each with its separate suit of quotation marks. The only quotations that should be cut up are those that are familiar enough to need no quotation marks, so that the effect is not so jerky.

The 'pigmy body' seemed 'fretted to decay' by the 'fiery soul' within it.—J. R. GREEN. (The original is:—

> A fiery soul which, working out its way,
> Fretted the pygmy-body to decay.—DRYDEN.)

18. TRITE QUOTATION

Quotation may be material or formal. With the first, the writer quotes to support himself by the authority (or to impugn the authority) of the person quoted; this does not concern us. With the second, he quotes to add some charm of striking expression or of association to his own writing. To the reader, those quotations are agreeable that neither strike him as hackneyed, nor rebuke his ignorance by their complete novelty, but rouse dormant memories. Quotation, then, should be adapted to the probable reader's cultivation. To deal in trite quotations and phrases therefore amounts to a confession that the writer either is uncultivated himself, or is addressing the uncultivated. All who would not make this confession are recommended to avoid (unless in some really new or perverted application— notum si callida verbum reddiderit junctura novum) such things as:

Chartered libertine; balm in Gilead; my prophetic soul; harmless necessary; e pur si muove; there's the rub; the curate's egg; hinc illae lacrimae; fit audience though few; a consummation devoutly to be wished; more in sorrow than in anger; metal more attractive; heir of all the ages; curses not loud but deep; more sinned against than sinning; the irony of fate; the psychological moment; the man in the street; the sleep of the just; a work of supererogation; the pity of it; the scenes he loved so well; in her great sorrow; all that was mortal of—; few equals and no superior; leave severely alone; suffer a sea change.

The plan partook of the nature of that of those ingenious islanders who lived entirely by taking in each other's washing.—E. F. BENSON.

For he was but moderately given to 'the cups that cheer but not inebriate', and had already finished his tea.—ELIOT.

Austria forbids children to smoke in public places; and in German schools and military colleges there are laws upon the subject; France, Spain, Greece, and Portugal *leave* the matter *severely alone.—West-minster Gazette*. (*Severely* is much worse than pointless here)

They carried compulsory subdivision and restriction of all kinds of skilled labour down to a degree *that would have been laughable enough, if it had only been less destructive.—*MORLEY.

If Diderot had visited . . . Rome, even the mighty painter of the Last Judgment . . . would have found an interpreter worthy of him. *But it was not to be.—*MORLEY.

Mr. de Sélincourt has, of course, *the defects of his qualities.—Times.*

The beloved *lustige Wien* [Vienna, that is] of his youth had *suffered a sea-change*. The green glacis down which Sobieski drove the defeated besieging army of Kara Mustafa was blocked by ranges of grand new buildings.—*Westminster Gazette*.

In the household of a farmer is an adopted daughter, Marikke, whose conduct is influenced by the fact that she is daughter of a *vagrom* gipsy.—*Westminster Gazette*. (the precise addition made by *vagrom* to the meaning is: you see, reader, I know my Shakspere)

19. LATIN ABBREVIATIONS, &c.

No one should use these who is not sure that he will not expose his ignorance by making mistakes with them. Confusion is very common, for instance, between *i.e.* and *e.g.* Again, *sic* should never be used except when a reader might really suppose that there was a misprint or garbling; to insert it simply by way of drawing attention and conveying a sneer is a very heavy assumption of superiority. *Vide* is only in place when a book or dictionary article is being referred to.

Shaliapine, first bass at the same opera, has handed in his resignation in consequence of this affair, and also because of affairs in general, vide imprisonment of his great friend Gorki.—*Times*.

The industrialist organ is inclined to regret that the league did not fix some definite date such as the year 1910 (sic) or the year 1912, for the completion of this programme.—*Times*. (This is the true use of *sic*; as the years mentioned are not consecutive, a reader might suppose that something was wrong; *sic* tells him that it is not so)

The *Boersen Courier* . . . maintains that 'nothing remains for M. Delcassé but to cry Pater peccavi to Germany and to retrieve as quickly as possible his diplomatic mistake (sic)'.—*Times*.

Let your principal stops be the full stop and comma, with a judicious

use of the semicolon and of the other stops where they are absolutely
necessary (*i.e.* you could not dispense with the note of interrogation
in asking questions).—BYGOTT & JONES. (*e.g.* is wanted, not *i.e.*)

20. UNEQUAL YOKEFELLOWS AND DEFECTIVE
DOUBLE HARNESS

When a word admits of two constructions, to use both may
not be positively incorrect, but is generally as ugly as to drive
a horse and a mule in double harness.

They did not *linger in* the long scarlet colonnades of the temple
itself, nor *gazing* at the dancing for which it is famous.—SLADEN.

This undoubtedly caused prices to rise; but did it not also *cause* all
Lancashire to work short time, many *mills to close*, and a great *restriction*
in the purchases of all our customers for cotton goods?—*Times*.

. . . *set herself* quietly down *to the care* of her own household, and *to
assist* Benjamin in the concerns of his trade.—SCOTT.

This correspondent says that not only did the French Government
know that Germany recognized the privileges resulting for France from
her position in Algeria, but also her general *views* on the work of reform
which it would be the task of the conference to examine.—*Times*.

Teach them the '*character* of God' through the 'Son's Life of Love',
that conscience must not be outraged, not because they would be
punished if they did, or because they would be handsomely rewarded
if they didn't, but simply because they know a thing is right or wrong
. . .—*Daily Telegraph*.

And any one who permits himself this incongruity is likely to
be betrayed into actual blunders.

The popularity of the parlements was surely due to the detestation
felt for the absolute Monarchy, and because they seemed to half-
informed men to be the champions of . . .—*Times*. (Here *because they
seemed* does not really fit *the popularity . . . was*, but *parlements were
popular*)

A difference, this, which was not much considered where and when
the end of the war was thought to be two or three years off, and that
the last blow would be Russia's.—F. GREENWOOD. (The last clause does
not fit *the end of the war was thought*, but *it was thought*)

Attila and his armies, he said, came and disappeared in a very
mysterious manner, and *that* nothing could be said with positiveness
about them.—BORROW.

Save him accordingly she did: but no sooner *is he dismissed*, and *Faust has made* a remark on the multitude of arrows which she is darting forth on all sides, than Lynceus returns.—CARLYLE.

The short drives at the beginning of the course of instruction were intended gradually *to accustom* the novice to the speed, and *of giving* him in the pauses an opportunity to fix well in his mind the principles of the automobile.—*Times*.

The predecessors of Sir Antony MacDonnell . . . were, to use the words of the Prime Minister, 'the aiders, advisers, and suggesters of their official chiefs'.—*Times*. (The aiders and advisers of a chief are those who aid and advise him; the suggesters of a chief, then, are those who suggest him, *i.e.* who propose him as chief?)

My assiduities expose me rather to her scorn . . . than to the treatment due to a man.—RICHARDSON.

One worthy gentleman, who is, perhaps, *better known than popular* in City restaurants, is never known to have lavished even the humblest copper coin on a waiter.—*Titbits*.

Its hands require strengthening and its resources increased.—*Times*.

Analogous, but always incorrect, though excusable in various degrees, is the equipping of pairs that should be obviously in double harness with conjunctions or prepositions that do not match—following *neither* by *or*, *both* by *as well as*, and the like.

Diderot presented a bouquet which was *neither* well *or* ill received.—MORLEY.

Like the Persian noble of old, I ask, 'that I may *neither* command *or* obey'.—EMERSON.

She would hear *nothing* of a declaration of war, *or* give any judgment on . . .—J. R. GREEN.

It appears, then, that *neither* the mixed and incomplete empiricism considered in the third chapter, *still less* the pure empiricism considered in the second chapter, affords us . . .—BALFOUR.

Scarcely was the nice new drain finished *than* several of the children sickened with diphtheria.—*Spectator*.

Which differs from that and who in being used *both* as an adjective *as well as* a noun.—H. SWEET.

M. Shipoff *in one and the same breath* denounces innovations, *yet* bases the whole electoral system on the greatest innovation in Russian history.—*Times*.

It would be *equally* absurd to attend to all the other parts of an engine and to neglect the principal source of its energy—the firebox—

as it is ridiculous to pay particular attention to the cleanliness of the body and to neglect the mouth and teeth.—*Advertisement*.

The conception of God in their minds was not *that of* a Father, but *as* a dealer out of rewards and punishments.—*Daily Telegraph*.

Dr. Dillon, than whom no Englishman has a profounder and more accurate acquaintance *with* the seamy side—as, indeed, *of* all aspects of Russian life—assumes . . .—*Times*.

Sir,—*In view of* the controversy which has arisen concerning the 12 in. Mark VIII guns in the Navy, and especially *to* the suggestion which might give rise to some doubt as to the efficiency of the wire system of construction . . .—*Times*.

We add three sentences, in the first of which double harness should not have been used because it is too cumbrous, in the second of which it is not correctly possible, and in the third of which the failure to use it is very slovenly.

The odd part of it is that this childish confusion does not only not take from our pleasure, but does not even take from our sense of the author's talent.—H. JAMES. (far from diminishing our pleasure, does not . . .)

As to the duration of the Austro-Russian mandate, there seems *little disposition* here to treat the question in a hard-and-fast spirit, *but rather* to regard it as . . .—*Times*. (. . . spirit; it is rather regarded as . . .)

To the student of the history of religious opinions in England *few contrasts are more striking when he compares* the assurance and complacency with which men made profession of their beliefs at the beginning of the nineteenth century and the diffidence and hesitation with which the same are recited at the beginning of the twentieth.— *Daily Telegraph*. (more striking than that between the assurance . . .)

21. COMMON PARTS

When two sentences coupled by a conjunction (whether coordinating or subordinating) have one or more parts in common, there are two ways of avoiding the full repetition of the common parts. (*a*) 'I see through your villany and I detest your villany' can become 'I see through and detest your villany'; 'I have at least tried to bring about a reconciliation, though I may have failed to bring about a reconciliation' can become 'I have at least tried, though I may have failed, to bring about, &c.' (*b*) By substitution or ellipse, the sentences

become 'I see through your villany, and detest it' and 'I have
at least tried to bring about a reconciliation, though I may
have failed (to do so)'. Of these, the (a) form requires careful
handling: a word that is not common to both sentences must
not be treated as common; and one that is common, and whose
position declares that it is meant to do double duty, must not
be repeated. Violations of these rules are always more or less
unsightly, and are excusable only when the precise (a) form is
intolerably stiff and the (b) form not available. In our examples
below, the words placed in brackets are the two variants, each
of which, when the other is omitted, should, with the common
or unbracketed parts, form a complete sentence; the conjunctions being of course ignored for this purpose.

What other power (could) or (ever has) produced such changes?—
Daily Telegraph.

Things temporal (had) and (would) alter.—*Daily Telegraph.*

(It had), as (all houses should), been in tune with the pleasant,
mediocre charm of the island.—E. F. BENSON.

This type will almost always admit of the emphatic repetition
of the verb: 'could produce or ever has produced'.

Those of us who still believe in Greek as (one of the finest), if not
(the finest) instruments . . .—*Times.*

(One of the noblest), if not (the noblest), feelings an Englishman
could possess.—*Daily Telegraph.*

Use (b): 'One of the finest instruments, if not the finest'.

The games were looked upon as being (quite as important) or (perhaps more important) than drill.—*Times.*

The railway has done (all) and (more) than was expected of it.—
Spectator.

Use (b): 'as important as drill, if not more so'; 'all that was
expected of it, and more'.

All words that precede the first of two correlatives, such as
'not . . . but', 'both . . . and', 'neither . . . nor', are declared
by their position to be common; we bracket accordingly in
the next examples:

The pamphlet forms (not only a valuable addition to our works on

scientific subjects), but (is also of deep interest to German readers).—
Times. (not only forms . . . but is . . .)

Forty-five per cent. of the old Rossallians . . . received (either
decorations) (or were mentioned in despatches).—*Daily Telegraph.*
(Either received . . . or were)

The Senate, however, has (either passed) (or will pass) amendments
to every clause.—*Spectator.* (either has passed or will pass)

Cloth of gold (neither seems to elate) (nor cloth of frieze to depress)
him.—LAMB.

A curious extension, not to be mended in the active; for
neither cannot well precede the first of two subjects when
they have different verbs.

On the other hand, words placed between the two correlatives
are declared by their position not to be common:

Which neither (suits one purpose) (nor the other).—*Times.* (suits
neither . . . nor)

Not only (against my judgment), (but my inclination).—RICHARDSON.

Not only (in the matter of malaria), (but also beriberi).—*Times.*
(In the matter not of malaria only, but of . . .)

22. THE WRONG TURNING

It is not very uncommon, on regaining the high road after a
divergent clause or phrase, to get confused between the two,
and continue wrongly the subordinate construction instead of
that actually required.

I feel, however, that there never was a time when the people of this
country were more ready to believe than they are today, and would
openly believe if Christianity, with 'doctrine' subordinated, were
presented to them in the most convincing of all forms, viz. . . .—*Daily
Telegraph.* (*Would believe* is made parallel to *they are today*; it is really
parallel to *there never was a time*; and we should read *and that they
would openly believe*)

In the face of this statement either proofs should be adduced to show
that Coroner Troutbeck has stated facts 'soberly judged', and that they
contain 'warrant for the accusation of wholesale' ignorance on the part
of a trusted and eminently useful class of the community, or failing
this, that the offensive and unjust charge should be withdrawn.—
Times. (*The charge should be withdrawn* is made parallel to *Coroner
Troutbeck has stated* and *they contain*; it is really parallel to *proofs*

should be adduced; and we should omit *that*, and read *or failing this, the offensive . . .*)

We cannot part from Prof. Bury's work without expressing our unfeigned admiration for his complete control of the original authorities on which his narrative is based, and of the sound critical judgment he exhibits . . .—*Spectator*. (The judgment is admired, not controlled)

Sometimes the confusion is not merely of the pen, but is in the writer's thought; and it is then almost incurable.

. . . the privilege by which the mind, like the lamps of a mailcoach, moving rapidly through the midnight woods, illuminate, for one instant, the foliage or sleeping umbrage of the thickets, and, in the next instant, have quitted them, to carry their radiance forward upon endless successions of objects.—DE QUINCEY.

23. ELLIPSE IN SUBORDINATE CLAUSES

The missing subject and (with one exception) the missing verb of a subordinate clause can be supplied only from the sentence to which it is subordinate. The exception is the verb 'to be'. We can say 'The balls, when wet, do not bounce', 'When in doubt, play trumps', because the verb to be supplied is *are*, and the subject is that of the principal sentence. Other violations of the rule occur, but are scarcely tolerable even in the spoken language. The following are undesirable instances:

For, though summer, I knew . . . Mr. Rochester would like to see a cheerful hearth.—C. BRONTË.

We can supply *was*, but not *it*; the natural subject is *I*.

I have now seen him, and though not for long, he is a man who speaks with Bismarckian frankness.—*Times*.

'Though I did not see him for long', we are meant to understand. But the *though* clause is not subordinate to the sentence containing that subject and verb: *and* always joins coordinates and announces the transition from one coordinate to another. Consequently, the *though* clause must be a part (a subordinate part) of the second coordinate, and must draw from that its subject and verb: 'though he is not a man of Bismarckian frankness for long, . . .'. Even if we could supply *I saw* with the clause in its present place, we should still have the absurd implication that the man's habitual frankness (not the writer's perception of it) depended on the duration of the interview. We offer three conjectural emendations: 'I have now seen him, though not for long; and he is a man who . . .'; 'I have now seen him, and though I did not see him for long, I perceived that he was a man who . . .'; 'I have now seen him, and though I did not see him for long, I found out what he thought; for he is a man who . . .'.

24. SOME ILLEGITIMATE INFINITIVES

Claim is not followed by an infinitive except when the subject of *claim* is also that of the infinitive. Thus, *I claim to be honest*, but not *I claim this to be honest*. The *Oxford Dictionary* (1893) does not mention the latter use even to condemn it, but it is now becoming very common, and calls for strong protest. The corresponding passive use is equally wrong. The same applies to *pretend*.

'This entirely new experiment' which you claim to have 'solved the problem of combining . . .'—*Times*.

Usage, therefore, is not, as it is often claimed to be, the absolute law of language.—R. G. WHITE.

The gun which made its first public appearance on Saturday is claimed to be the most serviceable weapon of its kind in use in any army.—*Times*.

The constant failure to live up to what we claim to be our most serious convictions proves that we do not hold them at all.—*Daily Telegraph*.

The anonymous and masked delators whose creation the Opposition pretends to be an abuse of power on the part of M. Combes.—*Times*.

Possible and *probable* are not to be completed by an infinitive. For *are possible to* read *can*; and for *probable* read *likely*.

But no such questions are possible, as it seems to me, to arise between your nation and ours.—CHOATE.

Should Germany meditate anything of the kind it would look uncommonly like a deliberate provocation of France, and for that reason it seems scarcely probable to be borne out by events.—*Times*.

Prefer has two constructions: I prefer this (living) *to* that (dying), and I prefer to do this *rather than* that. The infinitive construction must not be used without *rather* (unless, of course, the second alternative is suppressed altogether).

Other things being equal, I should prefer to marry a rich man than a poor one.—E. F. BENSON.

The following infinitives are perhaps by false analogy from those that might follow *forbade*, *seen*, *ask*. It may be noticed generally that slovenly and hurried writers find the infinitive a great resource.

Marshal Oyama strictly *prohibited* his troops *to take* quarter within the walls.—*Times*.

The Chinese held a chou-chou, during which the devil was exorcised and duly *witnessed* by several believers *to take* his flight in divers guises. —*Times*.

Third, they might *demand* from Germany, all flushed as she was with military pride, *to tell* us plainly whether . . .—MORLEY.

25. 'SPLIT' INFINITIVES

The 'split' infinitive has taken such hold upon the consciences of journalists that, instead of warning the novice against splitting his infinitives, we must warn him against the curious superstition that the splitting or not splitting makes the difference between a good and a bad writer. The split infinitive is an ugly thing, as will be seen from our examples below; but it is one among several hundred ugly things, and the novice should not allow it to occupy his mind exclusively. Even that mysterious quality, 'distinction' of style, may in modest measure be attained by a splitter of infinitives: 'The book is written with a distinction (save in the matter of split infinitives) unusual in such works.'—*Times*.

The time has come to once again voice the general discontent.—*Times*.
It should be authorized to immediately put in hand such work.—*Times*.
Important negotiations are even now proceeding to further cement trade relations.—*Times*.
We were not as yet strong enough in numbers to seriously influence the poll.—*Times*.
Keep competition with you unless you wish to once more see a similar state of things to those prevalent prior to the inauguration . . .—*Guernsey Evening Press*.

And that she should force me, by the magic of her pen to mentally acknowledge, albeit with wrath and shame, my own inferiority.— CORELLI.

The oil lamp my landlady was good enough to still allow me the use of.—CORELLI.

The 'persistent agitation' . . . is to so arouse public opinion on the subject as to . . .—*Times*.

In order to slightly extend that duration in the case of a few.—*Times*.

To thus prevent a constant accretion to the Jewish population of Russia from this country would be nobler work . . .—*Times*.

26. COMPOUND PASSIVES

Corresponding to the active construction '. . . have attempted to justify this step', we get two passive constructions: (1) 'This step has been attempted to be justified', (2) 'It has been attempted to justify this step'. Of these (1), although licensed by usage, is an incorrect and slovenly makeshift: 'this step' is not the object of 'have attempted', and cannot be the subject of the corresponding passive. The true object of 'have attempted' is the whole phrase 'to justify this step', which in (2) rightly appears as the subject, in apposition to an introductory 'it'.—In point of clumsiness, there is perhaps not much to choose between the two passive constructions, neither of which should be used when it can be avoided. When the subject of the active verb 'have attempted' is definite, and can conveniently be stated, the active form should always be retained; to write 'it had been attempted by the founders of the study to supply' instead of 'the founders had attempted to supply' is mere perversity. When, as in some of our examples below, the subject of the active verb 'have attempted' is indefinite, the passive turn is sometimes difficult to avoid; but unless the object of 'justify' is a relative, and therefore necessarily placed at the beginning, 'an attempt has been made' can often be substituted for 'it has been attempted', and is less stiff and ugly.

The cutting down of 'saying lessons', by which it had been attempted by the founders of the study to supply the place of speech in the learning of Greek.—*Times*.

But when it was attempted to give practical effect to the popular exasperation, serious obstacles arose.—*Times*. (When an attempt was made to . . .)

He and his friends would make the government of Ireland a sheer impossibility, and it would be the duty of the Irish party to make it so if it was attempted to be run on the lines of . . .—*Times*. (if an attempt was made to run it on the . . .)

It is not however attempted to be denied.—HAZLITT. (No one attempts to deny)

As to the audience, we imagine that a large part of it, certainly all that part of it whose sympathies it was desired to enlist, . . .—*Times*. (whose sympathies were to be enlisted)

He will see the alterations that were proposed to be made, but rejected.—*Times*. (proposed, but rejected)

The argument by which this difficulty is sought to be evaded.—BALFOUR.

This and the following instances are not easily mended, unless we may supply the subject of 'seek', &c. ('some writers').

The arguments by which the abolition was attempted to be supported were founded on the rights of man.—*Times*.

Some mystery in regard to her birth, which, she was well informed, was assiduously, though vainly, endeavoured to be discovered.—FANNY BURNEY.

The close darkness of the shut-up house (forgotten to be opened, though it was long since day) yielded to the unexpected glare.—DICKENS.

Those whose hours of employment are proposed to be limited.—*Times*.

The insignificant duties proposed to be placed on food.—*Times*.

The anti-liberal principles which it was long ago attempted to embody in the Holy Alliance.—*Times*.

Considerable support was managed to be raised for Waldemar.—CARLYLE.

We may notice here a curious blunder that is sometimes made with the reflexive verb 'I avail myself of'. The passive of this is never used, because there is no occasion for it: 'I was availed of this by myself' would mean exactly the same as the active, and would be intolerably clumsy. The impossible passives quoted below imply that *it* and *staff* would be the direct objects of the active verb.

Watt and Fulton bethought themselves that, where was power was not devil, but was God; that it must be availed of, and not by any means let off and wasted.—EMERSON.

Used or *employed*, and so in the next:

No salvage appliances or staff could have been availed of in time to save the lives of the men.—*Times*.

27. CONFUSION WITH NEGATIVES

This is extraordinarily common. The instances are arranged in order of obviousness.

Yezd is not only the refuge of the most ancient of Persian religions, but it is one of the headquarters of the modern Babi propaganda, the far-reaching effects of which it is probably difficult to underestimate.—*Spectator*.

Not a whit undeterred by the disaster which overtook them at Cavendish-square last week . . . the suffragettes again made themselves prominent.—*Daily Mail*.

So far as medicine is concerned, I am not sure that physiology, such as it was down to the time of Harvey, might as well not have existed.—HUXLEY.

The generality of his countrymen are far more careful not to transgress the customs of what they call gentility, than to violate the laws of honour or morality.—BORROW.

France and Russia are allies, as are England and Japan. Is it impossible to imagine that, in consequence of the growing friendship between the two great peoples on both sides of the Channel, an agreement might not one day be realized between the four Powers?—*Times*.

I do not of course deny that in this, as in all moral principles, there may not be found, here and there, exceptional cases which may amuse a casuist.—L. STEPHEN.

In view of the doubts among professed theologians regarding the genuineness and authenticity of the Gospels in whole or in part, he is unable to say how much of the portraiture of Christ may not be due to the idealization of His life and character.—*Daily Telegraph*.

Is it quite inconceivable that if the smitten had always turned the other cheek the smiters would not long since have become so ashamed that their practice would have ceased?—*Daily Telegraph*.

I do not think it is possible that the traditions and doctrines of these two institutions should not fail to create rival, and perhaps warring, schools.—*Times*.

Any man—runs this terrible statute—denying the doctrine of the

Trinity or of the Divinity of Christ, or that the books of Scripture are not the 'Word of God', or . . . , 'shall suffer the pain of death'.— J. R. GREEN.

But it would not be at all surprising if, by attempting too much, and, it must be added, by indulging too much in a style the strained preciosity of which occasionally verges on rant and even hysteria, Mr. Sichel has not to some extent defeated his own object.—*Spectator*.

No one scarcely really believes.—*Daily Telegraph*.

Let them agree to differ; for who knows but what agreeing to differ may not be a form of agreement rather than a form of difference?— STEVENSON.

Lastly, how can Mr. Balfour tell but that two years hence he may not be too tired of official life to begin any new conflict?—F. GREENWOOD.

What sort of impression would it be likely to make upon the Boers? They could hardly fail to regard it as anything but an expression of want of confidence in our whole South-African policy.—*Times*.

My friend Mr. Bounderby could never see any difference between leaving the Coketown 'hands' exactly as they were and requiring them to be fed with turtle soup and venison out of gold spoons.—DICKENS.

But it is one thing to establish these conditions [the Chinese Ordinance], and another to remove them suddenly.—*Westminster Gazette*.

What economy of life and money would not have been spared the empire of the Tsars had it not rendered war certain.—*Times*. (*It* is the empire. The instance is not quoted for *not*, though that too is wrong, but for the confusion between loss and economy)

The question of 'raids' is one which necessarily comes home to every human being living within at least thirty miles of our enormously long coast line.—LONSDALE HALE. (An odd puzzle. *Within thirty* means less than thirty; *at least thirty* means not less than thirty. The meaning is clear enough, however, and perhaps the expression is defensible; but it would have been better to say: within a strip at least thirty miles broad along our enormous coast line)

The fact that a negative idea can often be either included in a word or kept separate from it leads to a special form of confusion, the construction proper to the resolved form being used with the compound and *vice versa*.

My feelings, Sir, are moderately unspeakable, and that is a fact.— American. (not moderately speakable: *moderately* belongs only to half of *unspeakable*)

. . . who did not aim, like the Presbyterians, at a change in Church government, but rejected the notion of a national Church at all.—

J. R. GREEN. (*Reject* is equivalent to *will not have*. I reject altogether: I will not have at all)

And your correspondent does not seem to know, or not to realize, the conditions of the problem.—*Times*. (*Seems*, not *does not seem*, has to be supplied in the second clause)

I confess myself altogether unable to formulate such a principle, much less to prove it.—BALFOUR. (*Less* does not suit *unable*, but *able*; but the usage of *much less* and *much more* is hopelessly chaotic)

War between these two great nations would be an inexplicable impossibility.—CHOATE. (*Inexplicable* does not qualify the whole of *impossibility*; to make sense we must divide *impossibility* into *impossible event*, and take *inexplicable* only with *event*)

And the cry has this justification,—that no age can see itself in a proper perspective, and is therefore incapable of giving its virtues and vices their relative places.—*Spectator*. (*No age* is equivalent to *not any age*, and out of this we have to take *any age* as subject to the last sentence; this is a common, but untidy and blameworthy device)

28. OMISSION OF 'AS'

This is very common, but quite contrary to good modern usage, after the verb *regard*, and others like it. In the first three instances the motive of the omission is obvious, but does not justify it; all that was necessary was to choose another verb, as *consider*, that does not require *as*. In the later instances the omission is gratuitous.

I regard it as important as anything.

Lord Bombie had run away with Lady Bombie 'in her sark'. This I could not help regarding both a most improper as well as a most uncomfortable proceeding.—CROCKETT.

So vital is this suggestion regarded.

Rare early editions of Shakespeare's plays and poems—editions which had long been regarded among the national heirlooms.—S. LEE.

The latter may now be expected to regard himself absolved from such obligation as he previously felt.—*Times*.

A memoir which was justly regarded of so much merit and importance that . . .—HUXLEY.

. . . what might be classed a 'horizontal' European triplice.—*Times*.

You would look upon yourself amply revenged if you knew what they have cost me.—RICHARDSON.

He also alluded to the bayonet, and observed that its main use was no longer a defence against cavalry, but it was for the final charge.—*Times*.

. . . I was rewarded with such a conception of the God-like majesty and infinite divinity which everywhere loomed up behind and shone through the humanity of the Son of Man that no false teaching or any power on earth or in hell itself will ever shake my firm faith in the combined divinity and humanity in the person of the Son of God, and *as sure am I* that I eat and drink and live to-day, so certain am I that this mysterious Divine Redeemer is in living . . .—*Daily Telegraph*.

The last example is of a different kind. Read *as sure as I am* for *as sure am I* as the least possible correction. Unpractised writers should beware of correlative clauses except in their very simplest forms.

29. OTHER LIBERTIES TAKEN WITH 'AS'

As must not be expected to do by itself the work of *such as*.

There were not two dragon sentries keeping ward before the gate of this abode, *as* in magic legend are usually found on duty over the wronged innocence imprisoned.—DICKENS.

The specialist is naturally best for his particular job; but if the particular specialist required is not on the spot, as must often be the case, the best substitute for him is not another specialist but the man trained to act for himself in all circumstances, *as* it has been the glory of our nation to produce both in the Army and elsewhere.—*Times*.

We question if throughout the French Revolution there was a single case of six or seven thousand insurgents blasted away by cannon shot, *as* is believed to have happened in Odessa.—*Spectator*. (This is much more defensible than the previous two; but when a definite noun—as here *case*—can be naturally supplied for the verb introduced by *as*, *such as* is better.)

The decision of the French Government to send a special mission to represent France at the marriage of the German Crown Prince is not intended as anything more than a mere act of international courtesy, *as* is customary on such occasions.—*Times*.

Neither *as* nor *such as* should be made to do the work of the relative pronoun where there would be no awkwardness in using the pronoun itself.

With a speed of eight knots, *as* [which] has been found practicable in the case of the Suez Canal, the passage would occupy five days.—*Times*.

The West Indian atmosphere is not of the limpid brightness **and** transparent purity *such as* [that] are found in the sketch entitled 'A Street in Kingston'.—*Times*.

The ideal statues and groups in this room and the next are scarcely so interesting as we have sometimes seen.—*Times*. (*As* is clearly here a relative adverb, answering to *so*; nevertheless the construction can be theoretically justified, the full form being *as we have sometimes seen groups interesting*. But it is very ugly; why not say instead *as some that we have seen*?)

The idiom *as who should say* must not be used unless the sentence to which it is appended has for subject a person to whom the person implied in *who* is compared. This seems reasonable, and is borne out, for instance, by all the Shakespeare passages—a dozen—that we have looked at. The type is: The cloudy messenger turns me his back, and hums, as who should say:—&c.

To think of the campaign without the scene is as who should read a play by candle-light among the ghosts of an empty theatre.—MORLEY.

30. BRACHYLOGY

1. Omission of a dependent noun in the second of two parallel series: 'The brim of my hat is wider than yours'. For this there is some justification: an ugly string of words is avoided, and the missing word is easily supplied from the first series; it has usually the effect, however, of attaching a preposition to the wrong noun:

I should be proud to lay an obligation upon my charmer to the amount of half, nay, to the whole of my estate.—RICHARDSON.

There is as much of the pure gospel in their teachings as in any other community of Christians in our land.

There cannot be the same reason for a prohibition of correspondence with me, as there was of mine with Mr. Lovelace.—RICHARDSON.

Here the right preposition is retained.

A man holding such a responsible position as Minister of the United States.—D. SLADEN.

2. A preposition is sometimes left out, quite unwarrantably, from a mistaken idea of euphony:

Without troubling myself as to what such self-absorption might *lead* in the future.—CORELLI. (lead to)

He chose to fancy that she was not suspicious of what all his acquaintance were perfectly aware—namely, that . . .—THACKERAY. (aware of)

3. Impossible compromises between two possible alternatives.

To be a Christian means to us one who has been regenerated.—*Daily Telegraph.* ('A Christian means one who has': 'to be a Christian means to have been')

To do what as far as human possibility has proved out of his power.—*Daily Telegraph.* ('As a matter of human possibility': 'as far as human possibility goes')

One compromise of this kind has come to be generally recognized:

So far from being annoyed, he agreed at once. ('So far was he from being annoyed that . . .': 'far from being annoyed, he agreed')

4. Mistaken assumption that the repetition in a later clause or sentence of what has been the subject of a previous verb cannot be necessary.

This was before he had learned to write fair English, and so was obliged to find a bazar letter-writer.—KIPLING. (and so *he* was)

It was as the lay champion that he desired to act, and believed that in such a position his influence would be much greater.—BEACONSFIELD. (and *he* believed)

Efforts made to recover a little girl named Gudrun, who suddenly disappeared from Christiania, and whose playfellow says was carried off by gipsies.—*Westminster Gazette.* (and *who* her playfellow says was; or, and whose playfellow says *she* was)

31. BETWEEN TWO STOOLS

The commonest form of indecision is that between statement and question. But the examples of this are followed by a few miscellaneous ones.

May I ask *that* if care should be taken of remains of buildings a thousand years old, *ought not* care to be taken of ancient British earthworks several thousand years old?—*Times*.

Can I not make you understand that you are ruining yourself and me, and *that* if you don't get reconciled to your father *what is* to become of you?—S. FERRIER.

We will only say *that* if it was undesirable for a private member to induce the Commons to pass a vote against Colonial Preference, *why was it* not undesirable for a private member . . .—*Spectator*.

Surely, then, if I am not claiming too much for our efforts at that time to maintain the Union, *am I* exaggerating our present ability to render him effectual aid in the contest that will be fought at the next election if I say that prudence alone should dictate to him the necessity for doing everything in his power to revive the spirit which the policy of Sir Antony MacDonnell, Lord Dudley, and Mr. Wyndham has done so much to weaken?—*Times*.

I then further observed *that* China having observed the laws of neutrality, *how could he* believe in the possibility of an alliance with Russia?—*Times*.

The next two use both the relative and the participle construction, instead of choosing between them.

Thus it befell that our high and low labour vote, *which* (if one might say so in the hearing of M. Jaurès and Herr Bebel) *being* vertical rather than horizontal, and quite unhindered in the United States, of course by an overwhelming majority elected President Roosevelt.—*Times*.

He replied to Mr. Chamberlain's Limehouse speech, the only part of *which* that he could endorse *being*, he said, the suggestion that the electorate should go to the root of the question at the next general election.—*Times*.

Who, in Europe, at least, would *forego* the delights of kissing,— (which the Japanese by-the-by consider a disgusting habit),—*without* embraces,—and all those other endearments which are supposed to dignify the progress of true love!—CORELLI.

Poor, bamboozled, patient public!—no wonder it is beginning to think *that* a halfpenny spent on a newspaper which is purchased to be thrown away, *enough* and more than enough.—CORELLI.

But hurriedly dismissing *whatever* shadow of earnestness, or faint confession of a purpose, laudable or wicked, *that* her face, or voice, or manner, had, for the moment betrayed, she lounged . . .—DICKENS.

At the Épée Team Competition for Dr. Savage's Challenge Cup, held on the 25th and 27th February last, *was won* by the Inns of Court team, consisting of . . .—*14th Middlesex Battalion Orders*.

32. THE IMPERSONAL 'ONE'

This should never be mixed up with other pronouns. Its possessive is *one's*, not *his*, and *one* should be repeated, if necessary, not be replaced by *him*, &c. Those who doubt their ability to handle it skilfully under these restrictions should only use it where no repetition or substitute is needed. The older experimental usage, which has now been practically decided against, is shown in the Lowell examples.

That inequality and incongruousness in his writing which makes *one* revise *his* judgment at every tenth page.—LOWELL.

As one grows older, *one* loses many idols, perhaps comes at last to have none at all, although *he* may honestly enough uncover in deference to the worshippers at any shrine.—LOWELL.

There are many passages which *one* is rather inclined to like than sure *he* would be right in liking.—LOWELL.

He is a man who speaks with Bismarckian frankness, and who directly impresses *one* with the impression that *you* are speaking to a man and not to an incarnate bluebook.—*Times*.

The merit of the book, and it is not a small one, is that it discusses every problem with fairness, with no perilous hankering after originality, and with a disposition to avail *oneself* of what has been done by *his* predecessors.—*Times*.

If *one* has an opinion on any subject, it is of little use to read books or papers which tell *you* what you know already.—*Times*.

. . . are all creations which make *one* laugh inwardly as *we* read.—HUTTON.

One's, on the other hand, is not the right possessive for the generic *man*; *man's* or *his* is required according to circumstances; *his* in the following example:

There is a natural desire in the mind of *man* to sit for *one's* picture.—HAZLITT.

33. BETWEEN . . . OR

This is a confusion between two ways of giving alternatives —*between . . . and*, and *either . . . or*. It is always wrong.

The choice Russia has is between payment for damages in money *or* in kind.—*Times*.

Forced to choose between the sacrifice of important interests on the one hand *or* the expansion of the Estimates on the other.—*Times*.

We have in that substance the link between organic *or* inorganic matter which abolishes the distinction between living *and* dead matter. —*Westminster Gazette*. (Observe the 'elegant variation')

The question lies between a God and a creed, *or* a God in such an abstract sense that does not signify.—*Daily Telegraph*.

The author of the last has been perplexed by the *and* in one of his alternatives. He should have used *on the one hand*, &c.

34. 'A' PLACED BETWEEN THE ADJECTIVE AND ITS NOUN

This is ugly when not necessary. Types of phrase in which it is necessary are: Many a youth; What a lie! How dreadful a fate! So lame an excuse. But there is no difficulty in placing *a* before ordinary qualifications of the adjective like *quite, more, much less*. In the following, read *quite a sufficient, a more valuable, a more glorious, a more serviceable, no different position, a greater or less degree.*

. . . adding that there was no suggestion of another raid against the Japanese flank, which was *quite sufficient an indication* of coming events for those capable of reading between the lines.—*Times*.

Can any one choose *more glorious an exit* than to die fighting for one's own country?—*Times*.

Of sympathy, of . . . Mr. Baring has a full measure, which, in his case, is *more valuable an asset* than familiarity with military textbooks. —*Times*.

No great additional expenditure is required in order to make Oxford *more serviceable a part* of our educational system.—*Westminster Gazette*.

And young undergraduates are in this respect in *no different a position* from that of any other Civil Servant.—*Westminster Gazette*.

The thousand and one adjuncts to devotion finding place in *more or less a degree* in all churches, are all . . .—*Daily Telegraph*.

The odd arrangement in the following will not do; we should have *a* either before *so* or before *degree*.

But what I do venture to protest against is the sacrificing of the interests of the country districts in *so ridiculously an unfair degree* to those of a small borough.—*Times*.

35. *DO* AS SUBSTITUTE VERB

Do cannot represent (1) *be*, (2) an active verb supplied from a passive, (3) an active verb in a compound tense, gerund, or infinitive; You made the very mistake that I *did*, but *have made, was afraid of making, expected to make, shall* (*make*).

It . . . ought to have been satisfying to the young man. And so, in a manner of speaking, it did.—CROCKETT.

It may justly be said, as Mr. Paul does, that . . .—*Westminster Gazette*.

To inflict upon themselves a disability which one day they will find the mistake and folly of doing.—*Westminster Gazette*.

We can of course say He lost his train, which I had warned him not to *do*; because *lose* is then represented not by *do*, but by *which* (thing).

36. FRESH STARTS

The trick of taking breath in the middle of a sentence by means of a resumptive *that* or the like should be avoided; especially when it is a confession rather of the writer's short-windedness than of the unwieldy length of his sentence.

It does not follow (as I pointed out by implication above) that if, according to the account of their origin given by the system, those fundamental beliefs are true, that therefore they are true.—BALFOUR.

Sir—Might I suggest that while this interesting question is being discussed that the hymn 'Rock of Ages' be sung in every church and chapel . . .?—*Daily Telegraph*.

A very short-winded correspondent.

It seems to be a fair deduction that when the Japanese gained their flank position immediately West of Mukden, and when, further, they took no immediate advantage of the fact, but, on the contrary, began to hold the villages in the plain as defensive positions, that a much more ambitious plan was in operation.—*Times*.

If the writer means what he says, and the grounds of the deduction are not included in the sentence, reconstruction is not obvious, and *that* is perhaps wanted to pick up the thread; but if, as may be suspected, the *when* clauses contain the grounds of the deduction, we may reconstruct as follows: 'When the Japanese . . . , and when . . . , it was natural to infer that . . . '.

37. VULGARISMS AND COLLOQUIALISMS

Like for *as*:

Sins that were degrading me, like they have many others.—*Daily Telegraph*.

They should not make a mad, reckless, frontal attack like General Buller made at the battle of Colenso.—*Daily Telegraph*.

Coming to God the loving Father for pardon, like the poor prodigal did.—*Daily Telegraph.*

There is no moral force in existence . . . which enlarges our outlook like suffering does.—*Daily Telegraph.*

What ever . . . ? is a colloquialism; *whatever . . . ?* a vulgarism:

· Whatever reason have we to suppose, as the vast majority of professing Christians appear to do, that the public worship of Almighty God . . .?—*Daily Telegraph.*

Whatever is the good in wrangling about bones when one is hungry and has nutritious food at hand?—*Daily Telegraph.*

'Those sort':

I know many of those sort of girls whom you call conjurors.—TROLLOPE.

Those sort of writers would merely take it as a first-class advertisement.—CORELLI.

---

38. TAUTOLOGY

Lord Rosebery has not budged from his position—splendid, no doubt—of (lonely) isolation.—*Times.*

Counsel admitted that that was a grave suggestion to make, but he submitted that it was borne out by the (surrounding) circumstances.—*Times.*

One can feel first the characteristics which men have in common and only afterward those which distinguish them (apart) from one another.—*Times.*

A final friendly agreement with Japan, which would be very welcome to Russia, is only possible if Japan (again) regains her liberty of action.—*Times.*

Miss Tox was (often) in the habit of assuring Mrs. Chick that . . .—DICKENS.

He had come up one morning, as was now (frequently) his wont.—TROLLOPE.

The counsellors of the Sultan (continue to) remain sceptical.—*Times.*

The Peresviet lost both her fighting-tops and (in appearance) looked the most damaged of all the ships.—*Times.*

They would, however, strengthen their position if they returned the (temporary) loan of Sir A. MacDonnell to his owners with thanks.—*Times.*

The score was taken to 136 when Mr. MacLaren, who had (evidently) seemed bent on hitting Mr. Armstrong off, was bowled.—*Times.*

. . . cannot prevent the diplomacy of the two countries from lending each other (mutual) support.—*Times*.

However, I judged that they would soon (mutually) find each other out.—CROCKETT.

Notwithstanding which, (however,) poor Polly embraced them all round.—DICKENS.

If any real remedy is to be found, we must first diagnose the true nature of the disease; (but) that, however, is not hard.—*Times*.

M. Delcassé contemplated an identical answer for France, Great Britain, and Spain, refusing, of course, the proposed conference, but his colleagues of the Cabinet were (, however,) opposed to identical replies.—*Times*.

The strong currents frequently shifted the mines, to the equal danger (both) of friend and foe.—*Times*.

And persecution on the part of the Bishops and the Presbyterians, to (both of) whom their opinions were equally hateful, drove flocks of refugees over sea.—J. R. GREEN.

But to the ordinary English Protestant (both) Latitudinarian and High Churchmen were equally hateful.—J. R. GREEN.

Seriously, (and apart from jesting,) this is no light matter.—BAGEHOT.

To go back to your own country . . . with (the consciousness that you go back with) the sense of duty done.—LORD HALSBURY.

No doubt my efforts were clumsy enough, but Togo had a capacity for taking pains, by which (said) quality genius is apt to triumph over early obstacles.—*Times*.

. . . as having created a (joint) partnership between the two Powers in the Morocco question.—*Times*.

Sir—As a working man it appears to me that to the question 'Do we believe?' the only sensible position (there seems to be) is to frankly acknowledge our ignorance of what lies beyond.—*Daily Telegraph*.

39. REDUNDANCIES

Dr. Redmond told his constituents that *by* reducing the National vote in the House of Commons they would not *thereby* get rid of obstruction.—*Times*.

It is not a thousand years *ago since* municipalities in Scotland were by no means free from the suspicion of corruption.—LORD ROSEBERY.

Some substance equally *as* yielding.—*Daily Mail*.

Had another expedition reached the Solomon Islands, who knows *but* that the Spaniards might *not* have gone on to colonize Australia and so turned the current of history?—*Spectator*.

As one *being* able to give full consent . . . I am yours faithfully . . .—*Daily Telegraph*.

But *to* where shall I look for some small ray of light that will illumine the darkness surrounding the mystery of my being?—*Daily Telegraph*.

It is quite *possible* that if they do that it *may* be *possible* to amend it in certain particulars.—*Westminster Gazette*.

Men and women who *professed to call* themselves Christians.— *Daily Telegraph*. (An echo, no doubt, of 'profess and call' themselves Christians')

The correspondence that you have published *abundantly* throws out into *bold* relief the false position assumed . . .—*Daily Telegraph*.

In the course of the *day, yesterday*, M. Rouvier was able to assure M. Delcassé . . .—*Times*.

Moreover, too, do we not all feel . . .?—J. C. COLLINS.

The doing nothing for a length of days after the first shock he sustained was *the reason of how it came that* Nesta knitted closer her acquaintance . . .—MEREDITH.

When the public adopt new inventions wholesale, . . . *some obligation is due* to lessen, so far as is possible, the hardships in which . . .— *Westminster Gazette*.

40. 'AS TO WHETHER'

This is a form that is seldom necessary, and should be reserved for sentences in which it is really difficult to find a substitute. Abstract nouns that cannot be followed immediately by *whether* should if possible be replaced by the corresponding verbs. Many writers seem to delight in this hideous combination, and employ it not only with abstracts that can be followed by *whether*, but even with verbs.

The Court declined to express any opinion *as to* whether the Russian Ambassador was justified in giving the assurances in question and *as to* whether the offences with which the accused were charged were punishable by German law.—*Times*. (Perhaps 'declined to say whether in their opinion'; but this is less easily mended than most)

The difficulties of this task were so great that I was in doubt *as to* whether it was possible.—*Times*.

His whole interest is concentrated on the question *as to* how his mission will affect his own fortunes.—*Times*.

A final decision has not yet been arrived at *as to* whether or not the proceedings shall be public.—*Times*. (It has not yet been finally decided whether)

You raise the question *as to* whether Admiral Rozhdestvensky will not return.—*Times*.

I have much pleasure in informing Rear Admiral Mather Byles *as to* where he could inspect a rifle of the type referred to.

The interesting question which such experiments tend to suggest is *as to* how far science may . . .—*Outlook.*

When we come to consider the question *as to* whether, upon the dissolution of the body, the spirit flies to some far-distant celestial realm . . .—*Daily Telegraph.*

He never told us to judge by the lives of professing Christians *as to* whether Christianity is true.—*Daily Telegraph.*

M. Delcassé did not allude to the debated question *as to* whether any official communication . . . was made by the French Government to Germany. It is also pointed out that he did not let fall the slightest intimation *as to* whether the French Government expected . . .—*Times.*

41. SUPERFLUOUS 'BUT' AND 'THOUGH'

Where there is a natural opposition between two sentences, adversative conjunctions may yet be made impossible by something in one of the sentences that does the work unaided. Thus, if *in vain, only,* and *reserves* and *sole,* had not been used in the following sentences, *but* and *though* would have been right; as it is, they are wrong.

(The author dreams that he is a horse being ridden) *In vain* did I rear and kick, attempting to get rid of my foe; *but* the surgeon remained as saddle-fast as ever.—BORROW.

But the substance of the story is probably true, *though* Voltaire has *only* made a slip in a name.—MORLEY.

Germany, it appears, *reserves* for herself the *sole* privilege of creating triple alliances and 'purely defensive' combinations of that character, *but* when the interests of other Powers bring them together their action is reprobated as aggressive and menacing.—*Times.*

Such mistakes probably result from altering the plan of a sentence in writing; and the cure is simply to read over every sentence after it is written.

42. 'IF AND WHEN'

This formula has enjoyed more popularity than it deserves; either 'when' or 'if' by itself would almost always give the meaning. Even where 'if' seems required to qualify 'when' (which by itself might be taken to exclude the possibility of the event's never happening at all), 'if ' and 'when' are clearly not coordinate, though both are subordinate to the main sentence: 'if and when he comes, I will write' means 'if he comes, I will write when he comes', or 'when he comes (if he comes at all), I will write', and the 'if' clause, whether parenthetic or not, is subordinate to the whole sentence 'I will write when he comes'. Our Gladstone instance below differs from the rest: 'when' with a past tense, unqualified by 'if', would make an admission that the writer does not choose to make; on the other hand, the time reference given by 'when' is essential; 'on the occasion on which it was done (if it really was done) it was done judicially'. The faulty coordination may be overlooked where there is real occasion for its use; but many writers seem to have persuaded themselves that neither 'if' nor 'when' is any longer capable of facing its responsibilities without the other word to keep it in countenance.

No doubt it will accept the experimental proof here alleged, if and when it is repeated under conditions . . .—*Times*.

The latter will include twelve army corps, six rifle brigades, and nine divisions or brigades of mounted troops, units which, if and when complete, will more than provide . . .—*Times*.

Unless and until we pound hardest we shall never beat the Boers.—*Spectator*.

It is only if, and when, our respective possessions become conterminous with those of great military states on land that we each . . .—*Times*.

If and when it was done, it was done so to speak judicially.— GLADSTONE.

No prudent seaman would undertake an invasion unless or until he had first disposed of the force preparing . . . to impeach him.—*Times*.

Its leaders decline to take office unless and until the 90 or 100 German words of command used . . . are replaced . . .—*Times*.

If and when employment is abundant . . .—*Westminster Gazette*.

It means nothing less, if Mr. Chamberlain has his way, than the final committal of one of the two great parties to a return to Protection, if and when it has the opportunity.—*Westminster Gazette*.

It is clear, however, that the work will gain much if and when she plays faster.—*Westminster Gazette*.

43. MALTREATED IDIOMS

1. Two existing idioms are fused into a non-existent one.

It did not take him much trouble.—SLADEN. (I take: it costs me)

An opportunity should be afforded the enemy of retiring northwards, more or less *of* their own *account.*—*Times.* (of my own accord; on my own account)

Dr. Kuyper admitted that his opinion had been consulted.—*Times.* (I consult you: take your opinion)

But it was in vain with the majority to attempt it.—BAGEHOT. (I attempt in vain: it is vain to attempt)

The captain got out the shutter of the door, shut it up, made it all fast, and locked the door itself.—DICKENS. (make it fast: make all fast)

The provisioning of the Russian Army would practically have to be drawn exclusively from the mother country.—*Times.* (draw provisions: do provisioning)

It gives me the greatest pleasure in adding my testimony.—*Daily Telegraph.* (I have pleasure in adding: it gives me pleasure to add)

And if we rejected a similar proposition made to us, was it not too much to expect that Canada might not turn in another direction?—CHAMBERLAIN (reported). (Might not Canada turn? . . . to expect that Canada would not turn)

I can speak from experience that . . . 'conversion' . . . was a very real and powerful thing.—*Daily Telegraph.* (speak to conversion's being: say that conversion was)

He certainly possessed, though in no great degree, the means of affording them more relief than he practised.—SCOTT. (preached more than he practised: had means of affording more than he did afford)

My position is one of a clerk, thirty-eight years of age, and married. —*Daily Telegraph.* (one that no one would envy: that of a clerk)

Abbot, indeed, had put the finishing stroke on all attempts at a higher ceremonial. Neither he nor his household would bow at the name of Christ.—J. R. GREEN. (put the finishing touches on: given the finishing stroke to)

In this chapter some of these words will be considered, and also some others against which purism has raised objections which do not seem to be well taken.—R. G. WHITE. (exceptions well taken: objections rightly made. *To take an objection well* can only mean to keep your temper when it is raised)

A woman would instinctively draw her cloak or dress closer to her, and a man leave by far an unnecessary amount of room for fear of coming into contact with those to whom . . . *Daily Telegraph.* (by far too great: quite an unnecessary)

The fines inflicted for excess of the legal speed.—*Times.* (excess of speed: exceeding the legal speed)

Notwithstanding the no inconsiderable distance by sea.—*Guernsey*

Advertiser. (it is no inconsiderable distance: the—or a—not inconsiderable distance)

His whim had been gratified at a trifling cost of ten thousand pounds. —CRAWFORD. (a trifling cost—unspecified: a trifle of ten thousand *or so*: the trifling cost of ten thousand. So in the next)

Dying at a ripe old age of eighty-three.—*Westminster Gazette.*

That question is the present solvency or insolvency of the Russian State. The answer to it depends not upon the fact whether Russia has or has not . . .—*Times.* (the fact that: the question whether. But *depends not upon whether* would be best here)

To all those who had thus so self-sacrificingly and energetically promoted the organization of this fund he desired to accord in the name of the diocese their deep obligation.—*Guernsey Advertiser.* (accord thanks: acknowledge obligation)

The allies frittered away in sieges the force which was ready for an advance into the heart of France until the revolt of the West and South was alike drowned in blood.—*Times.* (the revolts were alike drowned: the revolt was drowned)

2. Of two distinct idioms the wrong is chosen.

When, too, it was my pleasure to address a public meeting of more than 2,000 at the Royal Theatre the organized opposition numbered less than seven score.—*Times.*

It is our pleasure to present to you the enclosed notification of the proportion of profits which has been placed to the credit of your account.—Company circular. (I had, we have, the pleasure of—. The form chosen is proper to royal personages expressing their gracious will)

In the face of it the rule appears a most advisable one.—*Guernsey Advertiser.* (*On the face of it* means prima facie: the other means in spite of)

3. The form of an idiom is distorted, without confusion with another.

However, towards evening the wind and the waves subsided and the night became quiet and starlight.—*Times.* (*Starlight* is a noun, which can be used as an adjective immediately before another noun only; a starlight night)

Russia is now bitterly expiating her share in the infamy then visited upon Japan.—*Times.* (We visit upon a person his sins, or something for which he is responsible, and not we; or again, we may visit our indignation upon him)

He anticipated much towards Mary's recovery in her return to Japan.—SLADEN. (anticipate . . . from)

But both Governments have now requested Washington to be chosen as the place of meeting.—*Times*. (requested that Washington should)

For as its author in later years told the writer of this article, he had studied war for nine years before he put the pen to the paper.—*Times*. (Put pen to paper. This looks like imitation French; it is certainly not English)

4. The meaning of an idiom is mistaken without confusion with another.

For days and days, in such moods, he would stay within his cottage, never darkening the door or seeing other face than his own inmates.—TROLLOPE. (To darken the door is always to enter as a visitor, never to go out).

5. Some miscellaneous and unclassified violations are added, mostly without further comment than italics, to remind sanguine learners that there are small pitfalls in every direction.

If I *did not have* the most thorough dependence on your good sense and high principles, I should not speak to you in this way.—TROLLOPE.

Japan, while desiring the massacre of her own and Russia's subjects to be brought to an end, *has* nevertheless *every interest that* the war should go on.—*Times*.

The unpublished state, of which only *an extremely few* examples are in existence.—*Times*.

Once I *jested her* about it.—CROCKETT.

It *is significant to add* that when Mrs. Chesnut died in 1886 her servants were with her.—*Times*.

Herring boats, the drapery of whose black suspended nets *contrasted* with picturesque effect *the white sails* of the larger vessels.—S. FERRIER.

It is at least incumbent to be scrupulously accurate.—*Times*. (The metaphor in *incumbent* is so much alive that *upon*—is never dispensed with)

A measure *according Roman Catholic clergymen* who have passed through the local seminaries but have not yet passed the prescribed Russian language test *to hold* clerical appointments.—*Times*.

There will be established in this free England a commercial tyranny *the like of which* will not be inferior to the tyrannical Inquisition of the Dark Ages.—*Spectator*.

44. TRUISMS AND CONTRADICTIONS IN TERMS

A contradiction in terms is often little more than a truism

turned inside out; we shall therefore group the two together, and with them certain other illogical expressions, due to a similar confusion of thought.

Praise which perhaps was scarcely meant to be taken *too* literally.— BAGEHOT.

Where no standard of literalness is mentioned, *too literally* is 'more literally than was meant'. We may safely affirm, without the cautious reservations *perhaps* and *scarcely*, that the praise was not meant to be taken more literally than it was meant to be taken. Omit *too*.

He found what was *almost quite* as interesting.—*Times*.

If it was almost as interesting, we do not want *quite*: if quite, we do not want *almost*.

Splendid and elegant, but *somewhat bordering on* the antique fashion. —SCOTT.

Bordering on means not 'like' but 'very like'; 'somewhat very like'.

A *very unique* child, thought I.—C. BRONTË.
A *somewhat unique* gathering of our great profession.—HALSBURY.

There are no degrees in uniqueness.

Steady, respectable labouring men—*one and all, with rare exceptions*, married.—*Times*. (all without exception, with rare exceptions)
To *name* only a *few*, *take* Lord Rosebery, Lord Rendel, Lord . . . , . . . , . . . , . . . , and *many* others.—*Times*.

Take in this context means 'consider as instances'; we cannot consider them as instances unless we have their names; *take* must therefore mean 'let me name for your consideration'. Thus we get: 'To *name* only a *few*, let me *name* . . . and *many* others (whom I do *not* name)'.

More *led away* by a jingling antithesis of words than *an accurate perception* of ideas.—H. D. MACLEOD.

'Guided by an accurate perception' is what is meant. To be 'led away by accurate perception' is a misfortune that could happen only in a special sense, the sense in which it has happened, possibly, to the writer, whom sheer force of accurate perception may have hurried into inaccurate expression; but more probably he too is the victim of 'jingling antithesis'.

Long before the appointed hour for the commencement of the recital, standing room only fell to the lot of those who arrived *just previous* to Mr. K.'s appearance on the platform.—*Guernsey Advertiser*.

The necessary inference—that Mr. K., the reciter, appeared on the platform long before the appointed hour—is probably not in accordance with the facts.

The weather this week has for the most part been of that quality which the month of March so *strikingly* characterizes in the *ordinary* course of events.—*Guernsey Advertiser*.

What happens in the ordinary course of events can scarcely continue to be striking. Whether the month characterizes the weather, or the weather the month, we need not consider here.

He *forgot* that it was possible, that from a brief period of tumultuous disorder, there might issue a military despotism more compact, more disciplined, and more overpowering than any which had preceded it, or any which *has* followed it.—BAGEHOT.

He could not forget, because he could not know, anything about the despotisms which *have* in fact followed. He might know and forget something about all the despotisms that had preceded or *should* follow (in direct speech, 'that have preceded or shall follow'): 'this may result in the most compact despotism in all history, past and future'. But probably Bagehot does not even mean this: the last clause seems to contain a reflection of his own, falsely presented as a part of what *he* ought to have reflected.

Some people would say that my present manner of travelling is much the *most preferable*, riding as I do now, instead of leading my horse.—BORROW.

Only two modes of travelling are compared: *the most preferable* implies four, three of them preferable in different degrees to the fourth. A not uncommon vulgarism.

45. DOUBLE EMPHASIS

Attempts at packing double emphasis into a single sentence are apt to result in real weakening.

No government ever plunged *more* rapidly into a *deeper* quagmire.—
Outlook. (From the writer's evident wish to state the matter strongly,
we infer that several Governments have plunged more rapidly into as
deep quagmires, and as rapidly into deeper ones)

Mr. Justice Neville . . . will now have the very rare experience of
joining on the Bench a colleague whom he defeated on the polls *just
fourteen years ago.—Westminster Gazette*. (The *experience*, with exact
time-interval, is probably unique, like any individual thumb-print;
that does not make the *coincidence* more remarkable; and it is the
coincidence that we are to admire)

Nothing has brought out more strongly than motor-driving the
overbearing, selfish nature of too many motor-drivers and their utter
want of consideration for their fellow men.—LORD WEMYSS. (The
attempt to kill drivers and driving with one stone leaves both very
slightly wounded. For what should show up the drivers more than
the driving? and whom should the driving show up more than the
drivers?)

The commonest form of this is due to conscientious but
mistaken zeal for correctness, which prefers, for instance, *without oppressing or without plundering* to *without oppressing or
plundering*. The first form excludes only one of the offences,
and is therefore, though probably meant to be twice as emphatic,
actually much weaker than the second, which excludes both.
With *and* instead of *or*, it is another matter.

Actual experience has shown that a gun constructed on the wire
system can still be utilized effectively without the destruction of the
weapon *or without* dangerous effects, even with its inner tube split.—
Times.

The Union must be maintained without pandering to such prejudices
on the one hand, *or without* giving way on the other to the . . . schemes
of the Nationalists.—*Spectator*.

He inhibited him, on pain of excommunication, from seeking a
divorce in his own English Courts, *or from* contracting a new marriage.
—J. R. GREEN. (Half excused by the negative sense of *inhibit*)

46. 'SPLIT' AUXILIARIES

Some writers, holding that there is the same objection to
split compound verbs as to split infinitives, prefer to place any
adverb or qualifying phrase not between the auxiliary and the
other component, but before both. Provided that the adverb

is then separated from the auxiliary, no harm is done: 'Evidently he was mistaken' is often as good as 'He was evidently mistaken', and suits all requirements of accentuation. But the placing of the adverb immediately before or after the auxiliary depends, according to established usage, upon the relative importance of the two components. When the main accent is to fall upon the second component, the normal place of the adverb is between the two; it is only when the same verb is repeated with a change in the tense or mood of the auxiliary, that the adverb should come first. 'He evidently was deceived' implies, or should imply, that the verb *deceived* has been used before, and that the point of the sentence depends upon the emphatic auxiliary; accordingly we should write 'The possibility of his being deceived had never occurred to me; but he evidently was deceived', but 'I relied implicitly on his knowledge of the facts; but he was evidently deceived'. In our first two examples below the adverb is rightly placed first to secure the emphasis on the auxiliary: in all the others the above principle of accentuation is violated. The same order of words is required by the copula with whatever kind of complement.

I recognize this truth, and always have recognized it.

Refined policy ever has been the parent of confusion, and ever will be so, as long as the world endures.—BURKE.

They never are suffered to succeed in their opposition.—BURKE.

She had received the homage of . . . and occasionally had deigned to breathe forth . . .—BEACONSFIELD.

He ordered breakfast as calmly as if he never had left his home.—BEACONSFIELD.

Miss Becky, whose sympathetic powers never had been called into action before.—FERRIER.

They now were bent on taking the work into their own hands.—MORLEY.

There may have been a time when a king was a god, but he now is pretty much on a level with his subjects.—JOWETT.

They both are contradicted by all positive evidence.—W. H. MALLOCK.

Religious art at once complete and sincere never yet has existed.—RUSKIN.

Not mere empty ideas, but what were once realities, and that I long have thought decayed.—C. BRONTË.

So that he might assist at a Bible class, from which he never had been absent.—BEACONSFIELD.

If we would write an essay, we necessarily must have something to say.—BYGOTT JONES.

The protectionists lately have been affirming that the autumn session will be devoted to railway questions.—*Times*.

Visitors no longer can drive in open carriages along the littoral.—*Times*.

It still is the fact that his mind . . . was essentially the mind of a poet.—*Times*.

Benefit will accrue; they are essential to the country, but that will be felt not until we are no longer countrymen.—EMERSON.

To whom in any case its style would have not appealed.—*Times*.

To go wrong with *not* is an achievement possible only with triple compounds, where the principal division is of course between the finite (*would*) and the infinitive with participle (*have appealed*). 'Would not have appealed' must be written, though at an enormous sacrifice of 'distinction'.

This enhanced value of old English silver may be due partly to the increase in the number of collectors; but it also has been largely influenced by the publication . . .—*Times*.

Mr. Fry showed to a very great extent his power of defence . . . To-day, if runs are to be of importance. he very likely will show his powers of hitting.—*Times*.

47. OVERLOADING

A single sentence is sometimes made to carry a double burden:

So unique a man as Sir George Lewis has, in truth, rarely been lost to this country.—BAGEHOT.

The meaning is not 'Men like Sir G. Lewis have seldom been lost', but 'Men like the late Sir G. Lewis have seldom been found'. But instead of *the late* a word was required that should express proper concern; *lost* is a short cut to 'men so unique as he whose loss we now deplore'.

There are but few men whose lives abound in such wild and romantic adventure, and, for the most part, crowned with success.—PRESCOTT.

The writer does not mean 'adventures so wild, so romantic, and so successful in the main'; that is shown by the qualifying parenthesis, which is obviously one of comment on the individual case. What he does mean ought to have been given in two sentences: 'There are but few . . . adventure; —'s, moreover, was for the most part crowned with success'.

The Sultan regrets that the distance and the short notice alone prevent him from coming in person.—*Times*.

This is as much as to say that the Sultan wishes there were more obstacles. Read: 'The Sultan regrets that he cannot come in person; nothing but the distance and the short notice could prevent him'.

48. DEMONSTRATIVE, NOUN, AND PARTICIPLE OR ADJECTIVE

Of the forms, *persons interested, the persons interested, those interested, those who are interested*, one or another may better suit a particular phrase or context. *Those interested* is the least to be recommended, especially with an active participle or adjective. The form *those persons interested* is a hybrid, and is very seldom used by any good writer; but it is becoming so common in inferior work that it is thought necessary to give many examples. The first two, of the form *those interested*, will pass, though *those who were concerned, all who drive*, would be better. In the others *that* and *those* should be either replaced by *the* or (sometimes) simply omitted.

The idea of a shortage had hardly entered the heads even of *those* most immediately *concerned.*—*Times*.

They are the terror of all *those driving* or riding spirited horses.— *Times*.

At every time and in every place throughout *that* very limited *portion* of time and space *open* to human observation.—BALFOUR.

That part of the regular army *quartered* at home should be grouped by divisions.—*Times*.

Here they beheld acres of *that* stupendous *growth seen* only in the equinoctial regions.—PRESCOTT.

It is not likely that General Kuropatkine has amassed *those reserves* of military stores and supplies plainly *required* by the circumstances of his situation.—*Times*.

The insurrection had been general throughout the country, at least *that portion* of it *occupied* by the Spaniards.—PRESCOTT.

My amendment would be that *that part* of the report *dealing* with the dividend on the 'A' shares . . . be not adopted.—Company report.

We shall fail to secure *that unanimity* of thought and doctrine so *indispensable* both for . . .—*Times*.

. . . in order to minimize the effect produced by *that portion* of the Admirals' report *favourable* to England.—*Times*.

A struggle . . . which our nation must be prepared to face in the last resort, or else give way to *those countries* not *afraid* to accept the responsibilities and sacrifices inseparable from Empire.—*Times*.

Civil servants will not, nay, cannot, work with *that freedom* of action so *essential* to good work in the case of such persons, so long as . . .—*Times*.

To *those Colonies unable* to concur with these suggestions a warning should be addressed.—*Times*.

---

49. FALSE SCENT

It is most annoying to a reader to be misled about the construction, and therefore most foolish in a writer to mislead him. In the sentences that follow, *facilities* and *excesses* are naturally taken as in the same construction, and similarly *influences* and *nature*, until the ends of the sentences show us that we have gone wrong. These are very bad cases; but minor offences of the kind are very common, and should be carefully guarded against.

He gloats over the facilities the excesses and the blunders of the authorities have given his comrades for revolutionary action among the masses.—*Times*.

The influences of that age, his open, kind, susceptible nature, to say nothing of his highly untoward situation, made it more than usually difficult for him to cast aside or rightly subordinate.—CARLYLE.

That there is no comma between *facilities* and *the excesses* is no defence, seeing how often commas go wrong; indeed the comma after *age* in the second piece, which is strictly wrong, is a proof how little reliance is to be placed on such signs.

50. MISPLACEMENT OF WORDS

Generous interpretation will generally get at a writer's meaning; but for him to rely on that is to appeal *ad misericordiam*. Appended to the sentences, when necessary, is the result of supposing them to mean what they say.

It is with grief and pain, that, *as admirers of the British aristocracy*, we find ourselves obliged to admit the existence of so many ill qualities in a person whose name is in Debrett.—THACKERAY. (implies that admirers must admit this more than other people)

It is from this fate that the son of a commanding prime minister is *at any rate* preserved.—BAGEHOT. (implies that *preserved* is a weak word used instead of a stronger)

And even if we could suppose it to be our duty, it is not one which, *as was shown in the last chapter*, we are practically competent to perform.—BALFOUR.

The chairman said there was no sadder sight in the world than to see women drunk, because they seemed to lose *complete* control of themselves. (implies that losing complete control leaves you with less than if you lost incomplete control)

The soldiers are deeply chagrined at having had to give up positions, *in obedience to orders*, which the Japanese could not take.—*Times*.

Great and heroic men have existed, who had almost no other information than by the printed page. I *only* would say, that it needs a strong head to bear that diet.—EMERSON. (implies that no one else would say it)

Yes, the laziest of human beings, through the providence of God, *a being, too, of rather inferior capacity*, acquires the written part of a language so difficult that . . .—BORROW.

Right or wrong as his hypothesis may be, no one that knows him will suspect that he himself had not seen it, and seen over it . . . Neither, *as we often hear*, is there any superhuman faculty required to follow him.—CARLYLE. (implies that we often hear there is not)

This, we say to ourselves, may be all very true (for have we, *too*, not browsed in the Dictionary of National Biography?); but why does Tanner say it all, just at that moment, to . . .—*Times*. (implies that others have refrained from browsing)

But in 1798 the Irish rising was crushed in a defeat of the insurgents at Vinegar Hill; and Tippoo's death in the storm of his own capital, Seringapatam, *only* saved him from witnessing the English conquest of Mysore.—J. R. GREEN. (implies that that was all it saved him from)

51. AMBIGUOUS POSITION

In this matter judgement is required. A captious critic might find examples on almost every page of almost any writer; but most of them, though they may strictly be called ambiguous, would be quite justifiable. On the other hand a careless writer can nearly always plead, even for a bad offence, that an attentive reader would take the thing the right way. That is no defence; a rather inattentive and sleepy reader is the true test; if the run of the sentence is such that he at first sight refers whatever phrase is in question to the wrong government, then the ambiguity is to be condemned.

Louis XVIII, dying in 1824, was succeeded, as Charles X, by his brother the Count d'Artois.—E. SANDERSON. (The sleepy reader, assisted by memories of James the First and Sixth, concludes, though not without surprise, which perhaps finally puts him on the right track, that Louis XVIII of France was also Charles X of some other country)

In 1830 Paris overthrew monarchy by divine right.—MORLEY. (*By divine right* looks so much more like an adverbial than an adjectival phrase that the sleepy reader takes it with *overthrew*)

(From review of a book on ambidexterity) Two kinds of emphatic type are used, and both are liberally sprinkled about the pages on some principle which is not at all obvious. The practice may have its merits, like ambidexterity, but it is generally eschewed by good writers who know their business, although they are not ambidextrous.—*Times*. (The balance of the sentence is extremely bad if the *although* clause is subordinated to *who*; and the sleepy reader accordingly does not take it so, but with *is eschewed*, and so makes nonsense)

It was a temper not only legal, but pedantic in its legality, intolerant from its very sense of a moral order and law *of* the lawlessness and disorder of a personal tyranny.—J. R. GREEN.

The library over the porch of the church, which is large and handsome, contains one thousand printed books.—R. CURZON. (A large and handsome library, or porch, or church?)

Both these last are very unkind to the poor sleepy reader; it is true that in one of them he is inexcusable if he goes wrong, but we should for our own sakes give him as few chances of going wrong as possible.

Luck and dexterity always give more pleasure than intellect and knowledge; because they fill up what they fall *on to* the brim at once, and people run to them with acclamation at the splash.—LANDOR. (*On* and *to* so regularly belong together now, though they did not in Landor's time, that it is disconcerting to be asked to pause between them)

52. AMBIGUOUS ENUMERATION

In comma'd enumerations, care should be taken not to insert appositions that may be taken, even if only at first sight, for separate members.

Some high officials of the Headquarter Staff, including the officer who is primus inter pares, the Director of Military Operations, and the Director of Staff duties . . .—*Times*. (Two, or three, persons? Probably two; but those who can be sure of this do not need the descriptive clause, and those who need it cannot be sure)

Lord Curzon, Sir Edmond Elles, the present Military Member, and the Civilian Members of Council traverse the most material of Lord Kitchener's statements of fact.—*Times*. (Is Sir E. Elles the Military Member? No need to tell any one who knows; and any one who does not know is not told)

I here wish to remark that Lord Dufferin first formed the Mobilization Committee, of which the Commander-in-Chief is President, and the Military Member, Secretary, Military Department, and the heads of departments both at Army Headquarters and under the Government of India, are members with the express intention of . . .—*Times*. (Is the Military Member Secretary of the Mobilization Committee? Well, he may be, but a certain amount of patience shows us that the sentence we are reading does not tell us so)

---

53. ANTICS

A small selection must suffice. Straining after the dignified, the unusual, the poignant, the high-flown, the picturesque, the striking, often turns out badly. It is not worth while to attain any of these aims at the cost of being unnatural.

1. Use of stiff, full-dress, literary, or out-of-the-way words.

And in no direction was the slightest concern *evinced*.—*Times*.

The majority display *scant* anxiety for news.—*Times*.

. . . treating his characters on broader lines, occupying himself with more elemental emotions and types, and forsaking altogether his almost *meticulous* analysis of motive and temperament.—*Westminster Gazette*. (We recommend to this reviewer a more meticulous use of the dictionary)

And most probably he is voted a fool for not doing as many men in similar positions are doing—viz., making up for a lack of principle by an abundance of *bawbees* easily extracted from a large class of contractors who are only too willing . . .—*Times*.

It is Victor Hugo's people, the motives on which they act, the means they take to carry out their objects, their relations to one another, that strike us as so *monumentally* droll.—*Times*.

Nothing definite has been decided upon as to the exact date of the visits, the *venue* of the visits, the . . .—*Times*.

2. Pretentious circumlocution.

That life was brought to a close in November 1567, at an age, probably, not far from *the one fixed by the sacred writer as the term of human existence*.—PRESCOTT.

She skated extremely badly, but with an enjoyment that was almost pathetic, *in consideration of the persistence of 'frequent fall'*.—E. F. BENSON.

The question of an extension of the Zemstvos to the southwest provinces is believed to be under consideration. It is understood that the visit of General Kleigels to St. Petersburg is *not unconnected therewith*.—*Times*.

3. Poetic phraseology especially the Carlylese superlative. Almost any page of Milton's prose will show whence Carlyle had this; but it is most offensive in ordinary modern writing.

A period when, as she puts it, men and women of fashion 'tried not to be themselves, yet never so successfully displayed *the naked hearts of them*'.—*Times*.

The last week in February was harnessing her seven bright steeds in shining tandem in the silent courtyard of the time to be.—*The Lamp*.

Our enveloping movements since some days prove successful, and fiercest battle is now proceeding.—*Times*.

The unhappy man persuades himself that he has in truth become a new creature, of the wonderfullest symmetry.—CARLYLE.

4. Patronizing superiority expressed by describing simple things in long words.

The skating-rink, where happy folk all day slide with set purpose on the elusive material, and with great content perform mystic evolutions of the most complicated order.—E. F. BENSON.

5. The determined picturesque.

Across the street blank shutters flung back the gaslight in cold smears.—KIPLING.

The outflung white water at the foot of a homeward-bound China-man not a hundred yards away, and her shadow-slashed rope-purfled sails bulging sideways like insolent cheeks.—KIPLING.

An under-carry of grey woolly spindrift of a slaty colour flung itself noiselessly in the opposite direction, a little above the tree tops.—CROCKETT.

Then for a space the ground was more clayey, and a carpet of green water-weeds were combed and waved by the woven ropes of water.—E. F. BENSON.

At some distance off, in Winchester probably, which pricked the blue haze of heat with dim spires, a church bell came muffled and languid.—E. F. BENSON.

A carriage drive lay in long curves like a flicked whip lash, surmounting terrace after terrace set with nugatory nudities.—E. F. BENSON.

6. Recherché epithets.

Perhaps both Milton and Beethoven would live in our memories as writers of idylls, had not a *brusque* infirmity dreadfully shut them off from their fellow men.—*Times*.

The high *canorous* note of the north-easter.—STEVENSON.

By specious and *clamant* exceptions.—STEVENSON.

Then, on the first day that was illuminated by *anaemic* sunlight . . .—*Spectator*.

'I merely mean,' said John, with *thaumaturgic* airiness, 'that the man is on his way to Rome.'—HARLAND.

7. Formal antithesis or parallel. This particular form of artificiality is perhaps too much out of fashion to be dangerous at present. The great storehouse of it is in Macaulay.

He had neither the qualities which make dulness respectable, nor the qualities which make libertinism attractive.—MACAULAY.

The first two kings of the House of Hanover had neither those hereditary rights which have often supplied the place of merit, nor those personal qualities which have often supplied the defect of title.—MACAULAY.

But he was indolent and dissolute, and had early impaired a fine estate with the dice-box, and a fine constitution with the bottle.—MACAULAY.

The disclosure of the stores of Greek literature had wrought the revolution of the Renascence. The disclosure of the older mass of Hebrew literature wrought the revolution of the Reformation.—J. R. GREEN.

8. Author's self-consciousness.

'You mean it is,' she said—'about Bertie'. Charlie made the noise usually written 'Pshaw'.—E. F. BENSON.

John—convict me of damnable iteration if you must: Heaven has sent me a laughing hero—John laughed.—HARLAND.

9. Intrusive smartness—another form of self-consciousness.

Round her lay piles of press notices, which stripped the American variety of the English language bare of epithets.—E. F. BENSON.

Income-tax payers are always treated to the fine words which butter no parsnips, and are always assured that it is really a danger to the State to go on skinning them in time of peace to such an extent as to leave little integument to remove in time of war.—*Times*.

Yet in the relentless city, where no one may pause for a moment unless he wishes to be left behind in the great universal race for gold which begins as soon as a child can walk, and ceases not until he is long past walking, the climbing of the thermometer into the nineties *is an acrobatic feat which concerns the thermometer only*, and at the junction of Sixth Avenue and Broadway there was no slackening in the tides of the affairs of men.—E. F. BENSON.

54. MISCELLANEOUS TYPES OF JOURNALESE

Mr. Lionel Phillips maintained that it was impossible to introduce white unskilled *labour* on a large scale *as a payable proposition* without lowering the position of the white man.—*Times*.

How *labour* can be a *proposition*, and how a *proposition* can be *payable* it is not easy to say. The sentence seems to mean: 'to introduce . . . labour on a large scale and make it pay'. This is what comes of a fondness for abstracts.

They have not hitherto discovered the formula for the intelligent use of our unrivalled resources for the *satisfaction of our security*.—*Times*.

This perhaps means: 'They have not yet discovered how our unrivalled resources may be made to ensure our safety.'

An attempt to efface the ill-effects of the Czar's refusal to see the workmen has been made *by* the grant *of* an interview *by* the Czar *at* Tsarkoe Selo *to* a body *of* workmen officially selected to represent the masses.—*Spectator*.

The powerful and convincing article on the question of War Office administration as it affects the Volunteers to be found in this month's *National*.—*Spectator*.

The Russian Government is at last face to face with the greatest crisis of the war, *in the shape of the fact that* the Siberian railway . . .—*Spectator*.

No year passes now without evidence of the truth of the statement
that the work of government is becoming increasingly difficult.—
Spectator.

It has taken a leading part in protesting against the Congo State's
treatment of natives controlled by it, and in procuring the pressure
which the House of Commons has put upon our Government with a
view to international insistence on fulfilment of the obligations entered
upon by the Congo Government as regards native rights.—*Times*.

The outcome of a desire to convince the Government of the expediency of granting the return recently ordered by the House with
regard to the names, . . .—*Times*.

In default of information of the result of the deliberations which it
has been stated the Imperial Defence Committee have been engaged
in . . .—*Times*.

The volunteer does not volunteer to be compelled to suffer long,
filthy, and neglected illnesses and too often death, yet such was South
Africa on a vast scale, and is inevitable in war under the present official
indifference.—*Times*.

55. SOMEWHAT, ETC.

Indulgence in qualifying adverbs, as *perhaps*, *possibly*, *probably*, *rather*, *a little*, *somewhat*, amounts with English journalists
to a disease; the intemperate orgy of moderation is renewed
every morning. As *somewhat* is rapidly swallowing up the rest,
we shall almost confine our attention to it; and it is useless to
deprecate the use without copious illustration. Examples will
be classified under headings, though these are not quite mutually
exclusive.

1. *Somewhat* clearly illogical.

A number of questions to the Prime Minister have been put upon
the paper with the object of eliciting information as to the personnel
of the proposed Royal Commission and the scope of their inquiry.
These are now *somewhat belated* in view of the official announcement
made this morning.—*Times*. (The announcement contained both the
list of members and the full reference)

Thrills which gave him *rather a unique* pleasure.—HUTTON.

Russian despatches are *somewhat inconsistent*, one of them stating
that there is no change in the position of the armies, while another says
that the Japanese advance continues.—*Times*.

Being faint with hunger I was *somewhat in a listless condition* bordering on stupor.—CORELLI.

In the light of these, it would be hard to say what full belatedness, inconsistency, and listlessness may be.

2. *Somewhat* with essentially emphatic words.

We may call a thing dirty, or filthy; if we choose the latter, we mean to be emphatic; it is absurd to use the emphatic word and take away its emphasis with *somewhat*, when we might use the gentler word by itself.

A member of the Legislative Council is allowed now to speak in Dutch if he cannot express himself clearly in English; under the proposed arrangement he will be able to decide for himself in which medium he can express himself the more clearly. Surely a *somewhat infinitesimal* point.—*Times.*

Thirdly, it is *rather agonizing* at times to the philologist.—*Times.*

The distances at which the movements are being conducted receive a *somewhat startling* illustration from the statement that . . .—*Times.*

Under these circumstances it is *somewhat extraordinary* to endeavour to save the Government from blame.—*Times.*

In various evidently 'well-informed' journals the *somewhat amazing* proposition is set up that . . .—*Times.*

But unfortunately the word 'duties' got accidentally substituted for 'bounties' in two places, and made the utterance *somewhat unintelligible* to the general reader.—*Times.*

The songs are sung by students to the accompaniment of a *somewhat agonizing* band.—*Times.*

There is a mysterious man-killing orchid, a great Eastern jewel of State, and many other properties, some of them *a little well worn*, suitable for the staging of a tale of mystery.—*Spectator.*

Some of the instances in these two classes would be defended as humorous under-statement. But if this hackneyed trick is an example of the national humour, we had better cease making reflections on German want of humour.

3. *Somewhat* shyly announcing an epigrammatic or well-chosen phrase.

There is a very pretty problem awaiting the decision of Prince Bülow, and one which is entirely worthy of his *somewhat acrobatic* diplomacy.—*Times.*

Gaston engages in a controversy on the origin of evil, which terminated by his *somewhat abruptly quitting his Alma Mater.*—BEACONSFIELD.

Why even Tennyson became an amateur milkman to *somewhat conceal and excuse the shame and degradation of writing verse.*—CORELLI.

The virtuous but *somewhat unpleasing* type of the Roman nation.—*Times.*

The sight of these soldiers and sailors sitting round camp-fires in the midst of the snow in fashionable thoroughfares, transforming the city into an armed camp, is *somewhat weird.*—*Times.*

While Mary was trying to decipher these *somewhat mystic* lines.—S. FERRIER.

4. *Somewhat* conveying a sneer.

It is somewhat strange that any one connected with this institution should be so unfamiliar with its regulations.—*Times.*

. . . that the conclusion arrived at by the shortest route is to be accepted—a somewhat extravagant doctrine, according to which . . .—BALFOUR.

But very few points of general interest have been elicited in any quarter by these somewhat academic reflections.—*Times.*

This somewhat glowing advertisement of the new loan.—*Times.*

5. The genuine *somewhat*, merely tame, timid, undecided, conciliatory, or polite.

It is somewhat pitiful to see the efforts of a foreign State directed, not to the pursuit of its own aims by legitimate means, but to the gratification of personal hostility to a great public servant of France.—*Times.*

I am certain that the clergy themselves only too gladly acquiesce in this somewhat illogical division of labour.—*Times.*

This, no doubt, is what Professor Ray Lankester is driving at in his somewhat intemperate onslaught.—*Times.*

The *rather mysterious* visit of S. Tittoni, the Italian Foreign Minister, to Germany.—*Times.*

These are of *rather remarkable* promise; the head shows an unusual power of realizing character under a purely ideal conception.—*Times.*

The *rather finely* conceived statuette called 'The Human Task' by Mr. Oliver Wheatley.—*Times.*

It is somewhat the fashion to say that in these days . . .—*Times.*

A letter from one whose learning and experience entitle him to be heard, conceived, as I think, in a spirit of somewhat exaggerated pessimism.—*Times.*

The statement made by the writer is somewhat open to doubt.—*Times.*

I have read with much interest the letters on the subject of hush-money, especially as they account to me somewhat for the difficulties I have experienced.—*Times*.

It would be valuable if he would somewhat expand his ideas regarding local defence by Volunteers.—*Times*.

Sir,—I have been somewhat interested in the recent correspondence in your columns.—*Times*.

So many persons of undoubted integrity believe in 'dowsing' that he is a somewhat rash man who summarily dismisses the matter.—*Times*.

Sir Francis Bertie, whose dislike of unnecessary publicity is somewhat pronounced.—*Times*.

It is not too much to say that any one who hopes to write well had better begin by abjuring *somewhat* altogether.

We cannot tell whether this long list will have a dissuasive effect, or will be referred to foolish individual prejudice against an unoffending word. But on the first assumption we should like to add that a not less dissuasive collection might easily be made of the intensifier *distinctly* than of the qualifier *somewhat*. The use meant is that seen in:

The effect as the procession careers through the streets of Berlin is described as distinctly interesting.

Distinctly gives the patronizing interest, as *somewhat* gives the contemptuous indifference, with which a superior person is to be conceived surveying life; and context too often reveals that the superiority is imaginary.

56. CLUMSY PATCHING

When a writer detects a fault in what he has written or thought of writing, his best course is to recast the whole sentence. The next best is to leave it alone. The worst is to patch it in such a way that the reader has his attention drawn, works out the original version, and condemns his author for carelessness aggravated by too low an estimate of readers' intelligence.

Numerous allegations, too, were made of prejudiced treatment *measured out against* motorists by rural magistrates.—*Times*. (avoidance of the jingle in *meted* out to *motor*ists)

No crew proved to be of the very highest class; but this, perhaps, *led the racing to be* on the whole close and exciting.—*Times*. (avoidance of the jingle in led to the rac*ing* be*ing*)

The Lord Mayor last night entertained the Judges *to* a banquet at the Mansion House.—*Times*. (avoidance of double *at*)

The occupants talked, inspected the cars *of one another*, interchanged tales of . . .—*Times*. (avoidance, in grammatical pusillanimity, of *one another's cars*)

. . . who have only themselves in view *by* breaking through it.— RICHARDSON. (avoidance of double *in*)

He nodded, *as one who would say*, 'I have already thought of that'.— CROCKETT. (avoidance of the archaism, which however is the only natural form, *as who should say*)

It is now practically certain that the crews of Nebogatoff's squadron were in a state of mutiny, and that this is the explanation *for* the surrender *of* these vessels.—*Times*. (avoidance of double *of*)

And *for* the first time *after* twenty years the Whigs saw themselves again in power.—J. R. GREEN. (Avoidance of double *for*; if *after* had been originally intended, we should have had *at last* instead of *for the first time*)

And oppressive laws forced even these *few* with *scant* exceptions to profess Protestantism.—J. R. GREEN. (To avoid the repetition of *few* the affected word *scant* has been admitted)

Given competition, any line would vie with the others in mirrors and gilded furniture; but if there is none, why spend a penny? Not a passenger the less will travel because the mode of transit is *bestial*.— E. F. BENSON. (To avoid the overdone word *beastly*—which however happens to be the right one here; *bestial* describes character or conduct)

There is, indeed, a kind of timorous atheism in the man who dares not trust God to *render* all efforts to interpret his Word—and what is criticism but interpretation?—work together for good.—*Spectator*. (*Render* is substituted for *make* because *make efforts* might be taken as complete without the *work together* that is due. Unfortunately, *to render efforts work together* is not even English at all)

57. OMISSION OF THE CONJUNCTION 'THAT'

This is quite legitimate, but often unpleasant. It is partly a matter of idiom, as, *I presume you know*, but *I assume that you know*; partly of avoiding false scent, as in the sixth example below, where *scheme* might be object to *discover*. In particular it is undesirable to omit *that* when a long clause or phrase intervenes between it and the subject and verb it introduces, as in the first four examples.

And it is to be hoped, *as the tree-planting season has arrived,* Stepney will now put its scheme in hand.—*Times.*

Sir,—We notice *in a leading article in your issue to-day on the subject of the carriage of Australian mails* you imply that the increased price demanded by the Orient Pacific Line was due to . . .—*Times.*

Lord Balfour . . . moved that it is necessary, *before the constituencies are asked to determine upon the desirability of such conference,* they should be informed first . . .—*Times.*

Lord Spencer held that it was impossible *with regard to a question which had broken up the Government and disturbed the country* they could go into a conference which . . .—*Times.*

If the Australian is to be convinced that is an unreasonable wish, it will not be by arguments about taxation.—*Times.*

I think he would discover the scheme unfolded and explained in them is a perfectly intelligible and comprehensive one.—*Times.*

It is not till He cometh the ideal will be seen.—*Times.*

And it is only by faith the evils you mention as productive of war can be cast out of our hearts.—*Times.*

I do not wish it to be understood that I consider all those who applied for work during the past two winters and who are now seeking employment are impostors.—*Times.*

I assume Turkey would require such a cash payment of at least £500,000.—*Times.*

Tawno leaped into the saddle, where he really looked like Gunnar of Hlithárend, save and except the complexion of Gunnar was florid, whereas that of Tawno was of nearly Mulatto darkness.—BORROW.

In some of these the motive is obvious, to avoid one *that*-clause depending on another; the end was good, but the means bad; a more thorough recasting was called for.

58. MEANINGLESS 'WHILE'

While, originally temporal, has a legitimate use also in contrasts. The further colourless use of it, whether with verb or with participle, as a mere elegant variation for *and* is very characteristic of journalese, and much to be deprecated.

Of its value there can be no question. The editor's article on 'Constitutions', for example, and that of Mr. W. Wyse on 'Law' both well repay most careful study; *while* when Sir R. Jebb writes on 'Literature', Dr. Henry Jackson on 'Philosophy', or Professor Waldstein on 'Sculpture', their contributions must be regarded as authoritative.—*Spectator.*

The fireman was killed on the spot, and the driver as well as the guard of the passenger train was slightly injured; *while* the up-line was blocked for some time with débris from broken trucks of the goods train.—*Times*.

The deer on the island took some interest in the proceeding, while the peacocks on the lawn screamed at the right time.—*Birmingham Daily Post*.

It cannot be contended that it is more profitable to convey a passenger the twenty-four miles to Yarmouth for payment than to accept the same payment without performing the service; *while*, if the company wish to discourage the use of cheap week-end tickets, why issue them at all?—*Times*.

59. COMMERCIALISMS

Certain uses of *such*, *the same*, and other words, redolent of commerce and the law, should be reserved for commercial and legal contexts. *Anent*, which has been noticed in Part I, is a legalism of this kind. In the Brontë instances quoted, a twang of flippancy will be observed; the other writers are probably unconscious.

This gentleman's state of mind was very harrowing, and I was glad when he wound up his exposition of the same.—C. BRONTË.

The present was no occasion for showy array; my dun mist crape would suffice, and I sought the same in the great oak wardrobe in the dormitory.—C. BRONTË.

There are certain books that almost defy classification, and this volume . . . is one of such.—*Daily Telegraph*.

I am pleased to read the correspondence in your paper, and hope that good will be the result of the same.—*Daily Telegraph*.

The man who has approached nearest to the teaching of the Master, and carried the same to its logical and practical conclusion is General Booth.—*Daily Telegraph*.

Do I believe that by not having had the hands of a bishop laid upon my head I cannot engage in the outward and visible commemoration of the Lord's Supper as not being fit to receive the same?—*Daily Telegraph*.

But do the great majority of people let their belief in the hereafter affect their conduct with regard to the same. I think not.—*Daily Telegraph*.

Let us hope, Sir, that it may be possible in your own interests to continue the same till the subject has had a good innings.—*Daily Telegraph*.

I believe, and have believed since, a tiny child, made miserable by the loss of a shilling, I prayed my Heavenly Father to help me to recover the same.—*Daily Telegraph.*

It is of course possible, in this connexion, that the Prayer Book is responsible for 'the same'.

If I am refused the Sacrament I do not believe that I shall have less chance of entering the Kingdom of God than if I received such Sacrament.—*Daily Telegraph.*

But when it comes to us following his life and example, in all its intricate details, all will, I think, agree that such is impossible.—*Daily Telegraph.*

An appeal to philanthropy is hardly necessary, the grounds for such being so self-evident.—*Times.*

. . . such a desire it should be the purpose of a Unionist Government to foster ; but such will not be attained under the present regime in Dublin.—*Times.*

. . . regaling themselves on half-pints at the said village hostelries.—BORROW.

Having read with much interest the letters re 'believe only' now appearing in the *Daily Telegraph* . . .—*Daily Telegraph.*

He ruined himself and family by his continued experiments for the benefit of the British nation.—*Times.*

60. PET PHRASES

Vivid writers must be careful not to repeat any conspicuous phrase so soon that a reader of ordinary memory has not had time to forget it before it invites his attention again. Whatever its merits, to use it twice (unless deliberately and with point) is much worse than never to have thought of it. The pages below are those of Green's *Short History* (1875).

The temper of the first [King George] was that of a gentleman usher. p. 704.

Bute was a mere court favourite, with the abilities of a gentleman usher. p. 742.

'For weeks', laughs Horace Walpole, 'it rained gold boxes'. p. 729.

'We are forced to ask every morning what victory there is', laughed Horace Walpole. p. 737.

The two following passages occur on pp. 6 and 81 of *The Bride of Lammermoor* (Standard Edition).

In short, Dick Tinto's friends feared that he had acted like the animal called the sloth, which, having eaten up the last green leaf upon the tree where it has established itself, ends by tumbling down from the top, and dying of inanition.

'. . . but as for us, Caleb's excuses become longer as his diet turns more spare, and I fear we shall realize the stories they tell of the sloth: we have almost eaten up the last green leaf on the plant, and have nothing left for it but to drop from the tree and break our necks.'

61. 'ALSO' AS CONJUNCTION; AND 'ETC.'

Also is an adverb; the use of it as a conjunction is slovenly, if not illiterate.

We are giving these explanations gently as friends, also patiently as becomes neighbours.—*Times*.

'Special' is a much overworked word, it being used to mean great in degree, also peculiar in kind.—R. G. WHITE.

Mr. Sonnenschein's volume will show by parallel passages Shakespeare's obligations to the ancients, also the obligations of modern writers to Shakespeare.—*Times*.

The use of *&c.*, except in business communications and such contexts, has often the same sort of illiterate effect. This is very common, but one example must suffice.

There are others with faults of temper, &c., evident enough, beside whom we live content, as if the air about them did us good.—C. BRONTË.

62. ANACOLUTHON

We can hardly conclude even so desultory a survey of grammatical misdemeanours as this has been without mentioning the most notorious of all. The anacoluthon is a failure to follow on, an unconscious departure from the grammatical scheme with which a sentence was started, the getting switched off, imperceptibly to the writer, very noticeably to his readers, from one syntax track to another. There is little to be said on the matter. The uneducated are likely to produce anacolutha if they attempt sentences of any length, the educated if they will not read over what they have written; both classes are represented in the following extracts, in which *our* readers may like to test, unaided, the noticeableness we have spoken of:

Another illustration of the manner in which changes of system which, from the point of view of military efficiency alone, may be desirable, but which on other grounds are inexpedient, has been given by Lord Kitchener himself.—*Spectator.*

To sum his letter up, it is a wild conglomeration of statement and mis-statement, of wild and senseless accusation, and feebly ends his letter with a nom de plume.—*Daily Telegraph.*

Supposing I wished to have history taught at Eton, and a man offered himself for the post—one of those who, holding that there is no such thing as certainty as to facts of history, and therefore he never reads it—and then I were to say to him, ' . . .'—E. LYTTELTON.

To think of God in any other aspect than in that of Love drives man to the terrible conclusion which 'A. B.' has expressed in your issue of Oct. 17, as One to whom to pray is impertinent.—*Daily Telegraph.*

INDEX

In this index all references are to pages. Small italics are used for words and phrases; small roman type for subjects incidentally mentioned; capitals for subjects expressly, even if not fully, treated.